D1359930

COUNSELING ON
PERSONAL DECISIONS

COUNSELING ON PERSONAL DECISIONS:
Theory and Research on Short-term Helping Relationships

EDITED BY IRVING L. JANIS

New Haven and London   Yale University Press

Designed by Nancy Ovedovitz
and set in ITC Garamond type.
Printed in the United States of America by
The Murray Printing Co., Westford, Mass.

Library of Congress Cataloging in Publication Data
Main entry under title:
Counseling on personal decisions.
   Bibliography: p.
   Includes index.
   1. Counseling.   2. Psychotherapy, Brief.
I. Janis, Irving Lester, 1918–
[DNLM: 1. Counseling.   2. Decision making.
3. Interpersonal relations.   WM 55 C854]
BF637.C6C638   158.3   81-11632
ISBN 0-300-02484-3   AACR2

10   9   8   7   6   5   4   3   2   1

Contents

Tables and Figures

FIGURES

PART
1
THEORY

1 Problems of Short-term Counseling

IRVING L. JANIS

This book deals mainly with when, how, and why counselors can be effective in just a few sessions with clients who seek help when they are making vital decisions concerning their health, career, marriage, or other aspects of their personal lives. The theoretical analyses and many of the conclusions derived from the research studies presented in the chapters that follow may apply equally to the work of large numbers of professional men and women who have had no training at all in counseling but nevertheless find themselves in the role of adviser to clients who ask them what they should do.

In order to depict the context for the theory and research, the first part of this chapter presents a brief overview of the main issues that require investigation and the current state of knowledge (or lack of it) in the field of counseling. The second part of the chapter describes the research strategy used in the series of 23 naturalistic field experiments reported in this book.

DIVERSE FORMS AND STYLES OF COUNSELING

Actually, much of the counseling on personal decisions that goes on in America and throughout the Western world is carried out by persons who themselves might benefit greatly by consulting a specialist in the psychology of counseling; many of them have never read even a single book on helping relationships. Here I am referring to the vast numbers of physicians, attorneys, personnel managers, stockbrokers, accountants, teachers, clergymen, and other professionals whose primary expertise lies elsewhere than in counseling. Nevertheless they are the ones to whom people most often turn for guidance on important decisions.

It is difficult to estimate how effectively these professionals function as counselors. Professionals who give health-care counseling have been studied more intensively than the other professionals in this regard and the evidence indicates that there is vast room for improvement. A high incidence of failures has been well documented in studies of the effectiveness of counselors in clinics that offer professional help to heavy smokers and to overweight men and women. In the United States many of these clinics are part of a profitable industry. Each year hundreds of thousands of new consumers and recidivists pay for their services, but most of their successes appear to be short-lived. A high percentage of the men and women who come to the clinics do cut down on cigarette smoking or lose weight for a few weeks, but most of them fail to adhere to the prescribed regimen after supportive contact terminates (see Atthowe, 1973; Henderson, Hall, & Lipton, 1979; Lichtenstein & Danaher, 1976; Sackett & Haynes, 1977; Shewchuk, 1976). In a review of the literature on the effectiveness of clinics for heroin addicts and heavy drinkers, Hunt and Matarazzo (1973) found that, just as with heavy smokers, many people begin to abstain in response to whatever counseling treatment they receive, but a very high percentage relapse within a month or two after starting the program.

Numerous studies also indicate that physicians often fail to influence their patients to do what they recommend. (See reviews of the literature by Kasl, 1975; Kirscht & Rosenstock, 1979; Sackett, 1977; Stone, 1979.) In a study of 47 men and women treated at an outpatient clinic in Liverpool, England, more than half the medical instructions given by the physicians could not be recalled accurately by the patients immediately after they left the consulting room (Ley & Spelman, 1965). Investigations of American women with acutely ill children suffering from rheumatic fever, streptococcal pharyngitis, and otitis media revealed that from 34 to 82% were seriously endangering the health of their children because they were not giving them the proper doses of penicillin that had been explicitly prescribed by their physicians (Bergman & Werner, 1963; Charney, Bynum, Eldridge, MacWhinney, McNabb, Scheiner, Sumpter, & Iker, 1967). A study of 154 new adult patients in the general medical clinic of a large teaching hospital in a northeastern city of the United States showed that 37% failed to comply substantially with the physicians' recommendations and only 14% fully complied (Davis, 1971). Reviews of the large number of studies on patients' failure to comply with physicians' recommendations report wide variation in different circumstances, with noncompliance rates ranging from 15 to 93% (Davis, 1966; Sackett & Haynes, 1977).

These and many related findings indicate that physicians' instructions or recommendations concerning what to do about serious health problems frequently go unheeded. We have no clear indications, however, as to how often their lack of success as counselors is primarily attributable to insurmountable resistances of the patients or defective communications by the physician. Health care practitioners may fail to communicate their recommendations clearly enough to avoid being misunderstood by the patients. Or they may fail to motivate their patients sufficiently to overcome surmountable resistances arising from the unpleasantness and other costs of adhering to the recommendations. If for any reason the patients do not follow the medical advice they are given, the physicians' skills in diagnosing the illness and in prescribing appropriate treatments or regimens are of no use whatsoever. Similarly, attorneys, financial consultants, and other professional persons who advise large numbers of clients on personal decisions fail to fulfill their primary functions effectively insofar as their clients misunderstand what they are recommending or remain unmotivated to adopt the recommended course of action.

The various professional advisers to whom I have been referring generally give counseling on a short-term basis—that is to say, they see each client for only a few sessions, usually only one or two. Large numbers of educational guidance and career counselors are also providing brief forms of counseling. Sometimes counseling is limited to one well-structured session (Radloff, 1977). Thus the rationale for selecting short-term counseling as the focus for research on helping relationships is not just that it is more feasible to carry out field experiments on the effects of short-term rather than long-term treatments but also that short-term counseling is becoming a widely prevalent type of helping relationship (see Garfield, 1971).

The hypotheses and conclusions about effective short-term counseling that are most fully discussed in this book appear to have a good chance of being applicable to a large majority of advisers, whether they give short-term or long-term counseling, including many who do not consider themselves professional counselors. The new theory and research that are presented about when, how, and why clients are helped in short-term counseling may also increase the understanding and skill of even the best qualified practitioners, who have been well trained as clinical psychologists, psychiatrists, or social workers, or who have had extensive experience as marital, career, or educational guidance counselors. I hope that many of those practitioners will find useful suggestions about new ways of improving their effectiveness and will make use of the theoretical analyses and tentative conclusions from our research reports in the training courses, workshops, and personal consultations they provide for other practitioners who know little about the psychology of helping relationships.

I use the term *helping relationships* in the plural because they come in many different forms and styles, varying in the degree of directedness and other dimensions. At one extreme is the form practiced by clinicians who consistently follow the principles of "client-centered" counseling. At each session conducted once or twice a week over a period of several months, the counselor is nondirective. He or she listens attentively to what the client says about personal problems and consistently responds in an accepting and empathic manner, reflecting the emotional content of the client's statements. The counselor carefully abstains from offering any advice or specific recommendations as to what the client should do. Carl Rogers (1951), who developed the client-centered approach, proposes that essentially the same nondirective procedures should be used for counseling people who seek help in making a vital personal decision as are used for conducting psychotherapy with people who seek relief from anxiety attacks or other neurotic symptoms. He acknowledges, however, that counseling may involve asking more questions and giving more information than psychotherapy, with fewer attempts to give psychological interpretations of the latent content of what the client is saying. Other practitioners argue that psychotherapy differs in more fundamental ways, both in objectives and in effective techniques, from counseling; they assert that counseling generally requires an educational and a supportive stance in order to help people deal with specific dilemmas (see Brammer & Shastrom, 1968; Corsini, 1968).

At the opposite pole from the nondirective approach of Rogerian client-centered counseling is the authoritarian-directive approach, which frequently characterizes the counseling given by large numbers of professionals, such as physicians, attorneys, and financial advisers. These counselors generally listen to each client's statement of the problem at the start of the first session and then use their expertise to decide on the best course of action. Before the first session is over, the client is usually told exactly what to do. If the client returns to discuss any complication that has arisen, the authoritative counselor once again tells the client, in the same directive manner, what to do about it.

Other types of counseling fall somewhere between the two poles of completely nondirective and completely directive. One intermediate type, often practiced in health clinics for people who want to quit smoking or to lose weight, involves giving supportive guidance for executing and sticking with a difficult decision (see Bandura & Simon, 1977; Cormier & Cormier, 1979; Krumboltz, 1966). The client already knows what he or she would like to do but seeks help in carrying out the intended course of action. In one or two sessions the counselor offers direct suggestions, sometimes in an authoritarian manner (e.g., "You should follow carefully every day all the rules of this 1200-calorie diet") and sometimes not (e.g., "You may find it helpful to spend about 10 minutes every day in meditation about your reasons for dieting"). Usually in this type of supportive counseling the counselor also offers information and persuasive arguments to reinforce the decision that the client has already tentatively arrived at before coming to the first session (e.g., by presenting medical facts about the potentially harmful effects of remaining overweight).

Another intermediate type is a relatively new form of decision counseling, which involves the joint work of the counselor and the client in diagnosing and improving the latter's decision-making efforts (see Broadhurst, 1976; Janis & Mann, 1977). The counselor attempts to help the person resolve realistic conflicts that arise when he or she is facing a difficult choice, such as whether to be married or divorced, to switch to a different career, or to undergo elective surgery. This type of decision counseling is usually nondirective with respect to substantive issues involved in the decision: The counselor abstains from giving advice about which course of action the clients should choose and even avoids suggesting in any way that he or she regards certain choices as good or bad. Instead, the decision counselor tries to help clients make the fullest possible use of their own resources for arriving at the best possible decision in terms of their own value systems. Much of the counselor's work consists of making clients aware of the decision-making procedures that they are using and of alternative procedures that they are not using. The counselor may be somewhat directive, however, in suggesting where to go for pertinent information, how to take account of knowledge about alternative courses of action, how to find out if deadlines need to be taken at face value or can be negotiated, which risks might require preparing contingency plans, and the like.

Among counselors in many different types of settings there appears to be a trend away from the traditional "tell-them-what-they-should-do" approach toward the type of decision counseling just described (see Cormier & Cormier, 1979; Egan, 1975; Greenwald, 1973). In the five-county area around Syracuse, New York, for example, a new Regional Learning Service, funded by the Carnegie Corporation, offers decision counseling to adults who want more education in order to upgrade their job qualifications or to change to a new vocation. According to an account in *Carnegie Quarterly* (Radloff, 1977) the counselors in this organization do not attempt to sell clients on making any particular choice or on going to any one of the 15 institutions of higher education in the area but function mainly as resource persons. Instead of telling clients what they are best qualified to do, as many career guidance counselors do, these counselors help the clients answer for themselves, "What is the next thing I want to do with my life?" More than 70% of the 9000 clients seen during the period from 1974 to 1977 were given only one session; the rest were given somewhat more counseling in a series of individual sessions or in group counseling workshops. The testimony of some of the most satisfied clients suggests that interacting with the counselor provided them with more than just useful information to pilot them through the maze of available educational pathways. One client reported that he benefited from talking to "somebody who really believed in me" because until then "I wasn't sure I could make anything of my life." Another said, "There are a lot of people like me . . . all we need is a little information and a lot of support." Recognizing the importance of the social support dimension, the directors of the counseling organization selected their 20 part-time counselors from more than 400 applications by giving priority to "personalities that were warm, resourceful, and 'naturally helping'" (Radloff, 1977).

Decision counseling is currently used to some extent as a component in the treatments offered by psychotherapists, marital counselors, career counselors, and other clinicians who deal with people at a time when they are making important personal decisions (see Baudry & Wiener, 1974; May, 1969; McClean, 1976). It is also similar to an approach that is becoming popular among consultants whose work with executives in large organizations is oriented toward trying to improve the quality of policy-making decisions (see Schein, 1969; Hackman & Morris, 1975).

The theory and research in this book deal primarily with the two types of counseling I have just described: short-term guidance for carrying out a difficult decision and short-term decision counseling to help people arrive at a vital choice. The hypotheses and conclusions to be presented may also prove to be relevant across the entire range of counseling, including the nondirective and the authoritarian-directive approaches, and perhaps even to many forms of psychotherapy.

COUNSELING AS AN ART

In 1968 Corsini pointed out that "all varieties of symbolic helping relation-ships," including all types of counseling as well as standard forms of psychotherapy, are "currently an art, not a science" (p. 1113). Taking account of the few systematic research investigations that have been carried out in recent years, one might modify that harsh conclusion slightly by saying that at present *counseling is more of an art than a science.* The bulk of the scholarly literature on helping relationships is by psychotherapists or counselors who tell us about their hard-won guiding principles based on long years of clinical experience. Most of them provide practically no evidence that could withstand the challenges of skeptical critics and, instead, rely almost exclusively on what is presumed to be tacit knowledge. Much of the alleged wisdom in books and papers on career counseling, marital counseling, educational guidance, and case work may strike the critical reader as being either untested, implausible generalizations or nothing more than common sense. Like Polonius, they occasionally give us strikingly brilliant jewels ("To thine own self be true. . . .") that all too often are lost in a sandpile of platitudes. However, not all their trite homilies should be discarded. Edith Hamilton (1958), in commenting on the seemingly trite truisms uttered by the chorus of wise old men in Aeschylus's *Agamemnon,* says, "But truisms are truths when they are first discovered, and become trite only because they are so true" (p. 161). One might add the truism that some old sayings embody bits of wisdom that can be eye-openers when first encountered by the young in each successive generation. The same might be said of some of the platitudes uttered by the wise old men and women who today write many of the psychology books and articles on how people can be helped by change agents.

Examples of valuable truisms are presented in a fresh, untrite manner in an essay on "The art of being a failure as a consultant," by Quentin Rae-Grant (1972). The essay is directed to consultants in the field of mental health, including clinical psychologists, psychiatrists, and social workers. Rae-Grant points out that the dice are so heavily loaded in favor of the prestigeful mental health expert that it is difficult to fail unless he or she unwittingly works hard to do so. The blueprint that Rae-Grant lays out contains four fundamental rules for anyone who wishes to cultivate the art of failing in his or her work as a consultant in any mental health clinic; all four can be applied equally to counseling individual clients. The consultant or counselor must (1) present himself or herself as knowing all the answers, which means ignoring the clients' ideas, desires, and goals and never hesitating to use his or her professional status to deal devastatingly with anyone who raises skeptical questions or offers an alternative point of view; (2) carefully avoid learning any facts about the clients so that his or her interventions are unencumbered by any knowledge about their needs, their available resources, and their limited capabilities, such as their inability to understand the impressive technical jargon he or she enjoys spouting; (3) insist upon complete reliance on his or her authority as an expert; (4) seize on every opportunity to function as a crusader for redressing whatever personal grievances or for promoting whatever social causes he or she is inclined to put on a hidden agenda, which should always be arrived at and implemented as a one-person "conspiracy" (p. 74).

These four essential components of a self-defeating strategy have a number of important corollaries that counselors should heed, according to Rae-Grant, if they want no unexpected forward-sliding despite their best efforts to prevent clients from making progress. When not busy dazzling the client with dynamic interpretations, the would-be unsuccessful counselor should tell the client exactly what line of action to carry out. The counselor must guard against allowing any decisions to be brought up or elaborated by the client because then there is the danger that the client will become committed and implement the decision successfully. The consultant "can take those solutions proposed by the consultee and gently, or not so gently, indicate their inappropriateness, naivety, superficiality, or lack of dynamic relevance." When the client reports that he or she dutifully did what the counselor recommended but it did not work, the counselor need not be at a loss to exploit the ambiguities in whatever words of advice were given by showing how badly the client had misunderstood or had failed to do it in the right way. Similarly, if the client reports having succeeded in trying out something on his or her own, the counselor can deal with the alarming situation by claiming that the client has no reason to feel proud or take credit for it because the idea was an obvious implication of what the counselor had been proposing all along.

Above all, in pursuing a strategy for failure counselors must avoid the development of warm and trusting personal relationships because this would make it difficult for them to avoid empathizing with their clients and would incline them to take seriously their clients' sincere complaints or other forms of feedback that invite honest self-appraisal and modification of counseling procedures. But it must also be emphasized that the counselor who avoids building up such a relation is by no means guaranteed that his or her work will be worthless. On the contrary, under certain conditions (which we are just beginning to learn about) a counselor who makes no attempt to build up a warm and trusting relationship in short-term counseling may end up being more helpful than one who does. (This very complicated matter is discussed in detail in the next chapter and again in several later chapters.) For the present it suffices to point out as another corollary to Rae-Grant's rules that one of the subtlest ways for a counselor to court failure is to rely upon spontaneous warmth and empathy to the exclusion of any special counseling techniques that might better aid his or her clients to work out solutions to their dilemmas.

Blechman (1977) suggests that even the most gifted relationship-builders who are successful in helping most of their clients might find that on the average it will take fewer sessions to achieve the goals of their counseling work if they follow the research literature and add the new techniques that have been tested and found to be effective. And, of course, not all counselors are capable of developing the type of relationship that will have positive motivating effects for the vast majority of their clients. For these less talented counselors, avoidance of using fairly well validated techniques —such as the balance-sheet procedure for career counseling (to be described in chaps. 3, 9, and 17)—might lead them to fail completely, whereas if they tried out the new techniques instead of relying exclusively on their ill-fated attempts to build a favorable relationship, they might start to get fairly good results with some of their clients. From what has just been said, it is apparent that the inflexibility principle emphasized by Rae-Grant to ensure complete failure should be interpreted broadly so as to include the counselor's exclusive reliance on his or her unsystematic, improvised efforts to build a positive relationship, with total disregard of research reports on new procedures that have been found to be effective either for building a warm and empathic relationship with clients in an authentic way or for dealing with one or another of the special problems that arise in decision counseling.

THE ILLUSION OF SUCCESS

A further point about the blueprint for failure is that the consultant runs the risk of being rated as successful despite careful adherence to all the fundamental principles as set forth by Rae-Grant for achieving failure. The reason is that the process of evaluation is so poorly worked out that a completely unsuccessful consultant or counselor is likely to be rated favorably by colleagues, potential clients, and the community at large unless he or she goes out of the way to be outrageously obnoxious. In fact, it is very easy for the counselor—or any therapist dealing with problems of physical or mental health—to have the illusion of being a great success even in those instances when the clients would do just as well or perhaps somewhat better if they had never come for help. Neal Miller and Barry Dworkin (1977) point out that the vast majority of people with any type of problem fluctuate in the intensity of their discomfort or suffering over a period of several weeks or months. They generally come for help only when they are in one of the recurrent low points in the cycle, at a time when they feel most miserable, demoralized, depressed, inhibited, or lacking in whatever they think it takes to gain control over the causes of their distress. If a large number of sufferers who come for help were to receive no professional treatment of any kind but were to be reexamined after several days, weeks, or months, most of them would no longer be at their lowest point.

This source of error is extremely difficult to eliminate. It would still be there even if counselors or therapists kept careful records to avoid memory distortions in their favor and even if they tried to prevent other sources of bias when evaluating their own effectiveness by using behavioral measures and blind ratings by outside observers along with their clients' ratings. The results of a series of carefully documented case studies using objective measures of successful or unsuccessful outcomes would still greatly over-estimate the percentage of cases who benefit from the treatment.

The main way to determine accurately whether favorable changes observed in the clients can be attributed to a counseling treatment is to carry out a controlled field experiment in which half the people who come for help are randomly assigned to the specific counseling treatment and the other half do not receive that particular treatment but otherwise are given the same information, recommendations, and auxiliary procedures (see Fiske, Hunt, Luborsky, Orne, Parloff, Reiser, & Tuma, 1970). All the studies reported in this book use this type of experimental design.

TRANSFORMING AN ART INTO A SCIENCE

Rudimentary knowledge about social influence has slowly been accumulating to the point where the time may now be ripe for a major effort to transform the art of helping others into a science. Obviously, this requires stepping up two types of scholarly enterprises, both of which are in a very early stage of development. First, the theoretical schemas that practitioners claim to be useful either for explaining what goes on in successful counseling or for suggesting promising new techniques must be explicitly formulated in terms of the conditions under which a helping relationship allegedly will be effective. This is an enterprise to which we can expect Kurt Lewin's well-known adage to apply: *Nothing can be so practical as a good theory.* Second, systematic empirical research is required to examine the testable implications of the theoretical formulations and to discover whatever can be learned about what goes on when the outcome of a helping relationship is successful as against when it is unsuccessful. We need dependable evidence on the effectiveness of various counseling procedures that practitioners claim to be successful. For this phase of developing a rudimentary science, the reverse of Kurt Lewin's adage might also prove to be true: *Nothing can be so theoretical as good practice.*

The research reported in this book represents an attempt to move ahead on the two-fold task of formulating testable theoretical ideas and of obtaining systematic evidence bearing on them. In most of the studies we give priority to selecting for our research sites those short-term counseling situations that allow us to obtain clear-cut criteria of the effectiveness of a helper's interventions—such as a dieting clinic, where weight loss can be objectively measured, and a career counseling clinic, where behavioral measures of the degree to which the clients carry out the recommended information-seeking activities can be obtained unobtrusively.

The ultimate purpose of the research reported in this book is to try to increase our understanding of how and why the influence of one person operates in a constructive way to help another person achieve his or her own goals. The main objective is to test hypotheses concerning the conditions under which talking with a professional counselor or some other type of helper will aid a person when he or she wants to choose and adhere to a difficult course of action, such as giving up smoking, going on a diet, or switching to a new career. Typically such a decision is difficult because it entails suffering short-term losses in order to attain long-term gains.

More specifically, the studies are intended to enable us to explain and predict when only one or a few sessions with a counselor will succeed in helping a client to arrive at and adhere to a recommended course of action that appears to both participants to be in the client's own best interests, with a minimum of postdecisional backsliding and regret. The findings, as I have already suggested, may prove to have practical applications for improving the effectiveness of all sorts of face-to-face counseling in a variety of community settings—wherever psychologists, social workers, lawyers, physicians, nurses, professional counselors, or paraprofessional interviewers talk with people and give them advice about their personal decisions in an effort to help them achieve long-term goals of improving their competence, health, or welfare.

There are, of course, some practical and ethical constraints on the types of intervention that can be used in a setting that is committed to providing a genuine clinical service. One obvious ethical constraint is that no new procedure can be tried out for which there is reason to suspect potentially adverse effects on even a small percentage of the clients. Another less obvious one is that everyone who participates in a study as a client in a clinic must be given some genuine help, even though he or she might be assigned on a random basis to a control group. This requires us to set up a baseline control condition in which we use procedures that, in light of existing knowledge, are expected to help the clients achieve whichever of their goals the clinic is designed to facilitate. But these constraints have not prevented us from investigating the effects of various innovative psychological treatments that, on the basis of a theoretical analysis, we believe could prove to be more effective than the tried-and-true treatment given to the baseline control group.

By means of naturalistic field experiments, we investigated hypotheses concerning the mediating processes that may account for the main effects and interactions of *two basic types of intervention*: (1) *relationship-building* interventions, such as inducing self-disclosure and responding with explicit acceptance, which influence the client's attitude toward the counselor and motivation to follow the counselor's recommendations; and (2) *decisional-*

process interventions, such as inducing the client to make contingency plans for anticipated postdecisional setbacks, which can introduce qualitative changes in the way the person arrives at, implements, and sustains his or her personal decision.

The theoretical ideas that have guided our efforts to develop and test the two types of intervention are presented in the next two chapters. But first there are several methodological problems that should be taken into account by readers who are concerned about how sound research can be carried out in such a way as to help transform tacit knowledge about the art of counseling into at least rudimentary science. (Those who have no particular interest in research methodology can skip the remaining pages of this chapter and go directly to chap. 2.)

HOW CAN WE GET VALID EVIDENCE?

In our field experiments the effects of counselors' interventions are assessed by obtaining behavioral measures of commitment and adherence to a recommended course of action. Many of the studies, for example, are conducted in the weight-reduction clinic we set up at Yale University, where weight loss is the main behavioral measure of adherence, supplemented by other measures, such as number of weekly reports on dieting mailed back to the clinic during the months following the last interview. We also use other field settings that lend themselves to systematic research on the effects of a counselor's interventions and that can provide objective records of compliance with recommendations made by public health authorities, physicians, career counselors, or other experts—such as early morning exercise classes, which have notoriously high absenteeism and high dropout rates, hospital wards where surgical patients sometimes react so adversely to the stresses of the postoperative period that they resist recommended convalescent procedures, and a career decision clinic, whose clients often fail to carry out an adequate information search to find out about the expected consequences of choosing one of the alternatives they are considering.

In selecting naturalistic settings for our field experiments we take account of several fundamental considerations. In addition to the ethical issues of introducing the types of intervention we want to investigate, these considerations include the feasibility of assigning clients to experimental treatments on a random basis and of obtaining follow-up data on behavioral changes (3, 6, or 12 months after the last of the counselor's interventions).

In each of our field experiments, along with the behavioral measures, we use attitude scales, content analyses of interviews, and other measures that enable us to assess—or at least to obtain some clues to—the mediating psychological processes that might account for the success or failure of the counselor's interventions. In our investigations of mediating processes we try to take account of what Michael Scriven (1974) calls the "logic of the 'modus operandi' approach": formulating the alternative causal sequences that might conceivably account for the outcome and then attempting to discern which of them appears to be the most probable cause by examining the evidence in fine detail, looking for telltale signs or "signatures" indicating the step-by-step ways in which each particular cause operates. For example, in a number of our studies on relationship-building interventions we have used process interviews and a new scale developed by Quinlan and Janis for assessing temporary changes in level of self-esteem (see Appendix). We have also added other scales designed for assessing changes in perceived control, need for approval, trust of the counselor, and other motivational variables that might explain how and why a counselor can effectively help people carry out difficult decisions that they could not manage as well on their own. The studies also include personality measures to assess each client's chronic level of self-esteem and other predispositional attributes that might be related to individual differences in the degree to which the interventions are effective.

In the course of many years' work in collaboration with colleagues and graduate students on field experiments dealing with helping relationships, I have arrived at some tentative conclusions concerning the directions that research on counseling might profitably take. First of all, our experience indicates that it is entirely feasible and ethical to study people who are confronted with real-life decisions and to expose them to different counseling treatments so as to carry out rigorously controlled experiments. I am now convinced that by offering a free counseling service for people in the community who seek help on personal decisions, psychologists can carry out field investigations in a way that is clinically responsible and that can gain the fundamental advantages of laboratory experiments without suffering from the usual serious disadvantages.

Despite the limitations of rigorously adhering to ethical norms and offering a genuine clinical service to all clients who come to us for counseling, we have been able to carry out systematic investigations in which we apply analysis of variance designs and assign subjects on a purely random or stratified random basis to different treatment conditions. We have been able to control for the influence of extraneous sources of error that could impair the internal validity of the findings by adopting essentially the same techniques used in laboratory experiments. For example, in every field experiment we always try to use more than one experimenter, all of whom operate blind with regard to hypotheses and if possible with regard to experimental conditions. We also present instructions and recommendations in a standardized way by using tape recordings or videotapes and we use other systematic procedures that also help to eliminate the influence of artifacts, such as differential demand characteristics and unintended experimenter effects.

Some unique advantages are to be expected when the rigorous procedures that have been developed during the past quarter century in the field of experimental social psychology are brought to bear in field investigations of real-life decisions rather than confining them to laboratory studies of hypothetical or trivial decisions that typically evoke none of the ego involvement or stress that characterizes decision making outside the laboratory. By using behavioral measures, such as weight loss among persons who decide to go on a low-calorie diet, the investigators have little need to worry about their findings being trivialized by demand characteristics or by the subjects' apprehension about being evaluated. Furthermore, the subjects do not have to be deceived and then debriefed afterward. Right from the outset, the field investigator can honestly state that he or she is trying out and studying the effectiveness of different forms of treatment that are expected to be helpful. Because of their high ego involvement most clients in these investigations are very conscientious about doing whatever is requested of them, including time-consuming "homework" assignments preparing detailed reports about daily actions that are pertinent to their success or failure in carrying out whatever decision is under investigation. For the same reason it is not very difficult to get most of them to come back after many months for follow-up assessments, enabling the investigators to study long-term effects of different short-term treatments.

There is one outstanding advantage of conducting well-designed investigations of real-life decisions that outweighs the disadvantages of not being able to hold extraneous variables as constant as in a laboratory experiment. The advantage is being able to obtain evidence that will meet the requirements of external validity—that is, the conclusions from the studies should have a fairly good chance of being generalizable to a variety of real-life counseling settings in private practice and in public institutions. Time and again we encounter a large gap between the way people think and act when coping with the stresses of real-life decisions and the seemingly clear-cut psychological phenomena observed in typical laboratory experiments using hypothetical decisions or simple tasks that are supposed to represent appropriate analogues (see Janis & Mann, 1977, pp. 417–419; McGuire, 1973; Smith, 1973). Research psychologists who give the highest priority to attaining methodological rigor by confining themselves to meticulous laboratory experiments are likely to exceed other experts in learning more and more about less and less. All too often *rigor methodologicus* is the terminal stage before *rigor mortis.*

As I have already indicated, there is one particular research strategy currently used by behavioral scientists that I regard as most promising for investigating problems of social influence in helping relationships. The strategy involves selecting hypotheses for their *theoretical* relevance but testing them by controlled experiments in *field* settings.[1] The theoretical orientation need not be limited to simpleminded, "*a*-always-causes-*b*" conceptions but can include multiple causation, feedback loops, and other complexities that McGuire (1973) correctly urges us to build into our theoretical models. Once a model of complex social or psychological processes is developed, the next step is to find some way to intervene in the system to bring about an observable change in socially significant behavior. The more complete and valid the model, the more it will tell us about how to intervene successfully. The intervention hypotheses can take the form "Intervention *a* will cause observable change *b* under conditions *x* but not *y* or *z*," which enables the investigator to specify the independent and dependent variables in the most cogent experiment as well as the factors that need to be held constant and at roughly what level.

My main point is that experimentation on major theoretical issues in naturalistic settings will help to minimize or avoid many of the difficulties that so often reduce the external validity of laboratory experiments on interpersonal relationships and prevent them from yielding cumulative findings. Time and again the psychologist's laboratory findings on main effects and simple interactions that are expected to be dependable generalizations turn out to be will-o'-the-wisps because they fail to stand up in conceptual replications or turn out to be the product of higher order interactions with relatively trivial variables that are specific to the experimental setting (see McGuire, 1973; Smith, 1973). The same demoralizing fate can sometimes beset the field experimenter since nature will continue to be ingenious in finding new ways to fool even the most vigilant investigators. Nevertheless, the unsuspected artifacts that we can expect gradually to uncover in field research are much less likely to make the findings trivial than in laboratory research. This is one of the reasons why I believe that psychological studies will prove to have more lasting value when the findings come from observations of subjects who are grappling with genuine decisions: choices they perceive as having serious personal consequences.

Partly with this expectation in mind, I propose that research psychologists should try to devise their projects to meet both of the following criteria.

First, the particular procedures and measures should represent plausible instances of variables that are of theoretical interest as concepts that have potentially high generality embracing a wide variety of specific psychological phenomena.

Second, even if some or all of the assumptions that enter into the judgments made about the first criterion were to prove questionable or false, the empirically observed relationships that emerge from the investigation in any case should be of inherent interest as psychological phenomena. They should help to specify determinants of socially important behavior, as assessed in the investigation itself.

These two prescriptive rules are intended to supplement the well-known methodological principles that are generally emphasized in research training of graduate students. The formulation of these precepts should not be construed to imply that following a set of such rules is sufficient, in my opinion, to guarantee that one's research will be successful. I believe that productive experimental research requires a great deal of tacit knowledge and creative inventiveness along with a bit of good luck. As Sigmund Koch puts it,

> Once we give up a rule-regulated conception of science... we must perceive... the intensely creative character of genuine scientific advance... [and] acknowledge that a well conducted experiment is a work of art, often of a very high order.... Quite aside from the essentially connoisseurlike assessment determining the choice of a significant "consequence" for test, there is the largely open-ended creative task of arriving at a relevant, sensitively discriminating, and rigorous design, and the still more artistic task of shaping, out of the world-flux, a material context which "truly" realizes the theoretical variables selected for study and their appropriate ensemble of initial conditions. (Koch, 1976, p. 509)

Even though rules may not provide all the essential components for carrying out a highly creative piece of research that could be regarded as a great work of art, they can, nevertheless, increase the chances that an investigator will in the long run obtain some worthwhile results.

As an illustration to explicate the meaning of the above two prescriptive rules, I shall briefly summarize the judgments we made in selecting the main dependent variable of weight loss, which led me and my collaborators to decide to set up a diet clinic as one of the sites for our research. (Similar reasons can be given for other research sites we have set up or arranged to be invited to use—a career counseling clinic, a surgical ward, a teacher training workshop, and others.) With regard to the first criterion (selecting variables of theoretical interest and of potentially broad applicability), we regard weight loss in healthy people as an objectively measurable indicator of adherence to the decision to go on a low-calorie diet and this is a plausible instance of the general category of adherence to a personal decision. It seems reasonable to expect that whatever interpersonal factors we find to have a significant influence on weight loss will have broad generality for many other, if not all other, personal decisions. In applying the second criterion (investigating empirical relationships that are inherently important) we force ourselves temporarily to take the pessimistic view that the foregoing assumption will prove to be wrong—perhaps because adherence to the decision to lose weight is influenced to a much greater degree than we suppose by unique variables, such as physiological tolerance for hunger between meals—so that the findings will *not* apply to any other type of decision than the decision we are investigating. In that unfortunate case, in my judgment, the findings would still pertain to the conditions under which people will succeed or fail to carry out their decision to lose weight and this is a sufficiently important type of behavior in its own right to represent a worthwhile contribution.

With these considerations in mind we took the necessary steps to use our social psychology laboratory as a community weight-reduction clinic. At other times, the same laboratory space is used to run a decision counseling service for people who want help in giving up smoking or in choosing a new career. In each of these studies the laboratory has been transformed into a field setting. But unlike most other field settings, our clinics, which are set up within the department of psychology of a university, remain under the control of the experimenters. Thus within the previously discussed ethical and practical constraints, we can introduce new treatments, assign clients at random to different treatment conditions, and use standardized procedures in order to carry out properly designed experiments. It seems to me that this is an example of one of the feasible ways available to research psychologists to apply the two criteria in order to obtain dependable evidence for testing significant hypotheses and theories. I suspect that often it will be much more profitable to transform laboratories into field settings than to try to transform field settings into laboratories.

NOTES

1. Were there world enough and time, research psychologists who study the effects of counseling interventions would try to do all the various parametric experiments and replications that should be carried out to test each promising hypothesis in a variety of counseling settings, with different types of people who receive help from counselors with widely different kinds of social background, training, and personality. What such studies would show, I suspect, is that there are few, if any, main effects or simple interactions that turn out to be highly dependable generalizations. In other words, any finding of an effective intervention, indicating that a given independent variable has a positive effect in a particular study, will probably be found ultimately to be ineffective in some settings for some types of clients or counselors because they enter into high-order interactions, just as appears to be the case for each variable and simple combination of variables found to be effective in educational evaluation research, in attitude change research, and in other fields of human psychology (see Cronbach, 1975; McGuire, 1969). Nevertheless, this bleak prospect need not deter us from trying to pin down hitherto neglected variables that are effective at least some of the time and that increase our understanding of the conditions under which many, if not all, counselors are most likely to help clients achieve their goals.

2 Helping Relationships: A Preliminary Theoretical Analysis

IRVING L. JANIS

The theoretical analysis presented in this chapter pertains to the powerful social incentives that influence a person's actions when he or she interacts with a professional counselor or with anyone else who takes on the role of helper. Under what conditions are a helper's suggestions or recommendations most likely to be accepted? What interventions can a helper introduce to build up an effective relationship? First, these questions will be examined from a novel perspective based on the social psychology of interpersonal influence. I shall focus especially on the problem of how counselors, who have no power to prevent their clients from firing them anytime they wish, come to have sufficient power to exert a positive influence on many people who seek their help, sometimes enabling the clients to carry out burdensome decisions that they cannot implement on their own. Then I shall introduce explanatory theoretical concepts in the context of analyzing two closely related problems: What are the crises that typically jeopardize the outcome of a helping relationship? What does it take to surmount these crises successfully? To answer these two questions we must draw upon clinical psychology as well as social psychology (see Janis, 1975, 1980).

SOCIAL POWER OF SUPPORTIVE HELPERS

The present theoretical analysis takes as its point of departure some well-known assumptions about one of the primary bases of social power, as described by social psychologists: becoming a significant other, a reference person whose signs of approval and acceptance are highly rewarding. The widely used typology by French and Raven (1959) designates *referent power* as a major determinant of social influence.

Referent power was initially used to characterize a person who fulfills a "comparison reference function," which means that he or she is used by others as a "frame of reference" for evaluating themselves. More recently, social psychologists have extended the concept of referent power to apply to influential persons who have a "normative reference function" (see Marwell & Schmitt, 1967; Tedeschi & Lindskold, 1976). Each individual perceives contact with such persons as socially rewarding and is motivated to live up to whatever norms they convey in order to obtain their approval. Each of them is a "significant other" who is able to induce genuine internalized changes in attitudes, values, or decisions.

19

The concept of a normative reference function can be directly applied to the social power of professionals. It applies when their signs of approval have positive effects on their clients as incentives for adhering to the courses of action they prescribe. Professionals are most likely to have normative referent power when their clients perceive them not only as useful and likable but also as benevolent, admirable, and accepting.

French and Raven (1959) contrast referent power with four other bases of social influence that are effective in inducing acquiescence but are much less likely to create sustained change or internalization: coercive power, reward power, legitimate power, and expert power. In a review of systematic research bearing on these postulated bases of social influence Tedeschi and Lindskold (1976) conclude that the evidence supports a number of relatively independent dimensions pertaining to one person's influence on another, five of which correspond roughly to the French and Raven typology. Two additional components suggested by the empirical evidence are trustworthiness and credibility, which can be regarded as supplementary to the knowledge and skill components of expert power.

From a social psychological viewpoint, how would we characterize the power that a counselor typically exerts over the attitudes and actions of his or her clients? Of the various factors that have emerged from social psychological research, the one least pertinent to the helping relationship is coercive power, which pertains to the use of threats and punishments to induce compliance with authoritarian demands (see Strong & Matross, 1973). Many professional counselors also avoid introducing material rewards as inducements for compliance with their recommendations, although proponents of behavioral intervention techniques point to research indicating impressive successes from reinforcing desired actions with external rewards, such as special privileges in an institutional setting (see Bandura, 1969; Nay, 1976). Those who are opposed to offering any material rewards generally rely upon social rewards of a symbolic nature, which are embodied in their reassuring, empathic verbal statements and in their friendly gestures, smiles, eye contact, and other nonverbal communications, all of which augment referent power.

To some extent, all professional counselors take advantage of the expert and legitimate bases of their power to influence clients (e.g., by displaying their credentials and their affiliations with legitimizing professional associations). Most of them also conduct themselves in a forthright manner conducive to creating an authentic image of themselves as trustworthy and credible, which may contribute to their referent power as well as their expert power (see Strong & Schmidt, 1970).

ACQUIRING REFERENT POWER

What are the primary means available to a counselor for acquiring social power as a normative reference person? According to social psychological research on interpersonal attraction there are several different ways that counselors or anyone else can build the type of relationship that results in their becoming significant reference persons for the people they deal with (Bennis, Berlew, Schein, & Steele, 1973; Berscheid & Walster, 1978; Byrne, 1971; Levinger & Breedlove, 1966; Newcomb, 1961; Strong & Matross, 1973; Tedeschi & Lindskold, 1976). One way is to make salient the *similarities* between themselves and their clients, particularly with regard to beliefs, attitudes, and values. Another way is to give *contingent praises* for specific accomplishments, actions, or intentions that are in line with the goals of the counseling sessions. Suppose, for example, a woman who comes for help in a weight-reduction clinic says that she is not sure that she can give up her favorite rich desserts, but she will try. The counselor might say, "It's good that you intend to make a real effort to stop eating those desserts because if you were to continue to eat them you wouldn't really be on a low-calorie diet." A third way is to talk and act in a manner that conveys a *benevolent attitude* toward the client, an unselfish willingness to provide help out of a genuine sense of caring about the client's welfare (see Carkhuff, 1972; Truax & Mitchell, 1971). Still another extremely powerful way, which may overlap somewhat with the third way, is to give empathic *noncontingent acceptance* statements. Such statements bolster the client's self-esteem by conveying that he or she is held in high regard as a worthwhile person despite whatever weaknesses and shortcomings might be apparent (see Goldstein, 1975; Rogers & Dymond, 1954; Truax & Carkhuff, 1967). For example, in a weight-reduction clinic, if a client says something unfavorable about herself when reporting a distressing incident to illustrate her lack of self-control, the counselor might respond with an empathic comment that conveys continued acceptance, such as "You seem to have a good grasp of that serious problem of yours, which is an important first step toward finding a way to solve it." The counselor can build up self-esteem by consistently expressing the sincere belief that the client has whatever it takes to succeed at changing in the direction the client wants. To do so, counselors can adopt an approach that many psychotherapists use: viewing every client as a worthwhile person and focusing in an open-minded way on the person's assets that could represent real potentialities for change (Cormier & Cormier, 1979; Okun, 1976). This approach is facilitated by an empathic set such that the counselor constantly makes "an attempt to think *with,* rather than *for* or *about* the client" (Brammer & Shostrom, 1968, p. 180).

There are, of course, marked individual differences among counseling practitioners in the degree to which they use one means or another of building up their referent power and also in the extent to which they rely upon the other sources of social power. In fact the French and Raven typology of social power together with the four means of fostering referent power could provide a systematic basis for classifying different approaches to counseling. This expanded typology might ultimately prove to have some value for predicting success or failure for different types of clients and for different types of counseling objectives. Nondirective counselors have a markedly different profile from those directive counselors who use a behavior therapy approach: The nondirective approach of client-centered counselors in the Rogerian tradition relies most heavily on expressing "positive regard," which is equivalent to the fourth type of means (noncontingent acceptance) for building referent power; in contrast, the behavioral interventionist is likely to make relatively little use of that means and instead to rely primarily on contingent praise and external rewards. Some client-centered counselors, especially those who practice long-term psychotherapy, attempt to give insight-inducing interpretations in a way that conveys empathic noncontingent acceptance, including "advanced empathic" responses that formulate what the client seems to be getting at but is leaving unsaid (Carkhuff & Peirce, 1975; Cormier & Cormier, 1979; Egan, 1975). In short-term counseling, however, they are likely to rely much less on their inferences about the latent content of what the client is saying but communicate empathic noncontingent acceptance by reflecting feelings and attitudes expressed in the manifest content.

The profiles for professional counselors in general differ from those of mutual helpers who participate in a buddy system of the sort pioneered by Alcoholics Anonymous. Buddies lack the credentials that give the professionals a headstart in expert and legitimate power, have somewhat more difficulty conveying benevolent intent to one another, and usually do not realize how or why noncontingent acceptance can be used effectively. But they may find it much easier than the professionals to build up referent power by highlighting the similarities of their current frustrations, concerns, hopes, and aspirations (see chaps. 4 and 5).

Some counselors fail to do anything at all to build up their power as a reference person. They are to be found especially among those attorneys, physicians, nurses, and social workers who concentrate solely on their professional tasks. They tell their clients what they ought to do without paying much attention to the clients' psychological resistances. A few are so businesslike that they do not openly show any concern about the client's current plight or future welfare. Such counselors, in effect, rely heavily on legitimate, expert, and reward power but neglect the potential increase in their ability to influence clients that could come from acquiring referent power as well.

Even if a businesslike counselor is using the other sources of power to the very limit, his or her effectiveness would be expected to increase by adopting one of the means for acquiring social power as a significant reference person in the life of each client. By adding referent power to the other bases of social power, according to the foregoing analysis, a counselor would become an even more highly esteemed helper with whom the clients are more likely to identify. Then his or her recommendations would not only meet with less initial psychological resistance but would also be more likely to be internalized and conscientiously adhered to long after the counseling sessions have come to an end.

SOCIAL REINFORCEMENTS

A considerable body of prior social psychological research on affiliative behavior indicates that when people face actual or anticipated situations of stress, they generally become motivated to affiliate with others in order to satisfy a number of important psychological needs, which include seeking for social comparison, obtaining reassurance, and bolstering self-esteem (Darley & Aronson, 1966; Dittes, 1959; Festinger, 1954; Helmreich & Collins, 1967; Janis, 1968; Radloff & Helmreich, 1968; Schachter, 1959; Zimbardo & Formica, 1963). People are likely to be under stress whenever they are trying to arrive at or to implement a decision that they know will require them to undergo short-term deprivation in order to attain long-term gains—as when people decide to accept a physician's recommendation to undergo medical treatment, to go on a diet, to stop smoking, or to take some other preventive course of action in order to improve their health in the future (see Janis & Mann, 1977). Given the strong affiliation motivation of persons in stressful dilemmas who seek help from a decision counselor, the question of whether they will develop strong affiliative ties depends largely on the degree to which they receive positive social reinforcements, as Berscheid and Walster (1978) point out.

Of the four ways just discussed of building reference power via social reinforcement, three are part of the conventional wisdom of our times. Popular books, magazine articles, TV and radio soap operas repeatedly tell us that if we want to win friends and influence people we should try to talk about things we agree about rather than to dwell on disagreements, we should give plenty of praise whenever someone deserves it, and we should always be considerate in a way that shows we really care about what happens to any person we want as a friend. Except for a relatively small number of people with personality defects or with trained incapacities, these three types of social reward are commonly used spontaneously by persons who take on the role of helper, whether as friend, teacher, or professional counselor. But the fourth type—giving noncontingent acceptance—is not part of the conventional wisdom of the Western world and is not very popular among the vast majority of counselors, despite the best efforts of Carl Rogers and his followers to make it so.

One reason why people do not use noncontingent acceptance even when they have been trained in how to do it is that it seems to violate powerful social norms involving social justice and equity (see Walster, Berscheid, & Walster, 1976). Noncontingent acceptance is often seen as giving verbal rewards to someone who does not deserve them. Most counselors, like most middle-class people, can be expected to have a sense of social equity and to be reluctant to violate norms asserting that social rewards should be given only to those who have earned them or who are likely to reciprocate.

Another reason why professional counselors are deterred from giving noncontingent acceptance is that it is not easy to do so in an effective way. It requires the counselor to take account of the clients' point of view and to empathize with their feelings in order for his or her positive comments to be impressive and believable. But this is difficult for anyone, no matter how well trained, when a client is weak, miserable, and lacking in self-control. And yet this is the way that most clients appear to be. Frank (1972) points out that the vast majority of people come for professional help only as a last resort, when they are depressed and demoralized about not being able to help themselves and have exhausted all possibilities of getting help from others in their social networks.

Aside from the problem of empathy, exceptional skill is needed to avoid the pitfalls of using noncontingent acceptance. Clients are just as aware of the norms of social equity as counselors and they are likely to be suspicious when given unearned praise or compliments. The attempts of counselors to use noncontingent acceptance can have a boomerang effect if they lay it on so thick, from the standpoint of their clients, that they are presumed to be either habitually insincere or attempting to be ingratiating with hidden manipulative intent (see Jones, 1964).

Working with clients assigned to the buddy system in a weight-reduction clinic, Nowell and Janis observed that the partners remained uncomfortable and inept in their attempts to use noncontingent acceptance even after they had been given special training, including modeling by a staff psychologist and practice trials followed by critiques (see chap. 5 below). Obviously, a brief training session is not sufficient to enable novices to become skilled at giving noncontingent acceptance and if they remain inept it can do more harm than good. But perhaps large numbers of professional counselors could become more effective if they were to obtain the type of training recommended by Carl Rogers (1951). He emphasizes the importance of cultivating empathy and skill in presenting genuine and credible statements that convey unconditional positive regard.

The theoretical analysis of critical phases in helping relationships, to which we now turn, is intended to add something to our understanding of how a professional counselor or any other kind of helper can influence clients to attain their own goals. It attempts to answer the following question: What does it take, besides positive social reinforcement and the other factors already discussed, for a helper to build up and use effectively his or her power as a significant reference person?

THEORETICAL ANALYSIS OF CRITICAL
PHASES IN HELPING RELATIONSHIPS

Where do the theoretical ideas come from? Mainly from my own clinical observations in a variety of different counseling settings. In an effort to learn something more about the way professionals build up their referent power— or fail to do so—in their interactions with clients, I functioned as a professional counselor in many different kinds of clinics where clients seek help about marital problems, choosing or changing their careers, giving up smoking, going on a diet, or undergoing disagreeable medical treatments recommended by a physician (Janis, 1975). I met with each client once or twice a week for several weeks, usually from 3 to 12 sessions. Sometimes, as in the case of the dieting clinics, the goal of counseling was to help the clients carry out a difficult course of action in the face of temptations to backslide; in other clinics, the goal was to help the clients arrive at their own decisions concerning marriage or career by encouraging them to go through the necessary steps of exploring alternatives, seeking pertinent information, and making unbiased appraisals.

After comparing successful and unsuccessful cases in an impressionistic way, I tried to evaluate the plausibility of my inferences from these clinical observations in light of the social psychological literature on affiliation and social influence. The main hypotheses that emerge are consistent with findings from systematic studies indicating that social support from a significant person or group can facilitate marked changes in behavior when two primary conditions are met: (1) the relationship is characterized by a high degree of *cohesiveness,* which is determined by the participants' anticipations of socioemotional gains (such as friendship and esteem) as well as utilitarian gains (such as improved health or better career opportunities) resulting from the relationship with the significant person or group; and (2) the relationship entails being exposed to *norm-setting* communications, which convey the behavioral standards that the significant person or group expects one to live up to (Cartwright & Zander, 1968; Hare, 1976; Shaw, 1971).

The hypotheses to be presented pertain to crises that typically arise in helping relationships. These hypotheses specify a number of variables in addition to the more familiar ones pertaining to social power and positive social reinforcements that I have just discussed—variables that are often overlooked by many professional counselors but that nevertheless can affect the extent to which a client will be favorably influenced.

The key variables are listed in Table 2.1, organized according to critical phases. The variables are formulated in a way that makes it easy to see how they could be subjected to experimental investigation. (The list in Table 2.1, in fact, includes the principal variables investigated in the series of studies reported in chaps. 4–16 below.)

Each of the variables shown in Table 2.1 should be understood as representing a *moderate* range of values. For example, the first variable refers to encouraging (*versus* not encouraging) clients to make self-disclosures that are well below the upper limit with regard to amount and intensity of self-disclosure that the client feels to be appropriate and tolerable in the here-

and-now social situation. Encouraging a moderate amount and a moderate depth of self-disclosure, for reasons to be discussed shortly, is expected to contribute to the development of a positive relationship to the counselor.

Table 2.1. Critical phases and twelve key variables that determine the degree of referent power of counselors as change agents

Phase 1: Building up referent power	1. Encouraging clients to make self-disclosures *versus* not doing so
	2. Giving positive feedback (acceptance and understanding) *versus* giving neutral or negative feedback in response to self-disclosure
	3. Using self-disclosures to give insight and cognitive restructuring *versus* giving little insight or cognitive restructuring
Phase 2: Using referent power	4. Making directive statements or endorsing specific recommendations regarding actions the client should carry out *versus* abstaining from any directive statements or endorsements
	5. Eliciting commitment to the recommended course of action *versus* not eliciting commitment
	6. Attributing the norms being endorsed to a respected secondary group *versus* not doing so
	7. Giving selective positive feedback *versus* giving noncontingent acceptance or predominantly neutral or negative feedback*
	8. Giving communications and training procedures that build up a sense of personal responsibility *versus* giving no such communications or training
Phase 3: Retaining referent power after contact ends and promoting internalization	9. Giving reassurances that the counselor will continue to maintain an attitude of positive regard *versus* giving no such reassurances
	10. Making arrangements for phone calls, exchange of letters, or other forms of communication that foster hope for future contact, real or symbolic, at the time of terminating face-to-face meetings *versus* making no such arrangements
	11. Giving reminders that continue to foster a sense of personal responsibility *versus* giving no such reminders
	12. Building up the client's self-confidence about succeeding without the aid of the counselor *versus* not doing so

*By selective feedback is meant a combination of (a) negative feedback in response to any of the client's comments about being reluctant, unwilling, or failing to act in accordance with the recommendations and (b) positive feedback in response to all other comments, whether relevant to the decision or not.

But attempts by a counselor to induce very high levels of self-disclosure could have unfavorable rather than favorable effects (see Cozby, 1973; Jourard, 1971; Tedeschi & Lindskold, 1976).[1]

My observations suggest that there are three critical phases in almost every helping relationship. When these crises are surmounted, people are most likely to benefit from the attempts of a counselor to help them arrive at or adhere to a difficult decision.

Phase 1: Acquiring Motivating Power

The first critical phase involves overcoming the usual tendency toward reticence, suspiciousness, and defensiveness that prevents a person from trusting someone who purports to be trying to help change his or her behavior. Fears of being exploited, of being dominated, and of being rejected by the stranger who is supposed to be a professional helper constitute initial bases for ambivalence. On initial contact, the client cautiously appraises the competence and trustworthiness of the would-be helper: "Does this person know what it's all about?" "Does this person tell the truth or is the person trying to sell something?" When clients have not been coerced into attending the clinic but come on a voluntary basis, these initial hurdles are usually passed with flying colors by a counselor who conveys by professional manner, as well as by office setting with framed licenses on the wall, that he or she has all the proper credentials. The client may be only vaguely aware of processing information about the counselor when making these initial appraisals.

In addition to evaluating the counselor's competence and trustworthiness, the client also assesses the counselor's readiness to give social rewards in the form of approval and acceptance, which can profoundly enhance the client's self-esteem. Whether using a directive or a nondirective approach, the counselor's influence on the clients increases as soon as they develop an image of the counselor as a genuine helper (see Barrett-Leonard, 1962; Luborsky, 1976). The crucial questions the clients raise in their own minds are: "Does this person think well of me?" "Does this person really care about me?" To make these judgments, clients attend to verbal and nonverbal cues indicating whether the counselor has genuine positive regard for them and takes a personal interest in their welfare. Once a client decides that the helper really does care and can be counted on to express positive regard, his or her self-esteem is raised and the helper acquires a considerable amount of referent power (see Tedeschi & Lindskold, 1976). Serious complications can arise, however, from the sensitivity of the client to possible signs of disapproval by a counselor, especially at a time when the person has just taken the first step to obtain professional help, which requires admitting personal weaknesses and inability to handle one or more serious problems with his or her own resources.

At the very beginning of a relationship with a trustworthy person, as Bennis, Berlew, Schein, and Steele (1973) have pointed out, a man or woman starts to reveal personal defects and "bad" aspects of his or her self "in small increments, tentatively waiting for a response. If the response is disapproval or rejection, the relationship freezes at that point, is terminated, or the testing begins anew. If each [self-] exposure is met with acceptance, there is a continual buildup of trust. . . ." (p. 135). According to these authors, practically everyone is highly sensitive to signs of acceptance or rejection even from the very beginning of an initial encounter with a stranger because, as a result of socialization experiences early in life, he or she has acquired a chronic concern about "bad" aspects of the self, which makes for low self-esteem and fear of being unacceptable to others. "Maintaining self esteem is a life-long concern for most of us, and for many of us the possibility of even a single instance of rejection by another presents a terrible threat and one to be carefully guarded against" (p. 131). Many other behavioral scientists agree with the assumption that self-esteem maintenance is a basic feature of interpersonal relations and depends upon signs of acceptance, both verbal and nonverbal (see Becker, 1968; Rogers, 1961; Marlowe & Gergen, 1969; Wylie, 1961). Becker (1968, p. 328) goes so far as to formulate a "principle of self-esteem maintenance" which asserts that all persons strive in their interactions with others to feel "good" about themselves. He proposes this as a "universal principle for human action akin to gravitation in the physical sciences."

In line with the above assumptions about self-esteem dynamics, one would expect that the quality of the helper–client relationship depends to a substantial degree on how the helper responds to whatever self-disclosures are elicited. In a weight-reduction clinic, for example, when clients are asked to discuss their eating problems, they often make self-critical statements about their appearance, such as "Look how fat and ugly I am," and about their lack of self-control, such as "I'm such a pig I just can't resist rich desserts." After a client has started to reveal some personal weaknesses to a counselor, a major consequence of being given verbal and nonverbal acceptance responses that convey positive regard is a marked improvement in the client's self-regard, which makes for strong motivation to continue the relationship, with high reliance on the helper as a respected model (see Carkhuff, 1972; Goldstein, 1975). From this point on, the helper becomes a significant reference person for the client and has the potentiality of acquiring as much social power to influence the client's actions as the most cohesive of normative reference groups (see Collins & Raven, 1969). But there are some emotional hurdles the client has to get over before the helper can succeed in using his or her newly acquired social power to foster adherence to a difficult course of action.

One complicating factor to which Bennis and his collaborators (1973) call attention is the hope for *unconditional* acceptance. They assume that from early in life on, everyone has a longing for unconditional love: a wish for a loving caretaker or friend who will be uncritical and undemanding, who can always be counted on to be accepting and affectionate no matter what one does or says or thinks. The concept of unconditional love, they assert, is acquired from early socialization experiences and persists into adult life, even though it is rarely, if ever, attained. All adults, however, have learned that love is conditional, that one is treated affectionately and accepted at certain times and not at other times, depending on whether one's actions appear to be good or bad in the eyes of the person whose acceptance is being sought. And yet, coexisting with reality-testing and ego-autonomous mastery motives, most people retain a latent hope of finding someone who will supply them with something approximating unconditional acceptance.

Carrying the analysis by Bennis and his collaborators (1973) one step further, I assume that if a counselor encourages clients to disclose personal feelings, aspirations, troubles, or weaknesses and consistently responds to the self-disclosures with statements of noncontingent acceptance, the clients tend to develop an image of the counselor as an unconditional acceptor, which at least temporarily increases their self-esteem by producing a gratifying sense of moral worth and heightened self-confidence about solving whatever personal problems are under discussion. The important point is that a counselor will acquire much more social power as a normative reference person when a client sees the counselor as a dependable source of self-esteem enhancement.

When a professional counselor gives conditional acceptance from the outset, making it apparent that acceptance responses must always be earned, clients may nevertheless come to like the counselor if he or she expresses attitudes similar to their own, continues to be affable, gives approval when the person has met the required demands, and limits disapproval for failing to do so to specific criticism of the client's actions without implying total rejection of the client as a person. All of these are considerate ways of giving contingent acceptance and they contribute to the power of the counselor as a significant reference person. Counselors who use this pattern, combining contingent acceptance with consistent respect for each client, presumably will attain much more reference power than those who withhold approval when it is deserved or who give contingent approval but also use threats, ridicule, or other humiliating punishments when their clients do or say the wrong thing, which markedly lowers their self-esteem.

Whenever a contingent acceptor gives praise for a desirable action, the client's self-esteem is temporarily enhanced. But whenever the contingent acceptor gives justified criticisms or disapproval in response to the client's disclosures of failure to do what is expected, the client's temporary feelings of low self-regard remain low and may plummet much lower. Consequently, even the most consistently respectful contingent acceptors will be perceived by clients as *undependable* sources of self-esteem enhancement.

In contrast, the noncontingent acceptor who is consistently respectful of clients will usually be perceived as a *dependable enhancer*. That is to say, a counselor will generally be seen by clients as someone who can always be counted on to raise their self-esteem if he or she consistently responds by

making statements and nonverbal gestures of acceptance, not only expressing approval about the "good" things the clients report but also expressing
empathy, optimism, and reassurance when the clients talk about being
"bad" or reveal personal weaknesses. Their image of the counselor becomes
that of a warm, understanding, protective figure who will always accept
whatever personal defects are revealed (see Goldstein, 1975; Truax &
Carkhuff, 1967). This image is also reinforced if the counselor uses the
clients' self-disclosures to provide fresh insights or cognitive restructuring
that help them view their problems as soluble, regardless of how hopeless
or "awful" they characterize themselves. For example, a counselor in a
weight-reduction clinic can use a client's self-disclosures about overeating
to help the client reappraise his or her difficulties and to develop a more
facilitating set of cognitions that are incompatible with self-defeating
thoughts. A client who says, "I'm such a pig about desserts" can be given
insight into how this belief interferes with successful dieting—because
eating any dessert confirms the belief, leads to self-blame, and contributes
to demoralization. The client can be shown how to identify the situational
context where desserts are most troublesome and change the cognition to
one that is not demoralizing (e.g., "I'll have to avoid having any of those
irresistible pastries around because those are the desserts that turn me
on"). Many clients are quite capable of taking personal responsibility for
their actions, but it requires some elementary insights, which a counselor
can provide, about when, where, and how to do so. People are less likely to
be demoralized when the causes of their misbehaviors are seen as situational and not as due to permanent personal dispositions (Janoff-Bulman,
1978; Rodin, 1978).

The theoretical analysis based on the conception of unconditional acceptance formulated by Rogers (1961) and elaborated by Bennis and his
collaborators (1973) has some testable implications. One of the main predictions is that by encouraging a tolerable level of self-disclosure[2] and by
giving noncontingent acceptance in response to whatever disclosures are
made by the clients, a counselor will elicit a relatively high degree of adherence in response to any feasible recommendations. The mediating psychological change is the clients' increased reliance upon the counselor for
maintaining their self-esteem. This type of reliance will be much less likely
to occur if self-exposure is followed by neutral, ambiguous, or negative
feedback rather than explicit signs of acceptance conveyed verbally and
nonverbally.

A client who has developed an image of the counselor during an initial
session as someone who will provide unconditional acceptance may be
especially vulnerable to disappointment later on, as soon as the counselor
indicates that he or she expects the client to make a genuine effort to
change, to live up to whatever norms are being endorsed. If the client's
initial image of the counselor as a completely dependable enhancer of his or
her self-esteem changes to that of an undependable enhancer, the counselor

will lose normative reference power. But, as will be seen shortly, an image that is intermediate between these two extremes may be most facilitating from the standpoint of achieving the goals of decision counseling.

Phase 2: Using Motivating Power in the Role of Norm-Sender

A major assumption in the foregoing discussion of the first phase is that a client will be much more receptive to the counselor's suggestions and recommendations if he or she is initially given noncontingent acceptance, which builds up an image of the counselor as a reliable source of self-esteem enhancement. The relationship is likely to be impaired, however, once the helper makes it clear that the client is expected to carry out a stressful course of action, such as staying on a diet, or to perform a difficult task, such as engaging in a thorough search for information before making a career decision. Any such demand creates a crisis in the newly formed relationship because of the threat that henceforth acceptance will be provided on a strictly conditional basis, which adversely affects the affiliative bond.

After receiving the first unambiguous recommendations or directives from the helper, the client expects thereafter to receive criticism and dis-approval if he or she fails to do what is being urged. If the client concludes that henceforth approval will be contingent upon good behavior, any in-cipient hope for unconditional approval from the helper is likely to be shattered. After that the helper will no longer be seen as a dependable self-esteem enhancer. The client realizes that from now on acceptance will be contingent upon living up to the standards of the helper, who, like all other parental figures, will probably make more and more demands to the point where he or she will give few, if any, spontaneous signs of genuine positive regard. When this transformation of the image of the helper occurs, it is accompanied by disappointment, alienation, and withdrawal.

And yet, unless a counselor makes recommendations and elicits some degree of commitment to carry out a course of action, the clients are likely to remain relatively unaffected and they will derive little benefit from the relationship as far as the goals of decision counseling are concerned. If the practitioner makes no such demands, either explicitly or implicitly, the relationship of the client with the decisional counselor will continue in a warm, friendly way but will be ineffectual. Here is another of those human conditions where love is not enough.

When a counselor continues to express nothing but unconditional posi-tive regard no matter what the persons says or does, the client is not likely to be motivated to do the work of careful search and appraisal necessary for sound decision making or to carry out a difficult course of action after the person has announced that he or she wants to do so. Such treatment given regularly over a long period of time might sometimes be successful in bring-ing about an increase in self-esteem and other types of personality change that are sought in client-centered psychotherapy. But in the more restricted short-term type of counseling relationship I have been discussing, if the counselor errs on the side of being too nondirective he or she may fail just as badly as by being too directive.

In order to facilitate adherence to a stressful decision it is essential for the counselor to use his or her social power to reinforce, in a nonthreatening way, the norms or behavioral standards that are implicated by that decision (see Goldstein, 1975; Strong, 1968). For example, when clients want help living up to their decision to stop overeating, the counselors in a weight-reduction clinic can invoke the norms of the medical profession concerning the proper rules of dieting. The counselors can express approval of those acts and intentions that are in line with the decision (e.g., resisting social pressure at a party to eat rich desserts and other fattening foods) and can indicate that they do not approve of those acts and intentions that make for failure (e.g., overeating during a relaxed vacation weekend). Thus, in offering help to people who want to adhere to a stressful decision, counselors become norm-sending communicators. But in order to mitigate the crisis created by taking on this directive role, counselors may need to take certain additional steps, which I shall discuss shortly. Counselors can effectively convey behavioral norms and elicit commitment from their clients to live up to those norms without necessarily losing referent power by destroying the alliance created in the first phase of the helping relationship.

Eliciting from the clients a verbal commitment to strive to live up to the norms endorsed by the counselor increases their motivation to carry out the difficult course of action. The term *commitment,* which refers to "pledging or binding of the individual to behavioral acts" (Kiesler & Sakumura, 1966), is used in this context in the restricted sense of informing at least one other person (the helper) about one's intentions to perform a series of acts.

During the second critical phase, as the helper begins to use his or her motivating power by endorsing sound decision-making procedures or a specific course of action and eliciting commitment statements, the client focuses on a set of evaluative questions pertaining to the new demands that are implicitly or explicitly being made. The key questions, which the client tries to answer by processing the cues given by the norm-sender's verbal statements and expressive behavior, are: "What does the counselor really want me to do?" "Will the counselor find out whether I do it or not?" "Will the counselor be satisfied if I do the few things being asked of me or will there be more and more demands?"

There are obvious things a counselor can say to guide the clients' personal answers to these questions in the desired direction. The clients' answers to the third question, however, are much more difficult to influence than the other two. At this point it is necessary to introduce another major theoretical assumption, namely, that a *selective pattern of social reinforcement* can be used in a way that enables clients to regard the counselor as a quasi-dependable source of self-esteem enhancement who will make only a few demands. I postulate that when helpers are going to function as norm-senders, they are more likely to retain motivating power if they avoid both extremes by building a differentiated image through the judicious use of selective reinforcement. It can avoid the illusory overlay that enters into an image of the helper as someone who will always provide unconditional acceptance in all circumstances no matter what one does. It can also avoid the other extreme, an image of the counselor as a completely undependable source of self-esteem enhancement, which results in withdrawal from the relationship. Clients can come to realize that they will mostly receive spontaneous acceptance, including when they reveal personal weaknesses and shortcomings, *except* when they fail to make a sincere effort to live up to a *limited* set of norms. This modified expectation of partially contingent acceptance from the helper allows clients to look forward to receiving genuine acceptance and approval from the helper much of the time—and perhaps practically all the time, almost the same as when acceptance is invariably unconditional—provided that they make a sincere effort to follow just a few rules recommended by the helper pertaining to only a limited sphere of personal behavior.

The image of the helper as a *quasi-dependable enhancer of self-esteem* differs from that of the common-garden variety of undependable enhancer who offers acceptance on a strictly conditional basis. Clients expect little or no approval from the latter type of helper except at times when they clearly earn it by conforming to all sorts of rules that will continue to be laid down by the helper to govern many different spheres of personal behavior, much like the seemingly endless rules imposed by strict parents who demand conformity with their extensive code of moral behavior and of proper etiquette. Everyone knows that signs of acceptance from demanding authority figures are few and far between.

A major problem for the counselor during the second phase, then, is how to minimize the risk of provoking detachment or withdrawal from the relationship when it is necessary to make recommendations that specify behavioral norms, especially when he or she explicitly asks clients to commit themselves to those norms. The solution I have suggested—to use the pattern of selective verbal reinforcement—requires considerable sensitivity and artistry. The pattern consists of criticizing clients' counternorm actions or intentions in a nonthreatening way while expressing positive regard the rest of the time, including when clients talk about personal shortcomings that are irrelevant to the task at hand. In a dieting clinic, for example, the counselor would limit negative feedback to comments about the undesirability of counternorm behavior when a client admits having indulged in overeating or wanting to do so, which is incompatible with the agreed-upon norm of sticking to a low-calorie diet. This limited type of negative feedback can be effectively presented in a nonthreatening way by reminding the client of his or her goals, by calling attention to the negative consequences of the counternorm actions, and by praising the client's honesty about admitting counternorm tendencies. For all other admissions of personal weaknesses or defects that do not bear on adherence to the given decision, the helper can give explicit acceptance statements. And, of course, the helper can also give explicit praise for each instance mentioned by the client of successful adherence to the norm and for each spontaneous commitment statement concerning intentions to adhere to the norm in the future. In this way the helper may succeed in conveying an image of himself or herself as someone whom the client can rely on most of the time as a self-esteem enhancer, someone who will often spontaneously give noncontingent acceptance responses with only occasional instances of conditional approval or disapproval that pertain to a very limited set of demands. This differentiated image of the helper as supplying a nurturant diet of variable but basic acceptance, rather than either the meager bones of conditional acceptance or the rich but undigestible fare of unconditional acceptance, is assumed to be optimal for functioning effectively as a constructive motivator.

A counselor might succeed in creating an authentic image as a quasi-dependable enhancer of self-esteem either by starting to use selective reinforcement from the very beginning of the initial session or else by introducing it in a tactful way after consistent use of noncontingent acceptance responses during the first phase of the relationship. A counselor who chooses the former approach (selective reinforcement from the beginning) runs the risk of failing to surmount the first crisis and thereby never acquiring any motivating power as a self-esteem enhancer. A counselor who adopts the latter approach (noncontingent acceptance at the beginning followed by the gradual introduction of selective reinforcement) runs the equally serious risk of accentuating the second crisis and thereby losing whatever motivating power as a self-esteem enhancer he or she had just acquired. But the blow to the client of being confronted with the first contingent acceptance responses after an unbroken succession of noncontingent acceptance responses might be softened in various ways. One way is to attribute the norm being sponsored to a respected secondary group (e.g., by informing clients who come to a weight-reduction clinic that medical specialists regard the recommended diet as the safest and most dependable way to lose weight). Another way to soften the blow may be for the counselor to explain frankly what he or she is going to do in advance and to engage in explicit negotiations with the client to arrive at an agreement about adopting the norm (e.g., by discussing with the client whether and in what ways he or she wants to be committed to the recommended low-calorie diet). After the client has explicitly agreed to carry out the difficult course of actions, the helper's contingent approval and disapproval are more likely to be tolerated. Even so, however, the helper is unlikely to retain motivating power unless it is repeatedly made clear that contingent acceptance responses will be limited to the specific norm that the client has said he or she wants to live up to. It is especially important for the helper to convey that each failure to do so will elicit disapproval of the deviant act without changing the helper's basic attitude of positive regard toward the client as a person.

Counselors may be able to retain their status as quasi-dependable en-hancers indefinitely for most of their clients by continuing to make only a few demands, by abstaining from deliberate social pressure, and by giving positive evaluative feedback only when they genuinely believe what they are saying, so as to avoid inadvertently giving cues to deceit or simulation of feelings (see Rogers, 1961; Rubin, 1973). As long as clients ascribe this status to the helper, they will no longer be as defeatist about achieving their goals as they had been before developing the relationship. With their newly found self-confidence, constantly bolstered by signs of basic acceptance from the helper, clients will see new vistas of self-improvement opening up, which may enable them to make successful use of their own dormant resources.

Phase 3: Retaining Motivating Power after Termination of Contact

A third major crisis arises when direct contact between the helper and the client is terminated, as is bound to happen when a counselor arranges for a fixed number of sessions to help a client arrive at a difficult decision or to get started carrying one out. When the sessions come to an end, even if pre-arranged by a formal contract, the client will want to continue the relation-ship insofar as he or she has become dependent upon the counselor for bolstering self-esteem. The client is likely to regard the counselor's refusal to comply with the demand to maintain contact as a sign of rejection or indifference. If this unfavorable change in the image of the counselor occurs, the client will no longer be motivated to live up to the norms advo-cated by the counselor and will show little or no tendency to internalize those norms after their contact has ended. The client's disappointment may be so extreme that he or she will deliberately violate the counselor's norms. Feeling angry or aggrieved about being abandoned, clients sometimes deliberately avoid doing what the counselor recommended, which wipes out all the progress they had so painfully achieved while the counseling sessions were going on.

The separation crisis, like the crisis provoked by the norm-setting de-mands in Phase 2, may be minimized if the counselor gives assurances of continuing positive regard. It may also be more tolerable if the counselor arranges for gradual rather than abrupt termination of contact.

Backsliding is much less likely to occur after contact is terminated if the client internalizes the practitioner's norms. Little is known about the deter-minants of the internalization process, but it seems plausible that it might be facilitated by the counselor in two ways. One way is to give reminders that foster a sense of personal responsibility for adhering to whatever decisions the client has arrived at. A second way is to give attributions bearing on self-control that build up the client's self-confidence about suc-ceeding without the aid of the counselor. These two themes may be introduced by the helper in Phase 2, but in Phase 3 they require strong emphasis. Special effort is required to make clients feel fully confident that they are able to go forward on their own. In diet programs, for example, the health counselor can emphasize that the clients' initial weight loss and changes in eating habits demonstrate their capabilities for self-control. These attributions promote the client's self-confidence about successfully losing weight and increase the likelihood of long-term maintenance (Rodin, 1978; Rodin & Janis, 1979). If a client temporarily backslides, the failure usually can be attributed to situational factors such as overexposure to temptations during the holiday season, or to other changeable events in the environment, rather than to the client's chronic personality weaknesses. Recovery from a temporary failure can be used to illustrate the client's basic strengths and capabilities for long-term success. When clients try to attribute their success to the counselor, it is important to point out that it was they themselves who were able to give up eating their favorite high-calorie foods and to make the necessary behavioral commitment that led to successful changes.

These and related themes that build up the client's self-confidence about being able to succeed without the helper's aid can be appropriately emphasized before it is time to say good-bye. The client can be encouraged to discuss frankly his or her feelings about termination of contact, as is often done as a standard procedure in many forms of counseling and psychotherapy. In such a discussion the counselor has the opportunity to counteract explicitly a client's misinterpretations of termination as a sign of rejection, to point out the client's capabilities for self-control, and to talk about the future satisfactions to be expected from increased autonomy and mastery.

BECOMING A QUASI-DEPENDABLE ENHANCER

The foregoing account of three critical phases assumes that the chances of counseling sessions being effective will increase if the client develops a differentiated attitude of reliance on, respect for, and emotional attachment to the counselor. This is a much more complex attitude than simple "liking" for a stranger as measured by standard scales of interpersonal attraction in current social psychological research (see Berscheid & Walster, 1978; Byrne, 1971). One would expect that if clients reveal personal weaknesses to any type of practitioner—physician, nurse, lawyer, financial consultant, career counselor, psychotherapist, or whomever—noncontingent acceptance by the practitioner will result in improving their self-regard. This, in turn, will make for strong motivation to continue the relationship, with high reliance on the practitioner as a respected model. The clients will perceive the practitioner not merely as someone who sometimes dispenses positive reinforcements but also as a quasi-dependable enhancer of their self-esteem, worthy of deference, gratitude, and affection. From this point on, the helper becomes a significant reference person for the clients and has the potentiality of using his or her social power to influence their actions. This power can be used to encourage clients to go through the essential steps to arrive at a sound decision (see chap. 3). Or it can be used to elicit commitment to a difficult course of action and to overcome temptations to backslide. The vital point is that all sorts of practitioners, including decision counselors, can acquire social power as normative reference persons if clients see them as dependable sources for enhancing self-esteem rather than as purely conditional acceptors, who are undependable enhancers.

A vivid illustration of a client's response to a health-care practitioner who became a powerfully motivating norm-setter can be cited from the innovative work of Neal Miller and Barry Dworkin on biofeedback training. These investigators were pioneers in developing an instrumental conditioning technique with verbal rewards to help patients suffering from hypertension gain control over their blood pressure. A young woman who wrote down her impressions of an arduous 10-week training period, during which she temporarily succeeded in lowering her diastolic pressure from a dangerously high average of 97 to a satisfactory average of about 80, had this to say about her trainer:

> I always depend very heavily on Barry Dworkin's encouragement and on his personality. I think he could be an Olympic coach. He not only seems aware of my general condition but he is never satisfied with less than my best, and I cannot fool him. I feel we are friends and allies—it's really as though *we* were lowering my pressure. (Quoted by Jonas, 1972)

When the client regards the health-care practitioner as an Olympics coach, she conveys the idea that in some sense she thinks of the coach as treating her like an Olympics star. Not everyone who engages in professional work can expect to function like a successful Olympics coach with all clients. But perhaps a better understanding of the crucial ingredients of an effective helping relationship, including the variables listed in Table 2.1, eventually will lead large numbers of practitioners to adopt improved means for building the type of relationship that is most effective.

Unfortunately, there is much more to it than just becoming familiar with the crucial ingredients. For example, many physicians, nurses, and other health-care professionals who function as counselors are likely to resist changing their current ways of dealing with their patients in order to become more effective as change agents. One major deterrent is the extra effort needed to acquire the necessary interpersonal skills. Another, which is most salient of all, is the added time required, for which there appears to be little room in professional schedules that are already overfilled. Nevertheless, there is reason to expect that as more and more practitioners become aware of the demoralizing statistics on nonadherence to their recommendations, they will become *quality* oriented (see chap. 1). That is, they will renounce quantity ambitions in order to expend extra time and effort with their patients or clients in accordance with the primary goal of improving the well-being of each of them as far as possible.

IMPLICATIONS FOR SEX PARTNERS
AND OTHER DYADIC RELATIONSHIPS

The key theoretical concepts introduced in the analysis of the three critical phases, including those pertaining to the image of the helper as a quasi-dependable source of self-esteem enhancement, provide a general framework that might account for what happens in a variety of other dyadic relationships—between a student and a teacher, a novice and a guru, a pair of work colleagues, friends, lovers, or marital partners—and also in relationships between group members and their leaders. In all these relationships, self-disclosure may initially occur inadvertently from overt acts even though the discloser has no intention at the time of saying anything about personal desires, hopes, fears, aspirations, frustrations, personal strengths, or weaknesses. For example, in encounters with a teacher or work colleague, self-disclosure of personal weaknesses may occur inadvertently when the person makes errors in his or her work or fails to carry out an assignment. With a lover, disclosure of sexual desires and aspirations occurs when the first "pass" is made. If accepted, it may lead to mutual acts of literal self-exposure—with each partner revealing his or her body not just in all its glory but also in all its imperfections that deviate from the classic ideals of ancient Greece and modern Hollywood.

One consequence of the sexual revolution of our time is that the traditional sequence (the man and woman first becoming affectionate friends and later on becoming sexual partners) is often reversed. Admirable and regrettable features of the self are revealed by sex partners in the first manifestations of their preferred forms of sexual gratification as well as their sexual antipathies and inhibitions. Acts of lovemaking, therefore, entail a great deal of self-exposure as well as bodily exposure. Although many complex interacting factors enter in when sexual liaisons develop into love relationships, the three phases described for helping relationships may, nevertheless, be relevant for explaining some of the changes in attitudes and behavior. For example, the way each partner responds to the other's disclosures probably plays a role in determining whether a sexual affair will continue and deepen into an affectionate relationship (see Levinger & Rausch, 1977). During the first sexual encounter, if one partner is dispassionately objective, facetious, or coolly critical of the other's performance, the intimate relationship, not just intercourse itself, is likely to come to a halt. Even after a love affair is well under way and both partners have repeatedly enjoyed sexual intercourse, one of the lovers may start making so many complaints about the other's failure to comply with sexual or social demands that the image of that lover as a dependable source of self-esteem enhancement is shattered. Thereafter the verbal interchanges of the couple are likely to become increasingly corrosive and soon the little world of that particular liaison will come to an end not with a bang but a whimper.

If each lover responds to the other's inadvertent disclosures during their initial sexual encounter with admiring glances and other overt acts and gestures implying positive regard, even without a single word being spoken, the relationship may get off to a flying start and continue as long as the two essential conditions of Phase 1 (acquiring motivating power) continue to be met for each participant: disclosures are encouraged and the other person generally responds in an accepting way even though some of the disclosures may reveal personal weaknesses or shortcomings. Under these conditions, casual sex partners would become affectionate friends, gradually adding verbal disclosures and verbal acceptance statements to what they had initially been communicating by body language.

But the human condition is such that sooner or later, no matter how wonderful the elated lovers appear and try to be in each other's infatuated eyes during the first phase, the time will come when one of them makes a demand or begins to offer the faintest hint of withholding acceptance because of something the other has done that is not quite to his or her liking. Soon a typical crisis of Phase 2 (resistance to norm-sending) is under way and the fate of the relationship depends on what kind of image replaces the shared preconscious illusion that each partner will always give unconditional acceptance as a completely dependable source of self-esteem enhancement. If a partner replaces it with an image of the other as a completely conditional acceptor, he or she will no longer be willing to make many sacrifices to keep the relationship going, even though the two people may continue to provide sexual gratification to each other each time they are together. But if each partner comes to view the other as a quasi-dependable source of self-esteem enhancement, the relationship could continue with almost the same intensity of emotional involvement as before.

Later on, if it turns out that for any reason the lovers must be separated for a relatively long period of time, the separation crisis (Phase 3) may pose a serious threat, unless each can successfully reassure the other that he or she is not going to be abandoned, that affectionate feelings and positive regard will continue while they are apart, and that some means of symbolic contact will be maintained throughout the period when they will be deprived of physical contact.

The main point of this brief digression concerning sexual liaisons is to emphasize that the three critical phases and their consequences, as specified by the theoretical analysis, are not limited to professional helping relationships. They may arise in all sorts of other potentially close relationships.

IMPLICATIONS FOR COUNSELORS' TACTICS

A number of problems confront the counselor in each of the three phases if he or she is to establish the type of relationship that, according to the theoretical analysis, will be optimally effective from the standpoint of motivating clients to change their undesirable or self-defeating behavior. In the first phase, as I mentioned earlier, it may be efficacious to start introducing gradually very mild forms of contingent acceptance responses when the client talks about doing the "wrong things," while building up referent power by giving predominantly noncontingent acceptance responses to almost everything else the client says. The Phase 2 crisis (resistance to norm-sending) may be less difficult to surmount if it is introduced *gradually* instead of all at once.

During Phase 2, one of the essential tasks of the counselor, in terms of theoretical assumptions, is to convince the clients that they will continue to be regarded in a positive way even if the counselor's standards are not fully met, provided only that they make a genuine effort. This conception is probably facilitated when the counselor works more as a collaborator than as an instructor, using a minimum of social pressure by encouraging his or her clients to arrive at their own decisions, to which they will feel personally committed. Clients who decide to go on a diet, for example, will be less likely to go off the diet when they are tempted to overeat because they regard the restrictions as a matter of carrying out their own decision, not as compliance with a decision imposed by the counselor. This sense of personal responsibility for sticking to the decision, as I have already pointed out, has considerable advantages for Phase 3 (retaining motivating power after termination of contact).

The absolute amount of noncontingent acceptance that is required during Phases 1 and 2 for a counselor to acquire and maintain motivating power as a quasi-dependable enhancer will probably vary from one client to another, depending upon the client's level of self-esteem, social competence, and a number of other background characteristics. Among the crucial determinants of individual differences in this respect would be those social background factors that affect the client's *comparison level* (see Thibaut & Kelley, 1959). At one extreme would be an alcoholic ex-executive unable to get a job and long ago kicked out of his own home who is now generally treated as a worthless nobody. Just a few words of genuine noncontingent acceptance by an employment counselor might make a deep impression on someone in such a lowly state, even though the person might at first react in an indifferent or a hostile way on the surface in an effort to protect himself from further humiliation or disappointment. Such a person's comparison level is so low (expecting practically no acceptance at all from an authority figure) that an empathic comment gleams like a campfire in a bleak wilderness. The donor can very quickly become highly prized as the only potentially dependable source of self-esteem enhancement in the entire social world of the client.

For a client who is a successful executive, constantly surrounded by admirers, even a long series of noncontingent acceptance comments by a counselor may fail to make much of an impression because they do not reach or exceed the expected level of homage that the great personage is accustomed to receiving. Furthermore, superstars are supersensitive to signs of ingratiation and may be supersuspicious of genuine noncontingent acceptance as being nothing more than a phony smoke screen to cover manipulative intentions. Counselors may never succeed in becoming sufficiently valued persons to have any effect at all on the level of self-esteem of such clients unless they first prove their value in an extraordinary way, such as by giving uniquely illuminating insights. Consultants to high-level executives sometimes discover that they remain nonentities until they start offering some such rare gems, after which their approval and acceptance are sought.

The content of the empathic, appreciative, and approving comments that a counselor offers as noncontingent acceptance responses is probably another important determinant of success in building his or her motivating power as a reference person. Even ordinary citizens who find it difficult to imagine themselves as superstars in their most extravagant Walter Mitty fantasies have learned to be wary of encounters with manipulative pseudo-admirers, especially of the opposite sex (see Jones, 1964). Most people have had painful experiences of being elated by others who sound as if they mean it when they say, "I'm thrilled to meet you" and "I think you are a wonderful person," but who soon switch to contingent acceptance that is intended to evoke compliance with sexual, financial, or other demands ("I know you are such a wonderful and generous person that you will do this favor for me"). Thus, even though a counselor carefully avoids saying anything that sounds like an obviously ingratiating compliment, he or she nevertheless may arouse wariness by making positive statements that the client finds difficult to regard as credible or that might cue the client to manipulative intent. Probably the best policy in this regard, as well as for ethical purposes, is for the counselor to be completely honest in his or her acceptance statements, avoiding exaggerations or broad generalizations that might be unwarranted when making favorable comments that are likely to be construed as compliments. In order to formulate his or her acceptance statements in an appropriate way the counselor will no doubt have to use a great deal of tact as well as tacit knowledge about each client. This is another of the many aspects of counseling that will continue to require a high degree of artistry even if subsequent research proves to be highly successful in transforming counseling into something more of a science.

After a counselor has acquired a great deal of motivating power as a quasi-dependable enhancer, he or she must still exercise considerable skill to maintain referent power and to use it effectively. There is something fragile about a helping relationship, especially when contact is limited to only a few sessions. The counselor will no longer be perceived as a quasi-dependable enhancer of self-esteem if his or her demands exceed the bounds of what the client regards as legitimate and reasonable. This is one of the principal

reasons why counselors may find it advantageous to restrict their normative recommendations to only one specific sphere when trying to help
clients adhere to a stressful course of action, such as abstaining from alcohol
or hard drugs, giving up smoking, staying on a diet, or undergoing painful
medical treatments.

So long as a counselor continues to be regarded as a quasi-dependable
source of self-esteem enhancement who will not make too many demands,
his or her endorsements of a given course of action introduce powerful new
incentives that were not there before. The here-and-now reward value in
signs of acceptance from a respected helper, which enhance the client's
self-esteem, can tip the balance in favor of good intentions at times when
the client is tempted to avoid the here-and-now costs and suffering. The
new social incentive arising from self-esteem enhancement obtained in the
client–counselor relationship can compensate for the relative weakness of
anticipated long-term gains when the client is reluctant to be committed
wholeheartedly to a new course of action requiring short-term deprivations.

STATUS OF THE THEORETICAL FRAMEWORK

The foregoing theoretical analysis summarizes the initial ideas that guided
most of the research studies reported in this book. It should be regarded as a
mere beginning, a scaffold rather than a finished product. This preliminary
framework, like the decision-making model presented in the next chapter,
has been used primarily as a basis for selecting variables to be investigated.

Because the critical phases and the hypotheses related to them were
inferred from clinical observations of clients who came for a series of about
3 to 12 sessions with a professional counselor, serious questions can be
raised concerning generalizability. Are the hypotheses supported when
tested systematically in the various types of counseling settings like the
ones in which the clinical observations were originally made? Do the hypotheses hold for briefer forms of professional counseling that are limited
to only one or two sessions? Do the hypotheses apply to the peer partnerships that are set up when a buddy system is used which replaces or supple-
ments the counselor–client relationship with a client–client relationship?
Evidence bearing on these and a number of other empirical questions is
presented in the subsequent parts of this book. The research reported in
part 2 deals directly with the effectiveness of the buddy system and highlights certain of the key variables of the second critical phase under conditions where the key variables of Stages 1 and 3 are held constant (see Table
2.1). In parts 3 and 4, most of the studies are field experiments on counselor–
client relationships that provide systematic evidence on the effects of the
two main variables specified as crucial for Phase 1 (encouraging self-
disclosure and responding with noncontingent acceptance), this time under
conditions where the variables specified for Phases 2 and 3 are held constant. A few of the field experiments also bear on the effects of the variables

specified for Phase 3. However, not all of the 12 variables in Table 2.1 have as yet been systematically investigated.

In the final chapter of the book the preliminary theoretical framework presented in this chapter are reevaluated in light of the empirical evidence from all the studies. It will become apparent as we examine the entire series of studies that the main hypotheses that were tested are generally confirmed. That is to say, those key variables specified in the analysis of the three phases (Table 2.1) that are systematically investigated in the field experiments prove to have essentially the effects on attitudes and behavior that are predicted. But there are also some unpredicted findings that point up the need to specify limiting conditions or to modify certain of the assumptions. Accordingly, several modifications and reformulations will be presented. The final synthesis will also attempt to answer unsettled theoretical questions concerning other sources of motivating power that a counselor may acquire. For example, under what conditions can an authoritative counselor, such as a highly directive physician, nurse, behavior therapist, or social worker, effectively induce commitment and adherence to a stressful decision without forming the type of relationship with his or her clients that involves becoming a quasi-dependable source of self-esteem enhancement? The tentative answers to such questions will help to delimit the type of counseling situations in which the theoretical analysis of supportive helping relationships can be expected to apply.

The theoretical analysis of the three phases of an effective helping relationship is formulated in general terms as being applicable to every man, woman, and child, irrespective of personality differences. But the clinical observations on which it is based (and, as will be seen in the final chapter, most of the systematic research evidence that substantiates it) comes mainly from counseling relationships with adults who have difficulty making or carrying out their personal decisions, particularly clients who come to clinics for help on controlling their overeating or smoking behavior. Future studies of the processes of social influence in dyadic relationships among persons who do *not* come to clinics might show that they are different in important respects. For example, adults who seek help with problems of self-control may be much more sensitive than others to empathic acceptance responses from helpers, perhaps partly as a result of having received insufficient or faulty empathic responsiveness from their primary caretakers during crucial developmental periods in childhood (see Kohut, 1977). It is quite conceivable, therefore, that whatever validity the theoretical analysis may have is limited to only one or a few categories of persons. Even so, those limited categories might turn out to include large numbers of clients who seek professional help.

SUMMARY

The preliminary theoretical framework presented in this chapter attempts to describe how a nurturant helper can make a crucial difference in the way a client arrives at and adheres to a stressful decision. The theoretical analysis focuses on the conditions under which clients' interaction with a supportive counselor will increase the probability that they will follow a partially directive counselor's recommendations to carry out careful search and appraisal before arriving at a new decision, such as obtaining a divorce, or will adhere to a new decision endorsed by the counselor, such as going on a diet, even though it is difficult to carry out. Three critical phases are postulated that must be surmounted successfully in order for clients to benefit from the attempts of a counselor to help them arrive at a sound decision or to carry out a stressful decision when they are deterred by the short-term losses.

1. In the first phase the counselor must surmount the client's wariness and acquire motivating power as a significant "reference person," comparable to the motivating power of a normative reference group. The client will develop an attitude of reliance upon the helper for enhancing and maintaining his or her self-esteem if the helper encourages the person to reveal personal feelings, aspirations, troubles, or weaknesses and responds to the self-disclosures with noncontingent acceptance statements. Referent power is also increased if the counselor uses the client's unfavorable self-disclosures to give the client insights and cognitive restructuring that decrease self-disparagement.

2. In the second critical phase the relationship built up during the first phase is impaired as the helper begins to function as a norm-sending communicator. Even though preferring to be nondirective, a counselor does in fact endorse certain norms if he or she recommends sound decision-making procedures (such as an adequate information search) or encourages clients to act in accord with their resolve to carry out a desirable but stressful course of action (such as dieting). If a helper refrains from calling attention to any such norms and makes no other demands, either explicitly or implicitly, the relationship will continue in a warm, friendly way but will be totally ineffective in achieving the primary objective of helping the person arrive at or carry out a difficult decision. But when a helper endorses certain decision-making procedures or a particular course of action, it is at the risk of losing some of his or her motivating power and ultimately of being completely rejected by the client. The crisis probably can be successfully surmounted if the helper conveys that the demands are very limited in scope and that occasional failure to live up to those demands after a sincere attempt to do so will not change his or her basic attitude of acceptance toward the client. It is also helpful for the counselor to attribute the norms being endorsed to a respected secondary group, to negotiate an agreement with clients whereby they become committed to those norms, and to give communications or training procedures that build up a sense of personal responsibility for whatever decisions they arrive at. The norm-sending helper is

most likely to retain motivating power if he or she uses a selective pattern of social reinforcement. This pattern consists of giving negative reinforcement in a nonthreatening way when the client talks about failing to act in accordance with the counselor's recommendations, giving positive reinforcement when the client talks about carrying out those recommendations, and expressing positive regard the rest of the time, including when the client admits to personal weaknesses or shortcomings that are irrelevant to the task at hand. By expressing noncontingent acceptance most of the time and by restricting contingent acceptance to the agreed-upon task, it should be possible to build an authentic image of the helper in the client's mind as a quasi-dependable source of self-esteem enhancement, which will facilitate the helper's effectiveness.

3. In the third critical phase the influence of the supportive norm-sending helper is threatened by the client's disappointment and resentment about the termination of direct contact. After the contracted sessions with the helper have ended, clients will fail to internalize the norms the helper had been advocating if they interpret the termination of contact as a sign of rejection or indifference. These adverse reactions to separation may be minimized if the counselor offers assurances of continual positive regard, arranges for gradual rather than abrupt termination of contact, and gives reminders that continue to foster the clients' sense of personal responsibility for their own decisions. Internalization of the norms and adherence long after all contact has ended is also promoted if the helper builds up the client's self-confidence about being able to succeed without the helper's aid, which might be done in the context of encouraging the client to "work through" feelings about termination and to look forward to future satisfactions that can come from increased autonomy and mastery.

Part of the art of counseling may reside in dealing with each of the three critical phases in a way that minimizes adverse effects. Perhaps only a small proportion of counselors have the interpersonal skills required to deal successfully with all three phases for the majority of their clients. Nevertheless, counselors with modest amounts of talent and skill in dealing with people in trouble may be able to improve their percentage of successful cases by taking account of the prescriptive hypotheses that follow from the analysis of the three stages.

The initial theoretical framework presented in this chapter specifies a number of variables that are expected to affect the success of any supportive counselor in a clinical setting where people come for help on decisions that they find too difficult to arrive at or carry out on their own. The main variables, the 12 listed in Table 2.1, should be found—either separately or in combination—to affect the success of a counselor with regard to establishing, using, and maintaining his or her motivating power as a helper.

NOTES

1. All 12 variables in Table 2.1 are expected to have an upper limit beyond which the effect is no longer more positive than very low levels and in some instances the effect could become increasingly negative. But the upper limit itself is somewhat variable because what a person judges to be "tolerable" in one social situation may not be so in another, even with the same person. Such judgments depend on the type of person one is talking to, the purpose of the conversation, prior contact, and other circumstances. For example, the tolerable level of induced self-disclosure would not be expected to be as high with a professional counselor at the time of the first interview, when he or she is a stranger, as in later sessions, when the counselor is regarded as an esteemed helper or a friend. When the upper limit is exceeded by a counselor who asks questions that attempt to elicit a very high degree of intimate self-disclosure in the initial session, the client is likely to resent the invasion of his or her privacy and react by becoming wary and negativistic, which results in increased resistance (see Cozby, 1973; Tedeschi & Lindskold, 1976). Consequently, in order to achieve a positive effect with regard to building referent power, a counselor would have to limit his or her efforts to induce self-disclosure of highly intimate personal matters. For the same reason the need to restrict the self-disclosure variable to tolerable limits would require the counselor to accept silence and uninformative or evasive answers without further probing when clients are reluctant to talk about certain sensitive topics.

In many psychiatric hospitals and clinics, relatively high disclosure interviews involving a great many questions about personal defects, worries, and guilt feelings are regularly used in the initial intake session, which may exceed the optimal level for many clients. Sometimes clients are asked questions that encourage them to reveal personal secrets that are not even freely discussed with close friends. In such interviews the overall effect could in some instances still be positive if the interviewer abstains from putting the clients under pressure to answer the questions and makes it clear that they can evade revealing intimate details if they wish to do so. Nevertheless, it may be extremely risky to ask questions designed to induce very high disclosure in an initial counseling interview because of the unfavorable effect that asking such questions might have on the client's relationship to the would-be helper.

Similar considerations need to be taken into account for each of the other variables. For example, if positive feedback is given too frequently, too elaborately, or inappropriately, clients may become suspicious of the counselor's sincerity and the effect could be negative rather than positive.

2. By a "tolerable" level of self-disclosure is meant a moderate amount and intensity, well below the upper limit that the client regards as excessive for the current social situation. (For further discussion of the upper limit of tolerable self-disclosure see n. 1.)

3 A Theoretical Framework for Decision Counseling

IRVING L. JANIS AND LEON MANN

"Here I am," says the proverbial middle-aged man, "stuck with a miserable career chosen for me by an uninformed 19-year-old boy." Why do so many young people make poor choices they live to regret? Why do so many middle-aged men and women fail to correct their erroneous decisions of the past and continue to make poor choices? Similar questions can be raised about all sorts of ill-conceived decisions by people of all ages and in all walks of life. In recent years research investigators in social psychology, cognitive processes, and related areas of psychology have been trying to answer such questions, to explain why people so often make decisions in public or private life that give rise to fiascoes. Some of the theoretical concepts and findings that have emerged indicate ways to prevent gross miscalculations and to improve the quality of decision making. The counseling interventions suggested by those concepts and findings can be used with clients who seek help in making a difficult choice, such as whether or not to switch to a new career.

In the preceding chapter a number of relationship-building interventions were discussed that affect the client's motivation to follow the counselor's recommendations. It is quite clear what those recommendations will be when a client comes to a counselor for support in carrying out a difficult course of action, such as cutting down on smoking or sticking to a diet. But what recommendations does the counselor make when a client is seeking an answer to "What is the next step I am going to take in my life?" or to any other dilemma? Assuming that a decision counselor can succeed in building up motivation power, what will he or she use it for?

A major purpose of decision counseling, as was pointed out earlier, is to help clients use their own resources for arriving at their own decisions, to make the best possible choice with respect to whichever personal values and objectives they want to maximize. When a client is facing a vital decision—such as entering or quitting college, choosing a career, changing to a different job, getting married, obtaining a divorce, or moving to a different city—many counselors abstain from trying to make the choice for the

This chapter is based on the material relevant to decision counseling in our book entitled *Decision Making: A Psychological Analysis of Conflict, Choice, and Commitment* copyright © 1977 by the Free Press, Division of Macmillan Publishing Co., Inc., New York, 488 pp.

client. They do not recommend any particular course of action as the best one. Rather, these counselors limit their interventions to making recommendations about decision-making *procedures* that could improve the quality of the clients' search and appraisal activities in order to help them make sound choices they can live with. These decision counselors do not refrain from using their expert, legitimate, and referent power to convey norms, but the norms they talk about pertain to avoiding making a choice on an impulsive or a defensive basis. What they advocate to their clients is to spend the necessary time and effort seeking clarification of the issues involved, striving to be open-minded when deliberating, searching for relevant information about consequences of the alternatives, making contingency plans, and taking other specific steps in order to arrive at a decision that will not be regretted. In this chapter we present a systematic theoretical framework that counselors can use as a guide for this type of decision counseling and we describe several newly developed counseling interventions that may be useful aids.

FUNCTIONS OF DECISION COUNSELING

A great deal has been learned during the past 25 years about the cognitive limitations of the human mind in confronting the complexities of selecting among multivalued choice alternatives, including the inability to keep in mind more than a few chunks of information at one time (see Carroll & Payne, 1976; Miller, 1956; Shepard, 1964). More recent studies emphasize other flaws and limitations in human information processing, such as the propensity of decision makers to be distracted by irrelevant aspects of the alternatives, which leads to erroneous estimates of predictable outcomes (Abelson, 1976). Another source of error is the illusion of control, which makes for overoptimistic estimates of outcomes that are a matter of chance or luck (Langer, 1975). Tversky and Kahneman (1974) describe various other illusions, some notorious and others not yet well known, which arise from intuitive assessments of probabilities that may incline all but the most statistically sophisticated decision makers to make biased miscalculations in using evidence about the consequences of alternative courses of action. Some of the findings, for example, indicate that sound evidence about the low risks of a given course of action is likely to be ignored when possible unfavorable outcomes are easy to imagine and readily come to mind.

Another line of research bearing on sources of error is being pursued by attribution theorists (see Nisbett & Ross, 1980). Some of the studies reveal biases in attributing motives, abilities, and other dispositions to persons whose cooperation might be required to facilitate or implement one's decisions (see Jones & Nisbett, 1971). In studies of policy formation in large organizations, other common causes of defective decision making have been elucidated, including bureaucratic politics and group conformity pressures (see Etzioni, 1968; George, 1980; Janis, 1972).

Psychological stress is yet another major source of defective decision making. For example, a harassed decision maker is likely to suffer a decline in cognitive functioning as a result of the stress generated by being confronted with a task too complicated to manage, especially when it can entail material losses and damage to the person's reputation as a decision maker (George, 1974; Janis, 1959; Janis & Mann, 1977). Our analysis of the ways that people cope with the stresses of making vital decisions emphasizes the tendency of people to short-circuit the essential stages of search and appraisal when they become aware of undesirable consequences to be expected from whichever choice they make (Janis & Mann, 1977). Decision makers are often inclined to deceive themselves into thinking they have conducted a complete information search after brief contact with a so-called expert and perhaps a few informal discussions with friends and acquaintances. This sometimes happens even when the decision is a crucial one that could entail serious, lifelong consequences. In such instances a decision counselor can serve a number of valuable functions. Even highly experienced decision makers might benefit from professional guidance designed to help them to carry out a more effective information search, to correct some of their biased judgments, and to become aware of the consequences of inadequate courses of action that they might be tempted to choose. Decision makers who are threatened by a loss of self-esteem in the face of a decision dilemma that is extremely difficult to resolve can be helped by a counselor who builds up their confidence about being able to arrive at a sound decision and to adhere to it.

There is undoubtedly much room for improvement in the information-seeking and appraisal activities of most people. This has been a neglected social problem for which new solutions, in the form of special counseling services and innovative educational programs, are now being developed to aid people facing fundamental life decisions. A new type of counseling service might also help persons in low-income families to become aware of the hidden consequences of the limited alternatives available to them and to work out personal or collective strategies for opening up more choices.

Our theoretical analysis of defective patterns of coping with decisional conflict (Janis & Mann, 1977) has some direct implications for counseling designed to help people improve the quality of their decision making. Some of the main implications are discussed in this chapter after the theoretical analysis is presented. Other implications will be considered in later chapters, where outcome psychodrama and several other new types of intervention are described, all of which are applicable when a client is evading the unpleasant cognitive and emotional work of exploring the full range of probable consequences of each alternative course of action that is available. The proposed interventions were devised as aids that a counselor can use when a client seeks advice in making a vital personal decision. With appropriate changes, they probably can also be used by a consultant who is asked for advice by a chief executive or group of executives who want help in arriving at major decisions affecting the welfare of their organization.

At present the vast majority of counselors and consultants use a completely improvised approach, relying on their personal sensitivity, intuition, and clinical experience to determine what they say to their clients. In contrast we propose a more systematic approach, including a set of standard diagnostic procedures and corresponding interventions based on a theoretical analysis that relies heavily on what is now known about the psychology of decisional conflict. Although highly structured, the proposed counseling procedures still leave plenty of room for flexibility and improvisation.

THE CONFLICT-THEORY MODEL

We start with the assumption that stress engendered by decisional conflict frequently is a major determinant of failure to achieve high quality decision making. *Decisional conflict* refers to simultaneous opposing tendencies within the individual to accept and at the same time to reject a given course of action. The most prominent symptoms of such conflicts are hesitation, vacillation, feelings of uncertainty, and signs of acute psychological stress (anxiety, shame, guilt, or other unpleasant affect) whenever the decision comes to the focus of attention.

Psychological stress arising from decisional conflict stems from at least two sources. First, the decision maker is concerned about the material and social losses he or she might suffer from whichever course of action is chosen—including the costs of failing to live up to prior commitments. Second, the person recognizes that his or her reputation and self-esteem as a competent decision maker are at stake. The more severe the anticipated losses, the greater the stress. In assuming that the stress itself is frequently a major cause of errors in decision-making, we do not deny the influence of other common causes, such as information overload and the limitations of human information processing, group pressures, blinding prejudice, ignorance, organizational constraints, and bureaucratic politics. We maintain, however, that a major reason for many ill-conceived and poorly implemented decisions is the motivational consequences of decisional conflict, particularly attempts to ward off the stresses generated by agonizingly difficult choices.

In line with our initial assumption, we postulate that there are five basic patterns of coping with the stresses generated by any realistic challenge that confronts a person with a vital choice (Janis & Mann, 1977, chap. 3). Each pattern is associated with a specific set of antecedent conditions and a characteristic level of stress. These patterns were derived from an analysis of the research literature on psychological stress bearing on how people react to warnings that urge protective action to avert health hazards or other serious threats.

The five coping patterns are:

1. *Unconflicted adherence.* The decision maker complacently decides to continue whatever he or she has been doing, ignoring information about the risk of losses.
2. *Unconflicted change to a new course of action.* The decision maker uncritically adopts whichever new course of action is most salient or most strongly recommended.
3. *Defensive avoidance.* The decision maker escapes the conflict at least temporarily by procrastinating, shifting responsibility to someone else, or constructing wishful rationalizations to bolster the least objectionable alternative, remaining selectively inattentive to corrective information.
4. *Hypervigilance.* The decision maker searches frantically for a way out of the dilemma and impulsively seizes upon a hastily contrived solution that seems to promise immediate relief, overlooking the full range of consequences of his or her choice as a result of emotional excitement, perseveration, and cognitive constriction (manifested by reduction in immediate memory span and simplistic thinking). In its most extreme form, hypervigilance is referred to as "panic."
5. *Vigilance.* The decision maker searches painstakingly for relevant information, assimilates information in an unbiased manner, and appraises alternatives carefully before making a choice.

Although the first two patterns are occasionally adaptive in saving time, effort, and emotional wear and tear, especially for routine or minor decisions, they often lead to defective decisions if the person must make a choice that has serious consequences for himself, for his family, or for the organization he or she represents. Similarly, defensive avoidance and hypervigilance may occasionally be adaptive but generally reduce the decision maker's chances of averting serious losses. Consequently, all four are regarded as defective patterns of decision making. The fifth pattern, vigilance, although occasionally nonfunctional, generally leads to decisions that meet the basic criteria for high-quality decision making, which we shall discuss shortly.

The five coping patterns are represented in Figure 3.1, which is a schematic summary of our conflict theory of decision making. This conflict model specifies the psychological conditions responsible for the five coping patterns and the level of stress that accompanies them.

The coping patterns are determined by the presence or absence of three conditions: (1) awareness of serious risks for whichever alternative is chosen (i.e., arousal of conflict), (2) hope or optimism about finding a better alternative, and (3) belief that there is adequate time in which to search and deliberate before a decision is required. We assume that the same five coping patterns are in the repertoire of every person when he or she functions as a decision maker, that the use of one pattern rather than another is determined by the mediating psychological conditions shown in Figure 3.1, and that the five patterns lead to distinctive behavioral consequences, which are summarized in Table 3.1.

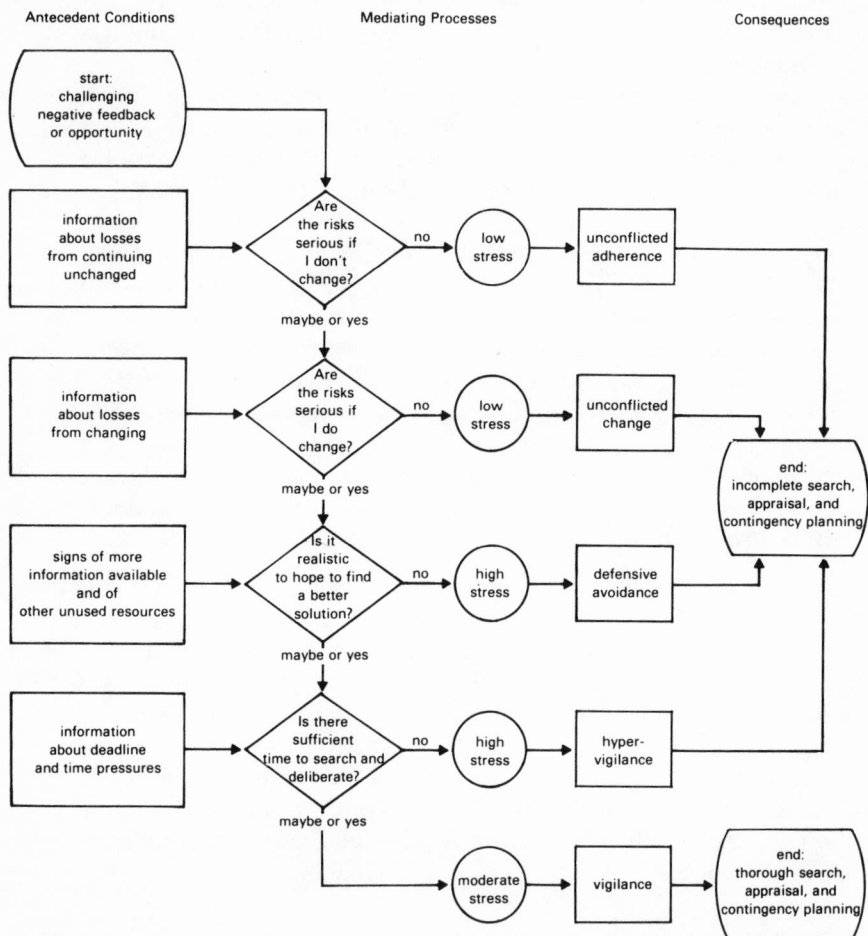

Figure 3.1. The conflict-theory model of decision making. (After Janis & Mann, 1977.)

The columns of the table represent the major criteria that can be used to judge whether a decision made by a person or a group is of high quality with regard to the problem-solving procedures that lead up to the act of commitment. These criteria were extracted from the extensive literature on effective decision making (see Janis & Mann, 1977, chaps. 1 and 2). The seven procedural criteria, which serve as the column headings in Table 3.1, are as follows. The decision maker (1) thoroughly canvasses a wide range of alternative courses of action; (2) takes account of the full range of objectives to

Table 3.1. Predecisional behavior characteristics of the five basic patterns of decision making

Pattern of coping with challenge	Thorough canvasing of alternatives	Thorough canvasing of objectives	Careful evaluation of consequences of		Thorough search for information	Unbiased assimilation of new information	Careful reevaluation of consequences	Thorough planning for implementation and contingencies
			(1) Current policy	(2) New policies				
Unconflicted adherence	-	-	-	-	-	+	-	-
Unconflicted change	-	-	+	-	-	+	-	-
Defensive avoidance	-	-	-	-	-	±	-	-
Hypervigilance	-	-	±	±	±	±	-	-
Vigilance	+	+	+	+	+	+	+	+

Source. Janis & Mann, 1977.

Note. + = the decision maker meets the criterion to the best of his or her ability, - = the decision maker fails to meet the criterion, ± = the decision maker's performance fluctuates, sometimes meeting the criterion to the best of his or her ability and sometimes not. All evaluative terms such as *thorough* and *unbiased* are to be understood as intrapersonal comparative assessments, relative to the person's performances under the most favorable conditions that enable the person to display his or her cognitive capabilities to the fullest degree.

be fulfilled and the values implicated by the choice; (3) carefully weighs whatever he or she knows about the costs or drawbacks and the uncertain risks of negative consequences, as well as the positive consequences, that could flow from each alternative; (4) intensively searches for new information relevant for further evaluation of the alternatives; (5) conscientiously takes account of any new information or expert judgment to which he or she is exposed, even when the information or judgment does not support the course or action he or she initially prefers; (6) reexamines the positive and negative consequences of all known alternatives, including those originally regarded as unacceptable, before making a final choice; and (7) makes detailed provisions for implementing or executing the chosen course of action, with special attention to contingency plans that might be required if various known risks were to materialize.

We assume that failure to meet any of these seven criteria is a defect in the decision-making process. The more such defects are present before the decision maker becomes committed, the greater the chances that he or she will undergo unanticipated setbacks and postdecisional regret, which make for instability and probable reversal of the decision. Although systematic data are not yet available on this point, it seems plausible to assume that "high quality" decisions (in the sense of satisfying these procedural criteria) have a better chance than others of attaining the decision maker's objectives and of being adhered to in the long run.

What is unique about the model is the specification of conditions relating to conflict, hope, and time pressure, which mediate the distinctive coping patterns. We do not claim that the five patterns occur *only* as a result of the specified conditions. A habitual procrastinator, for example, may almost invariably approach any decision, large or small, in a defensive manner; a flexible person may display vigilance in response to most threats but become hypervigilant each time he reencounters a situation in which he had once been traumatized. Our claim is that the patterns are linked dependably with the conditions specified in Figure 3.1—a claim that has testable implications about social circumstances that generate vigilance and about deliberate interventions that could counteract the beliefs and perceptions responsible for defective coping patterns. It follows from this theoretical analysis that information inputs and special intervention procedures used by a counselor when consulted by clients about making a vital choice can modify the way the clients cope with the stresses of decisional conflict in the direction of improving the quality of their decision-making activity. A number of testable implications of the model have been investigated and at least partially confirmed concerning the conditions that determine whether the decision makers' information search will be cursory or thorough, whether their deliberations will be biased or unbiased, and whether their adherence to their decisions will be short-lived or persistent. (The pertinent studies are reviewed in Janis & Mann, 1977, chaps. 4–12.) Decision counselors may find that their work is facilitated if they use the model to diagnose the coping patterns of their clients and to select appropriate interventions.

PREVENTING DEFECTIVE COPING PATTERNS

We propose to rely on the conflict model as the basis for a systematic approach to decision counseling. The diagnostic procedures and interventions suggested by the conflict-theory model, which usually require only one or two hours of counseling, appear to be potentially useful aids for certain types of clients, in light of evidence from studies of a variety of types of decisions. (The research bearing on them is discussed fully in Janis & Mann, 1977, chaps. 13 and 14.) One or two sessions of decision counseling obviously cannot be expected to overcome deep-seated neurotic disorders that give rise to chronic procrastination, chronic evasion of responsibility, or chronic denial of unfavorable outcomes. Probably some persons are predisposed to display time and again the same defective coping pattern, irrespective of the issues at stake or the situational opportunities and constraints that uniquely characterize each decision. If so, they require intensive psychotherapy or other psychological treatments far beyond the scope of decision counseling. But for people who are having unusual difficulty with a particular decision, a session or two with a skilled counselor might bring about a marked improvement in the quality of their decision-making procedures. It is primarily for such people, who occasionally display the common-garden varieties of defective coping patterns, that the decision counseling procedures are intended.

To start with, the counselor must conduct a structured interview during which the client is asked to explain the decisional dilemma he or she is facing and to discuss the steps the client is planning to take before making a final choice. To be effective, the decision counselor must apply a variety of clinical skills that help the client overcome the usual sources of obfuscation —such as efforts to present oneself in a socially accepted way, to restrict one's conversation to conventional modes of speech and superficial platitudes that cover up emotionally explosive conflicts, and to justify one's past and present actions by rationalizations.

Decision counseling, although different from psychotherapy, is probably facilitated by standard features of the clinical stance adopted by many well-trained psychotherapists (see Garfield & Bergin, 1978; Corsini, 1968). One component of this stance consists of making clear that the counselor has no intention of making moral judgments or of criticizing or admonishing any client. A second component involves conveying a genuine sense of interest in learning the truth for the purpose of helping the clients become fully aware of the truth about themselves, but not in order to satisfy the counselor's own egotistic needs. A third component, which is especially important when clients ask for help in selecting the best course of action, is consistent renunciation of the role of an authority figure who will tell the clients what to do. Over and over again, in many different contexts, the counselor can communicate the purpose of this abstention and demonstrate in his or her behavior the intentions that go along with it: that the counselor sincerely intends to refrain from making any judgment about what would be the best choice for the client to make, that the decision is being left entirely up to the client, and that what the client does to arrive at it is to be regarded as the client's own responsibility. Nevertheless, the decision counselor can strongly recommend careful appraisal of alternatives and effectively use interventions that are highly directive, as will become apparent when we review the evidence from systematic research.

Table 3.2. Diagnostic questions (based on the conflict-theory model) to be answered by the decision counselor in order to determine the most appropriate interventions

A. Reactions to the challenging threat or opportunity
1. Does the client believe that the risks are serious if his or her present course of action is not changed?
2. Does the client believe that the risks are serious if his or her present course of action is changed?
3. Does the client believe that it is realistic to *hope* to find a satisfactory alternative?
4. Does the client believe that there is sufficient *time* to search for and evaluate a satisfactory alternative?

B. The client's decisional balance sheet
For each of the alternatives he or she is contemplating, how completely and accurately has the client taken account of the full set of consequences pertaining to:
1. Utilitarian gains and losses for self?
2. Utilitarian gains and losses for significant others?
3. Self-approval or self-disapproval?
4. Social approval or disapproval from significant others?

C. Working through the appraisal and commitment stages
After appraising the challenge to his or her current course of action and surveying alternatives, how much time and effort has the client expended in deliberating with respect to:
1. Which alternative is best?
2. Can the best alternative meet all essential requirements?
3. If the best alternative is unsatisfactory, could one of the existing alternatives be modified to meet all essential requirements?
4. If the best alternative is satisfactory, what are the drawbacks or obstacles to implementing it and allowing others to know one's choice?

Source. Janis & Mann, 1977.

From a free-style diagnostic interview, using the items in part A of Table 3.2 as guidelines, the counselor should be able to diagnose the client's dominant coping pattern on the basis of answers to the four key questions from the conflict model. Those counselors who prefer to arrive at a diagnosis by using systematic procedures (and those who want to assess the effectiveness of decision counseling) may find it useful to carry out a systematic content analysis of a tape recording of the diagnostic interview, similar to the analysis Gottschalk and Gleser (1969) have proposed for psychotherapy interviews. Questionnaires may also prove to be useful in gaining diagnostic information, particularly self-assessment scales that measure variables related to the client's optimism or pessimism about finding an adequate solution to his decisional dilemma, e.g., the social assets scale (Luborsky, Todd, & Katcher, 1973), the social competence schedule (Phillips, 1968), and the state of self-esteem scale (Quinlan & Janis, Appendix). But even without using standardized tests, a skilled interviewer should be able to ascertain the client's expectations about the risks involved in changing and in not changing, as well as his or her degree of optimism about finding a satisfactory solution and expectations concerning deadlines. The counselor would then have to use this information to diagnose the client's dominant coping pattern.

One of the values of the conflict model is that it suggests a number of ways counselors can help their clients avoid defective coping patterns. The following prescriptive hypotheses specify counseling procedures for promoting vigilant search and appraisal:

1. If the counselor ascertains that the client sees no serious risks in persisting in the present course of action and surmises that this is an unrealistic assessment, he or she can attempt to prevent *unconflicted adherence* to whatever course of action or inaction the person has been pursuing. The counselor can raise questions about the potential significance of the negative feedback the client has already encountered, induce the client to consider possible unfavorable outcomes in the future, and encourage the client to obtain objective information and expert opinion about the costs and risks of not changing.
2. If the counselor ascertains that the client sees no serious risks in adopting an attractive new course of action and surmises that this is an unrealistic assessment, he or she can attempt to prevent *unconflicted change*. This requires encouraging the client to obtain objective information and expert opinion about the risks of making the intended change and inducing the client to consider the unfavorable outcomes that are being overlooked, including potential losses from failing to live up to prior commitments.
3. If the counselor ascertains that the client is in a state of acute conflict and that the client believes there is no realistic basis for hoping to resolve the conflict, he or she can try to counteract this pessimistic expectation in order to prevent *defensive avoidance*. The counselor might encourage the client to discuss the dilemma with respected individuals in his or her personal network of relatives, friends, and advisers who might supply

new perspectives that could help the client to maintain hope. The counselor can also suggest that more information is available and can tell the
client where he or she might find it by mentioning pertinent publica-
tions or by recommending professional experts who could be consulted.
Above all, the decision counselor can convey a sense of optimism about
the client's chances of finding a good solution to the problem.

4. If the counselor ascertains that the client is in a state of acute conflict and
that the client believes there is insufficient time to find a good solution,
he or she can try to counteract the panicky vacillation and impulsive
choice that characterizes *hypervigilance.* The counselor might give realistic reassurances about what can be accomplished before the final deadline is at hand. Or the counselor might encourage the client to find out if
the deadline is negotiable, to see if he or she can obtain an extension
without serious costs or risks.

The four prescriptive hypotheses are not necessarily mutually exclusive
if one considers the entire time span of the predecisional period. In early
sessions the major task may be to establish an understanding of the nature
of the alternatives and their associated gains and losses (hypotheses 1 and
2) while in later sessions attention is directed toward resolution, when
maintenance of optimism and morale (hypothesis 3) and realistic assessment of deadlines and time pressures (hypothesis 4) become the major
concerns. Thus, for example, in the first session after a counselor has successfully applied the first prescriptive hypothesis, he or she may soon discover that the second one has become applicable. In a later session the
other two might in turn become applicable, as the client changes answers to
the key questions in response to new information he or she has sought
about probable losses, resources available for working out a good solution,
and deadlines.

ENCOURAGING ADEQUATE SEARCH AND APPRAISAL

The diagnostic questions in parts B and C of Table 3.2 can be used by the
counselor to encourage the client to engage in adequate search and appraisal. Those questions are based on a model of five sequential stages
inferred from observations of people who displayed vigilance in reaching a
difficult personal decision that they subsequently carried out successfully
(Janis & Mann, 1977, chap. 7). We trace the five stages that vigilant decision
makers go through in the process of arriving at a stable decision.

Stage 1: Appraising the Challenge. Until people are challenged by some
disturbing information or event that calls attention to a real loss soon to be
expected, they will retain an attitude of complacency about whatever course
of action (or inaction) they have been pursuing. Being exposed to information about a threat or opportunity that effectively challenges a current
course of action marks the beginning of the decision-making process. The

challenging information produces a temporary personal crisis if the person begins to doubt the wisdom of continuing in that course. Once the decision maker gives a positive response to the first key question, he or she proceeds to search for alternatives.

Stage 2: Surveying Alternatives. After their confidence in the desirability of the old course of action has been shaken by the information contained in the challenge, decision makers start to focus attention on one or more alternatives. Having accepted the challenge, they begin a memory search for alternative courses of action and also seek advice and information from other people about ways of coping with the threat. Vigilant decision makers typically seek advice about how to avert the losses made salient by the challenge. They become more attentive to recommendations for coping with the challenge even though the advice may be inconsistent with their present commitments. Most decision makers are inclined, of course, to cling to the policy to which they are currently committed, if possible. But after being exposed to a powerful challenge they are hungry for fresh information about better alternatives.

Stage 3: Weighing Alternatives. Vigilant decision makers next proceed to a more thorough search and evaluation, focusing on the pros and cons of each of the surviving alternatives in an effort to select the best available course of action. They deliberate about the advantages and disadvantages of each alternative and strive to select the one that will best meet their objectives. During this stage the entries in a decision maker's balance sheet become much more fully elaborated. A vigilant decision maker usually becomes aware of certain gains and losses he or she had not previously taken into consideration. Consequently, the content of the balance sheet may change markedly, with corresponding changes in preference ratings of the alternatives. Any alternative for which the anticipated losses emerge as prohibitive or as incommensurate with the anticipated gains is rejected and precluded from further consideration.

Stage 4: Deliberating about Commitment. After having tacitly decided to adopt a new plan of action, the decision maker begins to deliberate about implementing it and conveying his or her intentions to others. Whether he or she is about to stop smoking, get married, change to a new job, or start a lawsuit, the decision maker realizes that sooner or later the people in his or her social network who are not directly implicated (family, friends, business associates, and casual acquaintances) will find out about it. As a vigilant decision maker the person becomes concerned about their possible disapproval, which he or she may not have thought about earlier. These fresh concerns deter the person from taking immediate action without first paving the way by giving intimates an inkling of the direction in which he or she is moving. Before letting others know about the chosen course of action —particularly if it is a controversial one, such as seeking a divorce—the person will be inclined to think up ways of avoiding disapproval from family, friends, and other reference groups. This often leads to working out social tactics and auxiliary contingency plans for ensuring the success of a new decision (e.g., preparing strong arguments to give those who might object).

Stage 5: Adhering despite Negative Feedback. Many decisions go through a honeymoon period in which the decision maker is quite happy about the choice and implements it without any qualms. All too often, however, this idyllic postdecisional state is rudely interrupted, sooner or later, by new threats or opportunities. Stage 5 then becomes equivalent to Stage 1 in the sense that each unfavorable event or communication that constitutes negative feedback is a potential challenge to the newly adopted policy. However, Stage 5 is different from Stage 1 in that the threshold for being challenged is much higher. Decision makers in this stage are only temporarily shaken and soon decide that despite the new threat or opportunity they prefer to stick with the original decision. They promptly discount minor challenging events and continue to display unconflicted adherence.

A person will remain in Stage 5 indefinitely, until he or she encounters a challenge that is so powerful as to provoke intense dissatisfaction with the chosen course of action. Then the decision maker embarks once again on a painful tour through the successive stages, this time seeking a different and hopefully better alternative. Obviously, the stability of a decision depends to a substantial degree upon the amount and intensity of negative feedback that the person encounters when he or she carries out the chosen course. But stability also depends upon the person's *capacity to tolerate negative feedback,* which, in turn, depends partly on how completely and accurately he or she has worked out the decisional balance sheet during the preceding stages of arriving at the decision.

We postulate that the five stages we have just outlined are fully developed only when the decision maker's dominant pattern is vigilance. The stages are greatly attenuated or short-circuited when a minor incremental decision is made on the basis of a pattern of unconflicted change, or when a major decision is made impulsively on the basis of a pattern of defensive avoidance or hypervigilance. If one of these nonvigilant patterns is dominant, Stages 2, 3, and 4 are perfunctory and sometimes almost entirely omitted.

Even when vigilance is the dominant pattern, the specific stage reached by a decision maker cannot always be sharply differentiated because earlier key questions keep cropping up if they have not been resolved. In presenting a schematic description of the stages of decision making, we do not intend to imply that a vigilant decision maker always proceeds in a completely orderly way. Some decisions appear to move along in linear fashion from Stage 1 to Stage 5, but many involve a great deal of fluctuation back and forth. Reverting to Stage 2 from Stage 3 or 4 is especially likely if the decision involves changing social affiliations, as when a person is contemplating divorce, converting to another religion, or switching membership from one organization to another.

With regard to the questions in part B of Table 3.2, the counselor can pinpoint the big gaps in the client's knowledge about the possible consequences of the alternatives under consideration and can make recommendations about where to go to obtain the missing information. The questions in part C can be explicitly discussed in order to help the client focus on pertinent issues that he or she needs to consider carefully before making a final choice and can be used in connection with recommendations to the client to spend sufficient time and effort deliberating about the decision at home.

In addition to the prescriptive hypotheses already discussed, others that have implications for specific counseling procedures can be derived from the conflict-theory model represented in Figure 3.1. In the remainder of this chapter we shall focus on these additional implications of the model by describing several new procedures that might prove to be useful for improving the quality of decision making among clients who seek advice or guidance when they are making vital choices.

INTERVENTIONS DESIGNED TO COUNTERACT DEFENSIVE AVOIDANCE

When people are required to make major decisions, defensive avoidance is probably the most pervasive defective pattern as well as the most difficult to prevent or correct. The combination of conflict and pessimism about finding an adequate solution leads to the all-too-human tendency to seek escape via wishful thinking. Defensive avoidance may take any of three distinct forms: (1) procrastinating, based on the wishful belief that nothing will be lost by putting off the decision indefinitely; (2) shifting responsibility, or "buck passing," based on the wishful belief that nothing will be lost by foisting the decision onto someone else; and (3) bolstering, based on wishful distortions of the gains and losses to be expected from adopting the least objectionable course of action. All three result in scanty search and inadequate appraisal. The special conditions that foster the first two forms are governed by cues as to whether the decision can be postponed at no great cost (e.g., absence of a deadline) and whether someone else is willing and able to take responsibility. When neither of these low-effort types of avoidance is available, bolstering, the classic mode of defensive avoidance, becomes the dominant mechanism for coping with the stress of a conflictful decision. Bolstering involves the well-known ways of reducing cognitive dissonance, including rationalizing, distorting, and denying in such a way as to play up the relative merits of the chosen alternative (see Festinger, 1964; Janis & Mann, 1977, chaps. 4 and 5).

In our research program we have been developing some new procedures to reduce defensiveness, all of which are based on the assumption that when defensive avoidance in any of its three forms is the dominant pattern, the person will actively resist new information about risks in an effort to avoid reactivating the distressing conflict.

Undermining Rationalizations

What can be done to help people who say over and over again that they want to change their behavior but in practice manage to continue with the same old, unacceptable course of action? In our antismoking and weight-reduction clinics we have interviewed scores of clients who say quite convincingly that they want to stop smoking or overeating in order to avoid damage to their health. But when the counselor probes to find out how seriously these clients really regard the health hazards, it soon becomes apparent that they actually have no intention of changing the old course of action. They bolster their decision to continue smoking or overeating with numerous rationalizations that prevent full acknowledgment of their vulnerability. Some men and women who smoke two or three packs of cigarettes a day, for example, rely heavily on rationalizations that explicitly minimize the chances of their becoming cancer victims ("It won't happen to me"). Others fully acknowledge the risk of lung disease but adopt a fatalistic attitude or claim that their addiction is so uncontrollable that they can do nothing about it. All such rationalizations by a heavy smoker dampen the impact of information about health hazards, with the result that the smoker does not fully take account of losses that could result from his or her present course of action.

People who cling to outworn decisions react in a characteristic way each time they are confronted with challenging information. They appear to go through the first two or three stages of decision making but then promptly return to accepting their outworn course of action. When shown a movie or pamphlet about the health hazards of smoking, for example, heavy smokers become momentarily concerned about the potential threat to themselves (Stage 1) but still display overt resistance, such as questioning the reliability of the information. Next they start to think about alternative courses of action that might counteract the threat, such as limiting themselves to only one cigarette every three hours (Stage 2). They assert that they *ought* to stop smoking entirely but that it is too difficult to do so. At this point their rationalizations about being hopelessly addicted or somehow invulnerable to the threat emerge with full force, and the upshot is that they resume their behavior as heavy smokers (old Stage 5). We have come to regard this repeated sequence through Stages 1 and 2 and then back to old Stage 5 as a *short-circuited* decision loop, which somehow has to be broken if the person is ever to move on to the appraisal and commitment stages required for making a new stable decision.

In an antismoking clinic Reed and Janis (1974) developed an *"awareness-of-rationalizations"* technique that helps to undermine some of the main rationalizations used by heavy smokers to bolster the decision to continue smoking. The technique, which is designed to make the heavy smoker more responsive to challenging information that he or she typically discounts, was tested in a field experiment at the Yale Antismoking Clinic on a sample of 74 men and women who wanted to cut down on cigarette consumption. Half the clients were randomly assigned to the experimental group that was given the awareness-of-rationalizations procedure, while the other half received a control treatment that included the same antismoking communications that were presented to the experimental group.

The counselor's introduction to the awareness-of-rationalizations procedure stressed the importance of "honest exploration and frank acknowledgment of basic, deep-down thoughts and feelings" about giving up smoking. The interviewer then presented the client with a list of eight statements (referred to as "excuses") and asked if he or she was aware of using any of the excuses. The list consisted of typical rationalizations made by heavy smokers, selected on the basis of pilot work with a sample of about 50 heavy smokers:

1. "It hasn't really been proven that cigarette smoking is a cause of lung cancer."
2. "The only possible health problem caused by cigarettes that one might face is lung cancer, and you don't really see a lot of that."
3. "I have been smoking for a fairly long time now, so it is probably too late to do anything anyway."
4. "If I stop smoking, I will gain too much weight."
5. "Smoking just seems to be an unbreakable habit for me."
6. "I need cigarettes to relax; I will become edgy, or irritable, without them."
7. "If I prefer to smoke, I am only hurting myself and nobody else."
8. "So smoking may be a risk; big deal! So is most of life! I enjoy smoking too much to give it up."

After that, the client was given a recorded lecture that refuted the eight rationalizations, followed by two dramatic antismoking films. At the end of the session each subject's reactions were assessed by means of questionnaires. The same refutation lecture, antismoking films, and questionnaires were presented to each client in the control group. Reed and Janis found that the smokers who had received the awareness-of-rationalizations treatment expressed greater feelings of susceptibility to lung cancer and emphysema. They also expressed stronger belief in the harmfulness of smoking and gave more complete endorsements of the antismoking films.

Follow-up interviews 2–3 months later revealed that, as far as the reported amount of smoking was concerned, the awareness-of-rationalizations treatment had a significant effect when given by one psychologist but not by the other. Hence it probably needs to be supplemented with additional procedures to bring about dependable changes in smoking behavior. But because this technique of inducing a decision maker to acknowledge his or her own tendencies to rationalize was found to have significant effects on feelings of vulnerability to lung diseases, it has considerable promise for reducing resistance to realistic warning messages. The technique has much in common with two other successful cognitive confrontation techniques, which have been used to undermine defensive attitudes that bolster social prejudices: Katz, Sarnoff, and McClintock's (1956) insight technique and Rokeach's (1971) awareness of inconsistency between values and actions.

Role Playing to Foster Vigilance

Two types of role-playing procedures have been developed for the purpose of stimulating vigilance at two different stages of decision making, both of which require the client to participate in a psychodrama similar to those widely used for educational purposes. One such technique, known as *emotional role playing,* is useful primarily for making persons who want to change their behavior more keenly aware of the unfavorable consequences of their current course of action. The counselor creates a scenario in which the client is confronted with an "as if" experience of being a victim of a specific disaster. For example, in our initial experiment, which was carried out with women who were heavy smokers, we asked each subject to play the role of a lung cancer patient at the moment when she is receiving the bad news from a physician (Janis & Mann, 1965, Mann & Janis, 1968). We soon found that this disquieting psychodramatic experience could be so realistic that heavy smokers would, for the first time, acknowledge their personal vulnerability to the threat of lung disease. The typical cognitive defense "It can't happen to me" or "It is impossible for me to change" can be undermined by this technique.

Sufficient research has been done on emotional role playing in antismoking clinics to show that this technique is capable of producing long-term changes in attitudes of personal vulnerability and in cigarette consumption among heavy smokers (see Janis & Mann, 1977, pp. 350-360). Additional studies suggest that the technique may prove to be effective for other types of decisions as well, for example, inducing heavy drinkers "to go on the wagon" (Toomey, 1972) and evoking student support for changes in university policy to provide special facilities to meet the needs of disabled students (Clore & McMillan, 1970). Modifications of the technique are now being explored as potentially effective interventions for other types of decisions, including policy decisions by executives.

Another role-playing technique that offers promise for counteracting defensive avoidance and stimulating vigilance is called *outcome psychodrama.* It was devised to aid people when they are approaching the point of making an irrevocable commitment to a final choice, when there is still time to reconsider or to work out contingency plans. The client is asked to participate in a scenario that requires projecting oneself into the future and improvising a vivid retrospective account of what has happened as a consequence of choosing each of the leading choice alternatives. The procedure is repeated as many times as necessary to explore the potential risks and consequences of the principal alternatives under consideration. The counselor refrains from mentioning any specific consequences, leaving it up to the client to use his or her imagination to improvise the specific losses (or gains) that might be sustained. The procedure is described in detail in chapter 18 by Janis and LaFlamme. That chapter summarizes the clinical case studies and the pilot research in which the procedure was first developed and then presents a large-scale field experiment carried out in the setting of a career counseling clinic.

The Balance-Sheet Procedure

Several additional interventions that are intended to foster the vigilant coping pattern have been developed. One is the *balance-sheet procedure,* a predecisional exercise requiring a decision maker to answer questions about potential risks as well as gains that he or she may not have previously contemplated. Without a systematic procedure, even the most vigilant and well-motivated decision maker will overlook vital aspects of the choice alternatives, remaining unaware of some of the losses that will ensue from the preferred course and maintaining unrealistic expectations about potential gains.

The decisional balance sheet schema takes account of both cognitive and motivational aspects of planning for future action. In this schema the expected consequences for each alternative course of action are classified into four basic categories (shown in part B of Table 3.2).

One of the main hypotheses that has grown out of our analysis of the balance sheets of persons making stressful decisions (such as choosing a career, getting a divorce, giving up smoking, going on a diet, and undergoing surgery or painful medical treatments) is the following: *The more errors of omission and commission in the decision maker's balance sheet at the time of becoming committed to a new course of action, the greater will be his or her vulnerability to negative feedback when the decision subsequently is implemented* (Janis & Mann, 1977, chap. 6). We refer to this hypothesis as the "defective-balance-sheet" hypothesis. Errors of omission include overlooking the losses that will ensue from the chosen course of action, which makes the balance sheet incomplete; errors of commission include unrealistic expectations about improbable gains that are overoptimistically expected, which are incorrect entries in the balance sheet.

A balance-sheet procedure designed primarily to prevent errors of omission was developed in a series of pilot studies by Janis and was pretested with Yale College seniors several months before graduation, when they were trying to decide what they would do during the subsequent year. The first step in the procedure is to ask the student to describe all the alternatives he or she is considering and to specify the pros and the cons for each alternative. Then the special procedure is introduced. The interviewer shows the student a balance-sheet grid with empty cells and explains the meaning of each of the four categories. The interviewer helps the student fill in the entries for the alternatives the student had rated as most preferable. After that the interviewer asks the student to examine each cell in the balance sheet again, this time trying to think of considerations that he or she has not yet mentioned. In order to focus on neglected pros and cons, the student is given a sheet listing various considerations that might be involved in a career choice of the type he or she is making (see Table 3.3). The bulk of the time spent on this exercise is usually devoted to those categories that start off with few or no entries, most often considerations pertaining to anticipated approval or disapproval of oneself.

Trial runs with 36 Yale College seniors who were making career choices suggested that the procedure is a feasible way of stimulating people to become aware of major gaps in their decisional balance sheets (particularly those pertaining to unfavorable consequences of the preferred courses of action) and can affect the decision makers' choices. This pilot work was followed up by field experiments on the effectiveness of using the balance-sheet procedure. One study dealt with the choice of a college by high school seniors (Mann, 1972). A second study, which obtained records of weight loss in the setting of a clinic for overweight women who decided to go on a diet, is reported by Colten and Janis in chapter 9. In the third study, reported by Hoyt and Janis in chapter 17, attendance records for healthy women who decided to sign up for an exercise class were unobtrusively collected. As will be seen, the results of the two controlled experiments described in chapters 9 and 17 support the earlier research indicating that the procedure is a promising type of intervention for decreasing postdecisional regret and for increasing the stability of the decision.

Why would it be beneficial for a decision counselor to ask a client to go through the laborious balance-sheet procedure after having already raised all the questions listed in parts B and C of Table 3.2? Why bother to dredge up from the hidden recesses of memory all the favorable and unfavorable consequences one can possibly think of and then write them all down? Our hunch is that a number of functions are served which are essential for preventing gross errors in decision making—so essential, we suspect, that in the not-too-distant future those managers and heads of households who make vital decisions without systematically recording all the entries they can think of in a balance sheet will be as rare as present-day managers and heads of households who do not record deposits and withdrawals in their bankbooks but try to keep a running balance in their heads.

It seems to us that three different types of functions are at least partly fulfilled by systematically going through the balance sheet and related procedures:

  1. *Stimulating more thorough search for essential information.* When drawing up a balance sheet, the decision maker becomes aware of consequences that had previously been neglected, and this can lead the person to seek out

Table 3.3. List of considerations that might affect career choice, used in the balance-sheet procedure as tested with college seniors facing a decision about what to do after graduation

1. Utilitarian considerations: gains and losses for self
   a. income
   b. difficulty of the work
   c. interest level of the work
   d. freedom to select work tasks
   e. chances of advancement
   f. security
   g. time available for personal interests, e.g., recreation
   h. other (e.g., special restrictions or opportunities with respect to social life; effect of the career or job demands on marriage; type of people you will come in contact with)
2. Utilitarian considerations: gains and losses for others
   a. income for family
   b. status for family
   c. time available for family
   d. kind of environment for family, e.g., stimulating, dull; safe, unsafe
   e. being in a position to help an organization or group (e.g., social, political, or religious)
   f. other (e.g., fringe benefits for family)
3. Self-approval or self-disapproval
   a. self-esteem from contributions to society or to good causes
   b. extent to which work tasks are ethically justifiable
   c. extent to which work will involve compromising oneself
   d. creativeness or originality of work
   e. extent to which job will involve a way of life that meets one's moral or ethical standards
   f. opportunity to fulfill long-range life goals
   g. other (e.g., extent to which work is "more than just a job")
4. Approval or disapproval from others (includes being criticized or being excluded from a group as well as being praised or obtaining prestige, admiration, and respect)
   a. parents
   b. college friends
   c. wife (or husband)
   d. colleagues
   e. community at large
   f. others (e.g., social, political, or religious groups)

Source. Janis & Mann, 1977.

crucial information that might otherwise not be encountered until it is too late. Combining the balance-sheet procedure with outcome psychodrama may be especially valuable for overcoming a decision maker's psychological resistances as well as the paucity of his or her imagination when confronted with a consequential decision. While going through these exercises the decision maker dredges up a number of fresh entries to record in the decisional balance sheet, which can temporarily heighten decisional conflict and motivate the person to engage in a more thorough search for the best course of action.

We do not assume that in all cases the more information seeking, the better. Occasionally a decision maker has already completed an adequate search, and more information might make for confusion or generate unnecessary procrastination because information about all sorts of minor unfavorable aspects of the preferred alternative is more salient or more available than information about compensatory positive aspects. But when decision makers have made little or no attempt to search for pertinent information that might be available, increasing their motivation to do so could be beneficial.

A decision maker's hunger for new information, stimulated by heightened awareness of the fresh entries in the decisional balance sheet, can generate intensive memory searches and self-scrutiny as well as requests for advice from experts or acquaintances. If a woman who is trying to make a career choice discovers that she has an "irrational" feeling of aversion toward the alternative that has emerged as best on the basis of the recorded pros and cons, she soon realizes that something important must be missing from her conscious views of the alternatives. Feelings of strong attraction to a seemingly inferior choice have the same effect of posing the question: Why do I feel that way—what am I leaving out of the picture?

Fleeting twinges of emotion may be experienced while the decision maker is writing down specific entries. These affective signals can function as goads to an *internal* information search, which may bring into the decision maker's consciousness a concrete image of enjoying a specific gratification or suffering a specific deprivation, which he or she can then begin to evaluate objectively. Even when the undifferentiated feelings churned up by the balance-sheet procedure cannot be pinned down in any way, the decision maker can at least acknowledge having those feelings and take them into account as significant items of self-knowledge. For example, if an ambitious man's internal search leads him to discover that he has the same "irrational" feeling of uneasiness every time he contemplates switching to a new administrative job that he consciously rates as desirable, safe, and good, he may come to realize that he can expect to suffer subjective discomfort (for some reason he does not know) if he chooses that alternative. Such recurrent feelings of "irrational" uneasiness can be represented in the balance sheet in the category of "anticipated utilitarian losses for self"; if the uneasiness has the emotional tone of guilt feelings, it can also be included in the category of "anticipated self-disapproval." Thus, before making the final choice, decision makers may be better able to take account of formerly preconscious anticipations and perhaps also of some manifestations of their unconscious motives. In general, fuller exploration of the consequences, including those that at first seem to be negligible, can lead a decision maker to move in a direction that better suits his or her objectives.

2. *Fostering more comprehensive appraisal of pros and cons.* Behavioral scientists know relatively little as yet about how people arrive at a sound overall judgment to select the "best" alternative in light of all the pros and cons that enter into a decisional matrix. Nevertheless, it seems safe to assume that, as they become increasingly aware of the consequences of a vital choice, they become less likely to rely upon an oversimplified decision rule for charting their course. A graduating law student who is about to choose among several job offers may feel fairly comfortable at the outset about using a simple heuristic, such as "Select the one that offers the highest initial salary, provided that the chances for promotion are at least as good as with any of the other offers." But he or she is apt to start using a more complex set of criteria after discovering (let us say with the help of the checklist in the balance-sheet procedure) that the available job that clearly meets this simple criterion will probably offer little opportunity to handle the types of cases he or she wants to work on and will involve exploiting loopholes in the law for purposes that he or she regards as ethically questionable.

When a decision maker is worried about a difficult decision and is inclined to avoid thinking about the most painful aspects, defensive avoidance is counteracted by systematic procedures for exploring the known consequences. Defensive avoidance flourishes when a decision maker relies exclusively on the salient considerations present in short-term memory, without being impelled to search his or her long-term memory, to ask others for pertinent information, and to record the findings from the information search.

3. *Inducing preparation for dealing with negative feedback when the decision is implemented.* The more conscientiously decision makers fill out their decisional balance sheet, the better prepared they are to withstand negative feedback once they start to implement consequential decisions. Psychological preparation is needed not only to cope with inherently unpleasant costs but also to avoid being demoralized by the social humiliation and loss of self-esteem that invariably confronts the decision maker at times when it looks as if his or her chosen course of action is turning out badly. By becoming aware of the potentially negative consequences of the chosen alternative before starting to implement the decision, the decision maker can make specific contingency plans. When a setback occurs, such as being asked by the boss to commit an illegal act shortly after having accepted the offer of a new job, the beleaguered decision maker is not caught by surprise and left to improvise on the spur of the moment; instead, he or she already has a plan that was carefully worked out in advance to counteract just such a threat, which can be implemented immediately.

Along with contingency planning and the heightening of confidence about having made the correct choice, there is a related effect resulting from exploring as many of the anticipated consequences as possible before they occur: a stress-inoculation effect, which is stimulated by becoming aware beforehand of the most threatening challenges to be encountered. When a decision counselor encourages clients to go through the exploratory work required by the procedures we have been discussing, he or she may to some extent be building up the stress tolerance of the clients. But the counselor may find it worthwhile to do much more than that—to present clients with various types of preparatory information and recommendations specifically designed to accomplish the goals of stress inoculation.

Stress Inoculation for Postdecisional Setbacks

The underlying principle of stress inoculation is that accurate preparatory communications about an impending crisis and how it can be dealt with gives decision makers the opportunity not only to make contingency plans but also to develop reassurances and other self statements that enable them to cope more adequately (see Janis, 1958, 1971; Meichenbaum, 1977; Meichenbaum & Turk, 1976). We would expect stress-inoculation procedures to be effective for any decision that entails moderate or severe short-term losses before substantial long-term gains are attained. Most decisions concerning personal health problems belong in this category because they usually require the person to undergo painful treatments and deprivations before his or her physical well-being improves.

A considerable body of research during the past 20 years has shown that stress inoculation can be effective with patients who have decided to undergo distressing medical treatments or surgery (e.g., Egbert, Battit, Welch, & Bartlett, 1964; Johnson & Leventhal, 1974; Schmidt, 1966; Schmitt & Wooldridge, 1973; Vernon & Bigelow, 1974). Although some of these studies did not use adequate controls and there are some partial inconsistencies among the findings, all of them provide evidence indicating that when someone on the hospital staff gives preoperative information about the stresses of surgery and ways of coping with those stresses, adult patients show more favorable reactions after the operation. They display less anger, less postoperative regret, more adherence to the postoperative medical regimen, and sometimes better recovery from surgery. Two other studies of surgical patients (Field, 1974; Langer, Janis, & Wolfer, 1975) reported no significant effect of a very brief message describing operative procedures or expected sequelae.

Positive results on the value of stress inoculation have been found in studies of childbirth (Levy & McGee, 1975; Breen, 1975) and noxious medical examinations requiring patients to swallow tubes (Johnson & Leventhal, 1974). Field experiments by Melamed and Siegel (1975), Moran (1963), and Wolfer and Visintainer (1975) with children on pediatric surgery wards yielded similar results. Preparatory communications given prior to relocation of elderly patients to a new nursing home or to a hospital have reportedly been found to be effective in reducing protests and debilitation (Schulz, 1976).

In a completely different area—that of work decisions—there is also evidence that stress inoculation can dampen postdecision stress and minimize the tendency to reverse the decision when setbacks are encountered (e.g., Gomersall & Myers, 1966; Wanous, 1973). New employees given realistic preparatory information at the time they are offered a job, or immediately after they accept it, have been found to be more likely to stay with the organization. All these findings support the conclusion that many people will display higher stress tolerance in response to undesirable consequences if they have been given warnings in advance about what to expect together with sufficient reassurances so that fear does not mount to an intolerably high level.

Recently, research has begun to focus on the psychological components of effective stress inoculation (Janis, 1981; Turk & Genest, 1979). One such component—reconceptualizing the stresses engendered by a stressful course of action—was investigated in a study of surgical patients by Langer, Janis, and Wolfer, which is reported in chapter 19. They found positive results for a counseling procedure that encourages clients to make an optimistic reappraisal of anxiety-provoking events so as to build up their realistic hopes of dealing effectively with whatever suffering or setbacks might be encountered.

In decision counseling for persons contemplating a divorce, a career change, retirement, or any other potentially stressful course of action, interventions of the type used in stress inoculation for surgical and medical patients might help clients to arrive at an accurate blueprint of the consequences that might be in store for them and the coping resources at their disposal. By using appropriate stress-inoculation interventions, a decision counselor may be able to help clients establish a basic attitude of self-confidence, maintain a vigilant approach throughout all the stages of decision making, and develop realistic reassurances. Those reassurances can prove to be effective cognitive coping responses that have a dampening effect whenever a postdecisional setback occurs, which otherwise might make the person regret his or her decision and try to reverse or undo it.

SUMMARY

Recent research indicates considerable room for improvement in the way people arrive at important decisions. A new approach to counseling is described that is designed to help people improve the quality of their search and appraisal procedures when they face choices concerning career, marriage, health, or other vital issues. Prescriptive hypotheses for decision counselors are derived from a theoretical analysis of the conditions making for effective and ineffective coping patterns. Sound procedures of search, appraisal, and contingency planning are most likely to be used, according to the theoretical model, when a *vigilant* coping pattern is dominant, which requires that the following three mediating conditions are met: The person (1) is aware of serious risks if any of the salient alternative courses of action is chosen, including no change from what he or she has been doing; (2) believes that there is some basis for hoping to find a better solution than the least objectionable alternative; and (3) expects to have sufficient time to search and deliberate before a final choice must be made. When one or another of these conditions is not met, a defective coping pattern will emerge, which generally leads to inadequate search and appraisal. The four defective patterns are:

1. *Unconflicted adherence* to the old course of action despite exposure to a challenging threat or opportunity;
2. *Unconflicted change* to a new course of action without considering its undesirable consequences;
3. *Defensive avoidance* of decisional conflict by procrastinating, shifting responsibility for the decision to someone else, or bolstering the least objectionable alternative with wishful rationalizations while remaining unresponsive to corrective information;
4. *Hypervigilance,* which takes the form of a frantic search for a way out of the dilemma and impulsive choice, without considering the full range of consequences, as a result of panic-like excitement, perseveration, and cognitive constriction.

Evidence from recent research was cited on the effectiveness of specific counseling intervention techniques for counteracting defensive avoidance and for fostering vigilance. These include an awareness-of-rationalizations procedure, new forms of role playing in structured psychodramas, a balance-sheet procedure devised to evoke awareness of the full range of consequences, and stress inoculation for postdecisional setbacks.

Decision counselors can use the conflict-theory schema (represented in Figure 3.1) for three purposes: (1) to explore the root causes of failure among clients who appear to be displaying a pattern of defective decision making, such as procrastination; (2) to help clients work more effectively on a specific decisional dilemma by introducing appropriate interventions; and (3) to devise new decision counseling techniques that take account of the three major determinants that, in combination, give rise to the coping patterns: intensity of conflict, degree of optimism about finding a solution, and perceived amount of time available for making the choice.

PARTNERSHIPS: A MEANS FOR INCREASING ADHERENCE TO THE COUNSELOR'S RECOMMENDATIONS

4 Effective Partnerships in a Clinic for Smokers

IRVING L. JANIS AND DAVID HOFFMAN

Proponents of Alcoholics Anonymous and Synanon have described the buddy system as contributing to their members' success in "staying on the wagon" or "kicking the habit" (Alcoholics Anonymous, 1939; Yablonsky, 1967). The potential value of forming a partnership has also been suggested by earlier research in Yale counseling clinics (Janis, 1965) on the effects of participating in a small discussion group with others who are trying to give up smoking or to stay on a diet. Those members who spontaneously acquired a buddy before the end of the group sessions, and who continued afterward to stay in telephone contact with the partner, reported less backsliding than those who did not acquire a partner.

The primary purpose of the present study was to investigate the effects of such partnerships systematically. We wanted to find out whether clients who come to an antismoking clinic would be more likely to adhere to their decision to cut down on smoking if a counselor induces pairs of clients to form partnerships and to have daily telephone contact, which gives them the opportunity to engage frequently in mutual self-disclosure during the critical period. A second purpose was to obtain observations bearing on two hypotheses that could explain the positive effects of partnerships, both of which were suggested by the earlier observations (Janis, 1965):

1. During the period that they are attending formal meetings with a counselor (or leader), partners who have daily conversations and disclose their problems of mutual concern as they are undergoing common sources of

Much of this chapter is a slightly revised version of an article published in the *Journal of Personality and Social Psychology* (1970, *17,* no. 1, 25–35). The data from the 10-year follow-up study, however, are new and are published here for the first time. The field experiment was originally funded by a grant to Irving Janis from the National Institute of Mental Health, United States Public Health Service. Funds for the 10-year follow-up study were provided by a grant to David Hoffman from the Academic Research Council of the Graduate School of Florida State University. The authors wish to thank Professor James C. Miller of George Washington University and Professor Howard Leventhal of the University of Wisconsin for valuable suggestions during the planning phases of this experiment. They are also grateful to Professor Thomas Crawford of the University of California for a detailed critique of the first draft of the article.

stress tend to become more cohesive than if they have no such contact; consequently they value the three-person group and its norms more highly. Thus, the increase in interpersonal attractiveness of the group members makes for stronger motivation to adhere to a group norm endorsed by the counselor, such as cutting down on heavy smoking or avoiding overeating.

2. After the three-person group has formally disbanded, partners who remain in contact and continue to discuss problems of mutual concern remind each other, intentionally or unintentionally, of their commitment to the group norm and provide mutual social support for living up to it.

These two hypotheses are linked with well-known social psychological phenomena that have been extensively investigated. The first combines two well-known principles. One is that interpersonal attraction increases as a consequence of increased communication between two persons who are facing common sources of stress; the other is that internalization of group norms increases as a consequence of increased attraction to a group that provides the rewards of mutual acceptance and friendship with one or more of its members (see Cartwright & Zander, 1968, pp. 47–62). The second hypothesis could be regarded as a special case of the positive relation between direct interaction with a group member and heightened salience of the group's norms.

With these two hypotheses in mind, we designed the present study as a field experiment in a smoking clinic in order to investigate the effects of different degrees of social contact. The dependent variables included measures of adherence to antismoking norms and process indicators that might provide a basis for evaluating the two explanatory hypotheses.

METHOD AND PROCEDURES

Design

This study was carried out with 30 adults (14 men and 16 women) who volunteered to come to our clinic for heavy smokers in the Department of Psychology at Yale University in response to newspaper articles and announcements offering free help for people who wanted to cut down on smoking in exchange for their participation in an ongoing program of research on smoking behavior. The mean age of the clients was 40 years. All were high school graduates; one-third of them had graduated from college. Twenty-one of the 30 were married.

The only criterion used in selecting the volunteers who phoned the clinic was their report that they smoked more than one pack of cigarettes daily. The mean for the 30 clients was 32 cigarettes per day. Eighteen reported that their physician had recommended cutting down for medical reasons and the other 12 also listed health hazards as a major consideration.

All clients were asked to attend a series of five weekly meetings at the clinic. At each of these meetings 3 persons were present: the clinic counselor and 2 male or 2 female clients. At the first meeting each pair of clients was assigned on a stratified random basis to one of three experimental groups: (a) *high-contact partners,* who were asked to talk with each other daily by telephone, in addition to attending the five weekly meetings; (b) *low-contact partners,* who spoke with each other only at the five weekly meetings, since they were asked *not* to have any telephone contact; (3) *controls,* who had no stable partner, each of whom was paired with a different person at each of the five weekly meetings. The three experimental groups, of 10 subjects each, were highly similar on relevant background characteristics: age, education, marital status, current cigarette consumption, and the number of years they had been heavy smokers.

Initial Interview and Assignment of Conditions

About 2 weeks before the first meeting, each client was individually interviewed by the counselor concerning general background information, current smoking behavior, smoking history, and reasons for wanting to cut down or stop smoking. The client was also asked to fill out a written questionnaire, which included two psychological scales: (a) a *smoking attitude* scale, consisting of 20 agree–disagree items that had been used in earlier studies of heavy smokers at the clinic and (b) an *anxiety symptom* scale, consisting of 10 multiple-choice items dealing with feelings of nervousness and psychosomatic complaints of the type that often accompany withdrawal from heavy smoking.

After completing the written questionnaire, the client listened to a tape-recorded description of the "new clinic program," which asked the client to come to the clinic once a week for 5 weeks, where he or she would meet with a fellow smoker of the same sex who was also trying to stop smoking. The client was told that at each weekly session the counselor would present the two smokers with recorded lectures and films designed to help them live up to their decision to cut down on smoking. This recorded talk also mentioned that the client would have an opportunity to discuss with a fellow smoker the problems of abstaining from cigarettes. The client was informed that the research aspect of the program consisted of evaluating various methods of helping people to cut down on smoking, and that for this purpose the weekly discussions would be tape-recorded. Also, he or she would be asked to fill out brief questionnaires after each session and to keep a smoking logbook or diary. The client was also informed that he or she would be asked to participate in an interview at the end of the fifth meeting. The client was assured that all questionnaires and tape recordings would be kept confidential. Finally, the client was told that although the clinic staff expected this program to be helpful, we did not know how helpful it would actually turn out to be; the only way we would be able to find out would be if everyone who came to the clinic was completely honest in answering the questions we asked.

The Five Meetings

Every one of the 30 subjects attended five meetings of a three-person group, for which the same psychologist (D. H.) always functioned as the counselor. Sessions 1–4 were deliberately structured in such a way that the counselor functioned as a norm-sender during the first half of each meeting by giving standard recommendations and by presenting persuasive communications about cutting down on smoking. The other half of these sessions was devoted entirely to a spontaneous discussion between the two clients, which gave them an opportunity to discuss the messages they had just received in relation to their own lives. This was done partly to encourage the clients to develop a sense of personal responsibility for carrying out the decision to cut down on smoking. While the two clients talked together, the counselor was outside the room, listening and watching through a one-way-vision screen. (Permission for recording and observing all these discussions was obtained from each client.) In order to minimize experimenter effects, the counselor presented all essential recommendations and information either by using a tape recording of his own voice or by reading aloud from a printed script. All the antismoking communications he presented were in the form of printed pamphlets, films, and tape-recorded lectures.

The counselor introduced the following specific procedures into the five meetings.

Session 1. The counselor presented to the two clients a brief lecture that he had tape-recorded on the nature of the smoking habit and how it could be broken. The tape recording included instructions about how to use the daily logbook to record smoking behavior. Then, after describing the clinic program in a standardized way, he gave somewhat different instructions to randomly assigned pairs of clients so as to create the three different experimental conditions: (a) for the high-contact condition, the standard instructions about the four subsequent meetings with the same partner were supplemented by an additional statement requesting the two clients to exchange their telephone numbers and to call each other every day in order to discuss their problems in connection with cutting down on smoking; the clients were also asked to make a notation in their daily smoking logbooks of each telephone call, indicating who initiated it, the content of the conversation, and how long it lasted; (b) for the low-contact condition, the same standard instructions about the four subsequent meetings were given, but the partners were asked *not* to telephone each other; (c) for the control (no stable partner) condition, the same standard instructions about the four subsequent meetings were given as in the other two conditions, except that the clients were told that they would be paired with a different fellow smoker at each meeting.

Session 2. The counselor played a tape-recorded lecture for the two clients summarizing numerous helpful hints offered in the psychological literature for people who wanted to stop smoking. The lecture also pointed out how relaxation and other gains from smoking can be obtained in other, more beneficial ways.

Session 3. The counselor played a tape recording of a documentary-like synthetic "case history," with an excerpt from a crucial session when the patient was told by his physician to stop smoking because his "smoker's cough" was due to a precancerous condition of his lungs (which was illustrated by a chest X-ray). This was followed by an excerpt from a session 2 months later in which the patient was informed by the same physician that as a result of his having stopped smoking, the X-rays now showed good recovery. The two clients were then given a pamphlet entitled "Your Health and Cigarettes" (distributed by the American Cancer Society), which was read aloud by the counselor while the clients underlined the main points in their own copies.

Session 4. The counselor presented a color film (*One in 20,000,* distributed by the American Cancer Society), which tells the story of a young smoker who becomes a victim of lung cancer. One scene takes place in the operating room and shows the gory details of the surgical removal of the patient's cancerous lung. This film was used because it has been found to be effective in motivating smokers to stop smoking (Leventhal & Niles, 1964; Niles, 1964).

Session 5. The counselor reversed the usual sequence by asking the two clients to have their spontaneous discussion during the first half-hour. He then used the last half of this session to give a posttreatment interview and questionnaire. Each client was interviewed privately in an adjoining room while the other member of the pair filled out a questionnaire.

The spontaneous discussions between the two clients, which in Sessions 1–4 were devoted mainly to talking over the material that had just been presented by the counselor, were tape-recorded. In addition the counselor kept a record of eye contact between subjects by observing them through a one-way-vision screen. The clients' chairs were so placed that it was necessary for them to turn slightly to look at each other in clear view of the observer, who held a button in each hand. He pushed one button or the other each time a client looked at the partner's face. These buttons activated timers that gave cumulative individual looking time for each client and total mutual looking time (when both clients simultaneously were looking at each other).

Posttreatment Interview

Posttreatment interviews were conducted at five different times with each client so as to follow the temporal course of changes in smoking behavior.

The first of these, which was the interview at the end of the final clinic session, contained questions concerning the client's expectations about his or her future smoking behavior, the client's impressions about the helpfulness of the meetings at the clinic, and the client's current feelings toward his or her partner. The questionnaire given at this time included a 10-item attitude-toward-partner(s) scale, together with the same two psychological scales that had been given during the initial interview 7 weeks earlier (the attitude-toward-smoking scale and the anxiety symptoms scale).

Three additional follow-up interviews were conducted at intervals of 6 weeks, 6 months, 1 year, and 10 years after the final clinic session. All except the last of these interviews were conducted over the telephone by the clinic's secretary. She explained that some people had been helped whereas others had not and that it would be valuable for us to know accurately how people were now doing so that we could evaluate the treatment methods we had been using. She asked each client about his or her smoking behavior since the end of the clinic and then asked how many cigarettes he or she had smoked the day before. The 6-month follow-up interview included some additional questions about the contacts, if any, he or she had had with the partner since the end of the clinic meetings.

RESULTS

Changes in Smoking Behavior during the First Year

The results in Figure 4.1 indicate that the treatments were differentially effective in producing changes in reported smoking behavior. At the end of the 5-week clinic (7 weeks after the before measure), all three treatment groups had cut down substantially on cigarette smoking ($p < .01$). The difference between the high-contact partners and the other two treatment groups were in the expected direction, although not large enough to be significant ($p < .15$).[1] By 6 weeks later, however, the differences among the three groups were highly significant ($p < .01$). The differences continued to be significant at the time of the 6-month follow-up ($p < .01$) and at the time of the 1-year follow-up ($p < .01$).

For the entire year, the high-contact partners reported continuing at a low level of cigarette consumption, ending up with an average of only 8.2 cigarettes per day (a reduction to one-fourth of their original smoking level).[2] In contrast, the low-contact partners reported stabilizing for the final 6 months of the year at an average of 23.6 cigarettes per day (three-fourths of their pretreatment level). The group with no stable partners reported returning to their starting level and thus showed no long-term benefit whatsoever from the clinic.

At the end of the year the high-contact partners differed significantly from both the low-contact group ($p < .01$) and the control group ($p < .001$). The difference between the low-contact partners and the controls with no

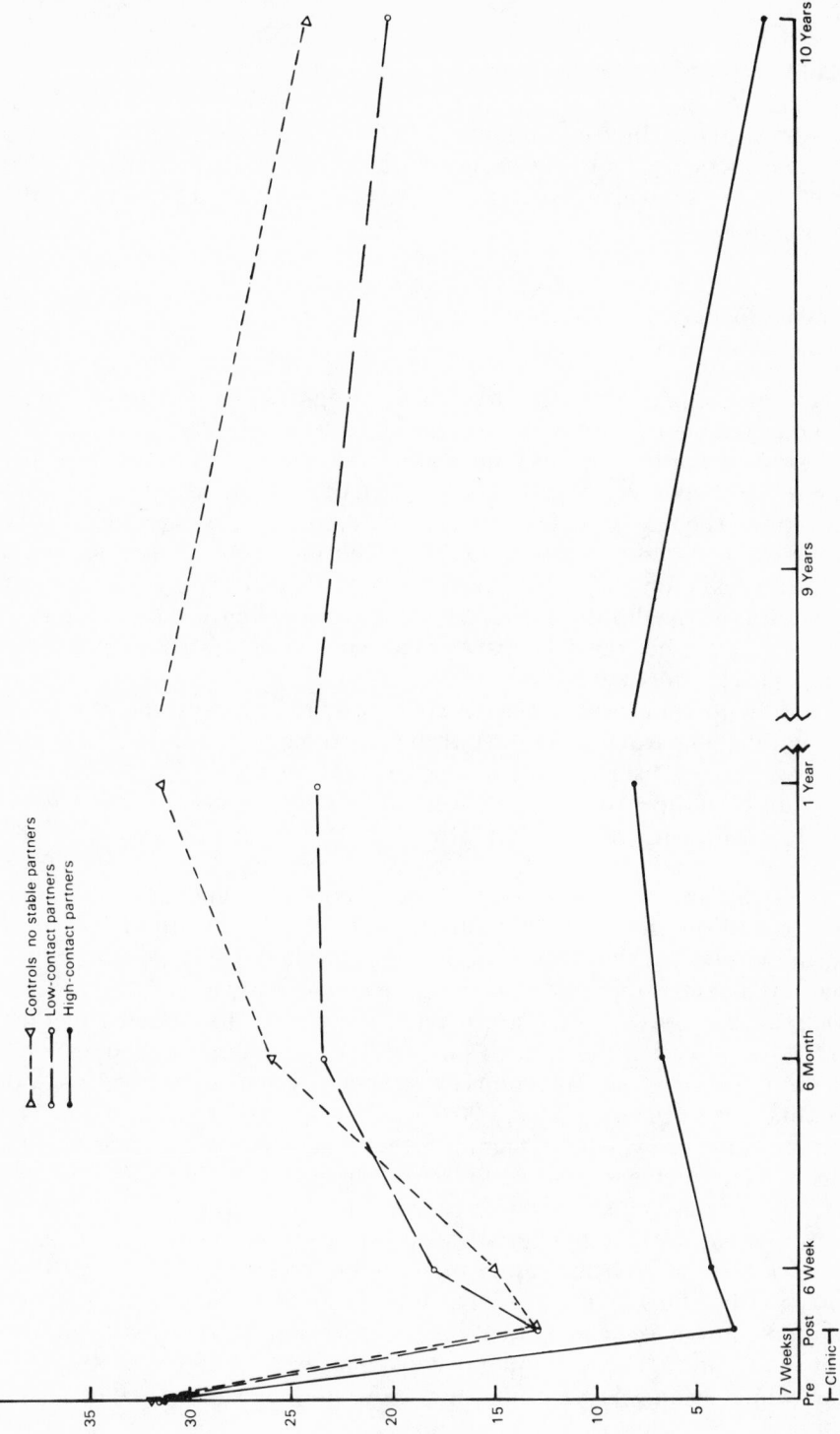

Figure 4.1. Changes in the reported number of cigarettes smoked daily.

stable partners still remained nonsignificant (p = approx. .15). Thus, the findings on reported smoking behavior indicate that one year after the final session with the clinic consultant, *only the high-contact partners continued to be highly successful in cutting down on cigarette smoking.* The other two groups failed to sustain the initial success they had shown at the end of the clinic sessions.

Smoking Behavior and Recollections of the Clinic Ten Years Later

Ten years and 3 months after the final meetings of the three groups, long-distance telephone interviews were conducted with the clients in the original experiment. In order to reduce any tendency to provide answers that might be thought to please the interviewer, the telephone interviews were presented as being part of a survey of health behavior being conducted by Florida State University (which was true). The questions about smoking and smoking cessation attempts were imbedded in a set of questions concerning a variety of health attitudes and behaviors, including diet, use of alcohol, and preventive health checkups. A female graduate research assistant conducted each interview.

Telephone companies in seven states assisted in the difficult task of tracing the 30 participants. Most of them had moved at least once during the 9-year period since they had last been contacted.

In all, 27 of the 30 participants were located by telephone and agreed to the 20-minute interview. Included in this follow-up study were all 10 of the high-contact partners; 9 of the 10 low-contact partners (one had died from an unascertainable cause), and 8 of the 10 controls (one had died of lung cancer and one refused to be interviewed). Nine of the 10 high-contact partners reported that they did not smoke at all and had not smoked for many years. One reported that she smoked currently approximately one pack (20 cigarettes) per day and had repeatedly tried to cut down over the previous 10 years without much success. The average reported number of cigarettes smoked per day for this experimental group, therefore, was only 2.0. In contrast the average was 20.0 for the low-contact partners and 24.0 for the controls, which are significantly higher than the average for the high-contact partners ($p < .01$ for both comparisons). Three of the 9 partners in the low-contact condition reported that they did not smoke at all; 2 of the 3 indicated that they had stopped during the past 5 years. The remaining 6 of the 9 smoked an average of 30 cigarettes a day, which is about the same as when they first came to the clinic more than 10 years earlier. Only 2 of the 8 interviewed members of the control group reported that they did not smoke at all. The remaining 6 smoked an average of 32 cigarettes per day, which again was about the same as when they had first come to the clinic.

When asked if they had ever participated in a smoking cessation clinic, all

10 high-contact subjects specifically mentioned the Yale Clinic. When asked for details, they gave detailed descriptions of the program, including an average of 5 distinctive features of the program (a partner, a group facilitator or psychologist, a film, role playing, weekly meetings, telephone contact with a partner, journals, and so forth). All 10 recalled at least the first name of their partner even though they had not had any contact for 10 years.

Of the 9 low-contact partners interviewed, all mentioned some formal program participation, and 8 specifically mentioned the Yale Clinic, but most had tried other programs as well. An average of only 2 features of the programs were recalled (usually the partner and the clinic facilitator), and only 2 of the 9 recalled their partner's first or second name.

Of the 8 controls who were interviewed, 5 mentioned the Yale Clinic and an average of 2.5 feates of the program was described. None of the controls recalled the first or second names of any of the 5 fellow smokers with whom each of them was paired at the five clinic sessions.

The recollection of their partners' names by all the high-contact participants, in contrast to recollection by only 2 of the low-contact participants, is consistent with the conclusion that there was higher interpersonal attraction between high-contact partners than between the low-contact partners. The high-contact partners also clearly recalled more details of the clinic program, which suggests that the program was a much more vivid experience for them than it was for the others.

Attitude Changes

The attitude-toward-smoking scale was given before and after the clinic sessions, with approximately a 7-week interval between administrations. (The interval between initial contact and the first of the five weekly meetings was about 2 weeks.) The attitude-change results are shown in the top row of Table 4.1. An analysis of covariance indicates significant differences in the degree to which the three treatment conditions succeeded in inducing antismoking attitudes ($p < .05$).[3] For all three treatment conditions there is a significant change from a slightly positive attitude concerning the desirability of smoking before the first meeting to a negative attitude at the end of the final meeting. But the high-contact partners changed significantly more in the negative direction than did either the low-contact partners ($p < .01$) or the controls ($p < .01$). Thus, the findings on attitude changes parallel the findings on long-term changes in reported smoking behavior, again indicating that the treatment in which the partners had daily telephone contact was superior to the other two types of treatment.

Some additional findings show the relation between attitudes toward smoking and reports of actual smoking behavior. We found that the clients' preclinic attitudes toward smoking were not related to their initial level of smoking (all subjects being very heavy smokers) or to their success in cutting down during the subsequent year. But the clients' postclinic attitude scores, obtained at the end of the last clinic session, turned out to be highly related to long-run success as assessed 1 year later. Those clients who scored above the median on the postclinic attitude test (indicating that they retained a relatively *favorable* attitude toward smoking) showed a rela-

Table 4.1. Mean scores on two scales: attitude-toward-smoking and withdrawal symptoms of anxiety

Scale	Type of group					
	High-contact partners		Low-contact partners		Controls	
	Before clinic	After clinic	Before clinic	After clinic	Before clinic	After clinic
Attitude toward smoking: total score on 20 agree–disagree items[a]	2.7	–12.0	2.2	–2.2	1.2	–4.8
Anxiety reactions: mean score on 10 multiple-choice items[b]	1.9	1.5	1.8	2.2	1.7	2.1

Note. N was 10 in each group.

  [a]Scores could range from –20 (for antismoking responses to all 20 items) to +20 (for prosmoking response to all 20 items).

  [b]Since there were five choices for each symptom, scores could range from 1 (for "practically never") to 5 (for "very often"). A score of 2 corresponds to the second lowest choice, "once in a while," and a score of 1 corresponds to "practically never."

tively small decrease in cigarette consumption after the clinic and then promptly returned to their preclinic level by 6 months later (smoking an average of 29 cigarettes per day) and remained there at the end of the year (smoking an average of 31 cigarettes per day). In contrast, those clients who scored below the median on the attitude posttest showed a very low rate of cigarette consumption (an average of only 2.5 cigarettes per day) at the time of the posttest and subsequently increased only slightly by 6 months later (to an average of 9.4 cigarettes per day) and by the end of the year (to an average of only 13 cigarettes per day, which is significantly less than the corresponding mean of 31 per day; $p < .05$). Thus, the findings consistently show that, across all three types of groups, those clients who were most influenced to adopt an antismoking attitude as a result of attending the five weekly sessions at the clinic turned out to be the ones who were most successful in cutting down on cigarette smoking throughout the following year. These correlational results do not, of course, enable us to draw a definite conclusion that the attitude changes were a cause of the changes in smoking behavior.

Anxiety Symptoms

Changes in sleeplessness, feelings of "nervousness," and related anxiety reactions are relevant for assessing the relative effectiveness of the three treatment conditions because some of the standard communications given by the counselor were intended to help the clients cope with the stresses engendered by relinquishing a well-established habit that was pleasurable, relaxing, and tension reducing. Preparatory information and reassurances were given for purposes of stress inoculation to counteract the adverse effects of feelings of "nervousness" or "irritability" that many heavy smokers experience when they try to cut down, which are similar to the more acute withdrawal symptoms that induce some smokers to give up the attempt.

The mean scores obtained from the anxiety symptoms scale are shown in the second row of Table 4.1. Before the first clinic session the mean scores for the three groups were almost equal, all being in the low range. At the time of the posttest, at the end of the final session, the high-contact partners showed a slight decrease in mean anxiety scores, whereas the other two treatment groups showed a slight increase. An analysis of covariance indicated that the differences among the three groups were significant ($p < .05$); the decrease in anxiety scores shown by the high-contact partners differed significantly from the increase shown by each of the other two groups ($p < .05$ for each of the two comparisons).

Attitudes toward Partners

Some indication of the qualitative differences in the social relationships among members of the high- and low-contact groups comes from a series of questions which asked the clients to rate their partners. The first key question asked how the client's feelings toward his or her partner had changed during the 5-week period. In the high-contact group, 7 of the 10 clients reported liking the partner "more and more" as they got to know the partner, whereas in the low-contact group, only 1 out of the 10 clients gave this response ($p < .05$).

Further evidence of the comparatively greater degree of mutual liking on the part of partners in the high-contact condition comes from a set of 10 multiple-choice questions in the postclinic questionnaire that asked for ratings of the partner's personal attractiveness. For each item the scale ranged from 1 for liking the partner "not at all" to 5 for liking the partner "very much." The mean ratings from the three groups were as follows: high-contact partners, 4.0; low-contact partners, 2.6; controls (no stable partners), 3.3. (Because none of the clients in the control group had a stable partner, each one in the control group was asked to answer the questions by giving a collective rating of the five partners with whom he or she had attended the five sessions.) An analysis of variance indicates significant differences among the three groups ($p < .01$). The high-contact partners expressed significantly more liking of their partners than did the clients in either of the other two treatment groups ($p < .001$ and $< .02$).

Similar findings were obtained from a behavioral measure based on observations of eye contact during the five sessions. An analysis of variance of the total time the partners spent in mutual eye contact shows significant differences among the three treatment groups ($p < .05$). The mean amount of mutual eye contact shown by the high-contact partners was significantly higher ($p < .05$) than the corresponding means for either of the other two groups. Although the counselor could not avoid knowing the condition the clients were in when he recorded the amount of eye contact as he observed them through a one-way-vision screen, he nevertheless followed a standard and highly reliable set of procedures in making these measurements. In any case the measurements of mutual eye contact were found to be highly correlated with the clients' own ratings of liking for their partners obtained from the postclinic questionnaire ($r = .67$, $p < .001$). These findings are consistent with prior findings indicating that eye contact is linked with interpersonal attraction (Exline & Winters, 1965).

Satisfaction with the Clinic Sessions

Open-ended questions about the value of the clinic's program, which were answered at the end of the final session, elicited uniformly positive comments from almost all clients in all three treatment groups. A significant difference ($p < .05$) was found, however, on one question that invited the clients to express criticisms of the clinic sessions: "What did you like *least* about the smoking clinic programs?" A larger number of favorable answers (asserting that nothing was disliked) was given by the high-contact partners than by the low-contact partners or by the control subjects. This finding implies that the high-contact partners felt more satisfied with the clinic sessions at the time of termination than did the others.

DISCUSSION

The foregoing findings consistently show that the treatment condition in which the counselor asked the partners to telephone each other daily and to disclose their mutual problems was much more effective in helping people to adhere to their decision to cut down on smoking than an equivalent treatment condition that did not allow for any contact between partners except at the five weekly meetings. The latter (low contact) treatment was no more effective than a control treatment, in which each client was paired with a different partner at each of the five weekly meetings. In fact, neither of these two treatments had any long-run effect on reported smoking behavior during the subsequent year or 10 years later, whereas the high-contact partners reported a marked and persistent decline in their cigarette consumption.

In seeking clues concerning psychological processes that may mediate the apparent success of the high-contact partnerships, we made a number of additional observations, some of which yield low-level evidence useful for obtaining preliminary leads. We shall discuss these additional observations, as well as the main findings, in the context of trying to answer the questions posed by the two explanatory hypotheses suggested at the beginning of the chapter.

Increased Interpersonal Attraction as a Mediating Factor

Did daily telephone contact increase interpersonal attraction between group members and produce a correlated increase in acceptance of the group's norms during the period when they were attending meetings with the counselor? Although we have no definitive evidence of the causal sequence, our study provides three pieces of relevant information that converge in giving a tentative positive answer to this question.

First, we have seen that the findings on attitudes toward partners support the assumption that the high-contact-partnership treatment produced a relatively high degree of mutual liking between the two group members, compared with the low-contact-partnership and control treatments. The mutual eye contact data also point to a relatively high degree of interpersonal attraction manifested by the high-contact partners at the weekly meetings.

Second, compared with clients in the other two groups, the high-contact partners showed a relatively greater amount of change in the direction of accepting antismoking attitudes when the clinic sessions came to an end (Table 4.1). Subsequently those who showed these attitude changes were more likely than the others to report that they had cut way down on their actual amount of cigarette smoking, in behavioral conformity with the antismoking norm, 1 year after termination. Hence, our findings reveal that the high-contact partners became more disposed than the others to accept and live up to the antismoking norm that the counselor constantly conveyed in the various lectures, pamphlets, and films he presented at the five meetings.

Third, supplementary observations based on the tape recordings of free discussions between partners at the five meetings indicate that the high-contact partners were more explicit than the others in expressing their commitment to live up to the antismoking norm. For example, by the final session, all 10 of the high-contact partners had spontaneously announced, "I am definitely going to cut way down, starting today," or an equivalent commitment statement; whereas only about one-half of the low-contact partners had made any such spontaneous announcement ($p < .05$). In addition the high-contact partners made many more statements that could be categorized as socially supportive of the counselor's norms than did the clients in the other two treatment groups.[4] Typically, these supportive statements were given when the partners reported some degree of success in cutting down on smoking (e.g., "You're really doing a good job, keep it up!"). But support was qualified and generally contingent on the partner's verbal adherence to the goal of giving up smoking. The high-contact partners, unlike the others, frequently criticized each other for backsliding and were skeptical about the partner's glib promises to be good in the future (e.g., "You don't really mean it, do you?" "Why aren't you honest with yourself?"). Such criticism and challenges were seldom made by the low-contact partners and were almost completely absent in the discussions held by the nonstable partners. Sometimes, in fact, the latter unintentionally supported counternorm tendencies. (For example, one woman in the control group told her partner in the final session, "I was terrible last week. . . . I just didn't have any will power or something, and I smoked more than before we started." Her partner replied, "Well, everyone deserves some time off, and you know you deserved it, so why worry?"). In general the interaction between the high-contact partners appears to have been qualitatively different from the more casual "chitchat" relationship that characterized the other two treatment groups: the high-contact partners directed their conversation much more to committing themselves to the group norm (within hearing of the counselor) and to giving selective social reinforcement—expressing approval when the partner conformed and expressing mild disapproval when the partner failed to do so.

There is the possibility, of course, that in their conversations and also in their answers on the attitude questionnaire, these clients were merely paying lip service to the norms. But the assumption that the antismoking attitudes we observed at the time of the final session were genuine, involving internalization of the norm, is supported by the auxiliary finding that these attitude scores proved to be inversely correlated with the number of cigarettes the subjects reported they were smoking *1 year later.* It should also be noted that across all three groups, the amount of liking the partners expressed toward each other was related to the amount of attitude change. Hence, although we cannot prove that the clients' verbal reports were valid, all the findings concerning changes in attitudes relevant to the antismoking norms are consistent with the hypothesis that increased contact of partners who engage in mutual disclosure during the period when they are attending meetings with the counselor makes for increased interpersonal attraction and results in greater adherence to the norms conveyed by the counselor.

Is Sustained Social Support a Mediating Factor?

The major question for the second explanatory hypothesis is: After the clinic meetings had ended, did the high-contact partners remain in touch over a long period of time and continue to provide social support for adhering to the decision to cut down on smoking? The answer appears to be no on the basis of what was revealed by the follow-up interview conducted approximately 6 months after the clinic sessions ended. In this interview all the high-contact partners informed us that they were no longer in contact with each other. They reported that after the last meeting they had continued to phone each other once or twice a week for 2–4 weeks and then stopped. It appears highly unlikely, therefore, that the long-term positive effects can be explained by continued contact or by anticipated future contact between partners in the formerly high-contact condition. All contact had ceased well before the significant differences in reported smoking behavior became apparent.

The long-term effects of the high-contact-partnership treatment apparently are not attributable to any long-term, ongoing interaction between the partners. The critical time period presumably was when the partners were interacting with the counselor: during the weeks when they were attending regular meetings at the clinic and perhaps for a few weeks thereafter, when the partners were still in telephone contact. Continued contact between the partners during the first 2 weeks after the final session may have provided mutual social support, which could help to counteract the disruptive effects of termination of contact with the counselor and the disbanding of the three-person group.

An Alternative Interpretation:
All One Needs Is a Buddy

In line with the preliminary theoretical analysis of effective helping relationships (chap. 2), the interpretations considered so far assume that attending meetings with a norm-sending counselor is a necessary condition for the success of high-contact partnerships. There is an alternative explanation, however, that attributes success entirely to the partnership itself, so that contact with a counselor or leader who communicates antismoking information and recommendations would not be essential. Perhaps when a person decides to undergo self-imposed deprivations, such as those resulting from giving up smoking, the availability of a buddy who can be contacted whenever social support is needed helps him or her to maintain the appropriate attitudes and to reduce withdrawal symptoms of anxiety, so that he or she is better able to carry out the intended action. If so, the most successful partnerships should be those in which each smoker has the opportunity to phone his or her buddy at any time he or she wants to, on an ad-lib basis, just as in Alcoholics Anonymous.

A subsequent pilot study by Hoffman, using 20 clients who had been on the waiting list for our antismoking clinic, obtained some preliminary results bearing on this hypothesis.[5] Hoffman randomly assigned the clients to two types of partnerships: (a) *ad-lib contact*: 10 clients were told that for 1 month they should phone the buddy whenever they wanted to, with a limit of once per day; and (b) *contact at a fixed time*; 10 clients were told that for 1 month they should phone the buddy every day at a specific time in the evening. None of the clients in either condition had any contact with the counselor at the clinic except for the initial phone call, in which he explained the buddy system and told them whom and when to call. Follow-up interviews showed that during the month both groups had kept up nearly daily contact with the buddy and had decreased their cigarette consumption by about 40%. But by 30 weeks later, both groups of buddies had returned to their initial smoking level of approximately 30 cigarettes per day on the average. Thus, unlike our high-contact partnerships, which functioned as a supplement to weekly meetings with the counselor, these high-contact partnerships had no sustained effect on reported smoking behavior. Hoffman's findings suggest that daily contact with a partner, whether on an ad-lib basis or on a fixed time schedule, is ineffective under conditions where the clients receive no antismoking communications and have no contact with a norm-sending counselor.

A similar interpretation can explain the results of a field experiment by Miller and Janis (1973) on the effects of partnerships set up with college students for the purpose of reducing maladaptive reactions to the stresses of college life, feelings of discouragement, and unfavorable attitudes that might incline a student to withdraw from academic activity or to drop out of college altogether. The partners were instructed to conduct intensive interviews with each other concerning their life history and personal adjustment. In contrast, a control group was set up of equivalent pairs who did not engage in mutual self-disclosure. A weekend t-group was conducted before the partnerships were formed. When the pairs met, however, they had no guidance from or contact with a psychological counselor. The results showed opposite outcomes for achievement and morale. On the one hand, the mutual student partnerships had beneficial effects on performance of the main task objectives (preparing psychobiographies of each other in a term paper for the introductory psychology course), as manifested by the grades received from the course instructors. The instructors had explicitly conveyed norms concerning the course work objectives and these were better fulfilled by students in the mutual partnerships. But, on the other hand, the mutual partnerships had demoralizing effects, as manifested by the students' answers to a series of questions about their feelings of adequacy for coping with the academic and social stresses of college life. A crucial factor that seems to account for the detrimental effects of the mutual self-disclosing partners on personal morale is the leaderless and unsupervised character of the students' interactions, which led them to reinforce each other's complaints about the college environment. Unlike what happens when a student seeks help from a counselor, no respected person encouraged the students to try to cope more adequately with current academic and social stresses.

Obviously, however, no definitive conclusions can be drawn on this issue until a full-scale factorial experiment is carried out in which the effects of various partnership treatments are investigated under contrasting conditions of being exposed versus not being exposed to antismoking communications and of having contact versus no contact with a counselor who endorses special behavioral norms. Studies with groups of varying sizes will also be needed to find out whether the outcome we observed is replicated when the groups meeting with the counselor are larger than the three-person groups used in the present study. The effects of variations in instructions given to the partners also require careful study in subsequent analytic experiments. For example, in order to determine whether sustained social contact contributes to the facilitating effects, one could observe the effects of instructing high-contact partners to continue phoning daily for, let us say, 6 months compared with telling such partners not to continue phoning after the last meeting or telling them nothing about what they are expected to do after the last meeting, as in the present experiment. Our finding that the high-contact partnerships had an extraordinarily powerful sustained effect on reported smoking behavior when assessed 1 year after and again 10 years after the clinic had ended opens up the possibility that investigations of variations in partnership instructions in similar clinics could yield results of both practical and theoretical significance. Such research should help to specify the conditions under which people are most likely to adhere to long-term decisions that originally had been bolstered by the norms conveyed by a counselor or group leader.

It must be emphasized that in this study the role of the counselor was primarily that of a resource person who presented a large number of mass-media-type communications urging the members of the group to stop smoking. In sponsoring these communications he was constantly making strong implicit demands for conformity to the clinic's antismoking norms. It seems unlikely, however, that the counselor introduced any *differential* demand characteristics that could account for the observed differences in reported smoking behavior and attitudes, since all three treatment groups in this experiment were given the same standard communications, and practically everything the counselor said was read aloud from a prepared script or was presented in a tape recording.

In view of all the various bits of evidence just discussed, the most likely explanation for the long-term success of the high-contact partners appears to involve increased internalization of the norms advocated by the counselor before the relationship with him had ended. From the data at hand from this study, the most plausible mediating factor is specified in the first explanatory hypothesis considered—namely, the increase in interpersonal attraction produced by daily contact with a fellow member who is sharing the stresses of cutting down on smoking, which makes for increased valuation of the group at the time when the members of the group are attending meetings together, and correspondingly greater internalization at that time of the norms conveyed by the group leader.

Our findings appear to be roughly in line with the broad conclusions suggested by Hunt and Bespalec (1974) on the basis of their survey of research on current counseling methods used to modify smoking behavior, including behavior modification, aversive conditioning, drug therapy, self-control training, role playing, education, and social support. Most treatment methods, they find, succeed only temporarily, with a very high relapse rate in the first 6 weeks after the treatment is completed. On the average, they find, only 40% of the smokers who have received some form of counseling treatment in antismoking clinics show a decrease in cigarette consumption 3 months after treatment; only 25% remain long-term abstainers. These authors conclude that of all the various methods they evaluated the most promising are education and group support. In our study the information and instructions given by the counselor were clear-cut instances of education; the high-contact partnerships, which were found to have comparatively favorable long-term effects, appear to be interpretable as increased group support. The supplementary bits of evidence concerning the effects of the high-contact partnerships appear to be compatible with an analysis in terms of the three critical phases involved in a counselor's acquiring and maintaining motivational power as leader of a three-person group (chap. 2). During the first critical phase the partners disclosed personal information bearing on their smoking problems to the counselor and to each other in the initial meeting of the three-person group. The counselor was empathic and accepting, which probably served as a model for the partners when they subsequently talked to each other. In Phase 2 the counselor clearly conveyed at each additional meeting his endorsement of the norm about cutting down on smoking and he gave selective feedback that reinforced the norm. There is evidence that the two partners did likewise in their conversations with each other when the counselor left them alone in the clinic room. In Phase 3 the partners decided to remain in contact with each other after the last meeting with the counselor and they continued to phone each other for several weeks, which may have reduced the unfavorable emotional impact of separation from the counselor and disbanding of the three-person group.

MAIN CONCLUSIONS

1. In a smoking clinic *high-contact* partners (who met once a week with the counselor and were instructed to phone each other every day for five weeks in order to disclose mutual problems) were more successful than *low-contact* partners (who spoke with each other only at the five weekly meetings with the counselor) or *controls* (who had a different partner at each of the five weekly meetings with the counselor). The superior effectiveness of the high-contact partnerships was manifested after the treatments by (a) more unfavorable attitudes toward smoking; (b) more favorable attitudes toward the clinic; (c) fewer withdrawal symptoms of anxiety reported after cutting down on smoking; and (d) markedly less smoking reported in

follow-up interviews during the year after termination of contact with the counselor and in a 10-year follow-up interview conducted as a general health survey by an independent organization based in a distant city.

2. The most plausible explanation for the greater long-term success of the high-contact partnerships appears to be the increase in interpersonal attraction produced by the daily contact, which makes for increased valuation of the clinic group when the members of the group are meeting and for correspondingly greater internalization of the norms conveyed by the counselor. In line with the preliminary theoretical analysis of effective helping relations (chap. 2), there is some low-level evidence that mutual disclosure alone is not enough and that attending meetings with a norm-sending counselor at the smoking clinic is a necessary condition for the long-term success of the high-contact partnerships.

NOTES

1. Analysis of covariance was used for each of the four posttreatment measures of smoking behavior to take account of the subject's pretreatment score on smoking behavior (number of cigarettes smoked the day before). (The four F-values were as follows: 2.25, 6.15, 13.17, and 15.87, respectively, with $df = 2/26$ in each instance.) None of the distributions was bimodal and the variances among the three groups were relatively homogeneous. Analysis of covariance was also used to take account of the subjects' pretreatment scores on the attitude-toward-smoking scale and the anxiety reactions scale. Using analysis of covariance as a significance test is conceptually equivalent to using an analysis of variance of change scores when (as in this case) there are no initial differences among treatment groups in pretreatment scores. (See Winer, 1962, pp. 578–588.)

2. The high-contact partners also reported in the 1-year follow-up interview that they had not gained weight as a result of cutting down on cigarette smoking.

3. For attitude toward smoking, $F(2, 26) = 4.82$; for anxiety reactions, $F(2, 26) = 4.08$. These were obtained from an analysis of covariance. (See also the last sentence in n. 1.)

4. A content analysis of the tape-recorded conversations showed that the high-contact partners made significantly more statements of the following two types than did the low-contact partners: (a) positive reinforcing or supporting statements when the partner reported some degree of success in adhering to the antismoking norm ($p < .01$) and (b) negative or disapproving statements when the partner reported reluctance or failure with respect to living up to the antismoking norm ($p < .05$). Similar differences in the same direction were obtained when the high-contact partners were compared with the controls. (For the two types of statements, $p < .07$ and $< .01$, respectively.) These content analysis results provide only low-level evidence because the analysis could not be carried out blind with respect to treatment conditions. The high-contact partners were often on a first-name basis and from time to time referred to their phone conversations, in contrast to the pairs in the other conditions, who spoke in a way that made it obvious that they had had less contact.

5. D. Hoffman, Effect of ad-lib and fixed daily contact between partners who agree to cut down on smoking. Unpublished research report, Yale University, 1968.

5 Effective and Ineffective Partnerships in a Weight-Reduction Clinic

CARLA NOWELL AND IRVING L. JANIS

In this chapter we describe two field experiments on partnerships carried out with women who wanted to lose weight. The experiments were designed to investigate the conditions under which giving overweight clients the opportunity to engage in mutual disclosures of their feelings about the problems of dieting with a partner facing the same type of stressful dilemma would strengthen adherence to the difficult decision. Our first field experiment was designed primarily as a conceptual replication of the one reported in the preceding chapter to see if the positive effects of assigning partners in an antismoking clinic would be repeated in a different counseling setting. The principal purpose of our second field experiment was to see if the positive effects would be enhanced by giving information that elicits a high degree of perceived similarity in the members of each pair.

THE FIRST EXPERIMENT: A CONCEPTUAL REPLICATION OF THE JANIS AND HOFFMAN EXPERIMENT

The main independent variable in this field experiment was high versus low contact with an assigned partner. The results reported by Janis and Hoffman in chapter 4 indicated substantial and enduring effects for high-contact compared with low-contact partners, but the investigators had to rely on the clients' self-reports concerning the number of cigarettes smoked per day. They could not definitively demonstrate that such measures corresponded to actual smoking behavior although they took precautions to minimize demand characteristics of the assessment procedures. This methodological problem was avoided in the present study in a weight-reduction clinic because we were able to use a direct behavioral measure of adherence to the diet as a dependent measure (amount of weight lost).

The predictions we tested were that high-contact subjects would show more weight loss (at the time of a follow-up interview) and would express more favorable attitudes toward their partners and the clinic at the end of the regular sessions than would low-contact partners. These predictions were based partly on the previous findings of Janis and Hoffman and also on a substantial body of literature showing positive effects of propinquity and contact on attraction (Byrne, 1961; Byrne & Buehler, 1955; Caplow &

95

Forman, 1950; Festinger, 1951; Gullahorn, 1952; Katz & Hill, 1958; Kennedy, 1943; Maisonneuve, Palmade, & Fourment, 1952; Newcomb, 1956). Studies by Darley and Berscheid (1967) and Berscheid, Boye, and Darley (1968) indicate that either induced contact or anticipation of future contact can generate increased attraction.

A second independent variable was introduced in this experiment to determine whether the effectiveness of partnerships could be enhanced if the partners are asked to use selective reinforcement in order to remind each other of their commitment to remain on the diet. The immediate and sustained effects found by Janis and Hoffman and the absence of such effects in the pilot study by Hoffman reported in chapter 4 as well as in the experiment on student partnerships by Miller and Janis (1973) suggest that contact with a norm-transmitting communicator is essential for a successful outcome. (See in chap. 2 the discussion of the second phase of a helping relationship, in which the helper uses his or her motivating power to endorse specific norms.) One of the purposes of the present study was to determine whether instructing the partners to give selective reinforcement to each other—which is tantamount to assigning them norm-transmitting functions—would result in increased adherence to the stressful decision. Half the pairs were told to give selective reinforcement to each other (expressing approval when the partner talks about adhering to the diet and withholding approval when he or she reports failures to stick to the diet or expresses the intention of eating foods that are not on the prescribed diet). The other half of the pairs were instructed to respond to each other in an unconditionally supportive manner, reacting to accounts of counternorm behavior (going off the diet) in an empathic way with no criticism or pressure (unconditional positive regard).

The two main predictions tested in this study were that greater weight loss would be found in those pairs who had been instructed: (1) to have a relatively high degree of contact (daily rather than weekly) and (2) to give each other selective reinforcement rather than unconditional positive regard.

METHODS AND PROCEDURES

The experimental conditions that were investigated consisted of two levels of contact (high vs. low) and two modes of interaction (selective reinforcement versus unconditional positive regard).[1] The subjects were 48 adult women who came to a weight-reduction clinic in the Department of Psychology at Yale University. Clients volunteered in response to a newspaper announcement offering free assistance to women with no special health problems who wanted help in beginning a diet in exchange for their participation in an ongoing program of research on effective counseling. The mean age of the subjects was 39.6 years. Most of them were high school graduates and a substantial minority had some college training. The only volunteers excluded were those who reported that they weighed over 200 pounds or had a special health problem such as heart disease. The mean weight for the subjects was approximately 165 pounds.

All volunteers were mailed three forms to be filled out: a life history questionnaire, the "need affiliation" subscale of the Personality Research Form (Jackson, 1967), and a blank time schedule on which each client was asked to indicate times when it would be possible for her to attend the clinic sessions. The answers on the questionnaires were used to set up pairs of subjects who would be similar in age, education, weight relative to height, and attitudes expressed about the problems of being overweight. At the first session with the counselor, each pair was assigned on a stratified random basis to one of the four experimental conditions. Six pairs (12 clients) were assigned to each condition. Mean levels of weight, education, and age did not differ significantly across conditions.

All clients were given mimeographed sheets outlining the recommended diet and a set of sample menus, all of which were obtained from the Department of Dietetics of the Yale–New Haven Hospital. After a tape recorded explanation of the diet, clients were asked to sign a commitment statement, agreeing to begin immediately on the 1200-calorie diet, to be weighed at each meeting, to attend the remaining meetings, and to inform the clinic of any new health problem. The commitment statements given to the high-contact subjects also included an agreement to call their partners daily for at least 10 minutes. Daily record sheets were given to each subject and participants were asked to fill them out daily.

Next the clients were given a taped communication which instructed them in one of two alternative modes of interaction whenever they spoke with each other. Clients in the selective reinforcement group were advised to encourage those statements about intentions and reported actions of the partner consistent with the goal of staying on the diet and not to encourage behavior inconsistent with that goal. They were asked to be warm and empathic in all instances *except* when it would undermine the common goal of adhering to the diet. Clients in the unconditional positive regard group were asked to be *invariably* accepting and sympathetic toward the partner, regardless of whether the partner was conforming to the diet recommendations. For example, a suitable response to backsliding by a partner in the unconditional-positive-regard condition would be, "I know it is very hard to stay on the diet sometimes"; whereas an appropriate response by a partner in the selective-reinforcement-condition would be, "I know it is very hard to stay on the diet sometimes, but do try to avoid going off it in the future." To ensure that clients understood the instructions and to give them practice in the assigned mode of interaction, the counselor, a female psychologist, asked them to role play a discussion in which typical problems arise, such as one partner reporting to the other a failure to resist tempting food that are not on the diet. The counselor encouraged, and whenever necessary modeled, the appropriate type of response.

One week later and again 2 weeks after that the two additional sessions were held with the counselor. These sessions provided continued contact with the counselor over a 3-week period and allowed the partners to have some face-to-face interaction. The procedures during the second and third sessions were the same for all clients in all conditions. The second session was devoted mainly to discussing the problems of dieting and the third session to administering questionnaires.[2] The clients were weighed at each of the three sessions.

Six weeks after the third session a different female counselor contacted subjects by telephone and arranged a follow-up interview. Clients were seen alone by the new interviewer rather than in pairs for this fourth interview. After being weighed at the beginning of the session, each client was asked to complete an attitude questionnaire. Included were questions asking them what feelings or attitudes they had toward the initial counselor, when they had last been in contact with their partner, how many times they had spoken with or seen their partner, how cooperative and how competitive their relationship had been, and how helpful the partnership was. Each question had a checklist of five multiple-choice alternatives.

RESULTS AND DISCUSSION

Effects of High versus Low Contact

As predicted, clients in the high-contact partnerships showed more weight loss than those in the low-contact condition at the time of the 9-week follow-up interview condition (see Table 5.1).[3] Over that time interval the high-contact partners lost about 3 pounds more, on the average, than the low-contact partners (main effect $F = 4.6$, $p < .05$).

Table 5.1. Mean weight loss (in pounds) for each treatment condition over a nine-week follow-up period

	High contact	Low contact	Combined
Selective reinforcement	8.6	5.0	6.8
Unconditional positive regard	8.2	5.8	7.0
Combined	8.4	5.4	6.9

Note. $N = 12$ in each of the 4 groups.

A second behavioral measure that was examined pertains to overt reluctance to return to the clinic for the follow-up weighing and interview (see Table 5.2). The measure used was a delay of 1 week or longer (including failure to come back at all). Of the 24 women in the low-contact condition 17 showed delay (71%); only 5 of the 24 women in the high-contact condition did so (21%). (The 50% difference is significant beyond the .01 confidence level.)

Table 5.2. Percentage of clients in each treatment condition who delayed one week or more coming back for their scheduled nine-week follow-up session

	High contact	Low contact	Combined
Selective reinforcement	25%	75%	50%
Unconditional positive regard	17%	67%	42%
Combined	21%	71%	46%

Note. $N = 12$ in each of the 4 groups.

Another measure on which the high-contact and low-contact partners differed, as expected, was the reported amount of spontaneous contact with the partner after the third session. This measure pertains to contact after the end of the period during which they were asked to be in contact, when they were free to be in contact or not as they wished. The data in Table 5.3 show that according to the clients' reports at the time of the 9-week follow-up interview, the average number of days since the partners were last in contact was significantly smaller for the high-contact pairs than for the low-contact pairs (21.0 vs. 38.0 days; $F = 6.96$; $df = 1, 20$; $p < .01$). These measures indicate that more spontaneous contact occurred among the high-contact partners during the 42 days that had elapsed since the high-contact partners had their third session (after which they were no longer required to contact each other). A closely related measure shows that 62% of the high-contact partners reported having had some spontaneous contact since the last clinic session as against only 29% of the low-contact pairs. (This 33% difference approaches significance at the .10 confidence level.)

Table 5.3. Mean number of days elapsed since partners had last spoken to each other (from verbal reports as of 42 days after the last clinic session)

	High contact	Low contact	Combined
Selective reinforcement	20.6	38.4	29.5
Unconditional positive regard	21.5	37.5	29.5
Combined	21.0	38.0	29.5

Note. $N = 6$ pairs in each of the 4 groups.

On a series of attitude items in the questionnaire given during the 9-week follow-up interview, we found no significant differences between the high-contact and low-contact groups. These included attitudes toward the partner and toward the counselor, on both of which we had expected to find more favorable attitudes expressed by the high-contact partners. Clients in all treatment conditions expressed extremely favorable attitudes on both attitude scales. The absence of differences is therefore most likely attributable to a ceiling effect: the low-contact partners obtained such high attitude scores that it was impossible for the high-contact partners to obtain significantly higher scores.

We did find a marginally significant difference ($p < .10$) between contact groups on attitude toward the weight-reduction clinic, which was assessed by a scale consisting of 3 items asking the clients how satisfactory they found the weight clinic's program as a whole, how useful they found the sessions, and how useful they found the 1200-calorie diet. On this scale the high-contact partners expressed somewhat more favorable attitudes than the low-contact partners.

Effects of Selective Reinforcement
versus Unconditional Positive Regard

The results in Tables 5.1–5.3 show that there were no significant differences between the two modes of interaction. Contrary to our expectations, selective reinforcement had no observable effect on weight loss, delay in returning for the 9-week follow-up interview, or amount of reported spontaneous contact between the partners. Two attitude scales (attitudes toward the partner and toward the clinic) also failed to show any significant differences. Clients in the unconditional positive regard condition expressed slightly more favorable attitudes toward their partners than did clients in the selective reinforcement condition ($p < .10$).

A clue as to why the two types of social reinforcement failed to have any important differential effects is provided by an additional attitude item which asked each client to indicate how much competitiveness had developed between herself and her partner. Clients in all experimental groups gave answers revealing only a slight amount of competitiveness, but statistically significant differences nevertheless emerged. Among the low-contact pairs, those who were instructed to give unconditional positive regard reported less competitiveness than those who were instructed to give selective reinforcement, just as expected. But for the high-contact pairs, the difference is unexpectedly in the reverse direction: Those instructed to give unconditional positive regard reported *more* competitiveness. (The interaction effect is significant at the .05 confidence level.)

Because the contact between low-contact pairs always occurred at the clinic, in the presence of the counselor, we know that the members of those pairs generally gave the type of social reinforcement they were instructed to give. For these pairs the competitiveness ratings came out as expected. But we could not monitor the daily 10-minute telephone conversations of the high-contact pairs, so we do not know to what extent they gave the type of social reinforcement they were instructed to give. The finding that those who were instructed to give unconditional positive regard during their telephone conversations reported feeling *more* competitiveness than those instructed to give selective reinforcement, which is not in line with prior research findings discussed in chapter 2, suggests that the instructions may not have been carried out in the expected way during the unmonitored telephone calls.

In summary the first experiment supports the main conclusion from the Janis and Hoffman study (chap. 4). Just as in the antismoking clinic, we found in our weight-reduction clinic that assigning clients to high-contact partnerships (requiring them to have a 10-minute telephone conversation every day for 3 weeks) led to a significant increase in adherence to the two main recommendations made by the counselor: Compared with the low-contact pairs, who talked together only at the clinic sessions, the high-contact pairs showed a significantly *greater amount of weight loss* at the 9-week follow-up interview and significantly *less delay* in returning for that interview. The high-contact partners also reported more spontaneous contact since the last clinic session and expressed somewhat more favorable attitudes toward the clinic than the low-contact partners.

The second variable investigated in this study, which involved instructing the pairs of subjects to give each other selective reinforcement versus unconditional positive regard, failed to yield significant differences on either of the two main behavioral measures. Anomalous results obtained on an attitude item dealing with feelings of competitiveness between partners suggests that during their unmonitored telephone calls, the high-contact partners may not have followed the instructions concerning social reinforcement in the way that was intended or else the instructions had a paradoxical effect.

THE SECOND EXPERIMENT: AN UNSUCCESSFUL ATTEMPT TO REPLICATE WHEN SIMILARITY OF THE PARTNERS IS EMPHASIZED

A second experiment, which was carried out concurrently with the first one, was an exact replication except for one variation that was expected to enhance the effectiveness of the high-contact partnerships. The one procedure that differed involved an attempt to induce a high degree of *perceived similarity* in the members of each pair, which, according to prior research, should have the effect of increasing liking, cohesiveness, and adherence to norms in dyadic or triadic groups whose members are in frequent contact.[4]

METHODS AND PROCEDURES

The second experiment used exactly the same experimental design and the same procedures as the first one, except for a modification in the explanation given to each client about the way partners were assigned. In our first experiment, clients were told truthfully that partners could not be closely matched up on all the attitudes they had expressed on the preliminary questionnaire. (This was similar to the type of statement made in the Janis and Hoffman experiment.) In our second experiment, however, the positive aspects of the matching attempts were emphasized by telling the subjects— again, without distorting the truth—that many of the feelings and attitudes which they had expressed on the questionnaires were very similar and that their reactions to the problem of being overweight were very much alike. Exactly the same criteria for assigning pairs were used as in the first experiment. Just as in the first experiment, the pairs were, in fact, fairly well matched on background factors (age, education, weight relative to height) and on attitude items concerning the problems of being overweight and the desire to lose weight.

RESULTS AND DISCUSSION

Contrary to expectations, neither of the two variables (high versus low contact and selective reinforcement versus unconditional positive regard) had any differential effects. (All p values are nonsignificant.) The amount of weight loss in the second experiment was less than in the first experiment. The overall mean weight loss of 5.0 pounds over the 9-week follow-up period is markedly lower than the corresponding mean of 6.9 for the first experiment ($p < .10$).

In the second experiment, at the time of the 3-week follow-up session the low-contact group had lost the same amount of weight (3.8 pounds) as in the first experiment, but the high-contact partners did not lose as much weight as in the first experiment (3.3 pounds vs. 5.5 pounds). These results indicate that emphasizing the similarity of the partners in the second experiment had an unintentionally adverse effect on the high-contact partners during the early weeks of dieting. It was more detrimental to those high-contact partners in the second experiment who received selective reinforcement than to those who received unconditional positive regard (2.3 pounds vs. 4.3 pounds).[5]

On the second behavioral measure—delay of 1 week or longer in returning for the final follow-up interview—we found that the percentage of high-contact partners who delayed was only very slightly different from the corresponding percentage of low-contact partners: 38 and 33%, respectively. For this behavioral measure, just as for weight loss, there were no significant effects of either amount of contact or type of reinforcement.

Additional data from the second experiment show that clients in both the high-contact and low-contact conditions felt that they were well matched with their partners and expressed extremely favorable attitudes toward their partners and toward the clinic psychologist. Just as in the first experiment, a ceiling effect apparently precluded any significant differences from emerging. And again, just as in the first experiment, the high-contact partners reported more spontaneous contact than the low-contact partners after the formal partnership period was over ($p < .01$ for the percentage who contacted each other at least once after the third session and $p < .01$ for the number of days since the partners last spoke to each other). On both indicators of amount of contact, the clients in the second experiment, in every subgroup, reported less spontaneous contact than in the first experiment, but the overall difference was not large enough to be statistically significant.

On the scale assessing attitude toward the weight-reduction clinic, the high-contact partners expressed somewhat *less* favorable attitudes than the low-contact partners ($p < .10$). This finding contrasts with the results on this scale obtained in Experiment 1, which showed a significant difference in the opposite direction. The information about close matching of the partners, which was intended to enhance the effectiveness of the high-contact partners by increasing perceived similarity, apparently resulted in less satisfaction. The *disappointment* implied by these results may account for the lack of success of the high-contact partnerships in the second experiment.

Disappointment reactions and the detrimental effects on weight loss that resulted from emphasizing the matching of the partners in the second experiment might have been a consequence of building up unrealistically high expectations. The clients who were told that their partners had similar attitudes and outlooks may have expected much more support from their partners and perhaps also expected dieting to be made very easy by sharing the experience with someone who would be very empathic and understanding. Thus, the clients in the second experiment may have failed to do the constructive "work of worrying." In chapter 3 Janis and Mann cite evidence indicating that, when people fail to worry about impending deprivations beforehand, their overoptimistic expectations are rudely shattered when they encounter pain or discomfort; as a result, they display a relatively low degree of stress tolerance. If dieters start out with highly optimistic expectations about the ease of losing weight because they believe that they are assigned an "ideal" partner, they would presumably react much more adversely to the subsequent hardships and setbacks of dieting, becoming more disappointed and discouraged than if they start out with more realistic expectations.

Whether the explanation we have just suggested proves to be the correct one, the fact remains that our second experiment failed to support the main findings of our first experiment, which inclines us to be cautious about drawing general conclusions about the value of high-contact partnerships. Although positive effects of high-contact partnerships are clearly manifested by our first experiment in the weight-reduction clinic and by the earlier experiment by Janis and Hoffman in an antismoking clinic (chap. 4), this outcome does not appear to be as robust as we had expected. The effects were wiped out completely by a change in procedure introduced in the second experiment that involved telling the clients, truthfully, that they had been matched up with their partners on the basis of the answers they gave on attitude questionnaires.

Obviously, additional studies are needed to try to pin down the conditions under which positive effects of high-contact partnerships will and will not occur. At this stage of research on helping relationships, however, we are not very optimistic about discovering the necessary and sufficient conditions because it is difficult to find out whether the partners in their daily conversations are carrying out the instructions given to them by the counselor. It will be recalled that in our first experiment we encountered anomalous findings concerning feelings of competitiveness between partners, which suggested that during the daily telephone conversations unconditional positive regard was not given in the way the high-contact partners had been instructed. In view of the difficulties of inducing partners to live up to the requirements necessary for investigating the effects of different types of social reinforcement or other important variables, we believe it might be more productive to postpone further research on partnerships until more is known about the effects of the crucial variables from other types of studies. In research using counselor–client pairs, for example, the experimenter, by taking on the role of a counselor, can vary the type of social reinforcement and many other variables in a highly dependable way and thereby obtain more precise data on the conditions under which the dyadic relationship has positive effects. Once the parameters are worked out in this type of helping relationship, it should be possible to resume studying partnerships between clients in a more sophisticated way, making use of whatever new knowledge is gained from studying relationships between counselors and clients. Similarities and differences between client partnerships and counselor–client pairs could then be investigated.

MAIN CONCLUSIONS

1. The first of our two field experiments provides a conceptual replication in a dieting clinic of the Janis and Hoffman antismoking experiment, with essentially the same outcome. High-contact partners (who were instructed to phone each other every day for 3 weeks and who attended three weekly meetings with the counselor at the clinic) were more successful than low-contact partners (who attended three weekly meetings with the counselor at the clinic but were instructed not to phone each other). The high-contact partners lost a significantly greater amount of weight and showed less delay

in returning for the 9-week follow-up interview. They also maintained more spontaneous contact with their partners after the last session and expressed more somewhat favorable attitudes toward the clinic. An important feature of this replication was that the clients were told truthfully, as in the Janis and Hoffman experiment, that partners could *not* be closely matched on all the various attitudes they had expressed in the preliminary questionnaire.

2. Instructing the partners to give each other selective reinforcement versus instructing them to express unconditional positive regard had no significant effects on weight loss or on any other of the behavioral measures investigated in our first experiment. There are indirect indications that some of the high-contact partners may have failed to follow the instructions in their unmonitored telephone conversations.

3. In our second experiment we did not find the expected positive effects of high-contact partnerships under conditions where the partners were told, again truthfully, that they had been paired on the basis of the similarity of many of the attitudes they had expressed in the preliminary question-naire. Except for emphasizing the apparent similarity of the partners, the second experiment used exactly the same procedures and the same measures as our first experiment, but no significant effects were found. A plausible explanation for this failure to replicate the prior results is that emphasizing the similarity of the partners led them to be overly optimistic at the outset about receiving empathy or support and thereafter to become disappointed, which undermined whatever advantages they could have obtained from the opportunity for added social support from the high-contact partnerships.

NOTES

1. A 2 × 2 factorial design was used with repeated measurement of the major dependent variable (weight) for each subject in each pair included in each cell of the design.

2. In the second session, after being weighed, the clients talked with the psychologist. They were encouraged to distinguish between hunger and boredom, restlessness, fatigue, depression, anxiety, and tension. Next, the clients were asked to suggest alternative satisfactions, sources of entertainment, or distractions that could be used when they felt tempted to eat as a result of restlessness or boredom. All clients were also taught a relaxation technique which could be employed when they felt tempted to eat in response to tension or anxiety.

After being weighed at the beginning of the third session, all clients were asked to complete a series of questionnaires. These included an attitude-toward-the-partner scale (4 items) and an attitude-toward-the-clinic scale (3 items).

3. In some treatment conditions there was a fairly large number of cases who delayed returning for the follow-up interview beyond the originally scheduled appointment at 9 weeks. Every effort was made to see clients at the time of their scheduled follow-up interviews, but in a field setting unforeseen events in individuals' lives are bound to occur that require rescheduling some of the appointments. In some cases this resulted in intervals between sessions not being identical to those recommended by the clinic. Furthermore, there is evidence (Table 5.2) that the percentage of clients who delayed returning was not the same in different treatment conditions. Weight loss would be expected to be correlated with time interval. As expected, a low but significant positive correlation was found between the amount of time the session had to be delayed and the amount of weight lost. Consequently, weight loss was corrected so that

the amount of weight lost would not be exaggerated due to rescheduling delays. Thus, if someone lost 10 pounds but had to be rescheduled for the follow-up session so it was 7 days later, with 70 rather than the recommended 63 days between the initial and final sessions, the person was assumed to have lost $(63/70) \times 10$ lbs. $= 9$ lbs. as of the originally scheduled session date, rather than the 10-pound weight loss recorded when the subject was weighed a week late. In all the analyses reported in this chapter, weight loss was corrected to eliminate the effects of such rescheduling delays. The uncorrected data on weight loss were also examined and were found to be very similar. The uncorrected data show the same trend, very slightly attenuated, as the corrected data in Table 5.1.

4. The success of the induction of interpersonal attraction through the manipulation of perceived similarity was expected on the basis of a considerable body of experimental literature. Increases in interpersonal attraction following manipulation of perceived and actual similarity of attitudes and personality variables have been reported both when subjects rate a hypothetical person (e.g., Byrne, & Griffitt, 1966, 1969) and when subjects rate an individual with whom they have actually interacted (e.g., Brewer & Brewer, 1968; Byrne, 1971; Levinger & Breedlove, 1966; McWhirter & Jecker, 1967; Rosenfeld & Jackson, 1965). Several studies have suggested additional reasons for predicting greater weight loss for subjects in the high-perceived-similarity group. Hillis (1969) found that the recipients' subjective estimation of the value of information transmitted increased as similarity between the recipients and the communicator increased. Reports indicate that subjects who perceive their partners as being similar also tend to perceive them as being more cooperative and are themselves more cooperative (Deignan, 1970; Kaufmann, 1967).

5. The data from the 3-week follow-up session show that for the low-contact partners in the second experiment, selective reinforcement resulted in *more* weight loss than unconditional positive regard (4.8 pounds vs. 2.8 pounds), whereas, for the high-contact partners, selective reinforcement resulted in *less* weight loss (2.3 pounds vs. 4.3 pounds). This interaction effect is statistically significant ($F = 5.44$, $df = 1/44$, $p < .05$). The corresponding interaction effect was not significant, however, in the weight loss data obtained from the 9-week follow-up session. No such interaction effect was found in the first experiment, either from the 3- or the 9-week follow-up session.

On a questionnaire item that asked about feelings of competitiveness between the partners, there were no significant main effects and there was no significant interaction effect. There was no trend in the data similar to the interaction effect observed in Experiment 1.

Additional data include comparisons between clients based on a question about *birth order* which was included in the initial questionnaire. We were able to test the predictions that first-born persons would have higher need affiliation scores and would respond more favorably to the partnership opportunities than would later-born persons. These predictions were based on Schachter's findings (1959) that first-borns tend to affiliate more readily under stress than do later-borns.

In Experiment 2 we found that, contrary to the predictions, when the first-born persons were compared with the later-born persons they (1) obtained significantly *lower* need affiliation scores ($p < .01$), (2) rated their partners *less* favorably ($p < .05$), and (3) rated the clinic *less* favorably ($p < .05$). There was no significant difference between first-borns and later-borns in the amount of weight loss. The birth-order comparisons from Experiment 1 did not duplicate the significant differences from Experiment 2, but the results again failed to support the predictions (based on Schachter's findings) that the first-borns would obtain significantly higher need affiliation scores. Furthermore, in Experiment 1 we found that the first-borns did not lose as much weight as the later-borns over the 9-week follow-up period (5.5 pounds vs. 8.2 pounds; $p < .05$).

3

COUNSELOR-CLIENT RELATIONSHIPS IN A WEIGHT-REDUCTION CLINIC

6 Effects of Acceptance by the Counselor

MURDO M. DOWDS, JR., IRVING L. JANIS, AND EDWARD S. CONOLLEY

The field experiment reported in this chapter was the first attempt to test systematically some of the main implications of the helping-relationship model presented earlier concerning the effects of acceptance by a counselor (chap. 2). According to the model, an essential feature of successful supportive counseling is that the client develops a cohesive relationship with the counselor. In the first phase of developing such a relationship, referred to as "acquiring motivational power," two factors are presumed to be crucial: *self disclosure* by the client and *positive feedback* from the counselor. More specifically, the theoretical analysis in chapter 2 postulates that a client who is conflicted about carrying out a stressful course of action, such as dieting or undergoing painful medical treatments, will display greater readiness to rely upon a counselor's recommendations if the following two conditions are met: first, that the counselor conducts an initial interview in which the client is encouraged to give confidential personal information (such as how the client feels about his or her current troubles); and second, that the counselor responds to all disclosures of personal information by giving positive feedback in the form of explicit acceptance responses, which is expected to have the immediate effect of enhancing the client's self-esteem.

In the present study we deal with the effects of variations in the second condition when the first one is held constant. (Later chapters present studies in which the first condition is varied.) The specific hypothesis we tested was that if counselors respond to the self-disclosures of their clients with genuine acceptance, they will be regarded with more esteem and affection by the clients and their recommendations will be more effective than if they respond in a neutral or noncommittal way. In order to test this hypothesis, we arranged for clients in all conditions to be given a standard intake interview that elicited a moderate degree of self-disclosure. On a random basis, half the clients who came to a weight-reduction clinic received positive feedback from the counselors in response to self-disclosures and half received neutral feedback.

Another key requirement for effective short-term counseling, according to the theoretical analysis in chapter 2, is that the counselor give norm-setting recommendations during the second phase of the development of the relationship. This requirement was met by arranging to have the counselors give all clients in the study a standard set of instructions concerning a 1200-calorie diet, together with recommendations to adhere to it regularly until they reached their target amount of weight loss.

Our expectation that a moderate self-disclosure interview will facilitate adherence to the counselor's recommendations runs counter to hypotheses put forth by other investigators. Several laboratory experiments with college students suggest that, when people are asked to disclose details about their lives, they feel threatened and tend to "clam up" or to dislike the interviewer (Hood & Back, 1971; Kaplan, Firestone, Degnore, & Moore, 1974; Taylor, Altman, & Sorrentino, 1969). Kaplan and his co-workers, for example, asked undergraduates in a psychology course to serve as subjects in order to give practice to graduate students who were being trained as interviewers. They found that the students expressed increased dislike of the interviewer as the amount of intimate questioning that required self-disclosure increased. On the basis of this outcome, the authors suggest that decreased liking is "the rule in situations where the impetus for disclosure comes from outside the person, with self-initiation of intimacy being the *sine qua non* of positive [reactions]" (p. 645).

On the basis of our own clinical observations we agree that self-initiated disclosures are less likely to result in dislike of the interviewer, but we expect the *type of feedback* given by the interviewer to be a far more important factor, sufficiently so to override the negative effects of the interviewer's probing questions. If the interviewer responds in an explicitly accepting manner, indicating that he or she is not critical of the client and not at all disapproving of the personal weaknesses or lapses that are revealed, the client's attitude toward the interviewer should become more favorable as the interview goes on, even though the interviewer asks probing questions that attempt to elicit self-disclosures about personal aspects of the client's life. But if the interviewer remains neutral or noncommittal, saying nothing at all, we would not expect as positive an attitude toward the interviewer to develop; rather, as the probing type of interview goes on we would expect either no change or (if the neutral feedback is interpreted as critical or unfriendly) an increase in dislike, as found by Kaplan and his co-workers. Thus, the outcome reported by the latter investigators would not hold, according to the hypothesis we are investigating, if the interviewer were to accompany his probing questions with positive feedback of the type that explicitly conveys acceptance and positive regard in response to the client's answers. (For a more direct test of the hypothesis, see the study by Mulligan in chap. 15, which reports the joint effects of variations in the level of self-disclosure induced by the counselor and the type of feedback given by the counselor.)

One problem that arises in testing any hypothesis about the effects of explicit acceptance statements is that if the counselor expresses approval when clients admit that they have done or are planning to do something undesirable (e.g., to ignore the counselor's recommendations), he or she will be reinforcing the wrong actions. An additional problem is that, as Jourard (1968) points out, acceptance statements given in a mechanical, nonempathic manner by someone who is playing a contrived role may have little effect, unlike acceptance statements given by someone who is authentically expressing goodwill and empathy. These problems can be avoided, as they were in the present study (and in the subsequent studies reported in later chapters), by limiting positive feedback to genuine praise of the client's honesty at times when he or she makes self-disclosures about undesirable actions. That is, the counselor expresses empathy and acceptance through the use of reflecting or restating responses only with those disclosures that do not refer to attitudes, intentions, or activities that would interfere with adherence to the recommended course of action. In this way we attempt to evoke what Deutsch and Solomon (1959) refer to as a "positivity effect" (the tendency to respond favorably to someone who gives positive evaluations), without saying anything that could be construed by the client as approval of acts or intentions that run counter to the counselor's recommendations. In typical counseling settings, if our hypothesis about the effectiveness of positive feedback is correct, it should be possible for the counselor to enhance the clients' self-esteem by giving predominantly noncontingent acceptance responses and, as a result, to increase their esteem and affection for the counselor and their adherence to the counselor's norms.

In the present study we introduced a second variable—positive versus negative feedback on an interpolated minor task—in order to investigate a second, more speculative, hypothesis. The second hypothesis is that once a counselor has acquired some degree of motivating power (by responding with acceptance to the self-disclosures elicited from the client in response to probing questions), the counselor can reduce the amount of resistance that will later be mobilized when recommendations are presented if he or she first makes a minor demand, indicates mild dissatisfaction with the client's failure to meet expected standards, and immediately thereafter returns to giving accepting feedback. This hypothesis is based on the following assumptions, which are consistent with the theoretical analysis of phases in the helping relationship (chap. 2). If the counselor's first recommendation is seen as making major demands that will be difficult to meet (such as adhering to a low-calorie diet), there is a serious risk that in Phase 2 the counselor will lose the motivational power acquired in Phase 1 because the clients will no longer see the counselor as a benign, dependably accepting helper who will continue to enhance their self-esteem. Instead, the image of the counselor will be that of a demanding authority figure who will give positive feedback only in response to compliant behavior. This unfavorable transformation of the image of the counselor is less likely to occur if clients are first given a minor demand that permits the clients to learn that, when the counselor makes a specific demand, he or she will continue to hold the client in high regard even if it is not met, and will continue to express acceptance on all other matters having nothing to do with the limited sphere to which the demand pertains.

These assumptions lead us to expect that a counselor's mild expression of dissatisfaction after a preliminary minor demand will prepare the client to accept more major demands later on, if the counselor promptly resumes giving positive feedback and continues to do so until the client has recovered from the temporary episode of mild negative feedback, before introducing the major recommendations. To put it more concretely, during a session when a counselor is building up a relationship with a client for the purpose of helping the client to carry out a difficult set of recommendations, such as sticking to a low-calorie diet, he or she may augment adherence to the major recommendations in the following way. First, the counselor can provide psychological preparation for the major demands (Phase 2) through the deliberate introduction of an initial task (such as a brief test of ability or motivation) and assert in a mild and objective manner that the client's performance on that task is unsatisfactory; then, after having indicated that the client has failed to meet the expected standard, the counselor can continue to express positive regard and basic acceptance. By giving a mild negative evaluation of the client, the counselor is more likely to be seen by the client as someone whose demands are not threatening, and who is capable of giving objective criticism without changing his or her basic attitude of positive regard as long as the client is making a sincere effort to adhere to the recommendations. Thus, a brief failure experience on a preliminary minor task might provide a form of stress inoculation that dampens the client's negative reaction to subsequent failure experiences on the main task (see chap. 3). But we must recognize that there are also plausible reasons for expecting the opposite outcome. Even if the contrived failure experience is completely plausible, mild, and smoothed over by prompt reassurances, the episode of negative feedback could still impair the client's attitude toward the counselor and therefore hinder rather than facilitate the counselor's ultimate objective of motivating the client to adhere to the major recommendations.

In order to obtain some preliminary evidence bearing on this issue, we added to the procedure in the present study a brief task requiring the client to hold a weight at arms' length as long as possible. It was introduced as a motivation test that was being included in the procedure because of the importance of motivation in successful dieting. The independent variable consisted of giving either negative or positive feedback on a random basis after each client performed the weight-lifting task: The counselor informed the client either that she had failed to meet the expected level of performance or that she had succeeded. (Because the norms for this test were ambiguous, the counselor could plausibly evaluate the client's performances in terms of relatively high or relatively low standards.)

Thus, the experiment was designed to test the effects of two independent situational variables: (1) giving noncontingent acceptance versus neutral feedback during a self-disclosure interview and (2) giving positive versus negative feedback following a preliminary minor task. We also included measures of three personality dimensions in order to investigate plausible sources of individual differences. The first of these, need for approval, has been shown to predict differential conformity, persuasibility, and general susceptibility to social influence in a variety of situations (Crowne & Marlowe, 1964) and thus is theoretically relevant to the social influence processes involved in this experiment. The second, personal boundary preference (assessed by a scale developed by Miller, 1968), pertains to each person's sense of separateness from others and similarly can be expected to affect susceptibility to social influence. The third, chronic level of self-esteem (assessed by a scale based on Janis & Field, 1959), has been discussed in chapter 2 as a factor expected to influence the amount of noncontingent acceptance necessary for the acquisition of motivating power in Phase 1 of a counseling relationship and is thus theoretically a determinant of responsiveness to the helping relationship.[1]

We introduced a major constraint into the counseling setting in order to eliminate the possibility that the effects of the counselor's acceptance statements might be influenced by the counselor's facial expressions, gestures, or other visual cues that could be confounding variables. The constraint was that the client could not see the counselor (as in counseling by telephone). More specifically, we used a counseling setting with a remote audio system whereby the client, who was alone in an interviewing room, heard the counselor's voice at normal speech level from a high-fidelity speaker and responded by talking into a microphone. This setup made the interview similar to talking with a counselor over the telephone, which is becoming a popular way of conducting counseling not only at suicide centers but also in organizations like Rescue, Inc., for the elderly and in other crisis intervention centers that have hotline services for troubled people who want help on problems concerning marriage, sex and pregnancy, family disputes, employment, or health (see Lester & Brockopp, 1973). In addition to resembling telephone counseling, the audio setup we used might become a common way of conducting intake interviews in clinics that adopt on-line computer diagnostic systems to treat large numbers of clients (see Cochran, Hoffman, Strand, & Warren, 1977; Harris, 1974).

METHODS AND PROCEDURES

Subjects

The clients in this study were 64 overweight women recruited for a weight-reduction clinic sponsored by the Yale Psychology Department, which was announced on posters in and around the Yale University campus and medical center. The announcements stated that the counseling service was offered free of charge in exchange for the clients' participating in a research study that involved filling out questionnaires and being interviewed.

Two male graduate students each interviewed 32 women. The 64 women who volunteered for the study ranged in age from 21 to 65 years (mean age 41 years). About 80% of them were married. Their educational background ranged from not having completed high school through having a college degree; fewer than 20% had graduated from college. The women reported themselves as being from 10 to 70 pounds overweight, the mean being about 30 pounds.

Sequence of Procedures[2]

Following written instructions mailed out beforehand, each client came to the interviewing room, where she saw a large printed notice informing her that her counselor would speak over a microphone in the next room and that she would hear his voice from the loudspeaker located above the table. The counselor then gave a standard introduction over the remote audio system, describing what would happen during the session. The counselor instructed the client to weigh herself on the balance scale (while he observed through a one-way-vision screen) and then asked her to sit down and fill out the questionnaires on the table (which included the three personality scales).

After completing the initial questionnaires, all clients were given the same standard interview on personal problems connected with being overweight and dieting. It took about 1 hour to complete. Two-thirds of the way through the interview all were given the same preliminary task, a motivation test that took about 5 minutes. After that the interview was resumed. Half the subjects were given positive feedback throughout the entire self-disclosing interview, whereas the other half were given neutral feedback (described below). Within each of these two experimental groups, half were given a positive evaluation and half were given a negative evaluation on the motivation test. Clients were assigned to the four treatment groups on a stratified random basis so as to make sure that the groups were comparable with respect to relevant background characteristics (age, education, and amount overweight). At the end of the interview clients in all four groups were given the same standard set of dieting recommendations.

The Self-disclosure Interview and the Recommendations

A schematic overview of the interview and other procedures is presented in Table 6.1. In the introduction to the session the client was told that she would not see the interviewer and that he was in an adjacent room separated by a one-way-vision screen. This arrangement was explained to clients as a special method of interviewing we were trying out that could have some advantages for women who find it easier to talk about their overweight problems when the interview is not face-to-face. The interview questions were intended to elicit a moderate amount of self-disclosure of the client's thoughts and feelings on a variety of topics related to being overweight and

Table 6.1. Schematic sequence of procedures and measures

Interview procedures	Measures
Start of first session	
1. Introduction	
	2. Weight on a balance scale
	3. Personality measures
Part 1	
	4. First rating of interviewer
5. Interview questions with either positive or neutral feedback	(time 1)
Part 2	
	6. Second rating of interviewer
7. Motivation test	(time 2)
8. Positive or negative evaluation of test performance	
Part 3	
	9. Third rating of interviewer
10. Interview questions continued with either positive or neutral feedback, as before	(time 3)
11. Dieting information and recommendations	
	12. Commitment form
Part 4	
	13. Fourth rating of interviewer (time 4)
	14. Attitude questionnaire
End of first session	
Follow-up period	
	15. Weekly report forms for 8 weeks
16. Two-month follow-up interview	
	17. Attitude questionnaire
	18. Weight on a balance scale

the problems of trying to lose weight: reasons for wanting to lose weight; the difficulties and disadvantages that might accompany dieting; the times and situations when they found themselves most likely to overeat; the reactions of family and friends to their overweight appearance and to their efforts to diet; and the anticipated effects of losing weight on their health, appearance, and life in general.[3] The final portion of the session was devoted to a 20-minute tape-recorded talk by the counselor in which he gave a standard set of recommendations to aid clients in losing weight through dieting. Each client was given an outline of a 1200-calorie diet (prepared by the Yale–New Haven Hospital's Department of Dietetics) and a series of sample menus conforming to the standards of the diet. Included among the recommendations was a "Plan for Dieters," a program that called for 10 minutes of silent thought every day about the problems of dieting and over-eating, to be carried out for at least 8 weeks in order to assist clients to remain on the diet. The clients were also given eight "Weekly Report" forms on which to record their adherence to the recommendations on a daily basis and to report their weight at the end of each of the 8 weeks. They were told that someone from the clinic would contact them near the end of the 2-month period to schedule a short follow-up interview to find out how well they had been losing weight.

Accepting versus Neutral Feedback

For the clients given accepting feedback during the interview, the counselor responded to all the client's statements in a positive, supportive way. Such responses include (a) favorable and sympathetic comments (e.g., "It's quite understandable why you feel that way"; "It's good that you are aware of that problem"); (b) rewarding statements about cooperation with the counselor (e.g., "You're being very frank about that"; "That's exactly the kind of thing I would like you to discuss"); (c) restatements of the client's answer to show that the counselor understands and is not critical of what the client is saying; and (d) comments indicating the counselor's interest and empathy (e.g., "Yes, that certainly is a problem"). The counselor's general tone while giving accepting statements was conversational and empathic. In the contrasting neutral feedback condition, the interviewer made no response at all to the client's statements. He simply paused for a few seconds and went on to the next interview question.

Positive versus Negative Evaluation of the Test Performance

The motivation test introduced just before the last third of the interview required each client to hold a 5-pound weight outstretched at arms' length for as long as possible. A preliminary trial was given after the counselor stated that the purpose of the test was to "give an indication of your general strength and muscle tone as shown by how quickly you become fatigued during physical exertion." (The counselor metioned that overweight people often complain of feeling in poor condition physically.) A second trial, the same as the first and with the weight held in the same hand, was introduced as a motivation test. The counselor stated that because of fatigue from the first trial, this time it "will not merely be a matter of your strength, but will require much more effort and motivation on your part."

All clients were told at the end of the second trial: "Holding the weight when your arm is already tired takes more effort and motivation than when your arm isn't tired. As you probably know, dieting also requires a great deal of effort and motivation. . . . We think that effort and motivation as measured by the second part of the [weight-holding] exercise may be related to the more general kind of effort and motivation required for dieting." Clients given the *positive* evaluation were then told: "It seems that you really *did* put a good deal of effort and motivation into holding the weight up during the second trial." Those given the *negative* evaluation were told: "It seems that you really *didn't* put anywhere near as much effort and motivation as I had hoped you would into holding the weight up during the second trial. I think you probably could have tried harder." After that the counselor then told every client that dieting requires a high level of motivation, and that in order to lose weight she will have to maintain a high level of effort and motivation. After the motivation test, clients were given the remaining interview questions with the same feedback as in their originally assigned feedback condition (accepting or neutral).

Measures

An "interviewer rating" of five questions was presented at four different times during the interview (as shown in Table 6.1). These questions were introduced as ones that would "help us in evaluating this special method of interviewing." They were presented by means of a tape-recorded woman's voice, preceded by the following explanation: "We have found that by having a different voice ask the questions it is much easier [for clients] to be frank and truthful in answering." The questions were (1) "How friendly and warm do you feel toward the psychologist?" (2) "Do you feel that the psychologist was expressing friendly and warm feelings toward you?" (3) "To what extent did you feel that the psychologist was judging or criticizing you?" (4) "Do you feel pleased or satisfied about this part of the interview?" and (5) "How much did you dislike the way the psychologist talked to you during this part of the interview?" Clients responded verbally on a 5-point scale, from "not at all" to "very much." Ratings on all five questions were averaged to produce the final measure for each part of the interview. (Ratings on questions 3 and 5 were reversed.)

During the final part of the interview, when clients were given the recommendations about dieting, they received a form on which they were asked to record their intentions to follow each of the counselor's recommendations. This "Commitment Form," on which each client was asked to sign her name, provided a 3-point scale (no = 0, undecided = 1, yes = 2) for each of six items, and a 4-point scale for a seventh item dealing with intended duration of adherence. The total score for the seven items was used as a measure of the immediate effects of the interview on intended adherence. Weight loss and the number of weekly report forms returned to the clinic over the 2-

month follow-up period were used as measures of actual behavioral adherence.

RESULTS

Clients' Ratings of the Counselor

Figure 6.1 shows the ratings at four time intervals during the initial counseling session. Clients who received accepting feedback gave consistently more favorable ratings of the counselor during and immediately after the interview than did those who received neutral feedback ($p < .01$).[4]

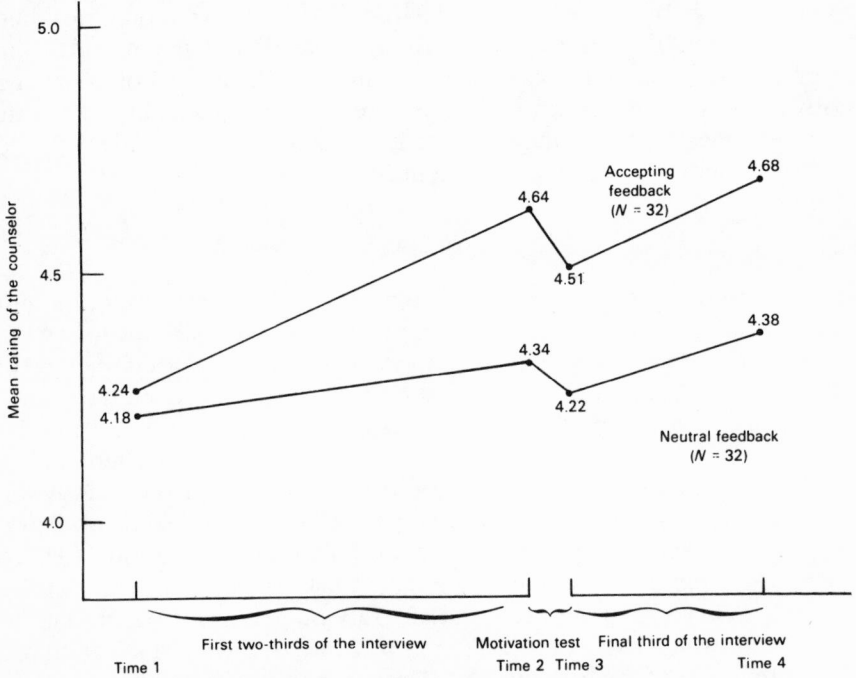

Figure 6.1. Ratings of the counselor at four times of measurement during the initial counseling session.

Commitment to Carry Out the Counselor's Recommendations

The accepting type of feedback not only had a favorable immediate effect on the clients' attitudes toward the counselor but also increased their willingness to commit themselves at the end of the interview to adhere to the recommendations made by the counselor. Although clients in all treatment groups reported highly compliant intentions on the commitment form (mean score of 12 or above on a scale from 0 to 15), those given accepting feedback reported significantly stronger intentions to follow the recommendations than those given neutral feedback. (The means were 13.7 and

12.9, respectively; $F(1, 56) = 6.97$, $p < .02$). Positive versus negative evaluation on the motivation test had no discernible effect on commitment.

Subsequent Weight Loss

Approximately 2 months after the interview session the clients were asked to return for a follow-up session, at which they were again weighed in order to determine the amount of weight they had lost. A small number of clients in each group failed to return to the clinic despite repeated phone calls (during which most of the nonreturners admitted that they had not lost weight). Because the follow-up returns were incomplete we used two different measures of weight loss: (1) the proportion who returned for the follow-up interview and showed a minimum weight loss of 4 pounds (one-half the amount of weight loss expected if each client had rigorously adhered to the recommended diet throughout the entire 2-month period); and (2) mean change in weight for each entire group (using mailed-in reports on weight loss from one to three clients in each group and assuming that those who did not respond remained unchanged).

The results are shown in Table 6.2. Both measures show the same pattern. First of all, there is essentially no overall difference between those who

Table 6.2. Weight change over a two-month period

Group	Type of feedback throughout the entire interview	Feedback on the motivation test	Percentage who returned and showed loss of 4 or more lbs.*	Mean change in weight for each entire group**
1	Accepting	Positive	38 } 28	-2.9 } -1.2
2	Accepting	Negative	19	+0.6
3	Neutral	Positive	6 } 18	+0.1 } -1.2
4	Neutral	Negative	31	-2.6

Note. $N = 16$ in each group.
* Interaction effect: $p < .10$.
** Interaction effect: $p < .05$.

received accepting and those who received neutral feedback. Second, the difference between the clients given positive and those given negative evaluations on the motivation test is slight and insignificant. But third, a significant interaction effect was found ($p < .10$ and $< .05$ on the two measures of weight loss shown in Table 6.2): For those clients who were given accepting feedback throughout the interview, weight loss was much *greater* if they were given a positive evaluation on the motivation test than if they were given a negative evaluation (a mean loss of 2.9 pounds versus a mean gain of 0.6 pounds). For the clients given neutral feedback, however, the outcome was the opposite: positive evaluation on the motivation test resulted in *less* weight loss than did negative evaluation (a mean gain of 0.1 pounds versus a mean loss of 2.6 pounds).[5] This same pattern was found when we compared the proportion of clients in each group who showed a weight loss of 4 pounds or more.

The data in Table 6.2 indicate that when positive feedback was given to the clients, it was much more effective in eliciting behavioral adherence to the counselor's main recommendations when given *consistently.* Group 1, which received consistently positive feedback, showed significantly greater mean weight loss ($p < .05$) than Groups 2 and 3, which received some positive feedback, but *not consistently.* (Group 2 was given accepting feedback during the interview but with negative feedback on the motivation test; Group 3 was given positive feedback on the motivation test but with neutral feedback during the interview.)

Personality Differences

The self-esteem scale (based on Janis & Field, 1959) was the only one of the three personality measures that showed any significant relationship to the longer term adherence measures over the 2-month period. In all experimental conditions clients who scored low on this scale (below the median) showed more compliance with regard to mailing back weekly reports than those who scored high ($p < .05$). On those weekly reports, the clients with low scores on the self-esteem scale reported following the diet on a significantly larger number of days than the clients with high scores ($p < .05$).

These findings suggest that clients with low self-esteem tend to be more compliant with regard to carrying out the counselor's recommendations. But such a conclusion cannot be firmly drawn because comparison of clients who obtained high and low scores on self-esteem showed no significant difference in weight loss measures obtained 2 months after the initial session. On both weight loss measures shown in Table 6.2 the differences were in the same direction as those for the weekly reports but were not large enough to be statistically significant (for mean change in weight, $p < .15$).[6]

DISCUSSION

The results on the immediate effects of giving accepting versus neutral feedback throughout the interview tend to bear out some but not all of the expectations from the theoretical analysis in chapter 2 of the initial phase of building a supportive relationship. The evidence in Figure 6.1 indicates that accepting feedback from a counselor, when given during an interview that encourages a moderate degree of self-disclosure of personal strengths and weaknesses, produces a more favorable attitude toward the counselor during the interview than does neutral feedback. This finding in a clinical field setting helps to establish the generality of the tendency to respond favorably to a person who gives positive feedback, a tendency previously observed in laboratory experiments on interpersonal attraction (e.g., Deutsch & Solomon, 1959; Jones, Jones, & Gergen, 1963). Additional evidence in the present study shows that the observed changes in ratings of the interviewer fail to support the generalization put forth by Kaplan, Firestone, Degnore, and Moore (1974) that decreased liking of the interviewer is to be expected whenever self-disclosure is elicited by probing questions. We found that after the clients were induced to disclose personal information, even those who had been given neutral feedback did not show a decrease in liking for the interviewer, and those who had been given accepting feedback showed a marked increase. The unfavorable outcome described by Kaplan and his co-workers might occur, however, when the clients regard the self-disclosures elicited by the counselor as irrelevant to their problem or as revealing more intimate details than they had wanted to reveal (see chaps. 9–13 for findings on the positive and negative effects of inducing different amounts of self-disclosure).

Additional findings in the present study can be interpreted as manifestations of the expected immediate increase in the motivational power of the counselor resulting from his or her giving accepting feedback during an initial session. Immediately after the interview those clients who had been given accepting feedback expressed greater willingness than those given neutral feedback to commit themselves to carrying out the counselor's recommendations.

When we turn to the longer term effects bearing on the motivational power of the counselor, however, we find that matters are much more complicated. An unexpected interaction effect was observed when we examined the joint effects of the two independent variables on weight loss over a 2-month period (Table 6.2). Accepting feedback given in response to the clients' self-disclosures resulted in more weight loss when the clients were also given a positive evaluation on the motivation test but not when they were given a negative evaluation. The opposite outcome was found for those given neutral feedback. The findings suggest that when clients are given *consistent* feedback (all positive or all nonpositive throughout the entire initial session) they are more likely than otherwise to show subsequent adherence to the counselor's recommendations. Thus, the findings bearing on the first hypothesis under investigation suggest that the theoretical analysis of the increase in motivating power during Stage 1 of a supportive relationship should be modified to include the provision that *the positive feedback must be completely consistent*. The requirement seems to be that there never be even a single instance of a negative comment by the counselor that is capable of momentarily decreasing the client's favorable attitude toward the counselor.

The evidence clearly does not support the second hypothesis under investigation, namely, that when clients are given accepting feedback by the counselor, a mildly unfavorable evaluation of their performances on a minor task will facilitate adherence to his or her main recommendations. Contrary to the hypothesis, clients given an unsatisfactory rating on the motivation test by an otherwise accepting counselor did *worse* on the main task of losing weight than those given a satisfactory rating.

What is most surprising is the evidence of a facilitating effect of the negative evaluation on the motivation test for the clients who were given neutral feedback. This unexpected finding raises the possibility that a relatively detached counselor who demands a moderate amount of self-disclosure but gives no explicit acceptance statements to the clients will acquire greater motivating power if he or she explicitly expresses dissatisfaction with some aspects of the client's behavior. An image of a firm, demanding authority figure is likely to be conveyed when the counselor withholds positive feedback throughout the initial session and occasionally expresses explicit disapproval for the client's failure to live up to expected standards. This image would be markedly different from that of a nurturant, supportive figure who can be counted on to enhance one's self-esteem. It is the latter image that we expect to be fostered by explicit acceptance statements. Evidently the nurturant type of image is impaired if a supportive counselor deviates sharply from an accepting stance by informing clients that they have failed to live up to an expected standard, whereas the image of the counselor as a demanding authority figure is enhanced by giving that kind of critical information. The image of the demanding authority figure seems to have functioned almost as effectiely as the nurturant image in motivating the clients to carry out the counselor's recommendations in the weight-reduction clinic.

If the foregoing inferences from our findings are confirmed in further research, two alternative prescriptive generalizations for effective counseling will follow. (1) If the counselor wants to function as a supportive, accepting type of adviser, his or her effectiveness can be increased by abstaining from any form of explicit negative feedback in order to develop the client's image of the counselor as a supportive quasi-dependable enhancer of self-esteem. (2) If the counselor wants to function as a detached authority figure, his or her effectiveness can be increased by abstaining from any form of positive feedback and by occasionally giving explicit negative feedback in the form of mild disapproval for the client's inadequacies.

We do not know whether the outcome of the present study is limited to situations like our weight-reduction clinic (where a self-disclosure interview and dieting recommendations are given in a single session and where the client is unable to see the counselor during the session, as in counseling by telephone) or whether the findings will hold equally for other types of counseling. This question obviously will require replications in a variety of counseling settings, including some that are similar to and others that are different from the particular setting we used in the present field experiment.

MAIN CONCLUSIONS

The results from this study, which was carried out in a weight-reduction clinic where clients were interviewed using a remote audio setup similar to counseling by telephone, support the following general conclusions.

1. When a counselor responds with positive feedback (noncontingent acceptance) rather than neutral feedback (no comment at all) throughout an initial interview that encourages a moderate amount of self-disclosure, the clients tend (a) to rate the counselor more favorably at the end of the interview and (b) to display greater willingness to commit themselves to the recommendations made by the counselor.

2. The clients' adherence to an accepting counselor's recommendations depends partly upon whether the counselor abstains from giving even a single instance of negative criticism. If the counselor gives one negative response (in this study a negative evaluation of the clients' performances on a motivation test), acceptance feedback is *less* effective in promoting subsequent adherence (as manifested by weight loss over a 2-month period) than neutral feedback. If, however, the empathic counselor gives nothing but positive responses throughout the interview (including a favorable evaluation of the clients' performances on the motivation test), the consistent acceptance feedback is *more* effective than neutral feedback in promoting subsequent adherence to the counselor's recommendations (as manifested by their losing more weight over a 2-month period).

3. When a counselor responds with neutral feedback throughout the initial interview, giving one unfavorable rating of the client's performance on a minor task (in this case a motivation test) temporarily produces less favorable attitudes toward the counselor than giving a favorable rating but it subsequently produces more adherence to the counselor's recommendations, as manifested by their losing more weight.

4. Some aspects of longer term adherence are partly determined by the clients' level of self-esteem regardless of the type of feedback they received. Clients scoring low on a self-esteem scale, compared with those scoring high, mailed back more weekly reports and reported dieting for a longer time (although their actual weight loss at the time of the 2-month follow-up session was not sufficiently greater to be statistically significant).

NOTES

1. The self-esteem scale we used is an adaptation of the feelings-of-inadequacy scale of the Janis–Field personality questionnaire, which was found to correlate positively with other measures of self-esteem and with measures of persuasibility (Janis & Field, 1959). In order to avoid response sets, some of the items were reworded so that the scale would include positive feelings of adequacy or self-esteem. The Miller boundary scale (1968) is a 15-item self-report instrument (factor analyzed from 150 items) calling for agreement or disagreement with statements indicating preferences for structured, delimited, well-controlled activities, for example,

"I allow plenty of time between tasks so I don't have to rush"; "On the whole I am successful at keeping my desk or work area tidy"; "I like getting high with my friends" (negatively scored). The need for approval scale was administered and scored according to the standard instructions by Crowne and Marlowe (1964).

2. The basic procedures were developed and pretested by Irving L. Janis in collaboration with Thomas Kohler.

3. The clients generally showed little or no reluctance about giving personal information in response to any of the questions; they frankly discussed their problems of being overweight and of dieting. We were satisfied from detailed inspection of their interview responses that, in accordance with the intent of the interview, the clients gave a fair number of personal disclosures and that the degree of intimacy of the disclosures was well within the range expected for a moderate degree of disclosure. The amount and depth (degree of intimacy) of the clients' disclosures in their answers to the interview in the present study were well above the corresponding scores obtained from the "low-disclosure" interviews used in subsequent studies in the same weight-reduction clinic (see, e.g., chap. 9, n. 1) and well below those obtained for the "high-disclosure" interview used in other subsequent studies (reported in chaps. 11-13).

4. Analysis of variance of the counselor ratings at the beginning of the interview (time 1), as expected, showed that there was not a significant main effect for feedback ($F(1, 56) = 0.19$, $p > .25$). At time 2, however, the main effect for feedback is highly significant ($F(1, 56) = 9.29$, $p < .01$) and it remains significant (at the .01 and .02 confidence levels) at the end of the interview. Changes in ratings of the counselor from time 1 to time 4 were further analyzed using the score at time 1 as covariate in an analysis of covariance. Change scores of clients who received accepting feedback were significantly more in the favorable direction throughout the entire interview than were those of clients who received neutral feedback ($p < .01$).

Analysis of variance revealed that although positive versus negative evaluation on the motivation test had no significant main effect on ratings of the counselor at the end of the session or at the time of the 8-week follow-up interview, there was a significant main effect for this variable immediately after the motivation test was given. The change in the ratings of the counselor from time 1 to time 3 is significantly different for the positive vs. negative evaluation conditions ($F(1, 56) = 5.08$, $p < .05$). Substantially the same result was obtained from an analysis of covariance using the time 1 score as covariate ($F(1, 56) = 4.68$, $p < .05$). Thus, clients who were given the negative evaluation on the motivation test lowered their ratings of the counselor just after receiving that evaluation, but not later on. Clients given the positive evaluation showed essentially no change from their preceding rating. There were no significant interaction effects of accepting versus neutral feedback with positive versus negative evaluations on the motivation test.

5. The number of cases who returned for the 2-month follow-up interview in the four groups as listed in Table 6.2 were 11, 11, 9, and 8, respectively. Among those who did not return, from 1 to 3 cases in each group responded to a request by mail and reported their current weight, which in most instances was zero weight loss. Those who did not respond were assumed to have remained unchanged and were counted as zero weight loss.

A separate analysis of mean change in weight that was restricted to those clients who returned for the 2-month follow-up session (eliminating those who failed to return) yielded the same significant result: the interaction effect was again significant below the .05 confidence level.

On two other indicators of longer term adherence to the counselor's recommendations, we noted a weak interaction tendency paralleling that found for weight loss. The clients given accepting feedback mailed back more weekly reports and reported having stayed on the diet for a longer period if the counselor gave them a positive evaluation rather than a negative evaluation on the motivation test, whereas the clients given neutral feedback showed the opposite effect, returning more weekly reports and reporting longer duration of dieting if the counselor gave them a negative evaluation on the motivation test. These interaction tendencies are not strong enough to be statistically significant ($p < .20$ and $< .15$, respectively), and there were no significant main effects. Clients who received accepting feedback returned a few more weekly reports during the 8-week follow-up period than did those who received neutral feedback (a mean of 6.0 vs. a mean of 5.6), but the difference is not large enough to approach statistical significance ($F(1, 56) = 2.3$, $p < .20$). Clients who had received accepting feedback also reported having stayed on the 1200-calorie diet for a longer time (19.2 days vs. 15.9), but again the difference is not large enough to approach statistical significance ($F(1, 56) = 2.61$, $p < .15$). For positive versus negative evaluation on the motivation test, the differences on both measures were very small and nonsignificant.

6. Analysis of variance results obtained for weight loss and other adherence measures show that self-esteem scores did not enter into any significant interaction effects either with accepting versus neutral feedback from the counselor or with positive versus negative evaluation on the motivation test.

The social desirability scale (Crowne & Marlowe, 1964) entered into a significant interaction with type of interview feedback as a determinant of ratings of the counselor during the first session. The low scoring subjects on the Crowne and Marlowe scale (below the median) reacted differentially, depending on the type of feedback they received throughout the interview, giving the counselor significantly higher ratings at times 2-4 during the interview in response to accepting feedback. The high scoring clients, however, gave highly favorable ratings to the counselor throughout the entire session irrespective of the type of feedback they were given. In interpreting this finding, we assume that all clients realized that the counselor would find out what ratings they gave. Those who were most strongly oriented toward gaining the approval of others evidently responded indiscriminately according to the conventional formula of saying only nice things about the professional counselor in order to please him. Clients who were less concerned about behaving in a socially approved way (low scorers on the social desirability scale) evidently felt somewhat freer to express their relatively unfavorable reaction to the neutral feedback.

Exactly the same interaction effect was found when scores on the personal boundary scale (Miller, 1968) were used as the sorting variable, as might be expected from our finding that the boundary scale and the social desirability scale were highly correlated ($r = .62$, $p < .01$). (Neither of the two scales was significantly correlated with the self-esteem scale.) From the manifest content of the items it seems probable that a high boundary scale score reflects a neat, orderly, obsessional style of life. Shapiro (1965) describes people with an obsessional style as being strongly motivated to behave in a conventionally proper manner and as being more concerned about what others expect them to do than what they would like to do. The results obtained on the boundary scale could therefore be interpreted in essentially the same way as those obtained on the Crowne and Marlowe social desirability scale.

7 Effects of Variations in the Type of Feedback Given by the Counselor

EDWARD S. CONOLLEY, IRVING L. JANIS, AND MURDO M. DOWDS, JR.

Taking account of findings from the experiment described in the preceding chapter, we carried out a similar experiment that was designed to replicate and extend the initial investigation. We used the same moderate self-disclosure interview in a weight-reduction clinic and the same variation in feedback from the counselor (positive vs. neutral). But we dropped the negative versus positive evaluation on the motivation test and replaced it with a modified procedure that we thought would have a better chance of facilitating a favorable outcome for a supportive type of counselor.

The results of the first experiment, as we have just seen, suggest that if counselors give consistently positive feedback during the initial interview with clients who come for help on a personal problem (such as dieting), they will be more effective than if they use inconsistently positive feedback (such as positive feedback throughout the interview but with a minor critical comment about the client's behavior, as exemplified by the brief negative evaluation given to the client following the motivation test). The consistently positive feedback proved to be relatively more effective both in inducing the clients to commit themselves to carry out the counselor's dieting recommendations at the end of the initial session and in influencing their dieting behavior during the next 2 months. Nevertheless, at the time of the follow-up study only a minority of the clients who had received consistently positive feedback were fully successful in carrying out the counselor's dieting recommendations over the entire 2-month period, even though the vast majority had originally committed themselves to do so at the end of the initial interview. We surmise that part of the backsliding problem might be partly explained in terms of the loss of motivating power described in the theoretical analysis of the second phase of a supportive relationship (chap. 2). After presenting himself as a warm, empathic, and supporting figure during the early part of the interview (Phase 1), the counselor may create disillusionment later on when he makes recommendations that are perceived as firm demands (Phase 2).

In the preceding experiment we attempted to build up tolerance for the blow inflicted by the counselor's strict dieting demands by introducing a preliminary minor demand that would function as a form of psychological preparation. This was the purpose of giving clients the weight-lifting task (which was presented as a test of motivation) with a negative evaluation of their performance and then returning to the accepting type of feedback for the remainder of the self-disclosure interview. But that attempt failed: the clients who received what was expected to be psychological preparation (temporary failure on the motivation test) along with positive feedback before and after it showed a temporarily unfavorable attitude change toward the counselor and subsequently did relatively poorly in adhering to the counselor's recommendations.

The present investigation includes a fresh attempt to provide psychological preparation intended to reduce the clients' resistances to the counselor's dieting recommendations in Phase 2. In this new attempt we used the same motivation test as in the first experiment but we eliminated the negative evaluation completely. This time the counselor restricted the preparation to making a minor demand that required the client to spend a few minutes carrying out an extraneous task, which was introduced during an interview in which the counselor gave either consistently positive or neutral feedback. One of the purposes of the research reported in this chapter was to determine whether our fresh attempt at creating an image of the counselor as a quasi-dependable enhancer of self-esteem would be successful in increasing the degree to which clients adhere to the counselor's dieting recommendations. Thus, whereas one independent variable was exactly the same as in the first experiment (accepting feedback vs. neutral feedback during a self-disclosing interview), the second independent variable was somewhat different (introducing a demand to perform a somewhat difficult extraneous task vs. a demand to perform a relatively easy task).

We regard our field experiment dealing with these two independent variables as essentially a replication of the Dowds, Janis, and Conolley experiment. After presenting the results of this experiment we shall describe a supplementary field experiment that included a third independent variable, along with the other two, in order to test additional hypotheses that were not investigated in the preceding field experiment. The third variable involves changing the type of feedback midway through the interview (from neutral to accepting or from accepting to neutral) in contrast to presenting the same type of feedback (either neutral or accepting) all the way through.

In these investigations we used the same remote audio setup as was used in the first experiment, with the counselor and the client in rooms separated by a one-way vision screen. Again, the purpose of this arrangement, which is similar to counseling by telephone, was to obtain experimental control over well-known sources of error arising from variations in the counselor's facial expressions, gestures, and other visual cues that could introduce unintended confounding effects on the client's reactions to the interventions under investigation.

REPLICATION OF THE DOWDS, JANIS, AND CONOLLEY EXPERIMENT

Using the same factorial design as in the preceding experiment (chap. 6), we investigated the effects of the two main independent variables just discussed. The procedures for the first variable (accepting feedback versus neutral feedback) were identical to those used in the first experiment (see pp. 114–116). The second variable (high versus low demand on a preliminary minor task) was introduced after two-thirds of the interview. The task (holding up a weight as long as possible) was the same one used in the first experiment and again was represented to the clients as a motivation test. This time, however, all the clients were given a positive evaluation of their performance. They were informed that we had just started to try it out and that "after we have given this test to a large number of dieters, we shall have a better idea of just how good a test of motivation it is." The clients assigned to the *high demand* condition were given (a) two initial trials in which they held up a 5-pound weight with outstretched arms until they became fatigued; and then (b) a third, much more difficult task in which, despite their muscular fatigue from the preceding two trials, they were asked to move the weight slowly up and down with their arm fully outstretched for as long a time as possible, trying not to give in to fatigue. Clients in the *low demand* condition were given only the two initial trials, with no additional demand. Immediately afterward, clients in both conditions were asked how much effort they felt they had to put into the task and the counselor agreed that they had done their best, indicating that he was satisfied with their performance. Then the clients were asked whether they thought that the determination required in holding the weight might be similar to the kind of motivation needed for staying on a diet. The last third of the interview was then completed, with each client being given the same type of feedback that she had received during the first two-thirds.

For the four groups in this replication experiment, the sequence of procedures was the same as the sequence shown in Table 6.1 for the Dowds, Janis, and Conolley experiment (except that instead of negative vs. positive feedback on the weight-holding test, the variation at that point in the sequence was making a high demand vs. a low demand). The experiment was again conducted in the Yale Weight-Reduction Clinic by three male counselors. The means and ranges of age, education, and initial weight of the 44 female subjects were approximately the same as in the first experiment, which was conducted in the same clinic. The same public announcements were used for recruiting volunteers.

RESULTS AND DISCUSSION

Clients' Ratings of the Counselor

The results for ratings of the counselor during the initial interview are essentially the same as shown in Figure 6.1 for the preceding experiment. As expected, at the beginning of the interview (Time 1) there was essentially no difference in the mean ratings given by the clients who were about to receive consistently accepting feedback and those who were about to receive neutral feedback. After 15 minutes (Time 2) the mean ratings of the counselor were significantly higher for the clients who received accepting feedback and remained so at the end of the interview ($p < .05$).[1]

Commitment to Carrying Out the Counselor's Recommendations

Again, just as in the preceding experiment (chap. 6), we found that at the end of the initial session those clients who had been given the accepting type of feedback throughout the interview showed significantly more willingness to commit themselves to comply with the counselor's recommendations than those who had been given neutral feedback. This was revealed by scores on the commitment form, which could range from 0 to 15; the means were 14.0 and 12.8, respectively ($F(1, 40) = 4.26$; $p < .05$).

Subsequent Weight Loss

On all four measures of long-term effects shown in the Table 7.1 the positive (accepting) type of feedback given throughout the initial interview produced more adherence to the counselor's recommendations over the follow-up period of 2 months. The clients who had been given accepting feedback (1) returned a significantly larger number of weekly reports ($p < .01$), (2) reported having adhered to the diet a significantly larger number of days ($p < .01$), and (3) demonstrated significantly greater success in dieting over the 2-month period on the objective measure of weight loss ($p < .05$).[2]

The sustained effects of the accepting type of feedback are much stronger in this experiment than in the preceding experiment. In the earlier experiment the differences on most measures were in the same direction as those shown in Table 7.1 but some were not large enough to be significant. The more powerful sustained effects of positive feedback found in the present experiment might be attributable to the complete omission of even a single instance of negative feedback. Remember that in the first experiment, half the clients given positive feedback throughout the interview received a bit of negative feedback: they were told that they had not performed well on the motivation test. This form of negative feedback appears to have reduced the main effect of the accepting feedback throughout the rest of the interview. The present experiment was intended to provide a purer exemplification of accepting feedback by eliminating the counselor's unfavorable evaluations of the clients' performance on the motivation test so that he never said anything that could be construed as a criticism. The comparable data from the earlier experiment, which are shown in Table 6.2, pertain to groups 1 and 3 (accepting vs. neutral feedback, with positive feedback on the motivation test held constant). The differences between these two groups are significant and are in the same direction as in the present experiment. These replicated results indicate that at least under the conditions

Table 7.1. Adherence assessed two months after the initial interview

Group	Type of feedback throughout initial interview	Type of demand made in motivation test	Mean number of weekly reports mailed to clinic*	Number of days of dieting reported by clients*	Percentage who returned for follow-up interview and showed weight loss of 4 lbs. or more*	Mean weight loss for each entire group*
1	Accepting	Low	6.3	21.3	67%	3.4
2	Accepting	High	6.0	18.0	45%	1.3
3	Neutral	Low	4.2	8.1	9%	0.1
4	Neutral	High	4.1	16.9	18%	1.0
1 + 2	Accepting groups combined		6.2	19.6	56%	2.3
3 + 4	Neutral groups combined		4.2	12.5	14%	0.5

Note. $N = 11$ in each group.
*Main effect of accepting versus neutral feedback, based on analysis of variance: $p < .05$.

that prevailed in these field experiments *consistently positive feedback from a counselor throughout an interview that elicits self-disclosure produces more sustained adherence to the counselor's recommendations than does neutral feedback*. Both experiments confirm this hypothesis under conditions where an hour-long session elicited a *moderate* degree of self-disclosure and included a brief motivation test after which the clients were told that they performed *satisfactorily*.

Effects of High versus Low Demand on the Motivation Test

The imposition of a high demand during the motivation test (requiring the clients to raise and lower a weight as long as possible after their arms had already become fatigued by two preceding weight-lifting trials) had an immediate effect on attitudes toward the counselor. Those given the high demand made less favorable ratings of the counselor just after the motivation test ($p < .05$) and also at the end of the interview ($p < .05$).[3]

The high versus low demands on the motivation test did not have a significant effect on the clients' willingness to commit themelves to the counselor's recommendations at the end of the initial session, and it did not produce a significant difference on any of the four long-term effect measures shown in Table 7.1. But we do find significant interaction effects in the number of days of dieting reported by the clients ($p < .01$) and on the objective weight loss measures ($p < .05$). For clients given *accepting* feedback throughout the interview, high demand on the motivation test resulted in somewhat *less* adherence to the counselor's dieting recommendations, whereas for clients given *neutral* feedback throughout the interview, high demand on the motivation test resulted in somewhat *more* adherence to those same dieting recommendations. Thus, on three of the four measures of adherence, the high demand made by the interviewer during the motivation test had a facilitating effect on those who received neutral feedback throughout the interview. This is similar to the effect of negative evaluation on the motivation test in the preceding experiment.

Originally we had expected that the high demand treatment would function as psychological preparation (for the even higher demands made in the dieting instructions), which would facilitate immediate commitment and long-term adherence among the clients given accepting feedback. The results certainly do not bear out this expectation. From the evidence now at hand we are led to conclude that a successful Phase 2 outcome is not likely to be facilitated by making a preliminary demand on the client during the initial interview even when the counselor abstains from saying anything negative. Consequently, we have abandoned the effort to use a preliminary demand like that made in the weight-lifting motivation test. It seems that an image of the counselor as someone who will be a quasi-dependable acceptor cannot be built up in this fashion, at least not with the type of interview and the type of demand we used in the present research. Perhaps a less rigorous preliminary demand or one that is more closely tied to the demands of dieting would prove to be more successful.

The findings from both experiments show greatest overall adherence to the counselor's recommendations when the clients were given positive feedback throughout the moderate self-disclosure interview, with positive evaluation on the motivation test and with no additional demand. These results are consistent with the theoretical analysis of Stage 1 of a supportive helping relationship, as presented in chapter 2, but additional findings suggest that some modifications of the analysis are needed.

The interaction effect replicated in the current experiment again impresses us with the necessity for postulating two different types of images that are likely to develop when the counselor uses different feedback styles. We surmise that when the counselor's style is to give consistently neutral feedback to the client's self-disclosures, adding either a strong demand or a critical evaluation on a preliminary task reinforces an image of the counselor as a strict, demanding authority figure who is hard to please and he or she becomes more effective in eliciting compliance. Further, we surmise that when the counselor's style is to give consistently accepting feedback, restricting the demands to those required by the main task at hand and abstaining from making any strong preliminary demand or any critical evaluation reinforces an image of the counselor as a nuturant parental figure who will enhance the client's self-esteem if the client lives up to the recommendations. The data on behavioral compliance in Table 7.1 suggest that the latter style is more effective for inducing adherence to the counselor's recommendations than the former, but this outcome might prove to be limited to the conditions of the present field experiment.

Personality Differences

Perhaps different types of personalities respond differently to the two types of feedback. If so, however, the personality measures we have tried out so far are the wrong ones to capture those differences, even though they are able to predict on a better-than-chance basis which clients will respond most positively to the recommendations of a counselor regardless of which type of feedback is given.

In the current study we used the same three personality scales that were used in the Dowds, Janis, and Conolley study. Again we found that as far as adherence is concerned, none of these personality measures was predictive of how different persons would respond to positive versus neutral feedback throughout the interview or to high versus low demand on the motivation test.

Just as in the Dowds, Janis, and Conolley study (chap. 6), the self-esteem scale was found to be significantly related to adherence over the 2-month period. Across all experimental conditions, clients with low-esteem scores (below the median) showed more adherence to the counselor's recommendations than those with high self-esteem scores on three follow-up measures: (1) number of weekly reports returned to the clinic ($p < .05$), (2) reported number of days of strict dieting ($p < .05$), and (3) mean weight loss ($p < .05$).[4]

A SUPPLEMENTARY EXPERIMENT: EFFECT OF CHANGING THE TYPE OF FEEDBACK DURING THE INITIAL INTERVIEW

There are two different theoretical orientations, one from clinical psychology and the other from experimental social psychology, which make different predictions about the effects of changing the type of social feedback during an initial interview. The theoretical model of counseling formulated by Carl Rogers (1957) asserts that the most effective helping relationship is one in which the counselor consistently gives unconditional positive regard, which is equivalent to presenting the accepting type of feedback throughout the entire interview (see chap. 2). This model is endorsed by other clinical investigators (e.g., Truax, 1963; Truax & Carkhuff, 1967). Many clinical psychologists and psychiatrists with somewhat different approaches to counseling and psychotherapy also use the unconditional acceptance type of feedback as an adjunct to other technical interventions, such as interpretations of resistance in psychoanalytically oriented psychotherapy. Some psychotherapists, although not all, agree with the main assumption of Rogers's client-centered therapy, namely, that unconditional positive regard is "a powerful therapeutic force in its own right" (Strupp, 1971, p. 42). According to Rogers's model, if a counselor waited until the middle of the initial interview with each client before starting to give accepting feedback, he or she would be somewhat less effective than if he or she started to do so right at the outset. The same prediction would be made by a simple exchange or equity theory of interpersonal influence (see Gergen, 1969; Homans, 1961; Walster, Walster, & Berscheid, 1978).

The opposite prediction would be made from the gain–loss model put forth by Elliot Aronson (1969, 1976) on the basis of social psychological experiments that he and his associates have carried out on changes in attitude toward a communicator and acceptance of a communicator's recommendations. The central theme of his theory, as Aronson has pointed out, was suggested over 300 years ago by Spinoza: "Hatred which is completely vanquished by love passes into love, and love is thereupon greater than if hatred had not preceded it."[5]

Aronson gives a more testable formulation:

> Increases in positive, rewarding behavior from another person have more impact on an individual than constant, invariant reward from that person. . . . Similarly, losses in rewarding behavior have more impact than constant punitive behavior from another person. Thus, a person whose esteem for us decreases over time will be disliked more than someone who has always disliked us—even if the number of punishments were greater from the latter person. (Aronson, 1976, p. 237)

According to Aronson's theory, when person A's liking for person B increases as a result of an increase in B's positive (rewarding) statements about A, B will exert a correspondingly greater influence on A; conversely, when A's liking for B decreases as a result of a decrease in B's positive statements about A, B's influence will correspondingly decrease (see Sigall & Aronson, 1967). In terms of Aronson's formulation, then, a counselor (or any other type of communicator) will be regarded more favorably and will have more influence on the plans and actions of his or her clients if he or she does *not* give consistently positive feedback from the outset, but instead starts off by giving neutral (or negative) feedback and later switches to positive feedback. Aronson's theory also makes the converse prediction regarding the unfavorable effects of negative or neutral feedback: A counselor will be regarded more unfavorably and will have less influence on his or her clients if he or she starts off giving positive feedback and then switches to neutral (or negative) feedback rather than giving consistently neutral (or negative) feedback from the outset.

By investigating the effects of different sequences of positive and neutral feedback we should find out, at least in a preliminary way, whether Rogers's

social reinforcement model, with its emphasis on consistent positive feedback, or Aronson's gain–loss model, with its emphasis on switching from
negative or neutral to positive feedback, is more applicable to effective
short-term counseling in diet clinics and in related types of helping relationships.[6] We expect that in the initial interview of a counselor with a
client, the effects that Aronson predicts do in fact occur at least temporarily
but may be subordinate to more powerful Rogerian factors that influence
the client's attitude toward a consistently accepting counselor, as specified by the theoretical analysis of Phases 1 and 2 in the development of an
effective helping relationship (see chap. 2).

DESIGN OF THE SUPPLEMENTARY EXPERIMENT

The supplementary experiment was designed to investigate the immediate
and sustained effects of three independent variables involving different
types of interaction between a counselor and client during the initial interview in a clinical setting: (1) positive versus neutral feedback during the
first two-thirds of the interview, (2) positive versus neutral feedback during
the last third of the interview, and (3) high versus low demand on a preliminary task imposed on the client right after the first two-thirds of the
interview. Accordingly, 88 clients who responded to announcements of the
Yale Weight-Reduction Clinic were assigned on a stratified random basis to
eight groups, each of which received a somewhat different pattern of treatments.

Four of the groups were used in the replication experiment described
earlier in this chapter. The four additional groups, which were treated concurrently by the same three male counselors, were given the same procedures during the first two-thirds of the interview, in the same sequence,
as the first four groups, but then, after the motivation test, the type of
feedback was changed for the last third of the interview. Two of the four
supplementary groups were given neutral feedback during the first two-
thirds of the interview and then were switched to accepting feedback
during the last third. The other two groups were given accepting feedback
during the first two-thirds of the interview and then were switched to
neutral feedback during the last third. Except for this switching from one
type of feedback to another, the treatments of the four supplementary
groups did not differ in any way from those given to the four groups in the
replication experiment. All the other procedures were exactly the same as
in the replication experiment described earlier in this chapter.

RESULTS AND DISCUSSION

Immediate Effects

The results on immediate effects of different patterns of feedback from the
counselor during the initial interview are shown in Table 7.2. When we

examine changes in ratings of the counselor from the beginning to the end of the interview, we find that the crucial factor is the type of feedback the clients received during the last third of the interview. Those who received

Table 7.2 Immediate effects of different patterns of feedback from the counselor during the initial interview

Type of feedback		Ratings of counselor			
During first two-thirds of the interview	During last third of the interview	Initial (before any feedback)	End of interview	Change	Commitment score
1. Accepting	Accepting	3.96	4.14	+.18	14.0
2. Accepting	Neutral	3.93	3.96	+.03	14.6
3. Neutral	Accepting	3.92	4.22	+.30	14.2
4. Neutral	Neutral	3.98	4.00	+.02	12.8

Note. N = 22 in each group, except that one case had to be discarded from the second group because of lack of comprehension of instructions.

accepting feedback during the last third gave significantly more favorable ratings to the counselor than those who received neutral feedback during the last third. (The mean changes are +.24 and +.025, respectively; $p < .05$).[7]

The results in Table 7.2 are not fully consistent with predictions from Aronson's gain–loss model. As we have seen, two main predictions follow from that model: (1) the group given neutral feedback during the first two-thirds of the interview followed by accepting feedback during the last third (a gain in esteem) should respond with significantly more favorable ratings than the group given accepting feedback throughout the entire interview, and (2) the group given accepting feedback during the first two-thirds of the interview followed by neutral feedback (a loss in esteem) should respond with significantly less favorable ratings than those given neutral feedback throughout the entire interview. For the first prediction the results on change in ratings of the counselor are in the predicted direction but are not large enough to be statistically significant. For the second prediction the results on change in ratings of the counselor show only a tiny difference and it is in the reverse direction. The only significant difference for ratings of the counselor is a main effect for positive versus neutral feedback during the last third of the interview. This finding was not predicted by Aronson's gain–loss model or by Rogers's consistent acceptance theory. For commitment scores, the largest difference is between accepting–neutral (14.6) and neutral–neutral (12.8), which is significantly different in the opposite direction from Aronson's second prediction ($p < .05$).

Adherence to Recommendations

In Table 7.3 we see a fairly consistent pattern for all measures of adherence over the 2-month period between the initial interview and the follow-up interview. On all four measures in Table 7.3 there is a trend suggesting that the more positive feedback given by the counselor during

Table 7.3. Adherence effects over a two-month period for different patterns of feedback from the counselor during the initial interview

Type of feedback		Number of weekly reports mailed in		Reported number of days on the diet		Percentage returning and demonstrating loss of 4 lbs. or more*		Weight loss for the entire group**	
During first two-thirds of the interview	During last third of the interview								
1. Accepting	Accepting	6.2	5.8	19.6	18.3	56%	49%	2.3	2.2
2. Accepting	Neutral	5.4		17.0		43%		2.0	
3. Neutral	Accepting	4.4	4.3	14.4	13.4	32%	23%	1.2	0.8
4. Neutral	Neutral	4.2		12.5		14%		0.5	

Note. N = 22 in each group, except that one case had to be discarded from the second group because of lack of comprehension of instructions.
  * The number of Ss who returned for follow-up were 16, 13, 11, and 11, respectively.
  ** Those who did not return were assigned zero weight loss.

the interview, the more effective he is. But for each measure, the only determining factor that proved to reach or approach the conventional level of statistical significance was the type of feedback given by the counselor during the *first part* (the first two-thirds) of the initial interview.[8] (Perhaps if the second part of the interview had been longer, the effect of positive feedback during that part of the interview, which is in the same direction, would also have been large enough to be statistically significant.) Because the only significant findings are for positive feedback during the first part of the self-disclosure interview, there appears to be a primacy effect. The unexpected findings pointing to a primacy effect, however, cannot be unequivocally interpreted as such because in this study the clients given positive feedback during the first part of the interview received a greater *total amount* of positive feedback than those given positive feedback during the second part of the interview. For example, in Table 7.3 the two middle groups look as if they should provide a crucial comparison for determining primacy versus recency effects but it must be remembered that the second group was given accepting feedback during the first *two-thirds* of the interview, which is about twice as much as that received by the third group (accepting feedback only during the last *one-third* of the interview). Nevertheless, one plausible interpretation of the findings is that the accepting type of feedback given by the counselor during the first part of the initial interview builds up a positive image of the counselor, which may be a crucial factor in sustaining a client's motivation to carry out the counselor's recommendations.

The findings on adherence can be unequivocally interpreted as failing to support the main predictions from Aronson's gain–loss model. According to that model, the counselor's influence should be (1) most strongly manifested by those who received neutral feedback during the first part of the interview followed by accepting positive feedback and (2) least apparent among those who received accepting feedback first followed by neutral feedback. But the results in Table 7.3 show that, contrary to these two predictions, the latter group, which was supposed to do relatively poorly, actually performed better than the former group, which was supposed to do better than all the others. The group that actually performed best was the one that received the accepting type of feedback throughout both parts of the interview; the group that actually performed worst was the one that received neutral feedback throughout both parts of the interview. These findings from our field experiment, like those from a laboratory experiment by Mettee (1971), do not bear out the predictions that follow from Aronson's gain–loss model.

We inferred from Rogers's model of counseling that the counselor's influence as a change agent should prove to be strongest if the counselor regularly gives clients accepting feedback throughout the entire initial interview. The results partially support this inference. As predicted by Rogers's model, the clients who were given the accepting type of feedback throughout the entire interview performed better on the various measures of adherence to the recommendations than those who received the accepting type of feedback only during the first two-thirds of the interview, but the differences were not large enough to be statistically significant. Consistent with Rogers's model is the finding that when counselors start off with the accepting type of feedback and use it all the way through the interview right up until they make their first dieting recommendations, they tend to be more effective in inducing sustained adherence to the recommendations than when they start off with neutral feedback and then either shift to the accepting type of feedback or continue to give neutral feedback. Also consistent with Rogers's model is the finding that accepting feedback given during the first two-thirds of the interview proved to be more effective than that given during the last part, which involved only half as much time.

If, on the other hand, subsequent research indicates that primacy is the basis of the observed findings, a plausible interpretation would be that many clients who come to a clinic for counseling are extremely impressed by initial accepting feedback because beforehand they are somewhat concerned about the possibility of encountering social disapproval or even being rejected or humiliated (e.g., being criticized by a counselor for being fat, lazy, and lacking in self-control). If the counselor starts off responding in a neutral way, making no comment one way or the other when the clients talk about personal weaknesses, their initial anxiety will mount because they are likely to regard the counselor's lack of response as a sign of unsympathetic or disdainful detachment (especially under conditions where they cannot see the counselor's facial expression). They will therefore tend to remain somewhat wary and withdrawn, which ultimately reduces the motivational power of the counselor. But if the counselor starts right off giving genuine accepting feedback, the clients' initial feelings of dejection and social anxiety will be promptly relieved and their self-esteem enhanced. As a result, they will develop warm, affectionate feelings toward the counselor from whom they are seeking help. Then, if the initial positive feedback is followed by neutral feedback, the clients will not be as likely to regard it as implying a lack of interest because the counselor has already demonstrated that he or she is a sympathetic listener. Having developed an image of the counselor as an enhancer of self-esteem, the clients will also be more likely to tolerate the threat of negative feedback that is conveyed as soon as the counselor makes specific recommendations (e.g., about dieting), which assert explicitly or implicitly that "I think you should change from what you are doing, which is unacceptable." Consequently the clients who receive accepting feedback from the outset will leave the initial session with a stronger motivation to maintain the counselor's positive regard and will show greater adherence to recommendations than if they encounter neutral feedback from the outset.

It seems plausible that alleviation of the client's feelings of dejection and social anxiety by giving accepting feedback at the beginning of the first session will often have a relatively more powerful effect than the gain effect postulated by Aronson from giving negative or neutral feedback at the outset before starting to give positive feedback. In some other types of social situations Aronson's predictions may well prove to be correct; they have, in fact, been borne out by several social psychological experiments which involve casual encounters in a laboratory with a stranger from whom the subject has no reason to expect any help (Aronson, 1976). But in a clinic, as a result of the clients' initial concerns about how they will be treated by a prestigeful authority figure from whom they are seeking help, a different outcome is likely to occur.[9]

Whether or not the latter interpretation of the findings in terms of a primacy effect and associated alleviation of dejection or social anxiety proves to be valid, the results of the present experiment by and large support the following prescriptive hypothesis, which is also supported by the findings from the Dowds, Janis, and Conolley experiment (chap. 6): If a counselor wants to build up a supportive relationship in order to increase the client's motivation to carry out a difficult course of action, he or she should give consistently positive feedback from the outset of the initial interview.

CONCLUSIONS

1. The first experiment described in this chapter was designed to be an exact replication of the experiment reported in the preceding chapter

except for a minor modification designed to eliminate negative feedback on the motivation test. As expected, the results obtained 2 months after the counseling session were in the same direction and were even stronger than in the initial experiment. This evidence further supports the hypothesis tested in chapter 6, namely, that if counselors give consistently positive feedback throughout an initial interview that elicits a moderate amount of self-disclosure, they will elicit more sustained adherence to their recommendations than if they give neutral feedback.

2. On three of the four measures of adherence, the extraneous high demand task (the weight-lifting motivation test) had a facilitating effect only on the clients who had been given neutral feedback throughout the interview, not on those who had been given positive feedback. These findings parallel those obtained for the motivation test in the preceding experiment. They indicate that introducing a preliminary demand (like that of the three-trial motivation test, which was intended to build up an image of the counselor as a quasi-dependable rather than completely dependable source of accepting feedback) is not likely to increase the clients' adherence to a supportive counselor's major recommendations (such as dieting instructions).

3. The differences between low and high self-esteem clients in adherence found in the preceding study (chap. 6) emerged also in this study, even more strongly. Low self-esteem clients lost more weight than high self-esteem clients (significantly so in this study), returned significantly more weekly reports, and reported staying on the diet for a significantly longer time.

4. A supplementary experiment on the effects of switching the type of feedback given by the counselor (from positive to neutral or vice versa) showed that the clients (a) expressed more favorable ratings of the counselor when they had been given positive (rather than neutral) feedback in the *last* part of the interview but (b) showed more adherence to the counselor's recommendations (including more weight loss 2 months later) when they had been given positive (rather than neutral) feedback during the *first* part of the interview. These findings are partially consistent with Rogers's assumption that the counselor's influence as a change agent will be strongest if the counselor regularly gives clients accepting feedback throughout the entire initial interview. They do not support Aronson's gain–loss model (which predicts, for example, that the strongest adherence effects will be produced by starting with neutral feedback and then shifting to positive feedback). A plausible interpretation of the outcome we observed for measures of adherence to the counselor's recommendations suggests the following hypothesis: When the counselor starts off with accepting feedback, the clients' initial feelings of dejection and social anxiety are promptly relieved; thereafter if the counselor switches to neutral feedback, the clients do not regard the change as implying lack of interest or rejection because

they have already developed an image of the counselor as an enhancer of self–esteem.

NOTES

1. Clients given accepting feedback increased their favorable ratings of the counselor (on a scale ranging from 1 to 5) from a mean of 3.96 at time 1 to 4.24 at time 2, whereas those given neutral feedback increased only very slightly from a mean of 3.98 to 4.07 (interaction $F(1, 40) = 5.21$, $p < .05$). After decreasing their ratings to a mean of 4.00 at time 3, the clients given accepting feedback went back up to a mean rating of 4.14 at time 4. Although the mean change of 0.18 from time 1 to time 4 was not large, it proved to be significantly larger than that shown by the clients given neutral feedback, whose mean rating at time 4 showed an increase of only 0.02 from time 1 (interaction $F(1, 40) = 4.31$, $p < .05$). Analysis of covariance of the change scores from the beginning to the end of the interview, with the initial score at time 1 as the covariate, also shows a significant main effect, with accepting feedback producing more positive change than neutral feedback ($F(1, 40) = 4.63$, $p < .05$).

2. The number of cases who returned for the follow-up interview in the four groups as listed in Table 7.1 were 9, 7, 5, and 6, respectively. When computing mean weight loss, we assumed that those who did not return remained unchanged and they were counted as zero weight loss. A separate analysis of mean changes in weight that was restricted to those clients who returned for the follow-up session (eliminating those who failed to return) yielded the same result: the main effect for accepting vs. neutral feedback was significant below the .05 confidence level.

3. Across both feedback conditions, the mean rating of the counselor given at Time 3 (just after the motivation test) by clients in the high demand condition was 3.94, whereas the mean rating given by those in the low demand condition was 4.10 ($F(1, 40) = 6.08$, $p < .05$). At Time 4 (end of the interview), the corresponding means were 3.94 and 4.19, respectively ($F(1, 40) = 4.31$, $p < .05$). Change scores from Time 1 to Time 3 and from Time 1 to Time 4, using ratings at Time 1 as a covariate, also show that the differences between high and low demand conditions are significant ($p < .05$).

4. As in the first study (chap. 6), the findings for the personality measures in the present study show that the social desirability scale (Crowne & Marlowe, 1964) and the personal boundary scale (Miller, 1968) were fairly highly correlated with each other ($r = .51$, with $N = 44$) but not with the modified Janis and Field (1959) self-esteem scale ($r = .19$ and .26, respectively). Neither the social desirability scale nor the personal boundary scale was significantly related to any of the measures of adherence.

An interaction effect was found by Dowds, Janis, and Conolley (chap. 6) for the social desirability scale (Crowne & Marlowe, 1964) and type of interviewer feedback as determinants of ratings of the counselor during the first session (see chap. 6, n. 4). This interaction effect was replicated in the present study ($p < .05$). We also found the same significant interaction effect for the personal boundary scale. These findings again support the familiar hypothesis mentioned in the first experiment, namely, that the clients who are most concerned about gaining approval say only nice things about the counselor in order to please him, regardless of what he says or does not say to them, whereas the clients who are less concerned about gaining approval express more freely their unfavorable reactions to neutral feedback.

An additional finding from the present study is that the clients who obtained relatively low scores on the social approval scale (below the median) were less likely than those who obtained higher scores to be willing to commit themselves to the counselor's recommendations on the commitment form ($p < .05$). But, as we already have mentioned, this immediate verbal response was not predictive of how well the clients would actually adhere to the counselor's recommendations when we assessed their behavioral adherence 2 months later.

5. Quoted by Aronson (1976) from Spinoza's *Ethics* (1678; edited by A. Boyle [New York: Dutton, 1910]).

6. Aronson (1976, p. 241) points out that three conditions must be met in order for his theory to apply. One is that the communicator not be suspected of intentional flattery when he or she gives positive feedback. This condition can be well satisfied in a diet clinic where clients receive treatment free of charge from professional counselors who are trained to give genuine acceptance responses. Such counselors are not likely to be suspected of engaging in flattery or ingratiation. Another condition is that the change in feedback should not pertain to markedly different attributes of the person being evaluated because it must imply a change in heart by the evaluator. In order to meet this condition, the interviews we conducted in the diet clinic included questions dealing with similar attributes in both parts of the interview. A third condition specified by Aronson is that the change in feedback should be gradual rather than abrupt, so as to avoid arousing the person's suspicion. We assume that the shift from neutral to positive feedback (or vice versa) is a gradual change and is certainly not in Aronson's prohibited category of an "abrupt about-face," which would be viewed "with confusion and suspicion" by the person being evaluated.

Aronson observes that when two people have an authentic affectionate relationship on a *long-term* basis, he does not expect predictions from his gain–loss model necessarily to hold. For marriages, friendships, and other long-term relationships, according to Aronson (1976, p. 244), when one partner switches from positive to neutral or negative feedback, the other partner does not immediately react in kind but attempts "to re-establish the positive intensity of the relationship." This exceptional case does not apply, however, to the present field experiment, which deals with an initial encounter between a counselor and client who are strangers, which is the type of social situation to which the gain–loss model is supposed to be applicable.

7. For the main effect of type of feedback, $F(1, 65) = 4.33$. An analysis of covariance was also carried out for change scores from time 1 (initial) to time 4 (end) using scores on time 1 as a covariate in order to take account of any initial differences among the 8 subgroups included in the $2 \times 2 \times 2$ factorial design (positive vs. neutral feedback during first two-thirds of the interview × positive vs. neutral feedback during last third × high vs. low demand on the motivation test given between the two parts of the interview). The analysis of covariance showed that in addition to a significant main effect for type of feedback during the last part of the interview there was a significant main effect for type of demand on the motivation test: Those who had been given the low demand gave significantly more favorable ratings to the counselor at the end of the session than those who had been given the high demand ($F = 7.01$, $p < .05$). This finding, based on all 8 subgroups, is in agreement with the significant effect of high versus low demand on ratings of the counselor reported earlier in this chapter, when the analysis of covariance was restricted to the 4 subgroups that had received no change in type of feedback during the interview. In the present analysis, as in the earlier one, there were no significant or near significant interaction effects.

Although the findings on immediate effects fail to give substantial support to Aronson's model, they do not unequivocally support an alternative model based on the postulate that the more positive acceptance a person is given by a counselor, the more favorable will be his attitude toward that counselor. One of the predictions which follows from this alternative model is that clients who receive the accepting type of feedback throughout the entire interview should respond with significantly more favorable ratings than those who receive the accepting type of feedback only during the last third of the interview. This prediction is not borne out when we compare the results in rows 1 and 3 of Table 7.2. The observed difference is not even in the predicted direction; it is not statistically significant.

Perhaps the ratings of the counselor obtained at the end of an interview are excessively influenced by what the counselor says during the last part of the interview and represent the client's momentary response, which might not be the same a short time later. More valid measures of sustained attitude changes might be obtained the day after the initial interview or maybe even just a few hours after. In any case, as can be seen in the final section of this chapter, the means ratings of the counselor obtained from each treatment group at the end of the initial interview did not prove to be valid predictors of how well those groups subsequently performed, as assessed by objective measures of sustained compliance with the counselor's recommendations. In contrast to the results on immediate responses to the various patterns of neutral or positive feedback (Table 7.2), which show a *recency* effect, the results on the sustained behavioral consequences (Table 7.3) show a *primacy* effect.

8. For number of weekly reports (5.8 vs. 4.3), $F(1, 65) = 6.70, p < .05$. For reported number of days of strict dieting (18.3 vs. 13.4), $F(1, 65) = 4.52, p < .05$. On the two measures of weight loss, the differences are in the same direction but of borderline significance. For percentages returning and demonstrating loss of 4 or more pounds (49% vs. 23%), $p < .10$. For mean weight loss for the entire group (2.2 vs. 0.8), $F(1, 65) = 3.99, p < .10$.

For high versus low demand on the motivation test we observed the same trends as in the replication experiment. But this independent variable did not have a significant main effect, and it did not enter into any significant interaction effect for any of the objective indicators of sustained adherence to recommendations shown in table 7.3.

9. One implication of our analysis of the primacy effect of positive feedback in terms of alleviating initial dejection and social anxiety is that the gain–loss effect observed by Aronson and his co-workers is not a main effect to be expected in all fresh encounters with strangers but depends upon the person's initial hopes and fears about the encounter. Thus, we expect that predictions from the gain–loss model will be confirmed when the person has relatively little initial concern about the stranger's evaluations but will not be confirmed when the person is worried about making a good impression on the stranger because he or she wants the stranger's help. Hence, we expect that the subjects' pre-encounter concerns about the encounter will prove to be a significant interacting variable, which could be tested in a factorial experiment in which pre-encounter concerns are deliberately varied.

8 Effects of the Counselor's Verbal Feedback, Interpersonal Distance, and Clients' Field Dependence

LES R. GREENE

The influence of a counselor's facial expressions and other nonverbal communications on a client's responses to the counselor's verbal statements has been stressed by Bordin (1974) as a major new topic in counseling research. Although it is difficult to generalize from the relatively small number of studies reported so far, there are indications that the content of a counselor's verbal messages can be modified—at times enhanced and other times discounted—by accompanying nonverbal cues. Most of the prior laboratory studies have examined how sending contradictory and complementary messages via verbal and nonverbal channels affects perceptions of the communicator (Bugental, Kaswan, & Love, 1970; Lampel & Anderson, 1968; Mehrabian & Weiner, 1967; Shapiro, 1966). A few laboratory studies have examined the effects of mixed messages upon the recipients' emotional reactions (Ellsworth & Carlsmith, 1968; Mettee, Taylor, & Fisher, 1971) and overt behavior (Albert & Dabbs, 1970; Reece & Whitman, 1962). One aim of the present study was to extend the prior research by exploring in a real-life counseling setting the effects of verbal acceptance versus neutral feedback under two different conditions involving a nonverbal variable, namely, near versus remote physical distance between the counselor and client.

Using a formulation based upon self-esteem dynamics, Janis (chap. 2) has provided an analysis of the facilitating influence of verbal evaluative feedback in bolstering clients' decisions to carry out stressful courses of action. He posits that receiving accepting feedback from a counselor for one's self-disclosures results in a heightened sense of personal worth; this, in turn, makes for strong motivation to continue the relationship with the counselor. This fostered dependency can be used to strengthen a client's commitment to a stressful decision, provided that the counselor imposes only a limited set of behavioral demands and continues to express warmth and positive regard for all but a narrow category of counternorm behavior.

This chapter is based on a dissertation (supervised by James C. Miller, Irving L. Janis, and Donald Quinlan) submitted for the Ph.D. degree at Yale University. Portions of the dissertation have been published previously (Greene, 1976, 1977).

Studies reported in chapters 6, 7, and 15 indicate that adherence to a difficult decision, such as staying on a diet or donating blood, is strengthened when clients receive consistently accepting rather than neutral feedback.

The use of physical space in social interactions between a counselor and client might strengthen or weaken the influence of verbal feedback. Argyle and Dean (1965) have postulated that the regulation of interpersonal distance is one means for controlling intimacy and involvement. A related formulation states that appropriate spatial proximity can enhance the impact of evaluative verbal information (Albert & Dabbs, 1970; Berscheid & Walster, 1969; Storms & Thomas, 1977). Changes in interpersonal proximity are directly related to the nature of the evaluative feedback anticipated or perceived: greater distances are maintained when a person expects threatening or stressful information (Dosey & Meisels, 1969), whereas interpersonal proximity is increased when a person expects positive information (Little, 1965).

Specific hypotheses can be offered about the ways in which physical proximity, as an aspect of a counselor's nonverbal communication, might modify the impact of his or her verbal evaluative feedback to clients. Positive verbal feedback given by a counselor sitting near a client should be more effective in fostering adherence to the counselor's recommendations than the same positive feedback given when the counselor is sitting farther away. Similarly, neutral feedback should induce more resistance or confusion in clients when the counselor is close than when the counselor is more distant.

In addition to examining the effects of positive versus neutral feedback and near versus remote seating distance between counselor and client, this study also explored the effects of a relevant personality dimension, field dependence, which refers to the degree to which a person is influenced by the environmental (field) context when making perceptual and other cognitive judgments. Several studies suggest that field dependent persons are more socially dependent, more influenced by authoritative opinion, and less self-reliant than field independent individuals (Freedman, O'Hanlon, Oltman, & Witkin, 1972; Konstadt & Forman, 1965; Linton, 1955). Other findings suggest that those with a field independent style tend to withdraw from helpers, maintaining greater psychological distance and personal space (Justice, 1970; Pollack & Kiev, 1963; Schimek, 1968). Finally, there are findings which indicate that field independent persons perform more effectively on autonomous and impersonal tasks, while field dependent persons are superior in interpersonally oriented activities (Lefcourt & Seigel, 1970; Quinlan & Blatt, 1972).

In the present study field dependence was investigated in a natural setting involving a counselor–client relationship. The study was conducted in a weight-reduction clinic like the one described in the preceding chapters. An important feature of this clinical setting is the potential for a relatively high degree of psychological intimacy and dependence. Each female client was interviewed face-to-face by a male counselor who asked questions about personal problems and offered help in carrying out a difficult decision. If field independent and field dependent clients have contrasting reactions to closeness and social support, this context should readily evoke them. Based on previous empirical and theoretical contributions, the predictions investigated in this study were that field dependent clients, compared with their field independent counterparts, would display less psychological withdrawal, more positive attitudes toward the counselor, and greater dependency upon the counselor. But if field dependent clients have a greater need for the physical presence and emotional support of helpers, they should be found to react more negativistically to the termination of direct contact with the counselor. Consequently, they should prove to be less successful in losing weight under these conditions than the field independent clients.

METHOD

Overview

The effects of three variables—the counselor's verbal evaluative feedback, the physical distance between counselor and client, and the clients' field dependence—were studied by means of a factorial design. Structured interviews were individually administered to 80 female clients in the diet clinic. These face-to-face interviews were systematically varied in terms of (1) the verbal feedback given by the counselor (accepting vs. neutral) and (2) the physical proximity of the counselor to the client (near vs. remote distance). On the basis of a preliminary test (the Embedded Figures Test), half the clients were rated as field dependent and the other half as field independent. Two measures of behavioral adherence were used in addition to behavioral and self-report measures of clients' attitudes and emotional reactions.

Clients

Clients were recruited by means of standard newspaper announcements about the Yale Weight-Reduction Clinic. The only restrictions placed on respondents were that they have no weight-related medical problems and be no more than 45 pounds overweight. The first 80 female respondents who passed this initial screening were scheduled for individual appointments.

Procedures

At the beginning of the face-to-face interview, the counselor informed the client about the clinic's policies, recorded the client's height and weight, and then administered questionnaires to obtain relevant demographic and personality data, including the measure of field dependence. Next, the counselor explained that he wanted to explore several personal topics for their possible relevance to the problems of overeating and dieting. After informing the client that this interview would be videotaped for subsequent research analysis, he gave a moderate disclosure interview which included questions on such matters as personal feelings associated with food and eating, attitudes about personal appearance, and ways of coping with frustration and boredom. After the 20-minute interview the client completed 19 questionnaire items concerning her feelings and attitudes toward the counselor.

Then the client was handed mimeographed materials consisting of lists of kinds and amounts of food appropriate for maintaining a 1200-calorie diet and a series of planned menus. She listened to a tape recording prepared by the counselor which reviewed the dieting information and presented specific recommendations for her to follow over a 5-week period. One of the recommendations was that the client should keep the clinic informed of her progress by mailing in weekly reports indicating how well she adhered to the diet during each week.

At the end of the session each client was asked to complete five additional questionnaire items. These items assessed her willingness to comply with the dieting recommendations and her interest in returning to the clinic and seeing the same counselor in 5 weeks.

Experimental Conditions

Verbal Feedback

The two forms of verbal feedback were essentially the same as in the preceding studies (chaps. 6 and 7). In the positive feedback conditions the counselor offered approval (e.g., "I'm glad you're answering these questions so openly") and acceptance (e.g., "I can see how that would be difficult") after the clients' self-disclosures. He also provided such transitional comments as "Let's go on to another topic." In the neutral feedback conditions the counselor remained silent or offered only transitional statements.

Interpersonal Distance

This variable involved arranging the position of the counselor's chair in relation to the client's chair. Near and remote distances of 2 and 5 feet, respectively (as measured knee to knee), were chosen to correspond to Hall's (1966) categories of "personal" and "social" distances. At both interpersonal distances the chairs were angled 30° from a direct, face-to-face orientation.

In order to isolate the effects of this nonverbal dimension the counselor was trained not to emit behavioral cues during the interview that might reflect his own feelings or attitudes. He was instructed to sit upright, minimize facial expressiveness and gesturing, and maintain normal eye contact with the client.

Field Dependence
The Embedded Figures Test, administered according to the manual by
Witkin, Oltman, Raskin, and Karp (1971), was used near the beginning of the
session to assess field dependence.[1] Clients were informed that the test was
being tried out in order to assess its value in predicting dieting success.

Dependent Measures

Subsequent Behavioral Adherence
The primary measure of behavioral adherence was defined as success or
failure in returning to the clinic after 5 weeks and showing a 5-pound weight
loss.[2] A second behavioral measure was success or failure in completing and
returning the five weekly report forms.

Behavioral Measures of Affect
A videotape camera was stationed unobtrusively in a small opening in a wall
separating the interviewing room from an adjoining room. It recorded a
head-to-knee, front view of the seated client during the first 10 minutes of
the interview. All the nonverbal behaviors subsequently scored from these
recordings had been previously established in the literature as indicative of
withdrawal, positive feelings, and dependency. Nonverbal positions included for analysis were eye contact, forward leaning, arm crossing, and leg
crossing. Behavioral acts that were analyzed consisted of shoulder shrug-
ging, head nodding, hair grooming, smiling, "palms-up" gesturing, lip and
tongue movements, and hand-to-mouth movements. To assess clients' experienced discomfort or anxiety during the interview, a measure of speech
disturbances (Kasl & Mahl, 1965) was also derived from the videotape
recordings.

Self-report Measures of Affect
A 24-item questionnaire was constructed to tap the same three types of
affective reactions as are reflected by the behavioral measures. All self-
report items used 7-point rating scales.

RESULTS

Effects of Verbal Evaluative Feedback and Interpersonal Distance

The first question to be addressed is, How did differences in the counselor's
verbal feedback and interpersonal distance affect clients' adherence to his
dieting recommendations? Table 8.1 presents the percentage of clients who
successfully met the criteria of behavioral adherence under each of the four
situational conditions. The effect of the verbal feedback offered by the
counselor in this study was found to depend upon whether the counselor
was physically close or remote. When both near and remote conditions are
combined, overall conformity to dieting recommendations was as strong
for clients receiving neutral feedback as for those given accepting feedback.

Similarly, the physical distance between counselor and client failed to have a consistent overall effect on the degree of behavioral adherence. Significant interactions of evaluative feedback and interpersonal distance, consistent with expectation, were found, however, on both the weight loss criterion ($p < .05$) and the weekly reports criterion ($p < .06$).[3] When the counselor sat near his clients, he elicited *more* behavioral adherence if he gave consistently positive feedback (in the form of approval and acceptance) than if he gave neutral feedback. At the remote distance, however, positive feedback was *less* effective in eliciting adherence to dieting recommendations than was neutral feedback.

Table 8.1. Effects of feedback and distance on two measures of behavioral adherence

Measures	Accepting feedback		Neutral feedback	
	Near distance	Remote distance	Near distance	Remote distance
Percentage losing 5 pounds	50%	20%	30%	45%
Percentage returning 5 reports	45%	25%	20%	40%

Note. $N = 20$ in each of the 4 groups.

An attempt was made to explore the interpersonal dynamics mediating these interactions by looking at the relationships between the clients' adherence and their emotional reactions. Factor analyses were carried out with the behavioral measures and also with the questionnaire items. For the behavioral measures, three dimensions were abstracted and identified as (1) withdrawal (reflecting attempts to distance oneself from the counselor), (2) dependency (involving expressions of helplessness and desires for nurturance from the counselor), and (3) positive attitudes toward the counselor. Three factors were also abstracted from the set of self-report items and were labeled as follows: (1) concerns about self-disclosure (reflecting distrust about having been asked for and having revealed too much personal information), (2) willingness to adhere (including commitments to follow dieting recommendations, praise of the services of the clinic, and expressions of the need to obtain the counselor's approval by acting in a socially desirable manner), and (3) positive feelings toward the counselor.[4]

How do these six measures of clients' reactions derived from the factor analyses relate to behavioral adherence to dieting recommendations? None of the assessed attitudes and feelings of the clients turned out to be correlated with dieting success during the 5-week follow-up period. But positive results were found when the effects of the counselor's behavior on clients' affective states were explored by means of analyses of variance. For one of the affective measures (concerns about self-disclosure) an interaction pattern emerged paralleling that obtained from each of the two adherence measures ($p < .10$). When the counselor sat near the clients, his accepting feedback resulted in somewhat less concern about the amount of personal information disclosed than neutral feedback did. In contrast, at the more remote distance, the counselor's accepting feedback resulted in a marked increase in concern, as well as less behavioral adherence (Table 8.2).[5]

Table 8.2. Effects of feedback and distance on two measures of affective reactions

Factors based on questionnaire items	Accepting feedback		Neutral feedback	
	Near distance	Remote distance	Near distance	Remote distance
Concerns about self-disclosure	−.30	.54	−.19	−.05
Positive feelings toward the counselor	.43	−.04	−.10	−.27

Note. $N = 20$ in each of the 4 groups. Means for the two variables are of standardized factor scores, $T = 0.0$, S.D. $= 1.00$.

A second analysis of variance revealed that the counselor's accepting feedback produced more positive feelings toward the counselor (as assessed from the questionnaire items) at both interpersonal distances ($p < .10$). This effect was more pronounced, as anticipated, for the near distance than for the remote distance. The interaction effect was not strong enough, however, to reach statistical significance.

Correlates of Field Dependence

The next question is how the clients' degree of field dependence is related to their behavior during and after the interview. It was expected that field dependent clients would become more emotionally involved with the counselor than would the field independent clients. Consistent with this prediction, the field dependent clients showed significantly fewer signs of psychological withdrawal during the interview ($p < .005$). They also tended to express slightly more positive attitudes toward the counselor on both the behavioral and self-report measures although these effects were not statistically significant. On the self-report questionnaire the field dependent clients, as anticipated, also expressed greater willingness to adhere to the dieting recommendations ($p < .05$). That this attitude reflected more the need to receive social approval from the counselor than an actual commitment is suggested by the findings from the measures of subsequent behavioral adherence. During the 5-week dieting period, when the counselor was no longer in direct contact with them, fewer field dependent clients mailed in all the weekly reports to the clinic ($p < .06$).[6] Only 25% of the field dependent clients returned to the clinic after 5 weeks and showed at least a 5-pound weight loss, compared to 48% of the field independent clients ($p < .05$).

Several interactions of field dependence with aspects of the counselor's behavior were also found. Generally the field dependent clients were more sensitive to and dependent upon the counselor's support and closeness. When the counselor sat near his clients, the field dependent clients showed less withdrawal when given accepting feedback than when given neutral feedback; in contrast, field independent clients became more withdrawn under these same conditions ($p < .05$).

Another interaction on this behavioral withdrawal measure was found under conditions where the counselor sat at the remote distance. Unexpectedly, under these conditions the field dependent clients were less psychologically withdrawn when the counselor responded with neutral comments ($p < .05$).

A separate analysis was made of speech disturbances in order to assess differences in anxiety among the field dependent and field independent clients. The results parallel those for psychological withdrawal. When the counselor sat near, the number of speech irregularities of field dependent and field independent clients were differentially affected by evaluative feedback ($p < .10$): Field dependent clients displayed more speech disturbances when receiving neutral feedback while field independent clients displayed fewer.[7] These findings and those from the behavioral measure of withdrawal support the view that the interpersonal tensions evoked in an interview with a counselor differ for field independent and field dependent individuals. The results suggest that, when a counselor sits near, providing accepting feedback is more effective than giving neutral feedback for field dependent clients but less effective for field independent clients.

Another interaction effect was found for the behavioral measure of positive attitude toward the counselor ($p < .06$): Field dependent clients showed more positive attitudes when offered accepting feedback, compared to neutral feedback, whereas field independent clients were not significantly affected by this situational variable.

Finally, on the behavioral measure of aroused dependency needs, a significant interaction was also found ($p < .05$). Again, only the field dependent clients reacted differently to systematic changes in an aspect of the counselor's behavior. They showed greater needs for nurturance and closeness when the counselor sat at the remote distance.

DISCUSSION

Clients who were given positive verbal feedback in the form of acceptance and approval expressed more positive feelings toward the counselor, no matter where the counselor sat, whether near or remote. This result is similar to the earlier findings from Dowds, Janis, and Conolley (chap. 6) and from Conolley, Janis, and Dowds (chap. 7) on the effects of accepting feedback on the clients' ratings of their liking for the counselor. But in the present study, positive feelings toward the counselor proved to be unrelated to subsequent adherence to the counselor's recommendations. The results on weight loss and other measures of adherence are related in complex ways to type of feedback and spatial proximity, involving interaction effects instead of simple main effects. Some of the findings on adherence can be readily interpreted in terms of the self-esteem enhancement analysis formulated by Janis (chap. 2), but other findings apparently require additional or different theoretical assumptions.

The results from this study provide some support for the hypothesis that the clients' motivation to endure the stressful decision to diet is dependent upon both verbal and nonverbal aspects of the counselor's interpersonal behavior. But the significant interaction effects of the two measures of behavioral adherence (mailing back weekly reports and showing weight loss at the 5-week follow-up session) do not support the interpretation of spatial behavior as an intensifier of the verbal component of the counselor's communication. Furthermore, evaluative feedback did not have a significant main effect.

At the near distance, accepting feedback did evoke more behavioral adherence than neutral feedback, in line with the expected outcome resulting from self-esteem enhancement. The unexpected finding occurred at the more remote interpersonal distance. In this spatial arrangement neutral feedback was more effective than positive feedback in eliciting adherence. In fact, almost as many clients were compliant in the "remote distance–neutral feedback" condition as in the "near distance–positive feedback" condition.

The findings on the effects of acceptance feedback when the counselor sat near the client are essentially the same as the findings from Mulligan's first experiment on volunteering to donate blood to the Red Cross (chap. 15), obtained under similar seating conditions. A positive effect of acceptance feedback on adherence to dieting recommendations was also found in the weight-reduction studies reported in chapters 6 and 7, for those conditions in which the counselor abstained from making any criticism or any severe extraneous demand. In those two prior studies, however, the counselor was not in the same room and conducted the interview from an extremely remote distance by means of an audio intercom, similar to a telephone conversation. Perhaps the finding in the current study that positive feedback was less effective than neutral feedback for the remote seating condition occurs only when the counselor is in the same room, where he is seen as being personally responsible for choosing to sit farther away from the client than is expected in a friendly conversation. When the counselor speaks from outside the room by means of an audio system, his physical remoteness is more likely to be interpreted by the clients as a standard operating procedure of the clinic (which is the way it is explained to the clients) and therefore is not used as a cue concerning the counselor's warmth or friendliness.

In the present study the two experimental conditions that were most effective in producing adherence to the counselor's dieting recommendations (i.e., "near distance with accepting feedback" and "remote distance with neutral feedback") also turned out to produce less distrust and less concern among the clients about the amount of information they disclosed. One interpretation which may account for both their greater trust and their behavioral adherence derives from the notion of consistency in the communication of evaluative information. If interpersonal proximity is regarded as an implicit message of the counselor's attitude, as several prior studies suggest (Kelly, 1972; Mehrabian & Ferris, 1961; Mehrabian & Weiner, 1967), the two "successful" conditions can be characterized as ones in which the counselor's image was fairly consistent across verbal and nonverbal channels. When sitting at the remote distance and offering neutral feedback, the counselor may foster a consistent image of a detached authority figure. Considering the impassive facial expression and neutral posture of the counselor, one would single out this condition as a situation where all aspects of the counselor's behavior would be perceived as most uniform and consistent. It may require two communicative channels (i.e., sitting nearby and offering acceptance) to overcome the other neutral aspects of the counselor's behavior (e.g., unsmiling, impassive, facial expressions) in order that he be perceived as a warm, accepting helper.

In the two "unsuccessful" conditions (i.e., near distance with neutral feedback and remote distance with positive feedback) an implicit communication of the counselor's attitude contradicted his verbal message. In both these conditions, only one aspect of the counselor's behavior is positively expressive. Janis has postulated that in the initial phase of a helping relationship a counselor can acquire motivating power by being perceived as a trustworthy and genuine helper (see chap. 2). According to the present interpretation, inconsistency in communicative channels may arouse clients' suspicion and consequently diminish the counselor's influence. More specifically, it may be that in those situations where *one* channel contradicts other communicative channels (e.g., the offering of accepting feedback by a physically remote, impassive counselor or the close physical proximity of an impassive counselor who provides neutral verbal feedback) that clients' mistrust is strongest.

Although these conclusions are tentative, prior studies provide supporting evidence. In the Dowds, Janis, and Conolley study (chap. 6), consistency of the counselor's feedback turned out to be a crucial determinant when the counselor gave verbal evaluations of two different aspects of the client's behavior (i.e., self-disclosures and performance on an extraneous motivation test). They found that behavioral compliance was enhanced in the experimental condition in which positive feedback was expressed for both kinds of behavior and in the condition in which it was withheld for both kinds of behavior. Taking account of these findings on consistency and similar findings obtained by Conolley, Janis, and Dowds (chap. 7), these researchers suggest that the communication of a consistent image (in one case, of a nurturant, supportive figure and in the other case, of a detached, demanding authority figure) may strengthen adherence. In a counseling-analogue study, Reece and Whitman (1962) found that verbal expressions of approval unaccompanied by consistent nonverbal cues were less effective as social reinforcers than combined verbal and nonverbal cues of approval. Finally, other studies suggest that consistency in communicative channels has a positive effect on interpersonal attraction (Ellsworth & Carlsmith, 1968; Mettee, Taylor, & Fisher, 1971). The nonverbal cues that are used, however, may be different for women than for men (see Ellsworth & Ross, 1975).

The present findings, considered in light of the prior research, point up the importance of including an analysis of the consistency of the counselor's communications when assessing the effectiveness of any counseling treatment. In addition, the findings may have implications for the training of counselors with regard to increasing their sensitivity to inconsistent messages communicated by the nonverbal cues they inadvertently display to their clients (see Jacobs, 1973).

The results of this study bearing on the personality dimension of field dependence contribute to the growing literature on predispositions related to adherence. Of particular interest are the data indicating a relationship between field dependence and withdrawal behavior. In comparison to those with a field dependent approach, the field independent clients tended to display more psychological withdrawal during the interviews. This finding corroborates a study by Justice (1970), who found that field independent subjects maintain greater personal space than field dependent subjects when communicating with another person. If these distancing or "proxemic" behaviors, as they have been called, are conceptualized as regulators of personal involvement in social contexts (Argyle & Dean, 1965; Scheflen, 1972), the present results provide further support for the association between perceptual style and preferred degree of psychological intimacy with others.

Other findings from the current study suggest that the observed differences in proxemic behaviors may reflect contrasting means of coping with dependency feelings involving approach toward or avoidance of warm, dependent relationships. It would be unwarranted, however, to conclude that field dependent persons are psychologically weak. They might simply be more openly accepting of their dependency feelings, with a preference for entering into dependency-gratifying relationships (see Nevill, 1974). The field independent individuals might prove to be "counterdependent," i.e., motivated to avoid feeling influenced by and dependent upon others.

Support for the notion that field dependence is linked to different styles of coping with opportunities to form dependent relationships comes from the results of the behavioral measure of withdrawal and the speech disturbance measure of anxiety. The present field setting, across all experimental conditions, was likely to arouse incipient dependency feelings: clients were explicitly seeking and receiving help for a personal problem. The combined situational effects of accepting feedback and close physical proximity were expected to augment their feelings of dependency upon the counselor. For the field independent clients this high degree of hospitable behavior did evoke, as anticipated, their strongest reactions of discomfort and withdrawal. Field dependent clients, in contrast, were favorably affected by this same hospitable treatment. These observations fit the characterization of field dependent persons as being more comfortable with and desirous of dependency-gratifying interpersonal relationships. But under certain conditions the field dependent clients did manifest relatively more withdrawal, namely, in the "near distance with neutral feedback" and "remote distance with positive feedback" conditions. As discussed earlier, in these two conditions the counselor may have appeared most self-contradictory and inconsistent. His mixed messages may be threatening for those who are most eager for support from others, although quite acceptable to field independent clients.

The two other significant interactions, involving positive attitudes toward and dependency upon the counselor, suggest that the field dependent clients are relatively more sensitive to the presence or absence of cues reflecting the emotional availability of the counselor. This greater reactivity of field dependent persons to the emotional climate, which extends findings reported by Konstadt and Forman (1965) and Nevill (1974), is compatible with the formulation of their greater external directedness and social dependence.

Finally, the results from the measures of adherence also lend support to the hypotheses about predispositional differences associated with perceptual style. The field dependent clients expressed greater readiness than the field independent clients to adhere to dieting recommendations during the interview but were less compliant during the dieting period. One way of understanding these two effects involves Janis's formulation (chap. 2) of the crisis likely to develop in a helping relationship at termination of contact. He postulates that a client, feeling attracted to and dependent on a counselor, may react with anger and depression to the termination of contact; these negative effects can lead to renunciation of the values and norms communicated by the counselor. In the present context the field dependent clients may have more strongly appreciated the supportive aspects of the clinic during the initial interview and then felt more abandoned during the dieting period, when there was neither face-to-face nor telephone contact with the counselor. Although there is no direct evidence for this conclusion, an additional correlational finding is consistent with it: the field dependent clients who manifested the most dependency behavior during the interview tended to send in the fewest weekly reports ($r = -.32$, $p < .05$). Perhaps when opportunities for receiving direct support from a counselor are not available after the counseling sessions have ended, field dependent clients more strongly reject the counselor's long-term recommendations. In light of the present set of findings, this hypothesis warrants further investigation in subsequent research on field dependence in relation to contrasting means of coping with dependency needs.

MAIN CONCLUSIONS

The results from this study on female clients' adherence to recommendations offered by male counselors in face-to-face interviews at a weight-reduction clinic lead to the following two general conclusions:

1. Adherence to dieting recommendations apparently depends on the degree of consistency between verbal and nonverbal components of a counselor's communications during a face-to-face interview. Positive verbal feedback offered by an impassive counselor to clients who disclosed personal information was found to be more effective than neutral feedback in increasing trust and in facilitating behavioral adherence when the counselor sat close to the clients. But when the counselor was seated at a more remote distance, neutral feedback proved to be more effective than positive feedback.

2. The effectiveness of the counseling procedures in this study also depended, in part, upon the personality dimension of field dependence. Field dependent clients, compared to field independent clients, generally were more sensitive to and gratified by the emotional support of the counselor during the one-session interview. They showed less adherence, however, to recommendations during the 5-week dieting period, during which there was no direct contact with the counselor.

NOTES

1. The score derived from the Embedded Figure Test is the time, averaged over 12 presentations, needed to outline a simple geometric figure within an embedding context. The distribution of scores of the 80 clients ranged from 23 to 180 seconds with a mean of 100.9 seconds. To form the field dependent and field independent groups, the scores were dichotomized at the median of 102 seconds.

2. Several factors went into the choosing of this criterion, which were mentioned in the footnotes for earlier chapters. On the basis of previous work using the same 1200-calorie diet it was expected that clients would lose, on the average, 1 pound per week. Previous experience in the weight-reduction clinic also suggested that not all the clients would return for a follow-up meeting. It seemed reasonable to assume that such clients failed to lose weight. This assumption was based on two observations: (1) many clients who did not return explicitly stated over the telephone that they lost no weight, and (2) other clients, fewer in number, repeatedly missed scheduled follow-up meetings, coming up with a variety of unconvincing excuses. Consequently, both the clients who did not return and those who did attend the follow-up meeting but who lost less than 5 pounds were classified together as "failures."

3. These probabilities are based on three-way factorial analyses of variance.

4. Detailed descriptions of the factor analyses are reported elsewhere (Greene, 1976).

5. An analysis of the actual amount of self-disclosure elicited during the interviews, based on Haymes's (1971) scoring system, yielded no systematic differences across the four experimental conditions. Because the interview questions became progressively more personal and probing, separate analyses were performed for the first and second halves of the interview. Again, however, no significant differences in amount of self-disclosure emerged.

6. Only 22.5% of the field dependent clients returned all the weekly reports, compared to 42.5% of the field independent clients ($F(1, 72) = 3.69$, $p < .06$). On the behavioral measure of psychological withdrawal, means across all conditions for the field dependent and field independent clients were $-.32$ and $.32$, respectively ($F(1, 72) = 10.14$, $p < .005$). Corresponding means on the behavioral measure of positive attitude toward the counselor were $.11$ and $-.11$ ($F(1, 72) = 1.00$, n.s.) and on the self-report measure of positive attitude were $.09$ and $-.09$ ($F(1, 72) < 1$, n.s.). On the willingness-to-adhere factor, means for the field dependent and field independent clients were $.23$ and $-.23$, respectively ($F(1, 72) = 4.27$, $p < .05$).

7. When the counselor sat at the remote distance, no significant differences in the number of speech disturbances were found. Findings from the behavioral measure of psychological withdrawal and from the measure of speech disturbances were derived from the analyses of simple two-way interactions (feedback × field dependence) at each interpersonal distance. These analyses were performed because significant or near significant three-way interactions (feedback × field dependence × interpersonal distance) had been obtained on the measure of withdrawal ($F(1, 72) = 9.36$, $p < .005$) and on the measure of speech disturbances ($F(1, 72) = 3.54$, $p < .10$).

9 Effects of Moderate Self-disclosure and the Balance-Sheet Procedure

MARY ELLEN COLTEN AND IRVING L. JANIS

The study reported in this chapter was designed to test one of the major hypotheses from the theoretical analysis in chapter 2. The hypothesis is that a person will display greater readiness to adhere to a counselor's recommendations about carrying out a stressful course of action (such as dieting) if the counselor conducts an initial interview in which he or she asks questions in a plausible context that elicit a moderate degree of self-disclosure, provided that the counselor responds to the self-disclosures by giving positive feedback in the form of explicit acceptance responses. The present study differs from those reported in the preceding three chapters because this time we varied the amount of self-disclosure rather than the type of feedback. In this study, which was carried out in the same weight-reduction clinic, we compare an interview that elicits a *moderate* degree of self-disclosure with one that elicits a *low* degree of self-disclosure, while holding positive feedback constant for both conditions.[1]

If it turns out that eliciting a moderate amount of self-disclosure evokes more adherence to the counselor's recommendations than does eliciting a low amount, we can be more secure about the key assumptions presented in the theoretical analysis of effective counseling for the supportive type of short-term helping relationship (see chap. 2). According to those assumptions, when clients describe their personal attitudes, aspirations, anxieties, strengths, and weaknesses to a counselor and in response to each of those self-disclosures receive acceptance (positive social reinforcement), they will value the counselor as someone who enhances their self-esteem. Such valuation is expected to be much weaker if the clients engage in little or no self-disclosure even though they are given the same kind and amount of positive social reinforcement. When a client makes an emotional investment in the relationship with the counselor by taking off his or her usual social mask and exposing personal feelings, the accepting counselor is more likely to acquire referent power as a significant other, which increases the client's motivation to adhere to whatever norms the counselor advocates.

In addition to testing the self-disclosure hypothesis we investigated the effects of a second type of procedure that we had reason to expect would

159

"beef up" the counselor's effectiveness. The second procedure involves introducing a "decisional balance sheet," which induces the clients to consider carefully the potential short-term and long-term gains and losses of the decision before committing themselves and starting to carry it out (see chap. 3). Prior pilot studies and field experiments suggest that people are more likely to adhere to a difficult decision if before beginning to implement the decision they are induced to scan all the pros and cons in the balance sheet systematically (see Janis & Mann, 1977, chap. 6).

One of the ways the balance-sheet procedure might reduce postdecisional regret is by providing stress inoculation for subsequent setbacks through anticipation of negative consequences. It also entails a fair amount of self-disclosure. The procedure requires the client to reveal personal preferences, fears, and antipathies in describing anticipated positive and negative consequences of alternative courses of action. The balance-sheet procedure may also allow more comprehensive appraisal of the favorable consequences of the chosen course of action, which the client is likely to perceive more clearly as outweighing the unfavorable consequences. The increase in salience of the favorable consequences can contribute to stabilizing a decision in the face of temptations to backslide. We expect these other effects to occur independently of a stress inoculation effect, which is not likely to predominate if the client is given other forms of stress inoculation. We did, in fact, give all clients in the current study a series of role-playing procedures and other exercises that were specifically designed to provide stress inoculation for the most common forms of unanticipated setbacks, as revealed by prior work with clients in the Yale Weight-Reduction Clinic. We expect, therefore, that whatever effects the balance-sheet procedure might have in the present context would more likely be mediated by self-disclosure or search and appraisal processes than by stress inoculation. In order to obtain indications of the mediating processes that might account for the effects of the balance-sheet procedure and of the moderate versus low self-disclosure interviews, we introduced several attitude measures into the study.

METHOD

Overall Design

The clients were given a face-to-face interview that was divided into two parts. During the first part each client was given either a moderate or a low self-disclosure interview; during the second part, the client was given either a structured balance-sheet procedure or a control procedure that held constant the type and amount of information given by the counselor. Thus, there were four treatment groups to which clients were randomly assigned: moderate self-disclosure interview with the balance sheet, moderate self-disclosure interview with no balance sheet, low self-disclosure interview with the balance sheet, low self-disclosure interview with no balance sheet. The clients were also randomly assigned to one of two female counselors, both of whom had been trained in systematic interviewing procedures.

Subjects and Procedures

Eighty female residents of the New Haven area were chosen randomly from a group of women who responded to a newspaper announcement of a weight-reduction clinic offered by Yale psychologists. The women, who had no other particular health problems, wanted to lose between 15 and 50 pounds, with a median desired weight loss of 29 pounds. They ranged in age from 22 to 66 years; the median age was 41. There were no significant or near significant differences among the treatment groups in weight, age, marital status, or educational level.

Each client was seen individually in a face-to-face interview during a single 75-minute clinic session. First the clients filled out a health questionnaire and a general information form and were weighed. Then they were randomly assigned to one of the two interview treatments (moderate or low self-disclosure). For both conditions the interview lasted about 30 minutes. Following the interview all clients were asked to listen carefully to a tape recording that explained the diet and gave specific recommendations for adhering to the dieting plan. After that each client was randomly assigned to either the balance-sheet treatment or the control treatment, which gave essentially the same information without suggesting that the client should examine the consequences of the alternatives.

All clients in all treatment conditions were then given a set of standard stress inoculation procedures, described in detail below. At the end of the session, arrangements were made for a follow-up interview.

In all cases the counselors consistently gave positive feedback throughout all interviews, expressing both verbal and nonverbal acceptance of the clients' attitudes and feelings. The counselors attempted to convey a strong interest in helping the clients with their overweight problems and optimism about the prospects of their dieting successfully.

The Moderate Self-disclosure Interview

Each client was asked a series of open-ended questions, designed primarily to elicit personal information relevant to her overweight problem. The questions ranged from what kinds of unpleasant feelings might occur in connection with overeating and dieting to how being overweight affects her family life and relationships with friends. The interview was standardized, with minor changes in wording to take into consideration the client's age, marital status, and answers to prior questions. The counselors were trained to ask the questions in a way which made the interview seem more like a natural conversation than a standardized questionnaire.

All statements made by each client were received with acceptance, which was expressed not only by the counselor's words but also by nodding and smiling at her. At several appropriate times during each interview the counselor made positive comments about the client's cooperative attitude and behavior.

The Low Self-disclosure Interview

Each client in this condition was asked questions about her food habits, which were designed to elicit as little affect-laden or confidential personal information as possible. Questions centered around specific eating be- havior in specific situations. As in the moderate disclosure condition the standardized interview was adapted to the client when necessary and con- ducted in a conversational manner. In the rare cases where a client seemed eager to talk in more personal terms than was called for by this condition, the counselor's standard procedure was to say, without implying any criti- cism or lack of interest in the client's problems, that right now we need to focus on the question that was being asked. Positive feedback, both verbal and nonverbal, was consistently given, just as in the moderate self-disclosure interview.

Diet Recommendations

All clients in all four treatment conditions listened to a 15-minute tape recording made by the counselor explaining the recommended 1200-calorie diet (see chap. 5). The recording contained additional pointers on how to keep caloric intake down, a pep talk, and other information designed to assure the women of the potential success of the diet if followed properly. The counselor's tape recording also presented three specific recommenda- tions in addition to endorsing the recommended diet: (1) to try starting out with a stricter diet of 1000 calories; (2) to engage daily in 10 minutes of silent thought concerning dieting, and (3) to fill out and mail to the clinic a standard form every week for 4 weeks, reporting on dieting behavior, weight loss, and adherence to the silent-thought plan. Before playing the tape recording, the counselor handed each client a copy of the recom- mended diet, a list of suggested meal plans, and weekly report forms in addressed, stamped envelopes. Afterward the client was asked if she thought she would follow the diet and whether she planned to try the stricter diet.

The Balance-Sheet Procedure

After the tape recording the counselor explained to each client that women who plan to follow a strict diet frequently find themselves making rationali- zations for going on some kind of haphazard or partial diet that allows them to continue overeating. Then the client was asked to discuss in general terms the costs and pay-offs for her of going on the recommended low-calorie diet and of going on a partial (haphazard) diet. She was then given a list of various types of favorable and unfavorable consequences that might result from the decision to go on the clinic's recommended diet or on the client's own partial diet. The various consequences (such as effects on health, wardrobe, self-pride, and how her family might react) were listed in the following categories:

1. utilitarian gains and losses for self,
2. utilitarian gains and losses for significant others,
3. self-approval or disapproval,
4. approval or disapproval from significant others.

These categories were explained to the client and she was asked to use them in order to fill out her personal balance sheet as completely as possible. The client was given a balance-sheet grid and was asked to write in as many entries as she could think of, which included personal hopes, wishes, fears, and self-doubts that the client had not previously disclosed. After the client finished, the counselor once again endorsed the recommended low-calorie diet by mentioning that there were many strong positive considerations in its favor.

Control for the Balance-Sheet Procedure

All the statements about dieting given in connection with the balance-sheet procedure were presented, but the client was neither given a list of the positive and negative consequences of following the clinic's diet nor asked to discuss the pros and cons or to fill out a grid. At the end of this control procedure, essentially the same positive statement about the recommended diet was presented as in the balance-sheet procedure.

Commitment and Stress Inoculation Procedures

The following additional procedures were given in the same sequence to clients in all conditions after the balance-sheet or control procedure:

Pledge Cards. Each client was asked to sign two pledge cards. One specified the date she would begin the diet (usually the following day). The other stated that she would stay on the diet until she achieved her goal of losing a given number of pounds and that, if she were to fail to adhere to the diet one day, she would return to it again the next day.

Role Playing of a Typical Setback. For purposes of stress inoculation, each client was asked to role play herself in a setback situation, imagining that she gave in to typical temptations and went off the diet one day. She was asked to verbalize her thoughts and feelings about the setback and how she would overcome it.

Information about Negative Consequences with Imaginative Rehearsal. For purposes of giving additional stress inoculation, each client was presented with two statements about unfavorable consequences of dieting, based on experiences of other women who had dieted successfully. In one statement a former client was quoted on an unexpected negative reaction from her husband: "Now that other men pay attention to me when we go out and I am much more willing to be seen in public, suddenly all he wants to do is stay at home. Although he insists that he's very happy with my weight loss, I think he's really threatened about it and dislikes the fact that other men might consider me to be attractive." The second quotation from another former client described a variety of unexpected sources of social embarrassment: "It's difficult for me to have company for dinner, go to someone's house for a party or for dinner, or to go to restaurants. I know it's silly, but when I'm eating less than everyone else I feel like they're all watching me. When people come to my house, I can't serve them food that I'm not eating myself. Of course, it's worth all this trouble to know I'm actually losing weight, but I'm getting pretty tired of all the drawbacks and don't know how much longer I can keep it up. I wish you had warned me that this was going to happen." After reading each statement, the client was asked, "Is there any possibility of a similar thing happening in your case?" Then she was told to try "to imagine something like this happening to you because I would like you to tell me how you feel about it and what you would say to yourself."

Final Attitude Questionnaire. At the end of the session every client in all four treatment conditions was given a 19-item questionnaire about her reactions to the interview. Each client was told that the interviewer would not see her responses and she was instructed to place the completed form in a box in the corner of the room.

Follow-up Interview. Reminders of the appointment that had been made at the close of the initial session were mailed 1 week before the scheduled appointment. The follow-up interview, which occurred 1 month after the initial session, consisted of weighing the women, asking some general questions about their dieting experience, and then giving encouragement appropriate to the goal of long-term weight loss.

RESULTS AND DISCUSSION

Immediate Effects

The counselors' (nonblind) ratings revealed marked differences between the groups given the moderate and low disclosure interviews in the amount and degree of intimacy of self-disclosures, just as had been found when blind ratings were made of clients' interview responses in a preliminary pilot study of 14 clients (see n. 1). As an independent check on the effectiveness of the interventions designed to induce self-disclosure, all clients were asked on the final questionnaire, "Do you feel the psychologist knows what sort of person you *really* are?" The results are shown in Table 9.1. The main effects are significant for both the moderate versus low disclosure interview ($p < .001$) and for the balance-sheet versus control procedure ($p < .02$).

The women who received neither treatment and thus had the least opportunity to reveal their doubts and concerns about personal shortcomings gave significantly lower ratings than any of the others. These findings in Table 9.1 for the two types of interviews are consistent with the counselors'

Table 9.1. Mean scores obtained from answers to the question, "Do you feel that the psychologist knows what sort of person you *really* are?" (scores range from 1 for "Definitely no" to 5 for "Definitely yes")

Experimental treatment	Mean score
Group 1. Moderate disclosure with balance sheet	4.0
Group 2. Moderate disclosure with no balance sheet	3.6
Group 3. Low disclosure with balance sheet	3.4
Group 4. Low disclosure with no balance sheet	2.7

For moderate versus low disclosure, $F(1, 74) = 11.19$, $p < .001$.
For balance sheet versus no balance sheet, $F(1, 74) = 6.06$, $p < .02$.

Note. $N = 20$ in each group.

ratings of the interview responses and with the results of the pilot study in indicating that the moderate disclosure interview elicited more self-disclosure than the low disclosure interview. The results for the balance-sheet procedure in Table 9.1 are also consistent with an examination of what the clients wrote on their balance sheets, which contained personal information about hopes and concerns in connection with the problems of being overweight and going on a strict diet. The balance-sheet procedure, as well as the moderate disclosure interview, appears to have elicited a fair amount of self-disclosure, as was expected.

There were practically no discernible differences among the groups in the answers they gave to a question asking how frequently they thought the psychologist had made positive comments to them during the course of the interview. In all conditions the clients asserted that the counselor made many such comments, indicating that, as intended, clients felt they received about the same amount of positive feedback irrespective of the variations in other procedures. Similarly, clients in all four groups gave equally high ratings in answer to the question, "Do you feel that the psychologist was expressing warm and friendly feelings toward you?"

Except for one woman, all clients in all conditions showed immediate compliance by signing the pledge cards; hence there was a ceiling effect that prevented this dependent measure from being informative.

Adherence to Recommendations

Adherence, as assessed 1 month after the initial interview, was clearly affected by the variations in the counseling procedures. One type of action

to which the clients committed themselves in response to a recommendation by the counselor was to send in weekly reports during the month
following the interview. The results in the first column of Table 9.2 show

Table 9.2. Adherence to the counselor's recommendation to prepare and mail in a
dieting report each week during the month following the initial interview

Experimental treatment	Percentage who mailed back all 4 weekly reports	Mean number of weekly reports mailed back
1. Moderate disclosure with balance sheet	80%	3.6
2. Moderate disclosure with no balance sheet	55%	2.5
3. Low disclosure with balance sheet	50%	2.9
4. Low disclosure with no balance sheet	50%	2.8

Note. N = 20 in each group.

that 80% of the women who received both the moderate disclosure interview and the balance-sheet procedure mailed back all four weekly reports,
whereas only 50 to 55% of the women in the other groups did so. The mean
numbers of reports mailed back, given in the second column of the table,
display a similar pattern.[2]

Table 9.3. Weight loss over a period of one month

Experimental treatment	Percentage of each entire group who demon- strated a loss of 4 or more lbs.[*]	Mean weight loss for each entire group
1. Moderate disclosure interview with balance sheet	80%	6.4 ⎫ 5.4
2. Moderate disclosure interview with no balance sheet	45%	4.4 ⎭
3. Low disclosure interview with balance sheet	40%	4.2 ⎫ 3.7
4. Low disclosure interview with no balance sheet	40%	3.2 ⎭

Note. N = 20 in each group.
　*The percentage of women who returned 1 month after the initial interview for the follow-
up interview differed slightly but not significantly among the four groups. The number of cases
in each group was 18, 14, 14, and 15, respectively, in the order listed in the table.

Similar effects of the counseling treatments were found for weight loss
(Table 9.3). Here again, the women who were given both the moderate
disclosure interview and the balance-sheet procedure showed most adherence to the counselor's recommendations. One month after the initial interview they had lost more weight than the women in the other three treatment

groups, indicating greater adherence to the recommended low-calorie diet ($p < .05$). The best estimate of the amount of weight loss for each entire group is shown in the second column of the table. On this measure an analysis of variance revealed that the main effect of moderate versus low disclosure is significant at the .08 confidence level.[3] The main effect of the balance-sheet procedure, however, is not large enough to approach statistical significance ($p = .11$).

Overall the results on behavioral measures provide some slight support of the self-disclosure hypothesis but they are somewhat equivocal. The main effect of moderate versus low disclosure was found to be statistically significant at the 10% confidence level on a crucial behavioral measure, amount of weight loss, but not on the ancillary behavioral measure of number of weekly reports mailed in. The main effect of the balance-sheet procedure was found to be statistically significant at the 10% confidence level for the latter measure but not for the former one. The only consistently significant findings pertain to the behavioral effects of the *combination* of both treatments, which clearly produced more adherence to the counselor's recommendations on all the behavioral criteria we examined.

These findings are in line with confirmatory findings from a subsequent field experiment conducted in a weight-reduction clinic by Quinlan, Janis, and Bales (chap. 10) and also with the findings from Mulligan's first experiment, which was designed to test the self-disclosure hypothesis in a different field setting (chap. 15). In the context of the confirmations of the hypothesis provided by the two additional field experiments, the present study can be regarded as adding some supportive evidence.

Our conclusion from the present field experiment is that a moderate self-disclosure interview of about 30 minutes duration in a weight-reduction clinic, under conditions where clients receive positive feedback from the counselor, tends to increase adherence to the counselor's recommendations. The balance-sheet procedure, which provides an added disclosure opportunity, appears to reinforce the effect of the moderate disclosure interview. Perhaps a longer, more intensive self-disclosure interview could serve the same function.

Effects on Attitudes

A number of attitude items were included in the questionnaire given to the clients at the end of the initial session for the purpose of obtaining clues to mediating psychological processes that might account for the observed effects of the different treatments on adherence. The results for the first item shown in Table 9.4 suggest that the treatments may have differential effects in creating affectionate feelings toward the counselor. The clients who received the balance-sheet procedure gave slight but significantly more positive responses than those who did not ($p < .04$); the clients who received the moderate disclosure interview also gave slightly more positive

Table 9.4. Attitudes toward the counselor expressed at the end of the initial session (scores range from 1 to a maximum of 5 on each attitude measure)

| | Mean attitude scores | | | | |
| | Moderate disclosure | | Low disclosure | | |
Attitude measures	Balance sheet	No balance sheet	Balance sheet	No balance sheet	Significant and near significant effects
Feelings toward the counselor					
1. Affectionate feelings	5.0	4.8	4.8	4.6	Main effect of disclosure: $p = .12$
					Main effect of balance sheet: $p < .04$
2. Satisfaction with counselor's behavior	3.8	3.6	3.7	3.4	Main effect of balance sheet: $p < .07$
Perceived characteristics of the counselor					
3. Caring about the client's success	4.4	4.6	4.3	4.0	Main effect of disclosure: $p < .03$
4. Sympathy toward the client	4.2	4.6	4.4	4.1	Interaction effect: $p < .02$
5. Personal interest in the client	4.5	4.6	4.6	4.2	Interaction effect: $p < .10$

Note. N = 20 in each of the 4 groups.

responses than those who received the low disclosure interview, but the difference is not large enough to be significant. Small differences among the treatment groups in the same direction were obtained on answers to a question concerning the client's feelings of satisfaction about the counselor's behavior during the interview (the second item in the table). A significant difference was found on the third item, which asked for each client's impression about the degree to which the counselor cares about whether the client succeeds in losing weight. On this item the clients who received the moderate disclosure interview gave significantly more favorable ratings than those who received the low disclosure interview ($p < .03$). The fourth and fifth items, which deal with the clients' perceptions of the counselor as sympathetic and personally interested in them, show no main effects at all but they do show one feature in common with all the other items dealing with attitudes toward or appraisals of the counselor. In each instance the clients who received neither the moderate disclosure interview nor the balance-sheet procedure (and hence were given practically no opportunity at all to disclose personal feelings) tended to give lower ratings to the counselor than those who received one or the other of the treatments that encouraged self-disclosure.

The results in Table 9.4 are not clear-cut because they do not show, as did the behavioral measures of adherence to the counselor's recommendations, that the clients who received both the high disclosure interview and the balance-sheet procedure consistently exceed all the other groups. On the measure of affection and esteem we used, most clients in every treatment group gave the highest possible rating, which may have created a ceiling effect. Once again we see a need for more sensitive measures to detect the effects of different interventions on attitudes toward the counselor. Nevertheless, the findings for the five measures dealing with attitude toward the counselor are compatible with the assumption that the differential effects of the two treatments are attributable to some extent to heightening of affection and esteem toward the counselor.

MAIN CONCLUSIONS

The following two conclusions are based on the convergence of the primary findings from this field experiment on adherence to recommendations by counselors in a weight-reduction clinic, but they must be regarded as tentative because some of the findings are of borderline significance and a few detailed bits of evidence are not wholly consistent with the main thrust of the findings. Both conclusions pertain to the effectiveness of counselors who consistently express *acceptance* in response to whatever their clients say in face-to-face interviews.

1. Counselors are more likely to evoke adherence to their recommendations, such as staying on a low-calorie diet, if they conduct a moderate self-disclosure interview during the initial session by asking questions about

personal problems and feelings. Such an interview was found to lead to more weight loss 1 month later than did a low disclosure type of interview that focused on routine eating habits and other objective topics relevant to overeating and that allowed the clients little or no opportunity for disclosing subjective thoughts and feelings. This finding bears on the following theoretical question posed by the results of the weight-reduction experiments reported in the preceding three chapters (which showed that consistently positive feedback by the counselor in response to whatever the clients say during a moderate disclosure interview is more effective than neutral or inconsistently positive feedback): Can counselors attain the same degree of effectiveness from giving consistently positive feedback during the initial session if the questions they ask elicit very little self-disclosure? The tentative answer indicated by the present experiment is *no*: Eliciting a moderate degree of self-disclosure makes a difference that approaches statistical significance in the direction predicted by the theoretical analysis of the crucial psychological components in the initial phase of a supportive helping relationship (chap. 2).

2. The effectiveness of a moderate self-disclosure type of interview is augmented if the counselor uses a balance-sheet procedure that requires the client to verbalize the pros and cons for each alternative course of action that is being considered. Self-disclosure appears to be one of the important psychological components of the balance-sheet procedure that may contribute to the increased effectiveness of the accepting type of counselor in inducing adherence to his or her recommendations.

NOTES

1. Pilot work on this study was started by Irving L. Janis and Thomas Kohler, who together worked out the basic procedures in a weight-reduction clinic at Yale University and began pretesting the self-disclosure interviews. Pretesting was continued by Janis with a number of research assistants who conducted interview sessions with 18 clients and tried out a series of modifications in order to improve the success of the interviews with regard to eliciting moderate versus low self-disclosure. Questions in the moderate disclosure interview that unexpectedly failed to elicit very much self-disclosure were replaced by new ones that proved to be more successful in subsequent pretests. Similarly, the questions in the low disclosure interview that induced more disclosure than we had expected were replaced by other questions that proved not to do so. When we felt quite certain that the low disclosure interview was eliciting much less disclosure than the moderate disclosure interview, we carried out a systematic pilot study which compared the responses of 7 clients who were given the moderate disclosure interview with those of 7 clients who were given the low disclosure interview. Clients in both groups were given consistently positive feedback of the type used in the studies reported in chaps. 6 and 7. Blind ratings of the clients' interview responses showed that there were huge differences on two basic dimensions of self-disclosure described by Cozby (1973): breadth or amount of personal information disclosed and depth or degree of intimacy of the information disclosed. On the two basic dimensions of self-disclosure (breadth and depth) there was little overlap between the scores of the two groups. On each measure the highest scores obtained by any of the clients given the low disclosure interview were about the same as the lowest score obtained by any of the clients given the moderate disclosure interview. More specifically, about 85% of the clients given the moderate disclosure interview obtained higher

self-disclosure scores than any of the clients given the low disclosure interview ($p < .05$).

By and large, the affective expressiveness of the clients given the moderate disclosure interview in the pilot study (and in the experiment proper) appeared to be appropriate to the personal information they were revealing. The interviewers rarely had the impression that any client was answering any of the questions in an indifferent or insincere manner.

2. In column 1 of Table 9.2 the percentage for the group that was given both the moderate disclosure interview and the balance-sheet procedure is significantly larger than that for the other three groups combined ($p < .05$). For the means in column 2 of the table, an analysis of variance, which included variations in the counselor as a third variable, showed that the only effect that approached the conventional level of statistical significance was the main effect of the balance-sheet procedure ($F(1, 71) = 3.13$, $p < .09$).

3. In order to demonstrate weight loss, the women had to return for the follow-up session to be weighed. Despite repeated efforts by the counselors to arrange for follow-up sessions at times that would suit the convenience of the clients, some of the women did not return. (The numbers of cases are shown in the note at the bottom of Table 9.3). There were no significant differences among treatment groups in the proportion of cases who did not return. Most of the women who did not reappear indicated in telephone interviews that they were not coming back because they had already dropped out of the program by failing to follow the diet and consequently had lost no weight.

A separate analysis (not shown in Table 9.3) was made of the mean weight loss only for those women in each group who did return for the follow-up interview. The outcome was essentially the same as that obtained from the means for each entire group (shown in column 2 of Table 9.3), which are based on the assumption that those who did not return had lost zero weight.

The pattern is the same when we use the proportion in each group who lost 4 or more pounds over the 1-month period (shown in column 1 of Table 9.3). According to the Yale Department of Dietetics, the minimum expected weight loss for women adhering to the 1200-calorie diet is about 1 pound per week. In effect the results in column 1 pertain to adherence to the two main recommendations made by the counselor, namely, that the women should return to the clinic to demonstrate their weight loss after adhering to the low-calorie diet for 1 month.

10 Effects of Moderate Self-disclosure and Amount of Contact with the Counselor

DONALD M. QUINLAN, IRVING L. JANIS, AND VIRGINIA BALES

Under what conditions will self-disclosure facilitate or hinder adherence to a stressful decision, such as staying on a diet? Studies carried out prior to this one (reported in chaps. 9 and 15) indicate that inducing a moderate amount of self-disclosure has a facilitating effect when the counselor gives consistently positive feedback to the client. In the pair of field experiments described in this chapter we attempt to tease out possible interacting variables that might affect the impact of a moderate versus low level of self-disclosure. One such variable we selected for study was the amount of contact the counselor has with the client after the initial interview. A second variable has to do with the type of material disclosed: a comparison between the standard personal interview, which elicits a combination of positive and negative self-disclosures, and a more restricted personal interview that elicits only positive self-disclosures. An assessment of changes in each client's current level of self-esteem was included in both experiments in order to evaluate possible mediating effects.

HYPOTHESES

Self-disclosure and Contact

In interviews conducted in our weight-reduction clinic some clients voice a wish for more frequent contact to help them in their struggles to stay with the diet. A few of them are quite explicit about wanting a "policeman" to monitor their weight and to serve as a source of social pressure at times when their internal motivation to adhere to the diet is not strong enough. A few others talk more in terms of a need for companionship with someone who will encourage and perhaps inspire them to keep up their efforts at weight control. If we take the clients' statements at face value, they suggest that more frequent contact with a counselor during the period of dieting might satisfy some of the clients' dependency needs in a constructive way that promotes adherence. In line with this supposition, prior studies suggest that maintenance of weight loss (Brownell, Heckerman, & Westlake, 1976) and smoking cessation (Shewchuk, 1976) can be facilitated by maintaining periodic contact with a counselor, even if contact is limited to brief telephone conversations.

But increasing the level of contact might also have detrimental effects. For example, the client may come to resent "being checked up on" by someone who started out as a supportive helper but has become a "policeman." Or, even when the added contact is wholeheartedly desired by the client, the sense of being abandoned when the supportive contact comes to an end may be more intense and result in disappointment, demoralization, and subsequent lack of success in maintaining weight loss. A study in an anti-smoking clinic by Best, Bass, and Owen (1977) found that smokers who were phoned by their counselors between sessions were more likely to relapse after termination of treatment than those who had been left entirely on their own.

These alternative effects pose an important theoretical issue that could have practical implications for a cost-benefit analysis of counselors' investment of additional time to keep in contact with their clients in order to follow their progress and to give them encouragement after the initial clinic interview: Does more frequent contact have a beneficial outcome? With this question in mind, we decided to examine the effects of a 1-month period of weekly telephone contact between the counselor and the client compared with no such contact after the initial session. We investigated this contact variable in a factorial study that included low versus moderate levels of self-disclosure in order to determine whether there were interaction effects between the two variables.

Type of Material Disclosed

The clients' self-perceptions are likely to be influenced by divulging personal weaknesses and failures (see chap. 2). Reassuring acceptance in response to such disclosures might temporarily lessen the client's demoralization and perhaps even result in a sustained increase in the client's level of self-esteem. Nevertheless, this type of counseling interaction may encourage the clients to express more and more negative feelings about themselves, which could increase guilt, shame, and self-derogatory attitudes to such a degree that they undermine the clients' confidence about being able to adhere to a counselor's recommendations, such as staying on a low-calorie diet. Another kind of unfavorable effect is suggested by Riskind (chap. 14). The reassurances given by the counselor when he or she prompts disclosures of personal liabilities and expresses a positive view of the client's assets might lead the client to expect unconditional acceptance, to become overconfident, and to remain relatively unmotivated with regard to obtaining further acceptance through adherence to the recommended diet.

In order to investigate these potentially positive and negative effects, we introduced a variation of the typical self-disclosure interview. In the standard version both favorable and unfavorable personal disclosures are elicited by asking clients questions about both their assets and their liabilities. Clients usually respond by talking mainly about their defects—in a weight-reduction clinic they most often talk about personal weaknesses, such as being unable to resist eating their favorite foods, which prevent them from keeping their weight down. In an alternative form of the interview, which we included in the present study, all the questions are designed to evoke self-reports only about positive feelings and personal assets, such as what aspects of daily life provide most satisfaction and which accomplishments are a source of pride. This alternative type of interview is similar to those in career-counseling sessions that focus on the clients' assets, aspirations, and capabilities.

PLAN OF THE RESEARCH

The investigations reported in this chapter can be described as two parallel studies on the effects of self-disclosure and level of contact. In our first study "*mixed*" (positive and negative) self-disclosures were elicited, comparable to the self-disclosures elicited in all the prior studies reported in the preceding chapters. In our second study *only positive* self-disclosures were elicited.[1] The two concurrent studies were designed to answer the following questions:

1. Does weekly telephone contact between the client and the counselor facilitate adherence to stressful decisions?

2. If the counselor gives consistently positive feedback, is moderate self-disclosure consistently more effective than low self-disclosure, irrespective of whether the content of the disclosures is (a) limited only to favorable information about the self or (b) a mixture of favorable and unfavorable personal information?

3. If the counselor gives consistently positive feedback, does eliciting personal information that is limited solely to positive attributes of the self facilitate adherence to the recommended course of action or, alternatively, does it produce overconfidence in the client, compared with eliciting a mixture of unfavorable and favorable personal information?

While these questions are phrased in terms of looking for simple main effects of the three experimental variables, theoretical speculations led us to anticipate that these variables might interact in significant ways.

Clients were recruited in New Haven, Connecticut, through newspaper announcements. All clients went through the standard intake procedures of the Yale Weight-Reduction Clinic (see chap. 6). After initial telephone screening, 144 clients were randomly assigned to the various conditions. At the beginning of the session with the counselor, clients completed an initial background data sheet and were weighed on the balance scale. Next they were given a 30- to 40-minute self-disclosure interview conducted face-to-face according to the format described below. After the interview the 1200-calorie diet was presented by means of an audio tape recording made by the counselor. Clients were handed mimeographed copies of the diet and examples of daily menus to take home. After the diet recording, the client's questions about the diet were answered. Then the clients were requested to fill out the weekly report forms, which they were given to take home. At the end of the session the client completed a final questionnaire.

After 4 weeks and again after 8 weeks the clients were asked to come back to the clinic to meet with the same counselor. In these follow-up sessions the clients were weighed, given a short interview about their dieting experience during the preceding month, and asked to fill out follow-up questionnaires.

EXPERIMENT 1

Method

In our first experiment, 72 clients were interviewed according to one of two self-disclosure interview schedules involving moderate or low disclosure. The interviews were constructed on a parallel question-by-question basis to cover comparable areas relevant to overeating and dieting but asking for different levels of disclosure. The type of disclosure induced by the questions in both the low and moderate interviews was a mixture of positive and negative aspects of the self, including strengths and abilities as well as weaknesses and anticipated difficulties.

Level of Self-disclosure
The moderate self-disclosure interview contained questions about the client's feelings, personal reactions, and motivation related to eating and physical activity, whereas the low self-disclosure interview was limited to questions asking for factual descriptions of and impersonal comments about the same daily activities. Moderate self-disclosure interviews encouraged the client to speak on a personal level; low disclosure interviews were on a more socially conventional level.

During the low disclosure interview some clients would occasionally start to disclose more than was expected and in the moderate disclosure interview a few clients were a bit reticent. With courtesy and tact the interviewers encouraged the appropriate levels of disclosure so that, on the whole, the level of disclosure matched that called for by the experimental design.[2]

Weekly vs. No Telephone Contact
On a random basis half the clients had relatively frequent contact with the counselor during the first month. They were told at the first interview that the interviewer would phone them once a week for the first 3 weeks of the program to find out how they were doing on the diet and to answer any questions they had about dieting. In contrast the other half of the clients had no telephone contact at all during the interval between the initial session and the first follow-up session 4 weeks later. The no-telephone-contact condition corresponds to the standard arrangement in all the other counselor–client studies in the Yale Weight-Reduction Clinic (chaps. 6–9 and 11–14). The weekly-telephone-contact condition, therefore, should be

regarded as a deviation from the usual procedure. Both the weekly- and no-telephone-contact groups were followed for 4 additional weeks without any contact except for the final follow-up interview at 8 weeks.

Questionnaires
The standard set of questionnaires included a background information sheet, questions on reactions to the interview, impressions of the interviewer, and the state-of-self-esteem questionnaire (see Appendix). At the follow-up sessions, conducted 4 and 8 weeks after the initial interview, the state-of-self-esteem questionnaire was readministered.

Results

Differences in Weight Loss
As in prior studies, we have placed primary reliance on physical measures of actual weight loss to determine the clients' adherence to the recommended program of dieting. The means showing amount of weight loss at 4 and 8 weeks are presented in Table 10.1. Within the condition comparable to all

Table 10.1. Mean amount of weight loss (pounds) for clients given interviews that elicited both positive and negative self-disclosures (Experiment 1)

	No telephone contact		Weekly telephone contact	
	4 weeks later	8 weeks later	4 weeks later	8 weeks later
Level of self-disclosure				
Moderate	5.5	7.5	3.3	5.4
Low	3.6	4.9	5.5	7.5

Note. $N = 15 \pm 1$ in each cell.

the prior studies (i.e., no telephone contact with the counselor after the initial session), the moderate disclosure interview proved to be more effective in helping clients to lose weight than the low disclosure interview. This finding replicates the main outcome of the preceding field experiment, in which moderate disclosure was compared with low disclosure in a weight-reduction clinic (chap. 9) and is consistent with results from another field experiment conducted in a different setting (chap. 15). For the weekly-telephone-contact condition, however, the relative effectiveness of moderate and low disclosure interviews was reversed. With weekly telephone contact, the *low* disclosure interview was more effective. Thus, the beneficial effect of a moderate level of self-disclosure was undercut by weekly telephone contact with the interviewer, whereas the relatively weak effect of low self-disclosure was augmented by weekly telephone contact.[3]

Differences in Self-reports
The clients' reactions to the counselor and their reported levels of self-esteem were examined for suggestive leads as to why the weight loss results

were found to depend on the combined influence of level of self-disclosure and frequency of contact. Although the clients' self-reports on questionnaires have dubious validity, they may nonetheless offer at least a suggestion of mediating processes.

Only two questionnaire measures yielded interaction effects which paralleled the weight loss data. One of the measures is based on a single item pertaining to the clients' feelings of shame. The other is based on a set of 9 items from the state-of-self-esteem scale, all of which deal with feelings of guilt (see Table 10.2). These results indicate that the clients in the groups

Table 10.2. Mean scores for shame and guilt reported by clients immediately after standard initial interviews that elicited both positive and negative self-disclosures (Experiment 1)

	Shame item*		Guilt scale*	
	No telephone contact	Weekly telephone contact	No telephone contact	Weekly telephone contact
Level of self-disclosure				
Moderate	3.0	2.8	30.8	28.1
Low	2.4	3.1	26.4	28.8

Note. $N = 15 \pm 1$ in each cell.

*The only significant finding obtained from the shame item and from the guilt scale is a statistically significant interaction effect: $F = 5.86$ $(p < .01)$ and $F = 4.02$ $(p < .05)$, respectively.

showing the greatest weight loss reported more feelings of shame and guilt immediately after the initial interview.[4] Before discussing the implications of these emotional reactions to the interviews, we shall examine the comparable results from the second experiment.

EXPERIMENT 2

Method

The methods and procedures for our second experiment were identical to those for the first experiment, with the single exception that the content of the low disclosure and moderate disclosure interviews was restricted to questions that elicit *positive self-disclosures* concerning the client's personal assets, sources of satisfaction in everyday life, and anticipations of positive outcomes. The interview schedules were constructed in parallel with the questions used in Experiment 1 and covered the same range of topics. This experiment was run concurrently with the first one in order to allow valid comparison of results. There were 18 clients in each of the treatment conditions.

Results

The weight loss results for clients given the positive disclosure interviews are presented in Table 10.3. The effects of self-disclosure and amount of

Table 10.3. Mean amount of weight loss (pounds) for clients given interviews that elicited only positive self-disclosures (Experiment 2)

	No telephone contact		Weekly telephone contact	
	4 weeks later	8 weeks later	4 weeks later	8 weeks later
Level of self-disclosure				
Moderate	2.6	3.7	6.2	10.0
Low	7.2	7.1	3.7	4.5

Note. N = 15±1 in each cell.

telephone contact interacted with each other, as in the first experiment, but in the opposite direction. In this experiment, when there was no telephone contact moderate self-disclosure of personal assets and other positive

Table 10.4. Self-reports obtained immediately after the positive disclosure interviews (means for each group in Experiment 2)

	Low disclosure		Moderate disclosure	
	No telephone contact	Weekly telephone contact	No telephone contact	Weekly telephone contact
1. Mood improved	4.4	4.1	3.8	4.4
2. Confident about losing weight	4.7	4.1	4.4	4.5
3. Self-critical	3.4	3.5	2.8	3.0
4. Guilt	3.3	3.4	2.8	3.1
5. Shame	3.1	2.7	2.7	2.4
6. Does interviewer respect you?	4.1	4.5	3.8	4.3
7. Do you like the interviewer?	4.3	4.7	4.5	4.7
8. Does the interviewer like you?	3.8	4.4	3.9	4.2
9. Self-derogation	20.9	22.4	19.6	21.9
10. Change in pride (8 weeks later)	3.1	–2.1	0.6	0.2
11. Change in self-confidence (8 weeks later)	2.7	–2.0	1.7	–1.0

Note. N = 15±1 in each of the 4 groups.

aspects of the self resulted in relatively little weight loss. When weekly telephone contact with the counselor was added, the amount of weight loss was much higher. In the low self-disclosure group the trend is in the opposite direction. The interaction effect is highly significant at 4 and 8 weeks after the initial interview.[5]

As in the first experiment we examined the self-report data for suggestive indications of possible mediating reactions. The mean ratings for each treatment condition obtained from questions about reactions to the interview and impressions of the interviewer that yielded significant differences are shown in Table 10.4. Only two of the questions showed significant interactions that parallel the subsequent weight losses, notably, *improvement in mood* ($p < .05$) and *confidence about losing weight* ($p < .05$). In the group that was told that there would be subsequent telephone contact with the counselor, the mean scores on both these reactions were higher if the clients had been given the moderate positive disclosure interview; but in the group that was told nothing about subsequent telephone contact, the mean scores were higher if the clients had been given the low positive disclosure interview. The same two groups showed the greatest amount of weight loss. Thus, the responses on the two questions obtained immediately after the initial interview suggest an immediately perceived difference that may have carried over during the subsequent 2 months to influence weight loss.[6]

DISCUSSION AND IMPLICATIONS

The pattern of results from these two studies at first appears confusing and inconsistent. Examination of individual variables, however, reveals a more orderly pattern.

Self-disclosure

Our results on the effects of a moderate versus low level of self-disclosure replicate the findings from previous studies if we look only at those conditions that are essentially the same as those of the other studies—namely, giving clients a standard (mixed positive and negative) self-disclosure interview with no telephone contact with the counselor during the follow-up period. Under those conditions (which were present only in Experiment 1), eliciting a moderate amount of self-disclosure was found to help the clients adhere to their decision to diet, as manifested by their greater success in losing weight. Clients who are encouraged to disclose a moderate amount of unfavorable as well as favorable personal material apparently form a relationship with the counselor that helps them stick with the deprivational regimen of the 1200-calorie diet. The facilitating effect of the moderate self-disclosure interview, however, is modified and may even be entirely eliminated as a result of other variables that give rise to significant interaction effects, which we shall summarize briefly and attempt to explain.

Positive Self-disclosure and Frequency of Contact

When the counselor elicited only positive, favorable disclosures from the client (Experiment 2), a complex set of outcomes was obtained. If the clients who had no telephone contact with the counselor were induced to disclose only a low level of favorable material, they were more likely to adhere to the diet than if they were induced to disclose a moderate level. This somewhat unexpected finding can be seen as similar to a finding by Riskind for his esteem enhancement treatment (chap. 14). In Riskind's study, when the clients were encouraged by the counselor to believe that they had many personal assets and could take pride in their past accomplishments, whether or not they lost weight, they showed *less* adherence to the diet program than if they were not given this form of self-esteem enhancement. Similar effects appear to be involved in the present study. Clients who were encouraged to speak a great deal about their personal assets may have lost a potential incentive, namely, approval (from the counselor and/or from the self) that is contingent on losing weight. Support for this interpretation is found in the self-reports on feelings of guilt and shame. In Experiment 1 and to some extent in Experiment 2 the groups that eventually lost the most weight reported feeling guiltier than the others immediately after the interview. The superior effectiveness of inducing a low level of positive disclosure compared with inducing a moderate level of positive disclosure can be interpreted as resulting from the feelings of complacency evoked in the latter type of interview, which counteracts feelings of shame and guilt that would otherwise motivate the client to adhere to her decision to stay on a diet.

The unfavorable effects of positive disclosure apparently are reversed when the counselor arranges for subsequent telephone contact. A moderate level of positive disclosure, when followed by weekly telephone contact with the counselor, turned out to be the condition under which most weight loss occurred. The group given this combination of treatments lost an average of 10.0 pounds during the 8-week period of observation. The least successful group, however, consisted of clients who were given the same type of interview (moderate level of positive self-disclosure) but who subsequently had no contact with the counselor until the follow-up sessions. This group lost an average of only 3.7 pounds during the 8-week period, which is significantly less than the amount lost by the first group. The magnitude of difference in adherence for these two groups is suggested by the corresponding difference in daily calorie intake. Since it takes a difference of about 3,500 kilocalories to make a 1-pound difference, the mean difference between these two groups is equivalent to about 400 calories of food a day, or 1/3 of the daily allotment, the equivalent of a lunch each day.

The findings pose a new pair of research problems that cannot be answered from the findings currently available: What is the nature of the facilitating "chemistry" of the moderate positive disclosure interview when it is followed by weekly telephone contact? Why are the effects of that type of interview reversed when the clients have no telephone contact with the counselor?

We can only speculate about why weekly telephone contact would enhance the effects of a moderate level of positive disclosure. One explanation might be that the clients who are induced to disclose a moderate amount of positive material do not fully believe the extent of their own personal assets because they have come to the clinic out of a sense of personal weakness, i.e., inability to lose weight on their own. Weekly telephone contact with the counselor may enhance the believability of their positive disclosures and mobilize them to live up to the positive self-images the counselor draws from them. Or the credibility of the counselor's acceptance of the positive disclosures may be enhanced by continued contact. The initial positive self-disclosure interview is unlike most other counseling contacts and may have gone against the clients' expectations. For this type of interview perhaps it is necessary to have further contact that repeats the initial type of acceptance before the client will regard the counselor as a consistent and genuine source of social support.

The contingent acceptance implied by the counselor's monitoring of weight loss by means of the phone calls is another factor that may contribute to the improved weight loss of clients given weekly telephone contact after a moderate self-disclosure interview restricted to positive content. The clients may come to believe that continued acceptance depends on whether they continue to diet successfully. During each weekly telephone interview the counselor included questions about the client's current weight. In the client's mind, continuation of the counselor's positive regard may be contingent on her losing weight. The quality of the relationship, then, may change because it is determined not only by the acceptance feedback from the interviewer during the initial interview but also by the subsequent contingent acceptance implied by the monitoring phone calls. In the low disclosure positive interview the initial superficial positive disclosures may have been too weak to create concern about the counselor's continued acceptance, and the subsequent monitoring by the repeated phone calls may have been regarded as intrusive checkups, which would elicit negative responses.

In general the introduction of weekly telephone contact yielded unexpected results and complex interactions. A reinforcing effect occurred only when the clients had been given the moderate positive disclosure interview, but the effects of telephone contact under other conditions were variable and remain puzzling.

Confidence, Self-esteem, and Weight Loss

Some leads concerning the mediating effects of telephone contact can be obtained from the results on clients' reported feelings of confidence. In Experiment 2, clients in the weekly-telephone-contact condition lowered their level of self-confidence during the 8-week interval, whereas those in the no-telephone-contact condition raised their level of self-confidence. One plausible interpretation is that with repeated contact clients regard the burden of losing weight—and the credit for success—as being more on the shoulders of the counselor and less on their own. Evidently, under some conditions this change in attribution of responsibility can inhibit weight loss, but under other conditions it can facilitate weight loss.

The results bearing on the probable role that feelings of confidence and self-esteem play in weight reduction seem to be somewhat inconsistent but they are at least partially understandable. First, the conditions under which the most weight loss occurred are those which apparently evoked an immediate reaction of relatively strong feelings of guilt and shame. Many clinicians think of such feelings as unhelpful and possibly harmful. Guilt and shame, however, are probably a powerful source of motivation for undertaking decisions such as dieting, stopping smoking, exercising daily, and other difficult courses of action.[7]

Complexity vs. Unpredictability

It is in some ways disappointing and certainly perplexing to find highly complex interaction effects among the different independent variables that affect the client–counselor relationship. One would hope that neat and clearly formulated prescriptions for effective counseling could be gleaned from the experimental data. Instead, the variables appear to be highly intertwined in seemingly incoherent ways that could not have been guessed on an a priori theoretical basis. For example, adding weekly telephone contact during the first month of dieting was expected to be a valuable addition which would enhance the capacity of most clients to stay on the diet. Instead, telephone contact was found to interact with other variables to produce detrimental results in certain conditions. Under one set of conditions the weekly contact can be experienced by the client as an undesirable "policing" form of observation initiated by the counselor; whereas under another set of conditions, the weekly contact can be seen as a sign of interest, which strengthens the relationship and enhances the counselor's motivational power.

If the results of this study do not produce a clear set of prescriptions for effective counseling, they nonetheless show that different combinations of the variables we investigated in the counseling relationship *do make a difference*. The trouble is that some of the differences are in a direction other than what our apparently oversimplified theoretical schema would predict. Eliciting positive feelings about the self, as an example, was expected to strengthen the relationship with the counselor among the vast majority of clients because they generally come to the clinic with a sense of personal inadequacy and want social support. We found that a low degree of positive disclosure did have a facilitating effect, but unexpectedly, a moderate level did not, *unless* there was subsequent telephone contact, which presumably bolstered the relationship. Moreover, the clients who were told that they would have weekly telephone contact with the counselor reported feeling more guilt and shame (immediately after the moderate *positive* disclosure interview) than those who were told that their next contact with the counselor would be at the follow-up interview. Evidently the mere *anticipation* of weekly telephone contact was sufficient to evoke concern among these clients that their weaknesses and untrustworthiness with regard to carrying out the dieting plan would be exposed and would belie all the good things they had just been saying about themselves.

One of the implications of the findings from this pair of experiments, when evaluated in the context of the prior studies, is that the optimal level of self-disclosure in a client–counselor relationship depends not only on the way the counselor responds to the client's self-disclosures but also on the content of what is revealed and the frequency of anticipated future contact with the counselor. Perhaps other variables also help to determine the optimal level. For some combinations of variables, the optimal level of self-disclosure may be quite low but for other combinations quite high. And so in research on counseling relationship we must start thinking in terms of a family of inverted U-shaped curves to represent the interacting variables. Those hypothetical curves can be taxing to work with in research since every study should have several points along a continuum, some above the expected optimal level as well as below, in order to find out what the "optimum" is. Although such a conception of research is difficult and costly to apply, it need not be discouraging if it enables us to discover the facilitating and inhibiting factors that affect the outcome of helping relationships.

MAIN CONCLUSIONS

1. The findings from Experiment 1, in which counselors gave a mixed type of self-disclosure interview (eliciting both positive and negative self-disclosures), confirm the findings from two prior studies (reported in chaps. 9 and 15). Clients given a *moderate* self-disclosure interview tend to be *more successful* in losing weight over an 8-week period of observation than those given a *low* self-disclosure interview (with consistently positive feedback held constant).

2. The superiority of the moderate level of the standard (mixed) type of self-disclosure interview appears to hold only under a limited set of conditions, however, which are the conditions that prevailed in the prior studies, namely, the counselor has *no contact* with the client during the weeks that intervene between the initial standard disclosure interview and the follow-up sessions. In Experiment 1, when the counselor had weekly telephone interviews with the clients during the first 4 weeks after the standard self-disclosure interview, the clients given the low self-disclosure interview were more successful in losing weight than those given the moderate self-disclosure interview.

3. In Experiment 1 the subgroups that were most successful in losing weight were those in which the clients reported feeling most shame and guilt on the self-report questionnaire given immediately after the mixed self-disclosure interview. These self-reports suggest that when counselors use a standard (mixed) type of self-disclosure interview, they will be most successful in helping their clients to lose weight when they mobilize self-confrontations that generate sufficient shame or guilt to motivate their clients to adhere to the stressful decision.

4. In Experiment 2 the clients were given an interview restricted to eliciting *only positive disclosures* and the outcome was entirely different from that obtained for the standard (mixed) disclosure interview. This time in the absence of any telephone contact with the counselor during the weeks between the initial and follow-up interviews, the clients given the *low* positive disclosure interview were *more successful* in losing weight than those given the *moderate* positive disclosure interview. But when the clients had weekly telephone contact with the counselor for 4 weeks following the initial positive disclosure interviews, the subgroup given the moderate positive disclosure interview was much more successful in losing weight over a period of 8 weeks than the subgroup given the low positive disclosure interview—more successful, in fact, than any of the other subgroups in the two experiments.

5. In Experiment 2 the subgroups that were most successful in losing weight were those in which the clients reported most self-confidence about being able to diet successfully on the self-report questionnaire given immediately after the positive self-disclosure interview. These self-reports suggest that if counselors use a nonstandard type of interview that elicits only positive self-disclosures about personal strengths and assets, they will be most successful in helping their clients to lose weight when they make comments that increase the clients' self-confidence about succeeding on the task of dieting. Taking account of the findings from both experiments, we suggest that an effective strategy might be for the counselor to attempt to stimulate a combination of guilt and self-confidence: eliciting self-disclosures about personal shortcomings to *induce guilt about past failures* and eliciting self-disclosures about personal assets to *build up self-confidence about achieving future success.*

NOTES

1. Questions were phrased so that, in each of the interviews, content areas would be equivalent—focusing on relevant daily life activities, eating, and exercise. Pilot work with pretest volunteer clients suggested that some of the questions in our preliminary versions of the two types of interviews were eliciting discussion of some topics that were not equivalent. The interviews were modified and further pretesting was done to equate the two interviews before the study began.

2. We have selected and trained research assistants who are skilled counselors; they are able to conduct interviews according to prescribed interview schedules and yet maintain spontaneity. The same two counselors conducted the sessions in both experiments and had equal

numbers of clients in each experimental condition. Their (nonblind) ratings of the clients' interview responses indicate that the vast majority of those given the moderate disclosure interview did, in fact, reveal more intimate personal information than did those given the low disclosure interview.

3. All clients had three face-to-face interviews and weigh-ins with their counselor: the initial interview and follow-ups at 4 and 8 weeks. This was the "normal" level of contact typical of all the prior studies. Clients in the telephone-contact condition, who received the three weekly phone calls from their counselor during the first 4 weeks of the program, were asked questions that were consistent with the level and type of self-disclosure in the initial interview. Thus, clients who initially received the moderate self-disclosure questions again received several moderate disclosure questions during the phone calls. Although some standard questions were asked of everyone, the same consistency in type of additional questions was maintained in the 4-week follow-up session.

Only a few clients did not appear for the 4- or 8-week follow-up interviews. Statistical analysis of these different frequencies in the various conditions are not significant ($p > .20$ for all main effects and interactions). Therefore, we report the actual weight loss of clients returning to the clinic.

The statistical results from analysis of variance of the weight loss data at 4 and 8 weeks in Table 10.1 yield no main effects for level of disclosure or amount of contact. A significant interaction is found at 4 weeks ($F = 4.52$, $p < .05$) and a near significant interaction at 8 weeks ($F = 2.91$, $p < .10$).

We recomputed the results on weight loss using the procedure of assigning zero weight loss to clients who failed to return for the follow-up session. The results were substantially the same as those in Table 10.1; the same significant and near significant interaction effects at 4 and 8 weeks were again found.

One explanatory hypothesis we investigated was that the greater amount of contact in the first 4 weeks might be effective during the period of high contact as long as the clients' wish for continued contact is being gratified, terminating in disappointment and a boomerang reaction when the amount of contact is reduced. If so, we would expect the clients given the weekly telephone calls to lose more weight than the clients in the no-telephone-contact condition during the first 4 weeks but then to lose less weight during the next 4 weeks, when there was no telephone contact. The results do not support the disappointment hypothesis. The group losing the most weight in the first 4 weeks continued to lose more weight (over 2 lbs.) in the second 4 weeks, while the group losing the least amount during the first 4 weeks continued to lose less weight (only 1.3 lbs.) during the second 4 weeks. Although the differences are not statistically significant, they are in the opposite direction from what would be expected on the basis of a disappointment hypothesis.

4. The specific question dealing with feelings of shame was as follows: "Do you feel more ashamed or less ashamed of your personal weaknesses and shortcomings [right now, as compared with the way you felt just before the interview]?" For this item the interaction effect was highly significant: ($p < .01$). The same interaction effect was found for the Guilt scale obtained from the Quinlan and Janis state-of-self-esteem questionnaire ($p < .05$). These findings indicate that among the clients who had no telephone contact with the counselor after the initial session (similar to all the other studies reported in the preceding chapters), those given the moderate disclosure interview reported that they felt more shame and guilt than those given the low disclosure interview; but among the clients who had weekly telephone contact, there was no such difference between those given the moderate disclosure and low disclosure interviews.

5. For the weight loss data in Table 10.3: At 4 weeks, interaction $F = 12.8$, $p < .01$. At 8 weeks, interaction $F = 8.9$, $p < .01$.

We also checked the level of statistical significance by combining the two experiments presented in this chapter in a single three-factor analysis of variance. It is warranted to combine them for the following two reasons. First, the procedures differ only in type of self-disclosure elicited during the initial interview (mixed vs. positive only). Second, the two experiments were run concurrently, with random assignment to conditions in both. In fact the clients were randomly assigned as if in a three-factor analysis of variance design. (In the initial analysis interviewer differences were examined as a fourth variable, but no significant main effects or interactions involving interviewer differences were found.)

The three-factor analysis of variance for the weight loss data (Tables 10.1 and 10.3 combined) yields highly significant results for the three-way interaction (level of self-disclosure × amount of contact × type of disclosure): $F = 16.5$, $p < .001$ at 4 weeks and $F = 11.2$, $p < .002$ at 8 weeks. This is exactly what one would expect to find after observing that there are interaction effects in opposite directions in Tables 10.1 and 10.3. There are no significant main effects or any significant lower order interactions. Thus, the treatments that were introduced as potential facilitators of weight loss—i.e., positive self-disclosure, increased contact, and moderate self-disclosure—do not yield any simple main effects but interact in an unexpected way.

In attempting to understand a three-way interaction it is useful to ask the following question about the 8 cells: Where are the largest differences? Using the Newman–Keuls procedure for a posteriori comparisons of the 8-week follow-up data suggests the area in which the largest differences occur. The only two cells that are significantly different from each other ($p < .05$) under the assumptions of this test are those with moderate levels of positive self-disclosure, which compare no telephone contact with weekly telephone contact (the second and the fourth means in the first row of Table 10.3, which are 3.7 and 10.0 pounds, respectively). The implications of this finding are examined in the Discussion and Implications section.

6. For Item 1 in Table 10.4, improvement in mood, interaction $F = 4.7$, $p < .05$. For Item 2, confidence about losing weight, interaction $F = 6.28$, $p < .05$.

Other significant differences for questionnaire measures shown in Table 10.4 do not show the same interaction pattern as weight loss. Significant differences between the moderate and low positive disclosure conditions were found for Item 3, feelings of self-criticism (main effect $F = 7.8$, $p < .01$) and Item 4, guilt (main effect $F = 5.52$, $p < .05$). As can be seen in rows 3 and 4 of Table 10.4, clients given the moderate level of positive self-disclosure interview reported that they felt less self-critical and less guilty than those given the low level of positive self-disclosure interview. Item 5, feelings of shame, which had yielded a significant interaction effect for the mixed type of disclosure interview in Experiment 1, did not yield any significant differences for the positive disclosure interview in Experiment 2.

The three questions about the interviewer (Items 6, 7, and 8) reveal significant differences as a function of the amount of anticipated contact. When the interviewer said that there would be weekly contact during the first 4 weeks of dieting (compared with saying nothing about telephone contact), the clients respected the interviewer more (F for contact = 6.2, $p < .05$), they liked the interviewer more (F for contact = 4.4, $p < .10$), and they felt that the interviewer liked them more (F for contact = 7.7, $p < .05$).

The clients' responses on the state-of-self-esteem questionnaire show a significant main effect ($F = 5.1$, $p < .05$) for self-derogation: Immediately after the interview, clients who were told that they would have weekly telephone contact with the counselor rated themselves in a more self-derogating fashion (Item 9). This is an unexpected negative consequence of providing the added contact. The differences between weekly and no telephone contact were also seen in changes in self-ratings of pride and self-confidence over the 8-week interval (Items 10 and 11). These results do not parallel the results on weight loss. Pride and self-confidence scores rose in the no-telephone-contact condition, while the scores dropped or remained the same in the weekly-telephone-contact condition. The main effect for telephone contact on these two measures of change in self-appraisal are significant: $F = 5.2$, $p < .05$ and $F = 7.8$, $p < .05$ for changes in pride and self-confidence, respectively. These changes indicate that added telephone contact is not necessarily helpful to the clients. In fact these data suggest that clients who were contacted weekly by the counselor experienced a decrease in feelings of self-sufficiency as compared to those who were allowed to "go it alone."

7. Although clients' self-esteem scores were affected by the variables we investigated, those scores (obtained at the end of the first session) did not predict subsequent weight loss. After 4 weeks of dieting, the initial effects of the variables on self-esteem scores disappeared. But self-

esteem scores (both guilt and self-confidence) at the time of the follow-up interview appear to be affected by amount of weight loss: Clients who lost weight were more likely than others to report less guilt and more confidence. The correlations between weight loss and self-esteem scores across all individuals in the study are highly significant after 4 weeks ($p < .01$) and after 8 weeks ($p < .001$).

11 Unfavorable Effects of High Levels of Self-disclosure

DONALD M. QUINLAN AND IRVING L. JANIS

The study reported in this chapter was designed primarily to examine two variables that could influence the effectiveness of short-term counseling: (1) encouraging a very high level of self-disclosure compared with a moderate level and (2) giving noncontingent acceptance throughout the interview compared with contingent acceptance that includes occasional critical comments about the client's negative intentions, attitudes, or actions.

According to the theoretical analysis of critical phases in a supportive relationship (chap. 2), encouraging the client to reveal personal material, including negative aspects of the self, can foster an effective working alliance. The first experiment on the effects of self-disclosure conducted in the Yale Weight-Reduction Clinic (reported in chapter 9) found some evidence, as expected, that adherence to the counselor's recommendations tended to be enhanced when the counselor elicited a moderate amount of self-disclosure compared with a low level. Confirmatory results on the facilitative effect of moderate self-disclosure on adherence to stressful decisions has also been found in two additional studies reported in the present volume, one of which was again in the setting of the weight-reduction clinic (chap. 10) and the other in the setting of a Red Cross blood donation campaign (chap. 15). In all three studies, the favorable effect of inducing a moderate degree of self-disclosure emerged under conditions where the counselor gave consistently positive feedback in the form of noncontingent acceptance in response to all the clients' disclosures.

The question arises as to whether encouraging a much higher level of self-disclosure in the initial interview would be more effective or less effective. On the one hand, high disclosure may augment self-esteem enhancement if a counselor responds to the disclosures with noncontingent acceptance. On the other hand, after revealing all sorts of personal weaknesses, the client may feel discouraged or develop negativistic reactions that could impair the counselor–client relationship (see Cozby, 1973; Kaplan, Firestone, Degnore, & Moor, 1974).

In the present study a moderate level of self-disclosure was induced by the counselor's standard interview questions designed to elicit a limited amount of personal information pertinent to the main task of the counseling, namely, losing weight. The questions dealt with realistic problems of dieting without probing to explore the affective meanings of the problems of overeating and lack of self-control. This moderate self-disclosure interview was compared with a high self-disclosure interview, which was similar to the intake diagnostic interviews often given by psychodynamically oriented counselors or therapists. It explored the same areas in much more personal terms, including affective meanings for the client. Always in the context of talking about the problems of overeating and dieting, the counselor asked a number of questions about intimate matters that were never mentioned in the questions asked in the moderate self-disclosure interview.

Previous studies of client–counselor interaction have generally contrasted noncontingent acceptance by the counselor with neutral responses (see chaps. 6–8 and 15). The model for such positive feedback is suggested by the "unconditional positive regard" of Rogers's client-centered approach (Rogers, 1961). But a problem arises when only positive reinforcement is given (see chap. 2). If, for example, the client reveals negative information about feeling unwilling to go on a strict diet or expresses self-deprecatory expectations about being unable to succeed at dieting, the counselor's consistently positive feedback may unintentionally encourage inappropriate attitudes and actions, despite the counselor's best efforts to avoid doing so.

In the present study we investigated a social reinforcement procedure that contrasted noncontingent acceptance with *contingent* acceptance. When giving contingent acceptance, the counselor responded to most of the client's statements in a generally positive manner but made mildly negative comments about specific attitudes or actions that were detrimental to the goal of successful dieting. This pattern of social reinforcement could be described as "mixed" in that each client received both positive and negative comments from the counselor. The negative comments were directed, however, solely to deterrents to dieting. Care was taken to avoid criticism of the client as a person and to convey an optimistic attitude about the client's ability to overcome the obstacles. Noncontingent acceptance consistently conveyed empathy and uncritical positive regard regardless of whatever weaknesses the clients talked about, but care was taken to avoid encouraging rejection of the recommended diet or defeatist attitudes. Contingent acceptance was somewhat more directive in that it explicitly conveyed the normative suggestion that the client should strive to overcome those weaknesses that might interfere with successful adherence to the diet.

METHOD AND PROCEDURES

Setting

In this study 58 clients were seen in face-to-face private interviews conducted by two female counselors at the Yale Weight-Reduction Clinic. Clients learned of the service through newspaper announcements offering psychological assistance in weight reduction. Women who were 15–45 pounds overweight and who had no medical conditions that would affect their losing weight were accepted for the study. (Those who were more severely overweight or who had conditions such as ulcers, diabetes, and colitis were not included but were told to consult their physician or to contact the appropriate clinic at the Yale–New Haven Hospital.) The counseling on weight reduction was offered as a free service, but in order to encourage the clients to return for a second session 4 weeks later a deposit of $5 was taken at the beginning of the first session as part of the informed consent procedure. The deposit was returned at the follow-up interview.

Interviews

Both counselors were trained to give two different structured interviews, one designed to elicit a high level of self-disclosure and the other to elicit a moderate level. The high self-disclosure interview consisted of questions dealing with personal attitudes and affective reactions to the problems of being overweight, including past failures at dieting and the effects of overweight on health, appearance, body image, social relations, and sex life. Several plausible probing questions were asked about each of these subtopics. Although the questions were specific, they were open-ended so as to allow the client to decline discussing any issue without embarrassment. The moderate disclosure interview tapped areas pertaining to reasons for dieting at a more fact-oriented level. In general the questions in the moderate self-disclosure interview were similar to those used in the prior studies (chaps. 6–9). Whenever a client responded to a moderate disclosure question by beginning to discuss more personal aspects of her problems, the counselor simply followed the rule of moving on to the next question as soon as tactfully possible. Examination of the clients' answers showed that, as intended, the ones who were given the high disclosure interview revealed much more intimate personal information than those given the low disclosure interview.[1]

Feedback

The two counselors were instructed to respond to the clients in one of two ways: noncontingent positive comments or contingent positive comments with mildly critical comments directed at specific attitudes or intended behaviors that were likely to cause problems in dieting. In the noncontingent positive condition the counselor responded to whatever aspects of the client's answers that could appropriately be positively commented upon, such as expressions of intentions to avoid fattening foods. Whenever there was no such opportunity, the counselor said, "I understand," or something equivalent in a warm, accepting manner. In the contingent positive condition the counselor responded in exactly the same way as in the noncontingent positive condition, except that when the client spoke about potentially diet-defeating behavior she made a mildly critical comment in terms of the goals of successful dieting. Records of the interviews showed that every client in the contingent positive feedback condition was given at least three such critical comments by the counselor and in some cases many more. An important distinction was made between criticizing the client and criticizing specific behavior. Critical comments were carefully worded to avoid implying lack of acceptance of the client as a person.

An example of the two different types of feedback can be seen in replies to a client's expressing doubt about being able to give up ice cream, chocolate candy, or other favorite foods. A noncontingent response would be, "It's quite understandable that you would feel that way about it right now." A contingent positive comment to the same disclosure would be "It's quite understandable that you would feel that way about it right now, but, of course, you will have to overcome those feelings because eating that kind of food will keep you from losing weight."

Measures of Adherence

The basic measure of adherence to the set of diet recommendations was the amount of weight lost after 4 weeks of dieting. Each client's weight was measured on a professional balance-type scale before the initial interview and again at the 4-week follow-up interview.

In order to obtain a second measure of short-term adherence, the counselor gave the client a pledge card in a stamped, preaddressed envelope. On the card was printed a pledge to go on the diet and to continue on the diet until the desired weight was reached. Clients were instructed to take the pledge card home and send it in the day they actually began the diet. All clients were encouraged to begin the diet as soon as possible.

A third measure of adherence to the counselor's recommendations was mailing back the weekly reports, which was requested by the counselor. On the report form there was a day-by-day checklist for compliance with the diet and another for a 10-minute period of "silent thought" (which was another recommendation made by the counselor). Three stamped, preaddressed envelopes were provided for three weekly reports; the fourth weekly report was to be returned at the follow-up session.

Self-report Questionnaires

Three self-report questionnaires were given to the clients immediately after the initial interview: (1) a scale assessing state of self-esteem (Quinlan and Janis, Appendix), (2) a series of questions on reactions to the interview, and (3) a series of questions on impressions of the interviewer.

Sequence of Procedures

At the beginning of the first session the client completed a brief form on health history (to screen out clients with medical complications that might not have been mentioned when the client phoned the clinic for an appointment). Then the counselor read aloud a description of the study and asked the client to sign a consent form. Next the counselor weighed the client. After that the self-disclosure interview was begun.

Clients were assigned on a random basis to one of the two counselors and to one of the four experimental conditions in the factorial design (high disclosure with noncontingent feedback, high disclosure with contingent feedback, moderate disclosure with noncontingent feedback, and moderate disclosure with contingent feedback).[2]

After the interview the recommended diet was explained in a taped message previously recorded by the counselor in order to assure uniformity across all conditions. The tape recording was stopped whenever a client indicated she had a question. The recommended diet was the standard 1200-calorie diet developed by the Department of Nutrition and Dietetics of the Yale–New Haven Hospital for gradual weight loss for women.

After the diet recording, the counselor left the room while the clients completed the three postinterview questionnaires. Finally, a follow-up appointment for 4 weeks later was scheduled. A written copy of the diet and sample menus were given to the client to take home along with the pledge card, the weekly report forms, and stamped envelopes.

After 4 weeks, at the follow-up appointment, each client was weighed and then briefly interviewed about the experience of dieting. As a final clinical service the client was given instructions and encouragement for maintaining her weight at a reduced level once her goal had been reached. At the end of the session the $5 deposit was returned and the client was invited to contact the clinic whenever questions about dieting arose.

RESULTS

Table 11.1 shows the average amount of weight loss for each of the experimental conditions. There is one significant finding: a main effect for level of

Table 11.1. Mean weight loss (pounds) after four weeks

| Amount of self-disclosure | Type of feedback from counselor | | |
	Noncontingent positive	Contingent positive	Combined
High	2.0	3.6	2.8
Moderate	6.0	4.8	5.4
Combined	4.0	4.2	4.1

Note. $N = 14$ or 15 in each of the 4 groups.

self-disclosure ($F = 4.14$, $p < .05$). Clients who had been given the *moderate* self-disclosure interview lost over 2½ pounds more weight, on the average, than those who had been given the high self-disclosure interview.[3]

A second variable measuring adherence to the counselor's recommendations was the number of weekly reports mailed back to the clinic (Table 11.2). The results are in agreement with those for weight loss. The difference between high and moderate self-disclosure conditions is significant at the 10% confidence level. Thus, on two independent behavioral measures, the clients given the moderate self-disclosure interview showed more adherence

Table 11.2. Mean number of weekly reports mailed back to the weight-reduction clinic

| Amount of self-disclosure | Type of feedback from counselor | | Combined |
	Noncontingent positive	Contingent positive	
High	1.2	1.7	1.4
Moderate	2.5	1.9	2.2
Combined	1.8	1.8	1.8

Note. N = 14 or 15 in each of the 4 groups.

to the counselor's recommendations than those given the high self-disclosure interview.

Self-report Questionnaires

The 18 items in the state of self-esteem scale were used to obtain two summary scores—self-confidence and guilt—based on previous factor analyses (see Appendix). Analysis of variance for each of the two scores indicated that level of self-disclosure had no effect on guilt but a significant effect on self-confidence: Clients given the high self-disclosure interview reported having less confidence in themselves immediately afterward than those given the moderate self-disclosure interview ($p < .08$). Similar results were obtained from two items in the other postinterview questionnaires: Clients given the high self-disclosure interview reported feeling that their personal weaknesses were more serious ($p < .01$) and that the counselor respected them less ($p < .05$) than those given the moderate self-disclosure interview.[4] Thus the results on immediate reactions to high vs. moderate self-disclosure parallel the data for adherence, indicating that clients were left with less self-confidence and a less favorable self-image after the high self-disclosure interview than after the moderate self-disclosure interview.

DISCUSSION

The principal results of this study pertain to the unfavorable effects of inducing a high level of self-disclosure on behavioral adherence to the counselor's recommendations. In many clinics where clients seek help in changing some currently unsatisfactory condition (such as excessive smoking, drinking, drug abuse, or overweight) an intake interview is conducted that elicits a considerable amount of personal information about the client's past failures and current weaknesses, just as in the high self-disclosure interview in the present study. Our results suggest that such intake interviews have a detrimental effect with respect to the behavioral changes that are the primary goal of short-term counseling.

Compared with the level of self-disclosure induced in all the previous studies, a much higher level of self-disclosure was induced in the present study with regard to sensitive personal topics, such as details about sex life. The total amount of confidential material discussed greatly exceeded that normally revealed to anyone except an intimate confidant. Taking account of the studies showing that moderate self-disclosure interviews were more effective than low (chaps. 9, 10, and 15), we infer that the effectiveness of the level of self-disclosure is not a simple linear function. Rather, just as with many other variables, such as induced anxiety and achievement motivation, self-disclosure appears to have both facilitating and inhibiting effects which combine in such a way that the curve for adherence is an inverted U-shaped function as the level of induced disclosure increases from low to moderate to high. This suggested curvilinear relationship is in line with comments by other investigators who have called attention to the potentially unfavorable consequences of too much disclosure as well as the favorable consequences of open, honest communication (see, e.g., Altman & Taylor, 1973; Cozby, 1973; Kaplan et al., 1974; Levinger & Snoek, 1972).

What are the possible sources of the detrimental effects of high self-disclosure? One plausible hypothesis is that a high level of self-disclosure elicits more negative feelings about the self. Examination of the clients' answers in the high disclosure interview indicate that much of the personal information revealed was, in fact, negative, some of which was accompanied by self-derogatory remarks. Despite positive feedback from the counselor, many clients given the high disclosure interview may have been left in a somewhat demoralized state. Their lowered self-confidence about being able to succeed on a task requiring self-control might account for the unfavorable effect of high self-disclosure on adherence to a diet.

High self-disclosure may make the task seem insurmountably difficult because the client's weaknesses and past failures become more salient as well as the temptations to be overcome and the other obstacles likely to be encountered. The postinterview questionnaire results showing that the high self-disclosure interview induced less self-confidence and more awareness of personal weaknesses are in line with this hypothesis. There is no difference, however, in feelings of guilt expressed by clients who received the high and moderate disclosure interviews.

A related source of unfavorable effects of high self-disclosure would be the client's sense of having revealed too much, which could impair the client's relationship with the counselor. The client might feel embarrassed or annoyed about having revealed so many personal weaknesses. The findings from the self-report questionnaires lend some indirect support to this hypothesis. Clients given the high compared with the moderate self-disclosure interview asserted that they felt not only that their personal weaknesses were more serious but also that the counselor respected them less. This hypothesis is similar to the hypothesis of lowered self-confidence, except that it places the locus of the client's negative feeling in anticipated disapproval from the counselor rather than from the self. It is difficult to distinguish the two similar hypotheses without more detailed inquiry into indicators of embarrassment and other mediating reactions.

Further evaluation of these hypotheses based on more sensitive and more detailed inquiries immediately following the self-disclosure interview are presented in chapter 13. However, we have not yet investigated the possibility that the reasons for negative effects of high self-disclosure might vary from client to client, depending on the client's initial level of self-esteem or the predisposition to interpret events as internally or externally controlled.

Another hypothesis to be assessed in subsequent research on mediating processes is that high self-disclosure is "too successful" in building up the relationship, leading to overdependency on the counselor. If the clients' disclosures of highly personal material deepens the relationship with the counselor (as suggested in the theoretical analysis presented in chap. 2), they are likely to become excessively frustrated and angry later on, when they wish that the counselor were available for support during the crucial weeks that they are required to diet on their own.

Initially we had expected that the clients' reactions to the high versus moderate disclosure interviews would be modified by the type of feedback they received from the counselor. But comparisons of the effects of contingent versus noncontingent positive feedback failed to bear out this expectation. The clients who received noncontingent positive feedback lost about the same amount of weight and mailed back about the same number of weekly reports as those who received contingent feedback. The evidence indicates that realistic criticism of the client's antidieting attitudes or intentions, when mixed with positive regard, did not facilitate or interfere with the effects of either the moderate or the high disclosure interviews. The clients given contingent feedback, however, felt guiltier and regarded their faults as more serious than did those given noncontingent positive feedback, according to the answers obtained from two questionnaire items. These observed differences suggest that contingent feedback had the effect of lowering self-esteem (or failing to raise self-esteem). But this interpretation is not supported by the findings from the state-of-self-esteem questionnaire, which yielded no significant differences between the two types of feedback on the self-confidence scale and a near significant difference in the opposite direction on the guilt scale. Our findings, therefore, indicate that the contingent feedback given in this study, compared with noncontingent positive feedback, had no consistent effects on the clients' attitudes or behavior and did not in any way modify the powerful negative effects of eliciting high disclosure.

MAIN CONCLUSIONS

1. The results from this study, which was carried out in a weight-reduction clinic where clients were given face-to-face interviews, support the following general conclusion: When counselors induce a high level of self-disclosure about personal problems in intake interviews, clients show less adherence to the counselors' recommendations than when counselors induce a moderate level, even if consistently accepting feedback is given throughout the entire interview. Clients given a high self-disclosure interview dealing with problems of overeating and dieting (which elicited relevant intimate information about past failures, current weaknesses, and feelings about sensitive topics such as sex life) mailed in fewer weekly reports and showed less weight loss 1 month later than did clients given a moderate self-disclosure interview (which elicited less intimate personal information about problems of overeating and dieting).

2. Questionnaire data obtained immediately after the interview indicate that clients given the high self-disclosure interview reported having less confidence in themselves than clients given the moderate disclosure interview. These results suggest that as a result of being induced to reveal negative information about themselves, the clients given the high self-disclosure interview were somewhat demoralized and were more likely to fail to adhere to the diet because of their lower self-confidence about being able to succeed on a task requiring self-control. A related mediating factor suggested by the questionnaire data involves expectations of social disapproval from the counselor. Clients given the high self-disclosure interview reported feeling that the counselor respected them less than clients given the moderate self-disclosure interview.

3. In this study we also compared the effects of contingent versus non-contingent feedback throughout the initial interview and found no observable differences in weight loss or in other behavioral measures of adherence. The finding that the two types of feedback are equally effective might hold only in certain limited types of clinical settings such as weight-reduction clinics, in which clients seldom express intentions that go counter to the counselor's recommendations.

NOTES

1. Considerable pretesting and preliminary research on the high versus moderate disclosure interview were carried out in the same way as the preliminary work on the moderate versus low disclosure interview in the earlier studies (see chap. 9, n. 1). In a preliminary study, 8 clients given the high disclosure interview were compared with 8 who were given the moderate disclosure interview. Blind ratings of their responses showed that both interviews

elicited a substantial amount of personal information but there was a large and statistically significant difference ($p < .05$) in the blind ratings of the amount of highly intimate self-disclosures. By "intimate" self-disclosures is meant items of personal information that received a rating of 4 or 5 on a 5-point scale of intimacy of self-disclosure, which ranged from 1 = routine information about self, such as place of residence, that would be freely given to any legitimate inquirer, to 5 = extremely sensitive information, such as details about sex life, family quarrels, and personal failures, which would not be discussed with anyone except a very close friend or a therapist.

Similar results were obtained from the interviewers' nonblind ratings of the responses of the clients in the present experiment. The 29 clients given the high disclosure interviews seldom evaded any of the questions and revealed far more intimate personal information than the 29 clients given the moderate disclosure interview ($p < .01$). Among the 29 clients given the high disclosure interview the 7 whose intimate self-disclosure ratings placed them in the *lowest* quartile had nevertheless revealed a considerable amount of intimate personal information, which was equal to or more than that revealed by the 7 clients who were in the *highest* quartile among the 29 clients given the moderate disclosure interview. Thus, there was relatively little overlap between the two distributions of scores on amount of intimate self-disclosure.

2. In addition to the 58 clients in the main experiment the same number of clients was randomly assigned to a replication experiment that was conducted simultaneously. The replication experiment was carried out in the same way, with the same four experimental conditions as the main experiment, except that the client was *not able to see the counselor* during the interview.

In the replication experiment an opaque partition was placed between the client and interviewer with the explanation that this procedure might allow the client to concentrate better on her answers. Such an interview is analogous to those conducted in confessionals in some religions, psychoanalytic sessions, and telephone counseling. The screen was removed after the interview for the remainder of the session.

Recent research on nonverbal communication has indicated the importance of cues such as eye contact and smiling on the affective tone of the interview (Ludwig & Ellsworth, 1976). Ellsworth and Carlsmith (1968) call attention to one particular aspect of eye contact that is especially relevant to the effects of contingent feedback investigated in the present study: When one person gives negative information to another (such as a message that the other person is failing on a task) eye contact increases the impact on the recipient. If so, under conditions of contingent feedback, the counselor's critical responses to a client's disclosure about noncompliant intentions should have a more powerful effect in a face-to-face interview than in an interview where the client cannot see the counselor.

The results of this supplementary experiment are summarized in n. 3, where they are discussed in relation to the findings from the main experiment.

3. The difference in weight loss between high and moderate self-disclosure was somewhat more pronounced in the noncontingent feedback condition than in the contingent feedback condition, but the interaction between self-disclosure and feedback was not statistically significant.

The mean weight loss shown for each experimental group in Table 11.1 is based on all the cases in each group. The few clients who failed to come for the follow-up interview were assumed to have lost zero weight. A chi-square analysis showed that there were no significant differences among the four experimental groups with regard to number of clients who failed to return for the follow-up interview.

An initial overall analysis of variance (with unweighted means) was carried out to see if there were any counselor effects. The results showed there was no main effect for the counselors or any interaction effects. Consequently all the analyses reported in this chapter are based on combined data from both counselors.

An overall analysis was carried out combining the results of the main experiment and the replication experiment (described in the preceding note). This was a three-factor analysis of variance, using viewing versus not viewing of the counselor as the third factor. The results of this analysis were essentially the same as the results for the two-factor analysis of variance for the main experiment (based on Table 11.1). Both analyses show that the only significant finding is a main effect for level of self-disclosure ($p < .05$ for the three-factor as well as for the two-factor analysis of variance).

When each of the two experiments (viewing and nonviewing) was analyzed separately, however, the main experiment (conducted under face-to-face viewing conditions) provided larger differences between the two self-disclosure groups. That is to say, the replication experiment conducted under conditions where the client could not see the counselor during the interview provided essentially the same results as the main experiment conducted under normal viewing conditions, with the difference in weight loss between high and moderate self-disclosure in the same direction but not so large. On the other dependent variables (number of weekly reports returned and so forth) the replication experiment also provided essentially the same, but somewhat weaker results, as the main experiment. Preventing the clients from viewing the counselor during the interview apparently introduces some "noise" into the client–counselor interaction and increases error variance. In future studies on the effects of visual cues in the counseling situation it may be more productive to examine the effects of variations in specific nonverbal cues emitted by the counselor, such as amount of eye contact, smiling, and facial expressions of tension versus relaxation.

4. Self-reports bearing on the immediate effects of contingent versus noncontingent feedback are inconsistent. An analysis of variance of guilt scores obtained from the state of self-esteem scale unexpectedly showed that clients given noncontingent positive feedback reported feeling guiltier immediately afterward than those given contingent feedback ($p = .08$). But, on two items in the other questionnaires the results came out in the opposite direction. Clients given noncontingent feedback reported that they felt *less* guilty ($p < .01$) and that their weaknesses were *less* serious ($p < .10$) than those given contingent feedback. Because of the inconsistencies in these findings no conclusions can be drawn concerning the immediate reactions of the clients to contingent versus noncontingent feedback.

12 Effects of High Self-disclosure and Approval Training Procedures

JOHN H. RISKIND AND IRVING L. JANIS

The present field study, which was carried out in the Yale Weight-Reduction Clinic, had two main purposes. First, it was designed to explore further the effects of self-disclosure. Included in the study is a comparison of a high versus a moderate level of induced disclosure of personal problems and current shortcomings, an aspect of this investigation which replicates the preceding study by Quinlan and Janis.

A second purpose, and the major feature of the study, was to determine the effectiveness of a new type of role-playing procedure in counteracting the negative effects observed by Quinlan and Janis for the high disclosure interview. The role-playing procedure is intended to orient the client toward the social approval of the counselor and was developed on the basis of hypotheses derived from the analysis of critical phases in the development of an effective helping relationship (chap. 2). According to the analysis, at the end of the first two critical phases, the client regards the counselor as a "significant other" from whom he or she seeks continued acceptance and social approval as a source of self-esteem enhancement. If this assumption is correct, the effectiveness of a counselor's initial interview might be increased by using a psychodramatic procedure toward the end of the session to get the client to focus attention on vivid images and verbalized expectations of obtaining the future approval of the counselor for diligently adhering to his or her recommendations. A social approval training procedure of this kind might minimize the unfavorable effects of high disclosure by encouraging the clients to anticipate social approval and acceptance from the counselor if they adhere to the diet recommendations. This would help to counteract their concerns about having lost the counselor's acceptance as a result of their having revealed too many past failures, personal weaknesses, sensitive current problems, and the like. The memory of the social approval role-playing exercise might subsequently function as a salient reminder of the powerful incentives to adhere to whatever behavioral norms are recommended by the counselor.

Prior research has shown that psychodramatic role playing can have a marked influence on perceptions and expectations of possible gains and losses from a future course of action—including anticipated social approval from significant others (see Janis & Mann, 1977, pp. 379–388). But the question arises as to whether the benefits of a psychodramatic procedure intended to influence expectations of social approval might be limited to *short-term effects* that are manifested only during the period when the counselor is in contact with the client. Once the supportive relationship with the counselor has been terminated, the positive behavioral effects of expecting the counselor's social approval might not be sustained.

A subsidiary purpose of this study was to explore the effects of a similar role-playing procedure designed to promote expectations of *self*-approval for adherence to the counselor's recommendations. We hypothesize that a type of motivation different from social approval motivation is needed to develop *long-term internalization* of the norms supported by the counselor. This internalization might be conceptualized as a transformation of social approval motivation into self-approval motivation. If so, one way to facilitate this transformation might be to focus the client's attention at the outset of the relationship on anticipations of self-approval and self-disapproval by means of role playing. In order to develop a self-approval training procedure that might do this, we tried out a psychodramatic procedure that resembles the social approval training procedure, but in this instance the client is asked to imagine and verbalize the increase in self-esteem that would result from self-approval for successful adherence to the decision.

The *social* approval procedure might counteract a client's expectation that, as a result of having listened to disclosures of so many past failures and current shortcomings, the counselor must regard him or her as pitiable and weak, a hopeless case, unworthy of true respect or acceptance. The client's disclosures of unfavorable aspects of the self might create this negative reaction despite the counselor's standard acceptance statements, which the client might dismiss by attributing them to the counselor's required professional role instead of to genuine acceptance. The *self*-approval training procedure, although intended primarily to promote long-term internalization of the counselor's recommendations after the counseling relationship has been terminated, might also counteract the short-term effects of a high disclosure interview by implicitly conveying that the client is not helpless and weak but is capable of succeeding.

Thus, either the self-approval or the social approval training procedure might mitigate the unfavorable effects of eliciting high disclosure by conveying the message that the client could be successful and is a worthwhile person. If so, the detrimental effects of a high disclosure interview that have been observed in prior research (chap. 11) might be counteracted if followed soon after by an approval training procedure. Accordingly, the current study was designed in such a way that we could examine possible interaction effects to see if the observed differences resulting from a high vs. a moderate self-disclosure interview in the initial session are reduced or even reversed by adding the social approval or the self-approval training procedure.

METHODS AND PROCEDURES

Design

The clients in this investigation were 74 overweight women (from 15 to 45 pounds overweight) from New Haven and the surrounding vicinity. All of them volunteered in response to a newspaper announcement of a free weight-reduction clinic connected with the Yale Psychology Department. As in the preceding studies, the sample of volunteers represented a broad range of ages, educational levels, and ethnic backgrounds.

In the initial session two independent experimental variations were introduced by the counselor: (1) an interview containing questions that induced either a high or moderate degree of self-disclosure and (2) social approval training or self-approval training (by means of the special role-playing procedures) or no approval training. Thus, in this field experiment we used a two-by-three factorial design. (In order to examine possible differences in reactions evoked by the three counselors [two males and one female] who conducted the interviews, we also included this additional factor in our analyses of variance.)

At the beginning of the initial session clients were assigned on a random basis to one of the six experimental conditions. After the self-disclosure interview and the approval training (or control) procedures, all clients were given exactly the same information and recommendations about the 1200-calorie diet. In order to make certain that the counselors did not unconsciously vary the way they presented the dietary recommendations to clients who had been given different treatments, each counselor made a tape recording of all the essential information and recommendations, which was played for each of his or her clients. After the tape recording the counselor volunteered to answer any questions the client might have. Counselors were instructed to answer the questions either by repeating the relevant material from the tape recording or by volunteering to obtain the information from the expert in the Yale Department of Dietetics who was a consultant to our weight-reduction clinic.

Five weeks later a follow-up interview was conducted. This enabled us to assess effects of the experimental variables on short-term adherence to the recommended diet. We also attempted to assess longer term adherence by conducting a follow-up interview 9 months after the initial session.

One potentially important difference between the Quinlan and Janis study (chap. 11) and the present study of high versus moderate disclosure should be noted. In the former study all three counselors had a great deal of prior clinical experience, including counseling of clients who were overweight or who had other health problems, whereas in the present study the three counselors were novices just starting their training as interviewers, having had little or no prior clinical experience. Partly because of their novice status, the interviewers were more formal and less inclined to display spontaneous warmth or empathy in response to the clients' disclosures, even though they were given some training designed to facilitate their carrying out the instructions to give consistently positive feedback in the form of acceptance statements in response to all disclosures.

Self-disclosure Interview Procedures

After being weighed and completing the standard background questionnaire, each client was given an interview that elicited either a high or moderate degree of self-disclosure.[1] The same introductory explanation was used for both types of interview (to the effect that the client's answers to the questions would aid the counselor to understand better the client's personal overeating problems, which might prove to be helpful to the client). For both types of interview the counselors were instructed to respond to each answer in a positive, accepting manner, using Rogerian reflective statements, empathic comments that acknowledge the client's feelings, and favorable remarks about the client's cooperation. (See the interview procedures for noncontingent positive feedback described in chaps. 6 and 11.)

The high disclosure interview, like the one used in the Quinlan and Janis study (chap. 11), was designed to elicit a much greater degree of self-disclosure than the earlier studies (reported in chaps. 6–9). It was modeled after the diagnostic intake interviews used in many psychological and psychiatric clinics where people come for help on personal problems.

In the context of exploring the linkage between problems of overeating and other personal difficulties, the high disclosure interview began with a general question asking the client to describe what the major problems were in her life at that time. Each problem was probed for details by further questions. Then specific questions were asked concerning marital and sexual problems and other personal troubles, including feelings of loneliness, dissatisfaction, depression, inferiority, and other self-deprecatory feelings that are seldom disclosed to others. The interviewer also asked the client to describe daydreams and favorite wishes.

The moderate disclosure interview began and ended with a general question about whether there were any personal matters that the client thought the counselor should know about, which allowed the client to disclose as much or as little about her personal problems as she wished. Most of the interview was devoted to a series of specific questions concerning the client's eating habits, daily life schedule, social life, and leisure activities.[2]

Approval Training

After the interview each client was given the standard information about three basic rules of dieting, which emphasized the necessity of sticking to the 1200-calorie diet, avoiding fattening foods, and resisting temptations to overeat. After that, each client was asked to engage in role-playing exercises referred to as "looking into the future." The basic scenario of the first exercise was that 4 weeks have gone by, and the client has *failed* to follow the dieting rules and knows that when she returns to the clinic in 2 days it will be apparent that she has not lost any weight. In the second exercise the client was asked to imagine that the same interval of 4 weeks has passed but that this time she has *succeeded* in following the dieting rules, and has lost 5 pounds. The role-playing instructions for the two exercises were varied in such a way that one-third of the clients were asked to emphasize their expectations of *social* disapproval or approval, and another third were asked to emphasize their expectations of *self*-disapproval or -approval.[3] The remaining third were not asked to emphasize either social or self-approval.

Table 12.1. Effects of self-disclosure and approval training on behavioral measures five weeks after the initial session

| Behavioral measures | Approval training | | | | Controls | |
| | Self-approval training | | Social approval training | | No approval training | |
	High disclosure	Moderate disclosure	High disclosure	Moderate disclosure	High disclosure	Moderate disclosure
1. Mean weight loss in pounds*	1.8	1.4	2.7	1.0	1.8	3.9
2. Percentage of failures: lost no weight or gained*	67%	58%	54%	73%	77%	18%
3. Mean no. of weekly reports mailed to clinic*	1.7	1.9	1.8	0.9	1.4	2.2
4. Percentage of dropouts**	25%	33%	38%	36%	54%	18%

Note. $N = 12 \pm 1$ in each of the 6 groups.

*An analysis of variance showed that the only significant finding was the interaction effects of self-disclosure with social approval training: for weight loss $F = 3.84, p < .10$; for percentage of failures: $F = 8.18, p < .01$; for weekly reports, $F = 3.77, p < .10$. There were no significant or near significant differences among the three counselors on any of the measures.

**An analysis of variance showed that for percentage of dropouts, the interaction effect of self-disclosure with self-approval training was not large enough to be statistically significant: $F = 2.68, p < .20$.

Clients in the latter third, constituting the role-playing *control* group, were merely asked to enact both the failure and the success scenario by saying out loud "the thoughts you would have about whether or not you would still try to follow the dieting rules during the following month."

Dependent Measures

Weight loss, the primary behavioral measure, was assessed by weighing each client on a standard balance scale at the time of the initial session and again at the two follow-up sessions about 5 weeks and 9 months later. Another behavioral measure was the number of weekly reports mailed to the clinic by the clients during the 4 weeks after the initial session. (All clients were given four weekly report forms to complete, along with stamped, addressed envelopes.) In addition to the behavioral measures, attitude and affect questionnaires were given at each session to obtain process measures relevant to explanatory hypotheses.

RESULTS AND DISCUSSION

Table 12.1 shows the behavioral effects of the treatments, as assessed at the time of the 5-week follow-up session. On the crucial measure of weight loss, we find no main effects for either degree of self-disclosure or approval training. However, as expected, there is a significant interaction effect. In the absence of any approval training the clients who had been given the moderate self-disclosure interview in the initial session lost more weight (a mean of 3.9 pounds) than those who had been given the high self-disclosure interview (a mean of only 1.8 pounds). This difference, which is statistically significant at the .05 level, replicates the findings of the Quinlan and Janis study reported in the preceding chapter, which did not use either form of approval training.[4] The principal finding in the latter study was essentially the same: Under conditions where there was no approval training, those clients who had been given the high self-disclosure interview showed significantly less weight loss 1 month later than those who had been given the moderate self-disclosure interview.

In the present experiment the relative advantage of giving a moderate rather than high disclosure interview disappears for those clients who were also given self- or social approval training. As can be seen in the first four columns of the first row in Table 12.1, for clients who received either social or self-approval training, the high disclosure interview resulted in somewhat more weight loss than the moderate disclosure interview. The interaction effect for *social* approval training is statistically significant below the 10% confidence level, indicating that the effect of the high disclosure interview on adherence to the counselor's dieting recommendations was favorable or unfavorable, depending on whether the clients were given the social approval training or no approval training. (The same conclusion cannot be drawn for *self*-approval training because in this instance the interaction effect is not large enough to approach statistical significance.)

Another measure based on the records of weight changes was obtained by observing how many women in each group failed to lose any weight at all or gained weight. The percentage of cases in each condition who failed to lose even 1 pound is shown in the second row of Table 12.1. For this measure the interaction effect of self-disclosure with social approval training is again statistically significant ($p < .01$). The results show that in the absence of any approval training many more failures to lose weight are manifested after 5 weeks among the clients who had been given the high disclosure initial interview (77%) than among the clients who had been given the moderate disclosure interview (18%). But when the clients received social approval training, the percentage of failures among the clients who had been given the high disclosure interview (54%) is smaller than among those who had been given the moderate disclosure interview (73%). Thus, both the percentages of failures as well as the means for amount of weight loss in Table 12.1 indicate that the relatively adverse effects of asking questions designed to induce a high degree of self-disclosure in an intake interview, of the type that is typically used for diagnostic purposes in many different clinical settings, are attenuated if the interview is followed by a role-playing procedure that provides social approval training. However, if the intake interview involves asking questions designed to induce only a moderate degree of self-disclosure, the social approval training procedure appears to have the adverse effect of increasing the chances that the clients will fail to adhere to the counselor's main recommendations.

The same conclusions are supported by the subsidiary behavioral measure of compliance with another recommendation made by the counselor: filling out and mailing to the clinic the weekly reports on adherence to the diet during the month following the initial interview. The results for mean number of weekly reports returned (row 3 of Table 12.1) show the same interaction effect as weight loss (at the 10% confidence level). The same trend occurs in the results for the proportion of clients in each group who dropped out of the program, i.e., failed to show up for the 5-week follow-up interview (row 4 of Table 12.1), but this interaction effect is not strong enough to be statistically significant.

Tables 12.2 and 12.3 show the results obtained from questionnaire measures bearing on three alternative hypotheses concerning changes in attitude, motivation, or affect that might help explain the results on the behavioral effects of self-disclosure and approval training:

Hypothesis 1. Eliciting a very high degree of self-disclosure, in the absence of social approval training, might produce *resentment or negativistic reactions toward the counselor.* This could be a result of the strong demands made on the client to reveal more than she wants to reveal, or a result of an increased need for personalized approval that is not satisfied by the standard acceptance statements made by the counselor. In either case we would expect to find that in the no-approval-training (control) condition the clients given the high self-disclosure interview would assert less favorable attitudes toward the counselor than those given the moderate self-disclosure interview. But the results in row 1 of Table 12.2 do not show the predicted

Table 12.2. Effects of self-disclosure and approval training on client's attitudes at the end of the initial session

	Self-approval training		Social approval training		No approval training	
	High disclosure	Moderate disclosure	High disclosure	Moderate disclosure	High disclosure	Moderate disclosure
1. Attitude toward counselor	0.4	−0.7	0.0	0.0	0.1	−0.3
2. Self-confidence about ability to diet successfully	0.5	0.3	0.8	1.0	1.0	1.2

Note. $N = 12 \pm 1$ in each of the 6 groups. An analysis of variance was carried out for both attitude measures. The findings that proved to be statistically significant or near significant were as follows: (1) attitude toward the counselor: a main effect for self-disclosure: $F = 3.08$, $p < .10$; (2) self-confidence about dieting: a main effect for self-approval training: $F = 5.98$, $p < .05$.

trend. The means across all conditions indicate that attitudes expressed toward the counselor by clients in all groups were generally close to neutral, with those who received the high self-disclosure interview tending to be slightly positive and those who received the moderate self-disclosure interview tending to be slightly negative. This main effect for disclosure is significant at the 8% confidence level.[5] Because the results are in the opposite direction from what is predicted by the resentment hypothesis, it does not appear to be a promising basis for explaining the weight loss differences or the other behavioral effects.

Hypothesis 2. By causing the clients' weaknesses and past failures to become more salient and by increasing their awareness of personal shortcomings, a high disclosure interview may produce an *immediate loss of self-confidence* about being able to carry out the diet, which is demoralizing. The analysis of critical phases (chap. 2) assumes that a major reason that clients are responsive to a counselor's recommendations is that the relationship bolsters their self-esteem. But rather than increasing the clients' self-esteem and self-confidence about their ability to succeed at dieting, the high disclosure interview may have had the opposite effect. The questionnaire results shown in row 2 of Table 12.2 are pertinent to the demoralization hypothesis. They do not, however, support the demoralization hypothesis. In all conditions the differences in immediate confidence between those who received the high disclosure and moderate disclosure interviews are very slight and nonsignificant.[6]

Hypothesis 3. The clients given the high disclosure interview might be relatively more easily shaken by the usual difficulties and setbacks when they actually start to diet as a result of their having become aware of many personal weaknesses made salient by that interview. This could produce a *delayed loss of self-confidence* about being able to diet successfully and perhaps a lower level of self-esteem in general. That is to say, the unfavorable effects of the high disclosure interview on self-confidence and self-esteem might not show up until after the clients were away from the reassuring counselor and were trying to live up to the recommended dieting rules. This hypothesis is partially supported by the results in the first two rows of Table 12.3, which are from two scales based on a factor analysis of responses to the

Table 12.3. Effects of self-disclosure and approval training on client's attitudes five weeks after the initial session

	Self-approval training		Social approval training		No approval training	
	High disclosure	Moderate disclosure	High disclosure	Moderate disclosure	High disclosure	Moderate disclosure
1. General self-confidence (Quinlan & Janis subscale)	0.0	7.0	4.0	6.0	5.0	11.0
2. Absence of self-derogation (Quinlan & Janis subscale)	11.0	2.0	1.0	14.0	7.0	12.0
3. Need for approval (Marlowe & Crowne scale)	16.7	16.2	15.1	19.3	19.1	21.7

Note. $N = 12\pm1$ in each of the 6 groups. An analysis of variance was carried out for each of the three attitude measures. The findings that proved to be statistically significant or near significant were as follows: (1) general self-confidence: a main effect for self-disclosure ($F = 3.62$, $p < .10$); (2) absence of self-derogation: an interaction effect of self-disclosure with self-approval training ($F = 5.29$, $p < .05$); (3) need for approval: a main effect for self-approval training ($F = 5.12$, $p < .05$) and a main effect for social approval training ($F = 3.14$, $p < .10$).

Quinlan and Janis state-of-self-esteem inventory administered to all clients in the 5-week follow-up interview. On the scale dealing with general self-confidence about coping with all sorts of personal problems (row 1 of the table), the clients who had received the high self-disclosure interview expressed less self-confidence than those who had received the moderate self-confidence interview. (Across all conditions the main effect for self-disclosure approaches significance below the 10% level.) On the other scale of the self-esteem inventory (row 2 of the table), the results show that when either social approval training or no approval training was given, the clients who had received the high self-disclosure interview expressed more self-derogation ($p < .01$).

The above findings for self-esteem indicate that in the absence of self-approval training the high self-disclosure interview tended to have a consistently adverse influence on the clients' self-appraisals, disposing them to lose their self-confidence and to be more self-derogatory after they had left the intake interview and were trying to carry out the recommended diet. A probable explanation for this demoralization effect would be an unintended process akin to self-persuasion, resulting from the clients' verbalizing and becoming vividly aware of their own weaknesses and past failures during the initial self-disclosure interview.

Although the delayed loss-of-esteem hypothesis offers a promising basis for interpreting the weight loss data, it cannot be considered definitive. Because we did not obtain a measure of general self-esteem at the end of the initial interview (it was measured for the first time at the 5-week follow-up interview), there is no conclusive way in the present study of determining whether the lower self-esteem of the clients given the high disclosure interview was a cause or a consequence of their failure to lose weight during the 5-week period between the initial interview and the first follow-up interview.[7]

THE NINE-MONTH FOLLOW-UP STUDY

The primary hypothesis explored with respect to the newly developed self-approval training was that it would have positive effects on the clients' long-term internalization of the dieting recommendations. In order to test this hypothesis and to investigate the long-term effects of the other treatment conditions, we attempted to carry out a 9-month follow-up study. Unfortunately, despite repeated efforts to get clients to come in, the extremely high incidence of "no shows" at the 9-month follow-up session and the significantly different rates among the three approval training groups make it impossible to draw any definitive conclusions from the results for weight loss. We were unable to contact about 20% of each group. Of those we were able to contact, the percentages of "no shows" for the three training conditions were as follows: self-approval training, 25%; social approval training, 65%; no approval training, 48%. Despite the very small samples involved these differences are large enough to be statistically significant ($p < .05$). They suggest that when dieting clients receive self-approval training, which induces them to look forward to their own reactions of self-approval or self-disapproval depending on their success or failure in adhering to the diet, they are more likely to show up for a 9-month follow-up session. Note that the clients given social approval training behave differently. Only a small minority came in for their appointments, fewer than half as many as in the group given self-approval training ($p < .01$).

Despite the impossibility of drawing dependable conclusions for long-term weight loss because of differential self-selected sample losses, the weight loss means were examined. They are not at all encouraging. The clients who received self-approval training showed a slight long-term weight *gain* over their initial weight (an average gain of 1.25 pounds for the 15 clients who attended the 9-month follow-up session). In comparison the 11 clients from the no-approval-training group who showed up had succeeded in losing an average of 3.90 pounds. The small minority of 7 clients from the social approval training group who showed up had an average weight loss of 2.10 pounds.

The relatively low incidence of "no shows" among the clients who had received self-approval training takes on added meaning when we consider the implications of the fact that most of the ones who came in for the 9-month follow-up session turned out to have *gained* rather than lost weight. Evidently these clients were much less socially defensive about their failure than those who did not receive self-approval training. This interpretation fits in with the earlier finding (in Table 12.3) indicating that the clients who had received self-approval training were less self-protective than the others, as manifested by their significantly lower scores on need for social approval (assessed on the Marlowe–Crowne scale at the time of the 5-week follow-up session). The two findings in combination suggest that the self-approval training, although unsuccessful in facilitating weight loss, nevertheless was partially effective in shifting clients away from a defensive social approval orientation, characterized by manifestations of a strong need for self-protection against criticism from others.

Because of the high incidence of "no shows" at the 9-month follow-up session it was also impossible to draw any conclusions about the long-term effects of the high disclosure interview compared with the moderate disclosure interview on weight loss or about the interaction effect that was observed in the 5-week follow-up data. (Of the 38 original cases in the high disclosure group, only 18 came to the 9-month interview; of the 36 original cases in the moderate disclosure group, only 15 came.) The mean differences in weight loss between the high and moderate disclosure groups were small and nonsignificant. However, we did note some significant long-term effects of self-disclosure on attitudes in the data obtained from a brief questionnaire given at the end of the 9-month follow-up session. In the questionnaire all clients were asked to rank order several common incentives for their importance in determining their own daily activities. The results show that clients who had been given the high disclosure interview gave significanty higher rankings than the clients who had been given the moderate disclosure interview when they were judging the importance of *social approval of others* as determinants of their daily activities ($p < .02$) and of their dietary activities in particular ($p < .01$). The clients given the high disclosure interview ranked concern about their physical health as a less important determinant of their eating activity ($p < .01$) than did clients given the moderate disclosure interview. Although findings from such questionnaire items cannot be considered conclusive evidence of differences in motivation, they suggest that clients given the high disclosure interview may have been induced to become more externally controlled in their behavior by the social approval of others, and less internally controlled by their assessment of threats to their physical health that are associated with overeating. This interpretation of the questionnaire findings is consistent with the hypothesis that when counselors use a high disclosure intake interview, their clients tend to become more dependent and subsequently attribute their attempts to comply with the counselors' recommendations to external social pressure rather than to their own motives.

MAIN CONCLUSIONS

1. In agreement with the findings reported by Quinlan and Janis (chap. 11), we found that, under conditions where no approval training was given, the use of a high self-disclosure intake interview, designed to induce clients to reveal a great deal about the negative aspects of their personality and past behavior, resulted in less weight loss over a 5-week period than the use of an intake interview designed to induce a moderate degree of self-disclosure.

2. A new psychodramatic procedure that we developed to provide clients with positive expectations and reminders that the supportive counselor would give further approval for adhering to the diet recommendations (*social* approval training) modified the strong negative effects of the high disclosure interview. A significant interaction effect was found indicating that although the high disclosure interview, compared with the moderate disclosure interview, had an unfavorable effect on adherence to the counselor's dieting recommendations when no approval training was given, it had a relatively favorable effect when social approval training was given. These results suggest that the negative effects of a high disclosure interview that encourages clients to disclose negative aspects of the self can be reduced when the counselor uses the social approval training procedure. Another new psychodramatic technique designed to orient clients toward *self*-approval rather than social approval did *not* significantly modify the effects of the high disclosure interview or have any other significant effect on adherence at the time of the 5-week follow-up session.

3. Questionnaire results indicate—if we take them at face value—that the adverse effects of the high disclosure interview on behavioral adherence (under conditions where no approval training is given) cannot be explained in terms of either resentment toward the counselor or an *immediate* loss of

self-confidence about being able to diet successfully. Rather, the results suggest that the mediating attitude change that accounts for the negative effects of the high disclosure interview on weight loss may be a *delayed* loss of self-esteem that becomes manifest only after the clients have tried to diet for several weeks, perhaps making its first appearance when hardships and setbacks are first encountered at home. This explanation, however, is highly tentative because there is no way of determining whether the delayed change in self-esteem ratings observed 5 weeks after the initial session were a cause or an effect of weight loss.

4. In this study we also investigated the hypothesis that the self-approval training procedure would have a positive long-term effect on internalization of the diet recommendations, as measured by weight loss and by attendance at a 9-month follow-up interview. The clients who had received the self-approval training were more conscientious about attending the 9-month follow-up session than the clients who had received social approval training or no approval training. The different rates for "no shows" among the approval training conditions make it impossible to draw any definitive conclusions about the long-term effects on weight loss obtained 9 months after the initial session, but the results for those who did return are in the opposite direction from what would be expected if the self-approval training were successful in increasing long-term adherence to the counselor's recommendations about avoiding overeating.

NOTES

1. The interviewer was blind to the self-disclosure treatment of each client until the time came for the interview, and remained blind to the subsequent approval training treatment until the time came to administer it. These blinding procedures, together with use of tape recordings of the interviewer's recommendations, were used in order to minimize possible experimenter biasing effects.

2. The high disclosure and moderate disclosure interviews in the present study were not the same as the ones used in the field experiment by Quinlan and Janis (chap. 11), so that the comparison of the effects of the two self-disclosure interviews constitutes a conceptual replication rather than an exact replication of the Quinlan and Janis experiment. As in the preceding studies on level of disclosure, the two self-disclosure interviews were carefully pretested and successive versions were modified in order to make sure that they elicited different amounts of intimate self-disclosure.

3. For the first *social* approval training exercise (failure to stick to the diet) the following instructions were given orally by the counselor:

"How would you feel about having to let the psychologist and clinic staff know about your not having had the self-control to follow the rules and to make your diet a success during the first four weeks? . . . When you think about *the thoughts and feelings the psychologist and clinic staff would have about* your not having stuck to your diet, you realize that you wouldn't feel proud of yourself. Try to say a few words out loud explaining how you would feel because of *the thoughts and feelings the psychologists and clinic staff would have about you and* your failure. Just try to say how that would make you feel, and why you would feel that way."

For the *self*-approval training exercises, the same instructions were given except that the phrases in italics were omitted. The second approval training exercise (success in sticking to the diet) used the same basic instructions except that negative terms were replaced by positive ones (e.g., instead of "you realize that you wouldn't feel proud of yourself," the positive version asserted, "you realize that you probably would feel very proud of yourself").

In order to reinforce the approval training exercises, the clients were given slightly different homework assignments in connection with the daily reports on dieting that every client was asked to prepare each day for the first 2 weeks of dieting. Clients who had received *social* approval training were asked to answer the following question after reporting on whether they had adhered to each of the three rules of dieting on that day: "When you think about *how the psychologist and clinic staff will feel about you because of* the self-control you have shown today, does this make you feel genuinely proud or not?" For those who had received the *self*-approval training, the question had the same form but omitted the phrase in italics (which was not italicized on the printed form given to the clients). Clients in the control condition were asked only to think about each rule and to place check marks in the appropriate box to show whether they had followed each of the rules. Envelopes were provided for mailing the daily reports to the clinic at the end of the first and second weeks of dieting.

Separate forms were used for the weekly progress reports, which each client was asked to mail back for 4 weeks. The client was instructed to fill out these forms at the end of each week and was asked to write a few sentences about how well she had followed the diet rules for that week. For those who had received the *social* approval training, the sentences were to focus on how proud and satisfied vs. ashamed and dissatisfied "you felt *when you consider the thoughts and feelings the psychologist and clinic staff would have* about your success or failure in carrying out the dieting decision." For those who had received the *self*-approval training, the same instructions were used except that the phrase in italics (about considering the reactions of the counselor or clinic staff) was omitted; the sentences therefore focused entirely on the client's feelings of pride vs. shame and self-satisfaction vs. self-dissatisfaction. For those in the *control* condition each client was simply asked to write a few sentences on how well she had followed the dieting rules.

4. Clients who did not return for the follow-up interview were scored as zero weight loss. As in the preceding studies, the assumption that they had not lost weight was borne out by those "no shows" who reported their weight to the interviewer during telephone calls.

The difference between the high and moderate disclosure groups within the control (no approval training) condition was tested for significance in two ways: a simple t-test for the two groups and a planned comparison using the error term from the overall analysis of variance based on the results for all treatment conditions. Both t-tests showed that the difference in mean weight loss was significant beyond the .05 level.

5. Attitude toward the counselor was assessed by using a composite measure, derived from a factor analysis, based on the following five items:

1. "At this moment, how much do you like the psychologist as a person?"
2. "How much do you respect the psychologist?"
3. "How much do you think the psychologist likes you?"
4. "How much do you think the psychologist respects you?"
5. "Do you feel the psychologist is really sympathetic and understanding of the problems you have been talking about?"

Each of the items had a 5-point scale (ranging from –2 to +2). The higher the composite scores, the greater the liking.

6. Self-confidence about ability to diet successfully was assessed by a composite measure, derived from a factor analysis, based on the following items:

1. "At this time, do you feel more able or less able to control your eating behavior—i.e., to stick to your diet and lose weight?"
2. "Do you feel more sure or less sure now than you did before the interview that you will stick to the diet and lose weight?"
3. "Right now, do you feel more critical of yourself or less critical of yourself?"

Each of the items had a 5-point scale (ranging from –2 to +2). The higher the composite score, the higher the client's level of self-confidence.

The results in Table 12.2 provide some incidental findings indicating that self-approval training had a discernibly unfavorable effect on the client's immediate self-attitudes, even though it did not have a main effect on weight loss at the time of the 5-week follow-up session. In Table 12.2 there is a significant main effect for self-approval training on self-confidence pertaining to the diet ($p < .05$), which indicates that this form of approval training unexpectedly lowered the client's self-confidence at the end of the initial session. But this immediate effect may have dissipated once the clients went home and started on their diet; no difference in weight loss or in self-confidence pertaining to the diet was found at the time of the 5-week session.

On the Marlowe–Crowne scale used to assess need for approval (see Table 12.3) there is a significant main effect ($p < .05$), indicating that 5 weeks later the clients who had been given the self-approval training, compared with the clients who were given no approval training, showed less tendency to be self-protective in order to prevent social disapproval. This appears to be a positive effect of the self-approval training procedure.

7. Another reason for being cautious about accepting the delayed loss-of-esteem hypothesis is that the self-esteem results (Table 12.3) do not show exactly the same interaction pattern as those for weight loss (Table 12.1). In particular the data on delayed loss of self-esteem in Table 12.3 cannot account for the moderating effects of social approval training shown by the weight loss data in Table 12.1: The clients who received social approval training show exactly the same pattern on both self-esteem measures as those who received no approval training, the level of self-esteem being lower for those who had been given the high self-disclosure interview.

Some of the questionnaire results can be used to assess another type of explanation that might account for the observed detrimental effects of the high disclosure interview. As a result of revealing many different personal shortcomings, the counselor's standard acceptance statements might have the unintended effect on the clients of creating self-satisfaction or very high confidence about obtaining the counselor's continued acceptance, which would reduce the incentive to live up to the norms endorsed by the counselor, such as the dieting rules. But the results in Tables 12.2 and 12.3 do not bear out any such explanation.

13 What Disclosing Means to the Client: Comparative Case Studies

IRVING L. JANIS AND DONALD M. QUINLAN

This chapter presents observations made in the Yale Weight-Reduction Clinic from a small series of intensive case studies that focus on the psychological reactions evoked in clients who were given a high self-disclosure interview. Their changes in attitude toward the counselor, self-evaluations, and expectations about the difficulties of the task of dieting are compared with those observed in a comparable small group of clients who were given a moderate self-disclosure interview.

The preceding two chapters have offered evidence of detrimental effects resulting when counselors ask questions designed to induce a high degree of self-disclosure from their clients. But the measures of state of self-esteem and various attitude changes obtained from the questionnaires are very crude indicators of mediating processes and sometimes turn out to be inconsistent or of dubious validity. People often give distorted answers that they believe to be socially desirable instead of genuine answers that indicate how they really feel. Obviously, more intensive and more sensitive assessments are needed.

METHODS AND PROCEDURES

This study was carried out as a small-scale controlled experiment with 18 women who came to the Yale Weight-Reduction Clinic for help in starting on a diet. They came in response to the same standard announcement in the local daily newspaper that we had used in the prior studies. Clients were assigned on a random basis to either of two treatment conditions. One was a *high* self-disclosure interview, during which the counselor asked questions about personal problems that might be linked with being overweight, including feelings of loneliness and depression, sources of anxiety, dissatisfaction with physical appearance, and effects of being overweight on the client's relationships with men and on her sex life. The other was a relatively *moderate* self-disclosure interview that concentrated on the client's past history of weight gains and weight losses, food preferences, daily life activities, temptations, and other circumstances linked with overeating. Equal numbers of high and moderate self-disclosure interviews were conducted

217

by two well-trained female counselors, both of whom had served as counselors in our earlier field experiments. During the first hour of the session, which was conducted as a face-to-face interview, the procedures were identical to those used in the original Quinlan and Janis field experiment (chap. 11), including the same high versus moderate interview questions, the same pre- and postinterview questionnaires, and the same standard dieting recommendations. Then the same interviewer carried out a process interview, a new procedure, unique to the present study. It was used with all clients in both the high and moderate disclosure groups. The process interview consisted of 25 questions, which took about one additional hour for each client to answer. The questions asked the clients to describe in detail their feelings during the preceding self-disclosure interview, their current mood, and their attitude with regard to succeeding on the diet.[1]

A follow-up session conducted about 1 month later included weighing the client and conducting a brief face-to-face interview about the client's experience on the diet and her outlook for the future. The counselor concluded the follow-up session by giving some specific recommendations about a maintenance diet after achieving the desired amount of weight loss and then repeating essentially what was said at the end of the first session about being optimistic and the importance of motivation.

The process interviews were tape-recorded (with each client's permission) and were typed up verbatim for purposes of blind analysis of the answers. Records of each client's success in losing weight were kept from the weekly progress reports and from the actual weighing at the 4-week follow-up session. However, we treat the follow-up measures as incidental observations of dubious validity because of the highly reactive character of the process interview. (Internal evidence from the process interview, as will be seen, tells us something about the way in which that interview itself changed the clients' psychological state from what it would have been if the process interview had not been given.)

The main results of this study pertain to the immediate effects of high versus low disclosure on self-confidence and attitudes toward the counselor, for which data were obtained from a blind analysis of the process interview protocols. After presenting some quantitative results, we shall devote the remainder of this chapter to comparative case studies that attempt to arrive at a coherent clinical picture of qualitative differences in the reactions of clients to the high and low disclosure interviews. The qualitative analysis is based on inferences from direct verbal reports of manifest attitudes and from indirect verbal and behavioral indicators of latent attitudes.

RESULTS AND DISCUSSION

Quantitative Comparisons

Amount of Self-disclosure Actually Elicited
Blind ratings were made of each client's interview responses in terms of

how much self-disclosure was actually elicited. A 5-point scale was used ranging from very low to very high. As expected, the ratings indicate that the level of actual disclosure elicited from the majority of clients who were given the high disclosure questions was much higher than that elicited from the majority of those who were given the moderate disclosure questions. In the moderate disclosure condition 1 client was rated "fairly low," 6 were rated "moderate," 2 "fairly high," and none "very high." In the high disclosure conditions, 6 were rated as "very high," 1 as "fairly high," and 2 "moderate." Thus, according to the blind ratings, 6 of the 9 clients (67%) who were given the high disclosure questions revealed more personal material than any of the clients who were given the low disclosure questions. Although the high disclosure interview did not induce a *uniformly* high level of self-disclosure among the 9 clients, it did, nevertheless, induce a *markedly higher level on the average* than did the moderate disclosure interview, just as in the preceding studies.

Self-confidence and Attitudes Expressed in the Process Interview
When we coded answers to specific questions on the process interview, we removed code numbers identifying the client and the type of interview she had received so that it was a *blind* analysis with regard to both: (a) whether the client had been given a high or low disclosure interview and (b) whether the client was successful in losing weight during the 4-week follow-up period.[2] Clients who had been given the high self-disclosure interview responded significantly differently from those who had been given the moderate self-disclosure interview on questions dealing with self-confidence about dieting successfully. One question, which asked whether the client thought that the counselor's optimism was realistic, drew partially or wholly negative replies from 7 clients, 6 of whom turned out to be in the high self-disclosure group. The difference (67% vs. 11%) is statistically significant beyond the 5% confidence level. Sizable differences in the same direction were found on the other two questions dealing with self-confidence, but the differences were not large enough to approach statistical significance for the small number of cases in the two groups.

When we consider answers to all the relevant questions about self-confidence combined (including the initial open-ended question), a significant difference again is found. Seven out of the 9 clients (78%) who had been given the high self-disclosure interview expressed some degree of doubt or uncertainty about being able to diet successfully compared with only 2 of the clients (22%) who had been given the moderate self-disclosure interview ($p < .05$).

Further, we find that on almost all questions throughout the process interview, clients in the moderate self-disclosure group express more favorable attitudes than those in the high disclosure group—asserting that the interview was helpful, that their mood was improved by the interview, that there was nothing about it that they disliked or that made them feel uncomfortable, that they do not feel dissatisfied in any way or disappointed in the counselor, that they feel encouraged rather than discouraged by the interview, and that they are "raring to go." Although none of the differences on individual items was large enough to be statistically significant, an overall significant difference ($p < .05$) was found on a combined measure: In the moderate self-disclosure group, 6 of the clients (67%) gave explicitly favorable answers to all the relevant questions, whereas only 1 (11%) in the high self-disclosure group did.

In summary the blind analysis of the process interviews reveals that the high self-disclosure interview had the immediate effect of producing *less* self-confidence and *less* favorable attitudes concerning the interview than the moderate self-disclosure interview.

Questionnaire Responses

In general almost all clients in both the high and moderate self-disclosure groups gave consistently favorable answers to the objective questionnaires that they filled out immediately after the initial interview, before the process interview. On the four questions dealing with self-confidence and motivation with respect to losing weight, only one client (who was in the high disclosure group) reported feeling *less* confidence as a result of the interview. The same client and two others (also in the high disclosure group) were the only ones who answered that they felt guiltier about past actions or that they felt more depressed than before the interview started. None of the differences on those questionnaire items (or any combination of them) is large enough to approach statistical significance. In answering the questions about impressions of the counselors, reactions to the interview, and feelings of self-esteem, almost all clients in both groups also gave uniformly favorable ratings throughout the questionnaires.

Thus, in contrast to the significant differences obtained from the process interviews, no significant or near significant differences were found in the self-report measures obtained from the questionnaires. If we had to rely entirely on the quantitative results from the questionnaires, as we did in the previously reported field experiments, we would have to conclude that high compared with moderate self-disclosure had no significant effect on self-confidence or any other attitudes. Practically all clients in both groups answered the questionnaires predominantly with socially desirable responses. (If you wanted to be polite to a counselor who has devoted some time to your troubles, it is most likely you would say that you like the interviewer, that the session was helpful, that you will try hard to succeed, and the like.)

We picked up the same tendency to say the polite thing in the process interviews, except that the clients would sometimes go on to elaborate or to make side comments that furnish the investigator with many additional indicators of whether this socially desirable response really is the client's attitude. In responding to the interview questions pertaining to self-confidence, for example, most of the clients who gave unfavorable responses started off their answers with a politely favorable sentiment, followed by a qualification: e.g., "I feel quite confident, *but*. . . ." It was from those qualifications that the significant differences were obtained in the blind analysis of the process interviews. The objective questionnaires, however, do not allow for such qualifications and therefore the client's check marks are likely to be more limited to conventional, socially desirable answers. In short, it seems probable that objective questionnaires are very crude measuring instruments of reactions to a counseling session, especially when the counselor is collecting the data, because they provide little opportunity for giving anything other than conventionally polite answers in response to the demand characteristics of the situation.

The findings from the process interviews have supported our emphasis on using objective behavioral criteria supplemented by open-ended interview questions to evaluate treatment effects rather than relying on verbal reports obtained from questionnaires. They reinforce our wariness about using self-report measures obtained from checklists for anything more than obtaining suggestive indications of possible mediating processes when signficant differences on objective behavioral measures have already been found. The process interviews, when compared with the questionnaire responses, show how unreliable and misleading unprobed self-report data can be for testing hypotheses.

Weight Loss
At the time of the follow-up session, conducted 4 weeks after the initial interview, the clients who had been given the moderate self-disclosure interview lost slightly more weight than those who had been given the high self-disclosure interview, but the difference is not large enough to be statistically significant. The mean weight loss for the two groups was 3.8 and 3.6 pounds, respectively. The amount of weight loss for both groups combined is of the same order of magnitude as in the original Quinlan and Janis study. But in that study, which involved almost twice as many cases in each group, the moderate disclosure group was found to have lost significantly more weight than the high disclosure group.

The absence of a significant difference in the present study may be attributable to the reactive effects of the process interview. There are some indications of a reactive leveling effect resulting from the process interviews which could reduce the differential behavioral effects of the high versus moderate disclosure interviews. We shall mention these indications from time to time in our qualitative analysis of the process interviews, to which the rest of this chapter is devoted.

Qualitative Analyses

Case Studies of Clients' Reactions to
the High Self-Disclosure Interview
We have seen that the quantitative results obtained from the process interviews indicate that clients given the high self-disclosure interview expressed

less self-confidence and less favorable attitudes about the session in general than those given the moderate self-disclosure interview. Those are the most obvious differences, which were detected by a blind analysis of the interview protocols. But a "sighted" analysis involving careful scrutiny of the interviews suggests, in addition, a number of less obvious qualitative differences. It is worthwhile to look over the process interviews in the context of all the other clinical observations and objective data available for each client, in order to discern subtler differences.

Admittedly, the qualitative case study evidence does not have the same status as evidence from a blind analysis of the results of a controlled field experiment. But it does provide some suggestive leads that fit in with and help to illuminate the prior quantitative findings on the detrimental effects of inducing high disclosure in the initial counseling interview, some of which are puzzling. The most unsuccessful cases with regard to losing weight will be examined first in some detail to try to discover what "went wrong"; then the comparative material concerning successful cases will be briefly summarized. In the summaries, we have mainly excerpted material relevant to the positive and negative reactions of the clients. The actual interviews did not have the sustained intensity of emotion conveyed by the condensed presentation of selected excerpts that are the product of our careful search for signs of positive or negative feelings. In fact, much of the time the interviews were quite neutral in tone, with only occasional expressions of strong affect.

Unsuccessful Cases

Case H-1. This married woman was in her early fifties and had not graduated from high school. She wanted to lose 25 pounds, but during the 4 weeks after the initial session she reported that she did not adhere to the diet at all and she failed to lose any weight.

At the outset of the initial interview she said, "You people do a lot of good." She added that she had a lot of respect for this Yale clinic because 5 years earlier she had come to a clinic at Yale for heavy smokers [actually as part of one of our earlier research studies] which helped her to cut down permanently from three packs of cigarettes a day to none at all. In the initial high self-disclosure interview she spoke freely about how unattractive she looks and about her concern that her sex life will deteriorate because she will not be able to keep a man interested in her. She revealed that her marriage is breaking up. She has been angry with her husband ever since they quarreled about her having an abortion. Every day, she said, he humiliates her and he constantly gets at her through their children. She would leave him if it were not for the children. She also revealed that she now has a boyfriend with whom she would like to run away. The counselor responded to each of these disclosures in a warm, accepting manner, in accordance with the standard procedure of consistently expressing positive regard, which was conscientiously followed by the counselors in all interviews in this study.

On the postinterview questionnaire this woman gave consistently favorable answers. According to her check marks, the interview made her feel better. She now feels less discouraged, more willing to diet, more able to control her eating behavior, and more confident that she will succeed in losing weight; she likes and respects the counselor and wants very much to talk to her again in a month; she believes that the counselor likes her, respects her, really wants her to succeed, and really cares what happens to her.

Quite a different picture emerges, however, from the process interview carried out immediately after this woman completed the questionnaire. She starts off many of her answers with conventionally polite compliments to the counselor (in agreement with her very positive answers to the questionnaire), but then she goes on to describe in much more vivid language the unfavorable feelings engendered by the interview. Here are several examples:

"[The interview] makes you step back and take a closer look at yourself and I think that can be helpful . . . *but* I'm unmerciful [to myself] at times.

I feel more confident right now than when I came in . . . [*but*] I don't know if I'm motivated enough to really get into this as I should.

I feel a lot happier right at the moment than I was [before the interview]. . . . I know it's all up to me *but* maybe I can do it [stick to the diet] if I really want to. It seems that it gets harder all the time; old age has a way of creeping up. . . .

[During the interview my mood was] apprehension and depression because I felt, 'Rats, I won't succeed. Do I really want to do this?' . . . I'm not sure and that's the truth."

In addition to expressing great conflict about undertaking a rigorous diet and strong doubts about having what it takes to succeed at it, she asserted that the interview generated other self-derogatory thoughts as well. This was most apparent in her response to the following question about feelings of discouragement. "A few women who have been here told me that they felt a bit discouraged or felt dissatisfied with themselves after the interview. Do you have any feelings like that?" Her answer was: "Yes, when I look back over this past year especially, I am much disappointed . . . with myself. . . . That came out very strongly at one point; I guess that's why I was close to tears."

Along with clear-cut signs of self-derogation and acute decisional conflict about the diet, there were numerous subtle manifestations of conflict about entering into an affectionate relationship with the counselor. Both the positive and negative components of her ambivalence appeared to be related to what she had revealed about herself during the high self-disclosure interview. On the positive side, she said at the beginning of the process interview: "I felt easy with you, which is good. Maybe that's why it all came out." Later on in the interview she added a comment about the counselor's consistent acceptance of her disclosures of personal weaknesses: "Well, you haven't stomped on me or hassled me at all. I like that! You've got a soft sell, I like that! . . . You're not trying to cram it down my throat and in the end everybody has got to decide for themselves."

But on the negative side, she also displays feelings of dissatisfaction because she wants more directive guidance from the counselor than she is getting, to help her with all her personal problems in addition to the problem of losing weight:

"I would have wished that you would have told me better how to cope with what's happening to me in all aspects that I mentioned. I would like it if you gave your impressions of . . . my problems. Well, I mean, what you would do in similar circumstances, or something. I don't know what I mean. . . . I wish you'd be more responsive in that area, whatever I brought up. . . . I guess you always hope someone else can help you cope."

The client went on to ask explicitly for more directive advice about how to deal with her marriage and her extramarital affairs. These requests were accompanied by implicit assertions of considerable uneasiness about the possibility of being badly hurt from becoming too affectionate and too dependent upon the counselor. She spoke about having had "few close women friends in my life," then added:

"I'm more upset than I thought. It just kind of popped out, I'm really quite astonished about that. Sometimes people are too kind and that hurts more. You can bear it more if they are unkind, you can cut them yourself. But if they are maybe too pleasant and kind when you are vulnerable, then, oh I don't know. It's easier to let things out and be hurt, I mean, or feel the hurt, I guess, I don't know. Am I making any sense at all? . . . Maybe you're as vulnerable as me, deep down."

The client's implicit reference to being "cut" by the counselor was not the only danger to which she alluded. Elsewhere during the process interview she asserted that although she was "prepared to bare my soul" to the counselor, she worried that doing so was making the counselor "uncomfortable" and she wondered if the counselor "can understand anything like that." Then she went on to say: "I don't know how to put it; I hoped you didn't have a big mouth anyway." After being reassured that everything she said is confidential and is kept within the clinic, the client responded:

"Yes, but people are only human . . . and sometimes I've been hurt by people I have trusted, quite often. I'm very gullible . . . I tend to always feel that people are better than they are or that they will do their best because that's what I do. But not everybody else does. You find out the hard way. . . . [During the interview] I had the fleeting thought, 'Oh fooey, here I am letting my soul hang out and what's she going to do with it? Maybe I made a mistake?' "

While talking about her sense of vulnerability from having revealed so much about herself, she asked with some urgency, "How *do* you feel about me?" "But how are you judging me?" After being reassured that the counselor felt that she understood her and thought that her problems could be solved, the client came out with the statement about being disappointed in herself, which made her close to tears.

One of the outstanding features, then, of this client's process interview is the repeated manifestations of ambivalence toward the counselor to whom she had "bared her soul," with some indications that she fears being hurt from allowing herself to become too affectionate and too trusting. Another key feature is her explicit expression of doubts about being able to succeed at the task of dieting along with feelings of depression and self-derogation, which contrasts sharply with her extremely positive assertions on the objective questionnaire she had filled out just before the process interview. During the process interview she said that she doubted that filling out the questionnaires was going to help her personally but she had no objections to helping out the counselor by doing what she was asked. This manifest attitude of polite compliance fits in with the fact that in answering the questionnaire items she uniformly gave socially desirable answers, always praising the counselor and the interview.

In the weekly reports she mailed in and again in the follow-up interview the client reported that she had started off dieting for a few days but soon went back to her usual eating habits. When she stepped on the scale at the 4-week follow-up session it became apparent that she had not lost even 1 pound. She claimed that she failed primarily because she had to be out of town, visiting at her father's home, where her stepmother "sabotaged" her diet. What she said about the sabotage, however, sounded very much like an excuse or a rationalization because it would account for only a few hidden calories—her stepmother secretly sprinkled a little sugar on the grapefruit before breakfast and denied doing so.

Signs of ambivalence toward the counselor were again present during the 4-week follow-up interview. On the positive side the client answered the question about what she remembered of the interview that took place a month earlier by stating that she really likes the counselor and then giving a glowing account of how wonderfully sympathetic, empathic, and receptive the counselor is. Throughout the follow-up interview the client seemed to be trying to reinstate that type of warm, accepting relationship by wandering off the subject, talking about a number of personal troubles, which required the counselor to bring her back to the specific issues of dieting. The client reported, however, that during the month since the initial session she never even once thought about the counselor or anything the counselor had said. Only vague, dim memories remained of the earlier session with the counselor: "It seems like I saw you six months ago instead of just a few weeks ago."

The client's attitudes and behavior in the follow-up interview consistently suggest that she had adopted a coping pattern of defensive avoidance: not thinking about the counselor or any of the counselor's specific recommendations about dieting. One gets the impression that she overreacted to her fear of being hurt from becoming too affectionately involved with the counselor, which was repeatedly expressed in the process interview at the end of the initial session, by suppressing memories and thoughts about the initial counseling session.

Case H-2. This 55-year-old woman had a high school education and was working full time as the secretary of a high-level executive. She wanted to lose 25 pounds. Despite several phone calls from the counselor, she refused to return for a follow-up interview, indicating that she had failed to lose weight and would find it "too upsetting" to be interviewed again.

In the high self-disclosure interview during the initial session the client frequently spoke about self-derogatory feelings and events: she "looks bloated and unsightly," she has "lost her pride," her husband calls her "fatty." She elaborated on her husband's rejection of her, her feelings of depression, and the boredom of her home life. She also admitted that her being overweight had adversely affected her sexual responsiveness. While disclosing the painful details she wept.

On the objective questionnaire, like the first case, she gave predominantly favorable responses, asserting that she now felt more confident, more satisfied with herself, less guilty, and less discouraged. She also asserted that she likes and respects the counselor very much. The only clue to a negative reaction was her answer to one question on the Quinlan-Janis state of self-esteem scale—she reported feeling *more ashamed* right now—but her overall self-esteem score was very high.

Again like the first case, this client's answers during the process interview were completely different from those given on the questionnaire. She made a number of polite references to how helpful the interview was (e.g., "It made me realize I have got to do something about it [being overweight]"), but she expressed massive doubts about succeeding—maybe at her age a woman is "just automatically going to put on weight and nothing you do will help"; besides, she had undergone a hysterectomy and everyone tells her, "Oh, then you don't have a hope in Hell; you're going to be fat." She also admitted that the interview had made her more worried because she had been hoping that this clinic would give her a "quick, easier way" of losing weight. And the interview had upset her: she had not expected so many questions, she had cried during the interview, and now she was feeling "annoyed at myself for having cried."

Ambivalent feelings toward the counselor were clearly manifested in her answer to a question about whether at any time she had felt dissatisfied with what was going on during the interview: "No," she responded. "I think you're marvelous to do this," but it must be a "monotonous job," because like doctors and dentists, you have to deal with "all the ugly things." She added that the counselor must despise her as "a fat old thing." When asked if she really thinks that is so, she responded, "Well, I wouldn't blame you if you thought that."

The feelings of shame about having revealed her ugly self to the counselor were also linked with her allegedly positive motivation to succeed on the diet ("I'll be very ashamed if I don't [succeed]") and presumably made its reappearance when she refused to come back for the follow-up session on the grounds that it would be too upsetting. One receives the impression that the painfulness of the initial interview, including the feelings of shame and frustrated longings for the affection of the helper, reduced the effectiveness of the helping relationship. The client presumably did not have a sufficiently positive image of the relationship, despite the counselor's consistent acceptance of all the "ugly things" revealed to her, to be motivated to comply with the helper's recommendations to stick with the low-calorie diet, to mail in weekly reports, or to return for the follow-up session.

Case H-3. This 30-year-old woman had a high school education and was working full time in a skilled trade. She wanted to lose 30 pounds. When the time came for the follow-up interview, she postponed coming back for 3 more weeks and when she returned her weight loss was only 2¾ pounds for the 7-week period (about 0.4 pounds per week, which is less than one-half the minimal criterion of 1 pound per week expected from adherence to the recommended diet). Another example of her lack of commitment to the diet recommended by the counselor was her report that she had just gone to a hospital clinic with the hope of obtaining plastic surgery to reduce the size of her thighs and buttocks but was told that first she should go on a diet.

The client had revealed a considerable amount of derogatory information about herself during the high self-disclosure interview. She described herself as lonely, lazy, and physically unattractive. She spoke a great deal about divorce and about breaking up with her most recent boyfriend. She said that she especially disliked the appearance of her thighs and buttocks and avoids displaying them by staying away from the beach and by insisting on total darkness whenever she engages in sexual intercourse.

Many of her statements in the process interview, like all her answers on the questionnaire, indicated a favorable reaction to the high self-disclosure interview. Nevertheless, as she elaborated on her feelings, she gave numerous indications of conflict and doubt. On the one hand, she said at the beginning of the process interview that the session gave her "a very good feeling about what's going to happen" and that she felt "very optimistic." On other hand, she also said that she was a bit disappointed that the counselor did not give her a completely new kind of diet that she had never seen before. She added that during the "very personal" interview she had the feeling that although her only trouble is her weight problem, the counselor was "trying to prove the opposite," to get her to admit that she feels "nervous" or "dissatisfied with myself as a person." She softened this criticism by asserting that "you didn't press the issue of—you know—when you're alone or unhappy do you eat. You asked it, but you went on to other things." She seemed to be saying that the counselor's asking such questions had a disturbing effect on her because she felt them to be accusations even though the counselor seemed to accept her answers without challenging any of them.

Despite her initial statement that she felt very optimistic about succeeding, her answers to later questions implied marked doubts. In response to the standard question about the counselor's optimism ("I'm very optimistic about your chances of succeeding on the diet. How *realistic* do you think my expectations are?"), she answered, "Well, I don't think they are really that realistic from your point of view." To the later direct question ("How confident do you feel about carrying out the diet?") she gave a manifestly positive response but qualified it by stating that the reason was that "now there is another person involved." She asserted that she feels she has "an obligation, not only to myself, but an obligation to other people for the time that they are investing in me for a program like this." This indirect way of referring to the counselor gives one the impression that she may have had mixed feelings about the "obligation."

When she was asked about her impressions of how helpful the interview might be, her answers again implied that she had mixed feelings but was unable to acknowledge them. She said that "there was nothing about it that unnerved me," that she does not "feel as though I mind being asked certain things that maybe somebody [else] would have mixed feelings about." She continued to protest too much about not minding by asserting that she thinks she is open enough to "not think about it after and say, 'Oh, gee, I shouldn't have said that!'" One gets the impression that this is precisely what she was thinking.

In line with the other indirect indications of uneasiness in relation to the counselor, this client hedged when asked to state frankly, "What do you think is my opinion of you?" She said that she "would hope that the person I talk to" would get a good impression of her and would "like me as a person, as far as you could get to like someone in this type of thing."

One month later she reported that she had stayed on the diet for 1 week and then "went on a binge." After that it was on again, off again, especially when doughnuts were available. When asked whether "at any time did you recall or think about any of the things we had spoken about the last time you were here," her answer again suggested mixed feelings, even more clearly than during the process interview. She had recalled her sense of obligation to the counselor because of the great amount of time devoted to helping her but she also recalled being surprised about some of the questions, such as those about her mother and her sex life. Evidently the "surprise" she spoke about was difficult for her to get over and may have reduced her motivation to adhere to the counselor's recommendations. Her formulation in terms of an "obligation" to repay the counselor for her time also implies at least a mild degree of ambivalence that might be linked with latent resistance or reactance.

Case H-4. This 21-year-old woman had completed 1 year of college and was looking for a job as a secretary. She wanted to lose 25 pounds. Like case H-2, she failed to send in any weekly reports, refused to return for the follow-up interview, and indicated that she had not been successful in losing any weight.

Most of this client's answers during the initial high self-disclosure interview centered upon her relationship with her fiancé—she was worried

about their impending marraige; she felt self-conscious about being overweight; she recalled how lonely and rejected she had felt before becoming
engaged. She also spoke about being worried about finding a job and having
enough money to meet her minimal needs. On the questionnaire she gave
consistently positive answers. Unlike the other unsuccessful cases she gave
predominantly positive answers throughout the process interview and the
counselor judged her to be completely sincere. She asserted that she had felt
nervous and depressed before the session but felt much better as a result of
the interview and felt grateful to the counselor. She claimed to be extremely
confident about succeeding on the diet. There was only one hint of a negative reaction: She reported having felt "uncomfortable" when the counselor
started to get into "the really personal questions." She added, "I don't
usually go blurting everything out," and "I disclosed things that I never told
anybody else."

Because of her subsequent refusal to continue with the clinic's weight-
reduction program, there is no way of knowing why this client failed to
comply with even the most elementary of the counselor's recommendations. Perhaps she was dissimulating during the process interview, but this
seems unlikely because the counselor was impressed by the repeated signs
of emotional relief, gratitude, and optimism that were conveyed by her
facial expressions and gestures as well as by her words. Perhaps some outside event disrupted her dieting plans, but we have no information at all
about what happened after she left the initial session. If we take her statements at face value, she left in a good mood, "raring to go," but felt a little
uneasy about having disclosed a great deal of personal material that she had
never told anyone before. Did she have a "slow burn" reaction, with a
gradual buildup of negative feelings about the interview and the counselor
as she mulled over various sensitive things about herself she had "blurted
out?" Perhaps even a mild sense of uneasiness about having disclosed too
much immediately after a personal counseling session, despite having
received consistent acceptance responses from the counselor that evoke a
predominantly favorable attitude in the client, is an indicator of a latent
negative reaction that will subsequently become sufficiently intense to
disrupt the client's motivation to adhere to the counselor's recommendations.

Successful Cases
The following five cases in the high self-disclosure group, all of whom were
successful in losing 1 pound or more per week, will be discussed very briefly
in terms of their similarities to and differences from the four unsuccessful
cases. In general the successful cases show signs of the same type of immediate negative reactions to the high disclosure interview as the unsuccessful ones, but they also show signs of overcoming those reactions as a
result of the process interview. At the end of the latter interview several
clients explicitly stated that they felt much better for having talked over
their reactions. From what they said, it seems plausible to assume that if the

process interview had not taken place, these clients would have been left with doubts about their ability to succeed at dieting, a sense of having disclosed too much, and mixed feelings about their relationship with the counselor, which might have interfered with their motivation to adhere to the recommended diet.

Case H-5. This 49-year-old married woman, who worked full time as a teacher, wanted to lose 25 pounds. During the high self-disclosure interview she was noncommittal in her answers to questions about her relationship with her husband and others, but she disclosed self-disparaging feelings about her appearance, her lack of self-control, and her readiness to get angry with her family at the end of each day when she is tired out from her work. At the beginning of the process interview she complained that the session had not got her "all fired up" as she had hoped. The interview was not helpful, she asserted, and now she felt pessimistic about succeeding. She said very little about her image of the counselor, just enough to imply that she thinks she is regarded as just another routine case: "I assume you think that I am someone who wants to lose some weight . . . and I fill the bill as far as being a candidate, I guess."

About midway through the process interview, after describing her negative reactions to the preceding interview, she began to express a more hopeful outlook: "I can't say that I am disappointed because, who knows, I may go home and find this works fine." At the end of the process interview she acknowledged that "maybe getting someone else involved in it would help." After having said good-bye, she delayed leaving to state that she probably had felt discouraged because she had obtained the recommended diet from a friend about a week earlier but had not been able to stick to it. She added, "I probably shouldn't have tried it without talking to you first."

The changes in her attitude from the first half to the second half of the process interview raise the possibility that the process interview itself played a determining role in reversing her negative reactions to the initial high-disclosure interview. What she seemed to be saying just before leaving was that, in contrast to the way she had felt at the beginning of the process interview, she now regarded the session as having some potential value and she was ready to make a conscientious effort to succeed.

In any case she did in fact succeed in losing 6 pounds during the next 4 weeks. She reported at the follow-up session that she went off the diet temporarily several times but resumed dieting because she had agreed to send weekly reports to the counselor; otherwise, "I might not have gotten back on." She recalled that during the initial session she had been disappointed and pessimistic because "I had expected to get more support and more psyching up." Yet, when she got home she was surprised to find herself refusing to eat rich food that was not on the recommended diet. Thereafter, according to her account, on most days she followed almost all the rules of the diet recommended by the counselor. When she gave in to a temptation every few days, she promptly got back on the diet by thinking about her obligation to return her progress report each week to the counselor.

Case H-6. This 60-year-old woman, who works full time in a professional role, wanted to lose 20 pounds. Like the preceding five clients, she responded to the high disclosure interview by revealing more intimate personal material than was elicited from any of the clients who were given the moderate self-disclosure interview.

At the outset of the process interview she described the counselor as understanding, sympathetic, and the kind of person with whom she was able to achieve close rapport. She said that she had disclosed much personal information that she would not have revealed to anyone else under other circumstances and that the interview made her feel that she should try to control her appetite. But she added, "I'm not absolutely convinced of being able to do it" because "I feel like I need a big crutch." She elaborated on her qualms and weaknesses in the following way, indicating that the interview had generated self-derogatory thoughts, that she was far from being confident about succeeding, and that the counselor was not offering enough support in the form of regular contact:

> "Sometimes I think I'm not so worthwhile as I like to think I am. Because why should I have these few weaknesses? I judge myself hard. . . . [The interview] did make me think of these bad times I have had. . . . you were able to evoke these feelings and thoughts in me. . . . I was chastising myself about why do I have to come to you. . . . I feel fairly confident, not absolutely, totally confident and I think to myself, 'Why not?' And I suppose why not is because . . . I have failed before and yet I feel that I should really be able to do it. . . . Your whole attitude was very helpful, very supportive. . . . This was a good start and I would have hoped that I would have more reinforcement, perhaps along the way, within [this coming] month. . . . You see I have this [the weekly report sheets] which is a paper reinforcement. . . . But perhaps more personal contact reinforcement, I mean, I think for me it would be good, you know, to discuss in the middle [of the month] what problems I have or just to say some of the things on my mind, even if it's not a problem. I would have liked that."

As the process interview went on, this client continued to complain about insufficient contact with the counselor, for example, "I'm not dissatisfied with you in any way . . . [but] I would perhaps say I might be disappointed with the clinic [because] I would like it much better if I were able to have some contact in this period of a month and perhaps subsequent to that . . . I'm just reaching out for any help that I can get."[3] At the end of the process interview, however, she asserted that she would have to "face up" to her own problems and that success would depend "really and truly [on] my motivation." She said that the counselor had "given me support which I felt that I needed and I am even more reinforced in my motivation. . . . I have gotten a prod and I feel also that you would like me to do it and so I would like to do it partly to oblige you as well as me." Thus, in this client's process interview, as in the preceding case, there are clear-cut signs of attitude change in a favorable direction. In this case there is a remarkable transformation from pleading for more contact with the counselor to a sense of inner resolution to control her own behavior, partly to please the counselor and partly to satisfy her own needs.

In the weekly reports she mailed back during the next few weeks there were additional signs of a change in attitude away from extreme dependency on the counselor in the direction of relying more on a sense of personal responsibility. Having lost 3½ pounds after the first week, she reported: "What a good feeling to be disciplined and in the groove again! I have confidence and have mentally accepted the fact of the diet—and surprised to feel no hunger at all." When she found herself on a plateau during subsequent weeks, she wrote, "I determined to start anew, lose more, and look and feel great by [the next meeting]."

At the 4-week follow-up interview, after expressing gratification about her success in having lost the expected amount of 4 pounds in 4 weeks, she asked if she could continue sending in her weekly reports for another month or so, because doing so had been very helpful. She made it clear that she still felt dependent upon the counselor but was willing to accept the termination of their direct contact without complaint and to rely on her own resources for continuing on the diet. "Seeing you today," she said, "will give me a new lease, which I need to get off this plateau. . . . It's hard [to diet] but not *that* hard; it's all mental." She added that the initial session had been helpful because she had to "dredge up things I hadn't ever specifically thought of before . . . about how I felt toward myself, about being fat but also my good points which I sometimes forgot. I have to think well of myself to succeed and your questions helped me to achieve that balance."

This final comment suggests that her motivation to diet may have benefited from disclosing her *positive* feelings about her assets during the initial session (which occurred during the process interview, as she thought over and revised what she referred to as "the very 'harsh judgments'" she had just made of herself when she had talked about her weaknesses during the high self-disclosure interview).

Case H-7. This 28-year-old woman with one child was a full-time student in a community college. She said that she wanted to lose weight mainly because she was worried about setting a bad example for her daughter. Her goal was to lose 40 pounds.

During the high self-disclosure interview she revealed a fairly large amount of personal material but relatively little about her specific weaknesses or difficulties. She presented herself mostly in positive terms, as an attractive, intelligent, and helpful person, well satisfied with her marriage and with her way of life. Nevertheless, she did admit to overeating occasionally when concerned about family problems.

In the process interview this woman asserted that she was surprised by many questions that she had never thought about before, especially those dealing with her sex life. Although they were "basically all logical questions," she was perturbed about some of her answers because she found out that "I'm weaker than I thought I was." She said she always had been proud of herself but now she wonders "if I'm so strong, then how come I can't keep to a diet which I logically want?" She said that she would try to diet but was not sure about succeeding: "I wouldn't bet money on me, but I have been know to come up from behind in a pinch."

Although she said many positive things about the counselor, she nevertheless made a large number of minor complaints: the counselor gave poor directions for finding the building, she could have made a better recording of her voice on the taped instructions, she ought to learn shorthand to take interview notes more rapidly, the interview room is stark, and "I don't care for your interior decorator at all." She said she noticed that the counselor was following a standard interview procedure of being accepting, "as taught in psychology classes," but it "was done well." When asked what she thought the counselor's opinion of her was, she became evasive after first making a joke of it, as she had done in making most of her minor criticisms: "*I* think I'm fantastic, therefore *you* must think that I am fantastic. But I logically know you have your own mind . . . that's your business, it doesn't affect me." Toward the end of the interview her surface manner of detached objectivity and mild bantering changed momentarily to much more serious bantering, implying an unsatisfied wish for a closer or more reciprocal relationship. Here is what she said when asked whether she felt in any way dissatisfied with the interview: "I don't feel we know enough about each other. . . . I don't know a *thing* about you and I'm not about to ask *you* about *your* sexual life." Nevertheless, she immediately returned to her seemingly detached, objective style, with her usual emphasis on being "logical," when responding to the last few questions.

The client conscientiously mailed in all her weekly reports, which indicated that she delayed starting for a few days, then gradually got onto the diet and adhered to it almost every day. In her weekly written reports she mentioned that her husband was exerting a bad influence on her dieting and that she wished the counselor had given her a diet "that works magic overnight." But she also wrote that "no one can do this for me."

Upon returning for the follow-up interview she was pleased to see that she had lost more than 6 pounds according to the clinic scale. She thought that the weekly reports were so helpful that she would keep some kind of record for herself from now on. She said at first that she could not remember the initial interview a month earlier but then added, "I don't think I was that honest in my answers." She explained that she cares more about being overweight than she had reported and that she was concerned about the first impression she was creating. She explained that she always has the latter concern, but "after that I have confidence that I have enough personality to make friends." She also asserted that many features of the prior session had been helpful, including the counselor's statement that "the diet was not magical," which she reported having thought about during her daily periods of silent thought. Overall, in the follow-up interview she was less evasive and less detached than she had been earlier.

In this case the high self-disclosure interview during the initial session seems to have evoked considerable resistance, which took the form of evasiveness, frequent presentation of her social mask to the counselor rather than her "real self," and efforts to maintain a mildly critical, detached stance toward the counselor despite longing for a warmer, affectionate relationship. Perhaps her realization that she was being excessively defensive during the process interview, as the counselor consistently accepted one provocative complaint after another, contributed to her autonomous attitude ("No one can do this for me"), which seems to have contributed to her success in dieting.

Case H-8. This 40-year-old, upper middle-class housewife was a college graduate and had been trained as a nurse. She wanted to lose 45 pounds.

The total amount of self-disclosure elicited from this client by the questions in the high disclosure interview was rated as moderate; she gave relatively sparse or noncommittal answers to most of the questions that asked about intimate aspects of her personal life. Nevertheless, she revealed that she is sometimes a bit bored with her daily life at home, that she feels anxious about her husband's health, and that she wants to lose weight partly out of a sense of family duty because she feels that she owes it to her children to improve her appearance by being less overweight.

In the process interview the client continued to give mainly noncommittal, vague answers. She said that the interview had been more or less what she had expected from doing case histories herself when she had worked as a nurse. She added that it made her a little more aware of what she already knew. What will be helpful, she said, is "knowing that I'll be checked," which she referred to as "an extra crutch." At the end of the process interview she admitted for the first time to feeling a bit dissatisfied with herself for not having gone on a diet sooner. She also expressed, for the first time, strongly positive feelings toward the counselor, in contrast to her earlier coolly polite statements to the effect that in her opinion the counselor was simply carrying out her role adequately. She said that at home her husband does not care at all whether she is fat or thin, but from this session she now knows "really that somebody cares." These final remarks suggest that the process interview once again had a reactive effect, this time transforming the client's withdrawn, evasive stance into a more open, emotionally responsive relationship with the counselor.

In her weekly reports the client indicated that she followed the diet rigorously during the first week and lost over 6 pounds. After that she was not so conscientious and lost only 1 more pound in the next 3 weeks, which nevertheless resulted in a very substantial amount of weight loss (7 pounds) at the time of the 4-week follow-up interview.

The client reported that she had thought about the initial interview while carrying out the diet during the intervening weeks and that the weekly reports were helpful. She was very enthusiastic about having had the opportunity to talk over her problems with the counselor: "That helped more than anything else." She came away from the first session, she said, feeling that the counselor was offering her genuine help but that dieting was something she would have to do for herself.

In this case there is a paradoxical contrast between the client's evasive answers during most of the initial attempted high disclosure interview and her subsequent glowing account of how much she learned about herself from that interview. There is no way of knowing to what extent, if any, the client's success in dieting was attributable to that apparently constricted interview or to the subsequent process interview during which she opened up much more and revealed a sense of loneliness and a wish for an emotional attachment to the counselor. In any case it is impressive to note that here again we have a successful case who reports that among her sustaining thoughts while adhering to the diet were the feeling that she was able to cope better with the demands of the diet because of the relationship with the counselor along with the realization that coping was nevertheless her own responsibility.

Case H-9. This 56-year-old housewife, who had less than an eighth grade education, was working part-time in a routine clerical job. She wanted to lose 25 pounds. Like the preceding case, she revealed only a moderate amount about herself during the attempted high disclosure interview. She said that she never feels lonely, depressed, worried, or bored, that she loves everyone in her family dearly and has a very happy married life. Being overweight was her only problem, she said, and it worried her a little. She admitted that she would like to look better and to cut down on serious health risks.

In the process interview this client continued to deny having any unpleasant feelings and gave conventionally polite answers to all questions about her reactions to the high self-disclosure interview and to the counselor. She said she "didn't mind the interview at all" and realized that the counselor had to "get some kind of idea of the type of person I am." She thought the counselor would "like to see me lose weight because your job here is to encourage and it would be good for your program here." This implicit assertion that the counselor was not interested in her personally was the closest she ever got to expressing any complaint. At the end of the interview she said she felt encouraged and was going "to give it a good try." She then repeated a recurrent theme that she had emphasized throughout the process interview, namely, that she was going to adopt a day-by-day approach rather than allow herself to think about the entire month ahead.

According to the client's weekly reports, she stuck to the diet almost every day and steadily lost weight throughout the month (for a total of 6 pounds). On the last report she wrote that she had thought about the coming appointment with the counselor, and that when she cheated on the diet she was "mad at myself for doing so." This low-level concern about external surveillance by the counselor, combined with a strong sense of internal personal standards that should not be violated, was again manifested in the follow-up interview. She spoke about being "mad" at herself for breaking the diet by eating sweets because she was "worse than an alcoholic about sweets" and had made up her mind to stay away from them completely. She said that she had never thought about the initial interview.

Perhaps the most impressive feature of this case is that, like the preceding case, we have here another instance of a client who *failed* to reveal more than a moderate amount about herself during the attempted high disclosure interview and yet completely *succeeded* in getting off to an excellent start on the diet. In contrast, the four clients who revealed the most personal material about their troubles and weaknesses in response to the high disclosure interview turned out to have failed on the diet. We surmise from these observations that at least in the present clinical setting of short-term counseling on weight reduction—with only a single interview session and a single follow-up session 1 month later—the detrimental effects of the counselor's attempts to elicit high self-disclosure are avoided when the client does not fully open up and, instead, responds with only a moderate level of disclosure.

Reactions to the Moderate Disclosure Interview
For comparative purposes we shall summarize briefly the reactions of clients given the moderate self-disclosure interview, focusing on the similarities and differences between these clients and those given the high self-disclosure interview.

Unsuccessful Cases

M-1. This 39-year-old college graduate was a housewife with two children. She wanted to lose 40 pounds. The most outstanding feature of this client's responses to the moderate disclosure interview is that, in the course of answering relatively neutral questions about her eating habits and other daily activities, she managed to disclose a relatively large amount of unfavorable information about herself, although not quite so much as that obtained in six of the nine high self-disclosure interviews. For example, she revealed an ambivalent attitude about being overweight. On the one hand she said that she is content to be fat and her only reason for dieting is that people and especially the men she encounters have a bad opinion of her for letting herself go. On the other hand she referred to herself as a "compulsive eater" and spoke about lacking will power. She portrayed herself as an unorganized person who was uncertain about whether she wanted to make the effort to lose weight.

Like most of the high disclosure cases, the client complained during the process interview that the session may not have been helpful. She reported that she had felt defensive and apprehensive at the beginning of the interview. She added, "I was amazed that you sort of picked up the areas that I was having problems [with], such as I was snacking a lot." Like the majority of high disclosure cases, she also expressed some discontent about the counseling relationship. She asserted that she thought the counselor was helpful but "maybe I need a little more help than just one interview." At the end of the process interview she continued to complain, especially about the questionnaire, which she said made her feel that the counselor was merely conducting a psychological study rather than treating her as a person who had her own personal reasons for seeking help.

This client sent in no weekly reports and, when the time came for the 1-month follow-up, she delayed week after week coming in for her session. When she finally did arrive after 2 months, the scale showed that she had gained almost 4 pounds. In the follow-up interview she asserted once again that she did not mind being fat but that she would like to try dieting conscientiously if the counselor would be willing to see her again in 4 weeks.

Case M-2. This 30-year-old high school graduate was a housewife with three children. She wanted to lose 35 pounds. Like the preceding case, she revealed somewhat more than was expected about her personal troubles during the moderate disclosure interview. She spoke about her health problems, difficulties with her children, a hectic daily schedule, and her indulgence in alcoholic drinks every night, which she felt she needed and deserved. In the blind analysis of her responses the interview was rated as a "fairly high level of self-disclosure." That the client regarded it as such is revealed by her comments in the process interview. "I guess," she said, "by asking me all those questions is a good way for you to find out what my problems are. . . . [Now] you *know* me."

Like the unsuccessful cases in the high disclosure group, this client expressed a self-derogatory attitude without any sign of change in attitude at the end of the process interview. One of her last comments was "I feel a little dissatisfied with myself, like I said." She expressed confidence about succeeding but nevertheless said that she was not going to tell anyone else about her decision to diet because they would notice it if she got out of line, implying reluctance to be fully committed. On questions bearing on her relationship with the counselor, she was evasive and gave conventionally favorable responses.

This client's weekly reports indicate that she dieted successfully the first week and lost over 1 pound, but for the next 4 weeks she was partly on and partly off the diet. At the follow-up session it turned out that she had lost only 2¼ pounds in 5 weeks, which is less than half the expected amount of weight loss from the recommended diet. After her first successful week, according to her account, her motivation was not sustained and thereafter she was dieting halfheartedly. She said that she was disappointed and wanted to get back on the diet, "to put my whole self into it."

Case M-3. This 35-year-old married woman was a high school graduate who was working full time in a clerical job. In the moderate self-disclosure interview she revealed relatively little personal information, except that she reported feeling nervous and under pressure at times, which she thought was related to overeating. In the process interview her reactions were consistently favorable. She claimed to be optimistic, determined, and self-confident about achieving her dieting goal of losing 30 pounds.

This client's weekly reports indicate that she started off well, adhering to the diet sufficiently to lose 1½ pounds each week for 2 weeks. After that, however, she reports having become ill and then gaining back some of the weight she had lost. She delayed returning for the follow-up session for a month. Her weight loss was only 1½ pounds for the 8-week period. According to her account in the follow-up interview, her illness and the medication it required prevented her from continuing on the diet. She felt ready to start dieting again and felt more confident than ever because, from the 2 weeks of successful dieting, "I found I can say no to junk foods." Nothing she said was inconsistent with her explanation of why she failed to continue losing weight after having gotten off to a good start.

Successful Cases

Cases M-4, M-5, M-6, and M-7. These four clients were middle-aged housewives, ranging in age from 42 to 57. All four responded to the moderate self-disclosure interview by revealing a moderate amount of personal material about their eating problems and related aspects of their lives. One of them, for example, said that at times she has an uncontrollable urge to eat, like an addict. During the process interview all four described themselves as highly motivated and confident about dieting. And they all said that the session with the counselor was definitely beneficial. There were hardly any signs of conflict or ambivalence toward the counselor to undercut their favorable comments about the counselor's interest and about the value of "knowing that someone will be checking on me," as one of the women put it.

All four lost the expected amount of weight, an average of approximately 1 pound a week for the 4 weeks. In the follow-up interview these four clients were confident that they would be able to continue dieting successfully and expressed gratitude to the counselor. Each one said that sending the weekly monitoring reports to the counselor had been helpful but each also showed signs of having internalized the norms, rather than being primarily dependent on the counselor's approval or disapproval. "I can't stand to cheat on the diet," one of them asserted, "because I don't want to do it in front of my kids . . . and it makes me sick."

The last two clients in the moderate disclosure group displayed somewhat different reactions from the four other successful cases. We shall present these two cases in somewhat more detail because they suggest a constructive type of dependency on the counselor that seems to facilitate autonomous self-control.

Case M-8. This 38-year-old housewife was a college graduate who wanted to lose 25 pounds. As expected, during the moderate self-disclosure interview she revealed a moderate amount about her daily life and personal problems.

She felt "weighed down" and somewhat resentful about excessive house-hold duties, which she thought was related to her inability to control her eating behavior.

At the outset of the process interview she said she felt relieved that she had not been put under pressure to admit to having all sorts of personal problems, because she had heard this was required of participants at the meetings of a popular national organization that offered help for over-weight people. She felt disappointed that the recommended diet was not very different from the diets she had been on before and that the only new gimmick was the recommended daily period of meditation about dieting. Nevertheless, she thought the interview was "well handled," felt confident about succeeding, and wanted to "hurry up and do it." She felt pleased that now she would be able to "report to somebody." She made it clear, however, that her view of the counselor was as a strictly detached professional per-son, not as a friend or a parental type of helper.

In the weekly reports this client wrote extensive notes indicating that she felt an inner compulsion to stick to the diet and to get back on it any time she deviated. In the 4-week follow-up interview she reported that her feel-ings of self-confidence helped her to keep going on the diet. And yet, despite these apparent signs of internalization of the dieting norms and despite the strong reinforcement of her self-confidence from her great success in losing approximately 8 pounds during the 4-week interval, she said that she was afraid of losing her momentum unless she could continue to be checked by the counselor. (She did, in fact, phone the counselor a few weeks later to report having lost an additional 2 pounds and to request another follow-up session.) In this case the client manifested a fairly high degree of inner control but apparently needed reinforcement in the form of external social support from the counselor as a dependable authority figure.

Case M-9. This 72-year-old unmarried woman had retired from a lifelong career as an administrative assistant. She wanted to lose about 25 pounds. Like most of the other clients given the moderate self-disclosure interview, she responded by revealing a moderate amount of personal information. When speaking about her inability to control her eating behavior, she said, "I know no measure; I'm hoggish." She complained about her "totally boring existence" of doing daily housework and participating in uninter-esting club work.

In the process interview the client characterized the counselor as firm, quiet, and dependable. She felt gratified that the counselor was willing to devote time and interest to her without "bawling her out." She was glad that the counselor was not trying to push her but was letting her make her own decision. She felt "inspired" by the counselor because the counselor's confidence in her gave her confidence in herself. She also said that she would be ashamed to face the counselor if she were to fail. Her remarks indi-cate that her image of the counselor, which appears to be similar to that of most of the other clients in the moderate disclosure group, was of a benign, dependable authority figure.

According to the client's weekly reports, she was highly successful in adhering to the diet during the first week and thereafter was slightly less rigorous but continued to lose weight. In the follow-up session she was pleased that the scale showed she had lost a total of 9½ pounds during the 1-month interval.

One of the main things that kept her going, she reported, was remembering that the counselor had said, "It won't be easy" and she had thought, "I'll show her!" She reported that she had gotten her brother and sister interested in following her dieting progress. She also said that she wants to continue filling out the weekly reports "for myself" because she intends to lose more weight. Here again, as in some of the other successful cases, the client seems to have displayed a fairly high degree of autonomous inner control but nevertheless manifested a continuing need for external surveillance, which this elderly lady arranged for herself by getting both her brother and sister involved.

DISCUSSION AND TENTATIVE CONCLUSIONS

When we look over the 18 case studies, the most impressive feature that emerges from the intensive process interviews is the emotional turmoil that seems to characterize the client's relationship to the helper, as manifested by numerous signs of apprehensiveness, humiliation, struggle, and resistance. Evidently the typical client experiences shame and lowered self-esteem from having come to a weight-reduction clinic, where she has to present herself not only as "fat" but as a weak and perhaps despicable person, lacking in self-control because she cannot stop overeating even though she desperately wants to. Whether the interview induces moderate or high self-disclosure, the client typically expresses much chagrin along with repeated concern about what the counselor "must think of me." A major problem for short-term counseling is to prevent shame or social anxiety from interfering with the helping relationship and, if possible, to transform it into an asset.

One of the main findings from the comparative case studies is that fewer signs of self-derogation and demoralization occur among the clients given the moderate self-disclosure interview than among those given the high self-disclosure interview. It seems as though the occasional revelations about relatively common personal weaknesses evoked by the moderate disclosure interview are about as much disclosure as these clients can bear in the initial session. If the counselor adds to their burdens by asking for fuller disclosure of personal weaknesses in the initial interview—as the pressure of a high caseload might lead psychiatrists, psychologists, or social workers to do in a typical community setting requiring rapid diagnostic workups—the clients' emotional disturbances may seriously impair their relationship with the would-be helpers. Although the number of cases is small, there is some suggestion that fairly high disclosure has unfavorable effects even if it occurs spontaneously in response to questions designed to elicit only a moderate level of disclosure.

In light of the observations from the comparative case studies, it seems most probable that the findings of the two earlier studies in the weight-reduction clinic on the effects of high self-disclosure (reported in chaps. 11 and 12) are attributable to these unfavorable emotional reactions. Those studies did not consistently show changes in self-derogation as assessed by the check marks the clients made in response to various questionnaire items. But we have seen in the present case studies that there was a strong tendency for the clients to give conventionally polite, socially desirable responses to the questionnaires, whereas they revealed considerable disturbances in answering the open-ended questions in a process interview. Hence the absence of signs of lowered self-confidence in the questionnaire data from one of the prior studies should not be regarded as dependable evidence.

Our observations have led us to a more cautious position in evaluating the outcome of counseling treatments. The reactions our clients gave us on written questionnaires and even in the early portions of the process interview would have caused us to believe that the high self-disclosure interview was a generally positive experience. In the later portions of the process interviews, however, we discovered that high self-disclosure evokes in the client ambivalent reactions with strong negative components, which might account for the adverse effects on adherence. We now consider such process interviews to be essential for understanding the effects of any new counseling treatment.

Most of the clients to whom we gave the lower disclosure interview actually disclosed a moderate amount of personal material about their daily lives, about their difficulties in controlling their eating behavior, and about related personal weaknesses. (That is why we refer to these as *moderate* disclosure rather than as low disclosure interviews.) The personal information elicited by the moderate disclosure interview in the current study resembles that elicited in the moderate disclosure interviews in prior studies (reported in chaps. 9 and 10), which were found to facilitate subsequent weight loss. Taking account of all the pertinent evidence, including Mulligan's study in the setting of a Red Cross campaign for blood donations (reported in chap. 15), we conclude that for most clients, a moderate degree of disclosure is likely to be the optimal level for short-term counseling sessions.

We had not realized until we examined the process interviews that eliciting high self-disclosure was perceived by the clients as making a rigorous *demand* on them during the initial session. We had thought that the clients would realize that they could evade answering if they wanted to because the counselors did not exert any direct pressure and consistently expressed acceptance of whatever they said. But it is apparent that the clients did feel under pressure to answer the personal questions and some said that they had disclosed more than they had wanted to. Perhaps the clients were right about this because of the general demand characteristics of the interview situation and also because of the selective probing questions that were asked whenever a client was evasive. (Counselors were instructed to respond to vague answers with a general probing question, such as "Can you tell me more about that?")

Insofar as the clients felt under pressure from the counselor to reveal personal information about themselves that they regarded as shameful or demeaning, the use of a high self-disclosure interview during the initial session could result in the counselor being perceived as excessively demanding. According to the theoretical analysis of critical phases in the helping relationship (chap. 2), the relationship will be impaired if the counselor at the outset, instead of being consistently accepting, makes strong demands on the client. The results from the field experiment by Conolley, Janis, and Dowds (chap. 7) provide empirical support for the assumption that an extraneous strong demand during the initial session results in unfavorable attitudes toward the counselor and in subsequent failure to adhere to the counselor's recommendations.

We must recognize, of course, that high disclosure interviews might have less detrimental effects and might even have facilitating effects if sensitive personal material emerges more spontaneously and more gradually over a larger number of sessions than in the present clinical study. But we are cautioned by some of the case study observations against assuming that *spontaneous* high disclosure during the initial session is less detrimental than induced high disclosure. We have seen that among the clients given the moderate disclosure interview, the ones who spontaneously disclosed the most prove to be least successful in losing weight.

The negative effects of an initial high disclosure interview on the clients' self-confidence and attitude toward the counselor may be the result of their being induced to disclose too much, too soon. In smaller doses, spread over a longer time period, in a less transient relationship with the counselor, a client might be able to speak more freely about his or her personal shortcomings and to come to terms with them without feeling humiliated or ashamed and without developing ambivalent feelings toward the person to whom the disclosures are made. There are even some indications in the present case material that the additional hour or so of interaction in the intensive process interview (which involved eliciting a fairly high degree of disclosure about current weaknesses, fears, conflicts, and aspirations) was sometimes successful in overcoming the detrimental effects of the initial high disclosure interview that had preceded it. At the end of the process interview, signs of increased self-confidence and other favorable attitude changes (compared with attitudes expressed at the beginning of the process interview) were clearly observed in four of the nine cases in the high disclosure group and those four were among the most successful in losing weight.

A crucial feature of the process interview—which may account for its effectiveness in undoing the unfavorable effects of the initial high disclosure interview—is that it gave the clients the opportunity to ventilate the misgivings generated by their answers to the counselor's prior questions and to receive consistent reassurance that the counselor had not developed a low opinion of them but felt confident that they had what it takes to succeed on the task of dieting. The same kind of mitigating effects might be found in other counselor–client settings, when the opportunities for self-disclosure are spread over a longer period of time in many sessions, as in longer term counseling treatments that are similar to psychotherapy.

In the absence of a second interview to discuss the emotional impact of the first one, a client who has just undergone a high disclosure intake interview may be left with the impression that the counselor is just doing his or her routine job but does not personally regard the client as a worthwhile person and has no confidence in the client's ability to succeed at self-control. This disturbing view of the counselor was expressed by a number of clients who had just disclosed a great deal about their personal weaknesses. In the Quinlan and Janis study (chap. 11) and in the Riskind and Janis study (chap. 12) the high disclosure interview was immediately followed by a tape recording of the dieting instructions, which would allow the clients to retain uncorrected the notion that the counselor was just going through the routine required by the role since there was practically no opportunity for this damaging view to be corrected in further face-to-face conversation.

From what the clients said in the process interview about their fears of being bawled out, despised, and rejected by the counselor, it is apparent that one of the principal functions of giving acceptance responses is to build an image of the counselor as a benign helper who is "on your side." But expressing a great deal of warmth and empathy seems also to sow seeds of discontent among some of the clients because they expressed vague fears of becoming too dependent or of somehow being hurt.

We get the impression that most of the successful cases saw the counselor as a detached, nonevaluating professional person who was genuinely interested in giving them the limited amount of help offered but could not be expected to do anything more than that. It is this type of image of the counselor that seems to go along with the clients' readiness to continue the task of dieting with a minimum of external social support (although routine surveillance by someone seems to be strongly desired by most of the successful clients).

An effective working relationship with the counselor apparently requires the client to come to terms with unrequited longings for a close relationship with the counselor. There are some faint indications here and there of fantasy images of what the desired relationship might be like. For some clients what seems to be involved is primarily a wish for unconditional acceptance by an all-loving maternal helper. For others it may be a wish to be guarded from temptations and helped to overcome other weaknesses by a powerful paternal authority who will somehow provide magical protection. Neither of these fantasy images seems to facilitate success in adhering to the task of dieting.

It must be repeated once again that all the observations concerning the detrimental effects of high disclosure come from the special form of counseling given in our weight-reduction clinic, where clients have only one session of treatment followed by a period of many weeks before the first follow-up session, which merely involves surveillance and a brief interview, with no further treatment. For some, if not most, clients given this brief form of counseling, a business-like, low-pressure interview may be more effective than an effort to build an affectionate relationship by inducing a high degree of self-disclosure and providing a great deal of warmth and empathy.

Consider, for example, case H-5, who had been given a high disclosure interview and was very successful in losing weight. She complained during the process interview that the counselor was not giving her enough, was not firing her up, but was treating her as just another eligible candidate for the counselor's professional services. She was clearly implying that what she wanted was a much more affectionate personal relationship. After discussing these reactions she seemed to be able to come to terms with her unfulfilled longings when she announced that she expected to benefit from "getting someone else involved." The latter statement might be freely translated as asserting that she will settle for having the continued surveillance of a professional who is interested only in helping her on the task at hand. This restricted image of the counselor appears to have provided sufficient positive incentive to keep her going, even though she might have wished for a more loving relationship. She reported that, when tempted to go off the diet, she was able to resist the temptation by thinking about the counselor receiving her weekly report.

Throughout this discussion we have been assuming that valid clues to the clients' reactions can be obtained by taking at face value what they said during the process interview. But, of course, it is possible that some of the clients were talking sincerely while others were merely wearing their social masks throughout the entire session. There is even the grim possibility that the clients who were given the high disclosure interview expressed a great deal of dissatisfaction with themselves and with the interview because they had been induced by the series of prior questions to become more and more candid, whereas the clients given the moderate disclosure interview may never have overcome their initial reticence. During the process interview the latter group may have continued to give more politely conventional answers to the effect that everything was just fine, even though they were just as perturbed as the others. Although there is no way of telling whether the differences are attributable to differential frankness, the fact remains that those clients who complained most about the interview and who expressed most conflict about the relationship with the counselor (fearing that maybe the counselor had no real interest in them, might despise them, or might in some way let them down) did *not* succeed as well in dieting as those who said that they regarded the counselor as an uninvolved professional person who was trying to help them. In other words it appears that when clients in the weight-reduction clinic give conventionally positive responses that imply an image of the counselor as a business-like professional person, they end up benefiting more from the initial counseling session than when they express longings for more intimacy or fears of becoming too deeply attached.

NOTES

1. The sequence of standard procedures for each client (prior to the process interview) was as follows:

1. Filling out the standard initial questionnaires containing inquiries about the client's health problems, reasons for wanting to lose weight, and expected difficulties in connection with dieting.
2. Signing a consent form, which includes agreeing to be interviewed with the understanding that the client is free to decline to answer any question and to withdraw from the study at any time.
3. Being weighed on a standard balance scale.
4. Answering the counselor's questions in a face-to-face interview (inducing high or moderate self-disclosure).
5. Being instructed about the recommended diet and additional recommendations (to spend 10 minutes each day meditating about the dieting and to fill out and mail back weekly progress reports on adherence to the diet), all of which are presented in a tape recording of the counselor's voice.
6. Filling out a standard postinterview questionnaire, including a self-esteem scale, questions about reactions to the interview, and attitude toward the interviewer.

The process interview began with an open-ended question in order to allow the client to describe any aspect of her experience in undergoing the preceding interview that impressed her.

"Suppose you wanted to tell a close friend about the interview here today. What would you tell your friend—what would you say about it? Pretend I am the friend."

Specific questions were then asked concerning what aspects of the interview the client liked, disliked, made her feel uncomfortable, affected her mood, evoked the feeling that she was revealing too much about herself, made her feel "raring to go," affected her motivation in any other ways, might have been helpful, and were *not* helpful. Several additional questions dealt specifically with the client's self-confidence about succeeding in losing the amount of weight she had set as her goal. The first of these was as follows:

"I've told you that I'm very optimistic about your chances of succeeding on the diet. How *realistic* do you think my expectations are?"

This wording was used in order to minimize the possibility that a more neutral wording might be construed by some clients as suggesting that the counselor was not optimistic about her chances of success. Despite the demand characteristic embodied in the wording of this question, as will be seen when the findings are described, there was sufficient variation in the clients' answers to discern differences between the two treatment groups. Two additional questions were included that explicitly dealt with self-confidence:

1. "How confident do you feel about carrying out the diet?"

2. "A few women have told me that as a result of the interview here they became aware of so many difficulties and problems about sticking to a diet that they feel worried now that they won't be able to do it successfully. Do you have any feelings like that?"

Many of the questions provided opportunities for the client to express her attitudes and expectations about the counselor, but two additional questions were included that bear specifically on the client's image of the counselor:

1. "Some of the women told me that at one time or another during the session here with me they felt somewhat dissatisfied about the interview and disappointed in me. Did you have that feeling at any time during today's interview?"
2. "You have told me many things about yourself and your problem of overeating. What do you think is my opinion of you? Please try to give me a frank answer and I will give you my answer as frankly as I can. So, what opinion do you think I have of you?"

After this second question the counselor gave a standard accepting statement to the effect that she realized that the client had some problems in connection with being overweight and that those problems were understandable and could be overcome. Again, in order to avoid possible negative effects of the process interview that might interfere with the primary clinical task, the last question was about whether the client felt "raring to go" with respect to starting on the diet, after which the counselor made a reassuring final statement about feeling confident that the client will be able to lose weight successfully if she makes a genuine effort to do so.

2. Both authors independently carried out a blind analysis of every interview. All the interviews had been conducted by research assistants, so there was no possibility that the authors could recollect anything that might enable them to identify which group a subject was in. Comparison of the two authors' blind ratings on the main results (reported in the initial part of the Results and Discussion section) revealed that they were in complete agreement on 95% of the ratings. The few ratings that were discrepant were re-scored after reaching mutual agreement through discussion.

3. This client's response is typical of a number of clients' requests for more intensive contact. The study reported in chap. 10, however, which compared the effects of more frequent with less frequent contact, revealed that such contact does not have a uniformly beneficial effect.

14 The Clients' Sense of Personal Mastery: Effects of Time Perspective and Self-esteem

JOHN H. RISKIND

The importance of a sense of personal mastery for coping with stress is a common theme in the psychological literature. Experimental and clinical evidence indicates that when people perceive that they can control the outcomes of their actions in stressful situations, they show improvement in their ability to plan and to execute their decisions efficiently; whereas when people perceive themselves as lacking in control, they show signs of increased stress and diminished effectiveness in active problem-solving (see DeCharms, 1968; Glass & Singer, 1972; Janis, 1958; Lazarus, 1966; Lefcourt, 1972, 1973; Rotter, 1966; Seligman, 1975).

Few studies have been made of the actual consequences of attempting to enhance the sense of mastery or perceived control among persons who feel debilitated by a sense of helplessness with regard to controlling major events in their lives. Recent studies indicate that an enhanced sense of personal control has positive effects on the institutionalized aged, who suffer from feelings of lack of control (Langer & Rodin, 1976; Rodin & Langer, 1977; Schulz, 1976).

The present investigation was undertaken to examine several specific features of a counselor–client relationship that may enhance clients' perceptions of their ability to exert control over their subsequent performances in actually trying to carry out a stressful course of action. The setting for the study was a weight-reduction clinic, where counselors try to help overweight women follow a low-calorie diet.

A vital but overlooked factor for enhancing a sense of mastery is the time perspective of a person who is ready to start carrying out a difficult decision. If people adopt a short-term orientation (such as a day-by-day approach) to a task like dieting, they structure their anticipations of the future and focus on small features of the task that can easily be mastered (such as

This chapter is based on a dissertation (supervised by Irving L. Janis, Donald Quinlan, and Irvin Child) submitted for the Ph.D. degree at Yale University. My thanks go to Irving Janis and to my committee for their help and constructive support. Thanks are also due to Anne Granger for typing the original manuscript, and to June Connolly, Donna LaFlamme, Aloen Townsend, William Wong-McCarthy, and other members of the staff of the Yale Weight-Reduction Clinic for their help in carrying out the project.

living up to a diet for the next 24 hours, which almost everyone can do). By deciding to carry out a stressful task for just one day at a time, many people may be able to enhance their sense of mastery. Small day-by-day steps provide a key to ultimate success if done successively on a repeated basis. But if people take a long-term approach to a stressful task and focus on the entire set of stressful problems that may arise in the vast expanse of time that lies ahead, the task may seem so endlessly difficult and demanding as to make them feel powerless and hopeless.

Based on the assumption that a day-by-day approach would enhance the clients' sense of mastery with regard to adhering to a weight-reduction diet, two different time perspectives were investigated in the present study. For half the clients the counselor recommended dieting on a day-by-day basis and for the other half the counselor recommended facing up to the necessity to diet for as long as necessary in the future in order to achieve the ultimate goal.

A relevant feature of the counselor–client relationship is the extent to which the client's current state of self-esteem is enhanced. In a field experiment by Smith (reported in chap. 16) self-esteem enhancement in the form of positive feedback from a counselor was found to have a favorable effect on teachers who attended a special workshop to learn a new teaching technique. It seems likely that such enhancement had the effect of increasing adherence to the recommended teaching technique because it increased the teachers' sense of mastery and control for the type of behavior that was the object of enhancement (see Eisenberger, Park, & Frank, 1976).

In the current study the effects of two different types of self-esteem enhancement were independently examined. In order to give these treatments, the counselor elicited positive self-disclosures from all clients, including personal accounts of their past accomplishments, successes, and personal strengths. In response to each self-disclosure about one of the client's strong points, the counselor attempted to build up the client's sense of mastery by enhancing either (1) the client's *task self-esteem* with regard to personal resources and strengths that would be of direct instrumental assistance to being successful in dieting (e.g., past evidence of perseverance), or (2) the client's *general self-esteem* with regard to personal resources and strong points that would help her to be generally successful in life despite any lack of immediate success in dieting.

Past studies in a diet clinic similar to the present one have suggested that persons whose chronic level of self-esteem is relatively high are not particularly helped by social support or counseling interventions, even when they themselves have sought the help of a counselor. The studies by Dowds, Janis, and Conolley (chap. 6) and Conolley, Janis, and Dowds (chap. 7) showed that clients with relatively low chronic self-esteem were fairly successful at carrying out a counselor's dieting recommendations, but clients with relatively high chronic self-esteem were not. These findings, although unexpected, may be in line with other observations indicating that in certain circumstances persons with low self-esteem are more responsive than others to persuasion or directive suggestions (Janis & Field, 1959; Marlowe & Crowne, 1961; Strickland & Crowne, 1962). Persons with high self-esteem, on the other hand, may be more generally motivated by internal factors and might be particularly responsive to those counseling interventions that enhance their perceptions of their own ability to exert autonomous control over future events. In the current study the interaction of chronic level of self-esteem with each treatment intervention was investigated as well as the main effects.

METHOD

Design Overview

The present investigation was conducted at the Yale Weight-Reduction Clinic, which offers overweight women free help in losing weight in exchange for their participation in research (see chap. 1). All women who participate are given the same 1200-calorie diet and instructions prepared by the Department of Dietetics at Yale–New Haven Hospital.

In the present study, at the beginning of the first of three meetings, clients completed a personality scale which measured their chronic level of self-esteem. They were then assigned on a random basis to three cross-cutting treatments. One treatment was designed to give the client either a short-term (day by day) or a long-term orientation to following the diet (*time perspective*). The other two treatments were designed to enhance the clients' self-esteem. One was intended to enhance their state of self-esteem with regard to strong points pertinent to successfully following a diet (*task self-esteem enhancement*). The other treatment was intended to enhance their state of self-esteem with regard to strong points pertinent to generally being successful in life, even if they were not immediately successful in following a diet (*general self-esteem enhancement*).[1] There was no reason to expect any of these treatments to be harmful to clients in any way, and from what little is known in light of existing psychological research a case could be made to expect advantages for each. Dependent variables, including weight loss and attitudes relevant to a sense of mastery, were measured at three meetings in the diet clinic over an 8-week period: at the initial meeting and at follow-up meetings at 4 and 8 weeks.

Clients

Clients were 105 women who responded to a local newspaper announcement of a free weight-reduction clinic for women who were between 15 and 50 pounds overweight and without serious health problems. Participating volunteers were screened (for disqualifying health problems) by telephone and informed about the research aspects of the project. Clients were from the New Haven area and varied considerably in age, ethnic group, and socio-economic class.

Procedures

Four counselors were employed in this study (two men and two women), all of whom were graduate students in psychology. After giving a brief intro-duction and explaining the informed consent form, the counselors collected a voluntary $8 deposit (which was subsequently returned) to increase each client's commitment to come back for the follow-up meetings.

The initial session, which was devoted largely to giving all clients a moderate self-disclosure interview, included the treatment interventions and the standardized procedures for providing all clients with details about the 1200-calorie diet and helpful recommendations for following the diet.

Assessment of Chronic Level of Self-esteem

At the beginning of the interview during the first meeting, after each client was weighed on a balance scale, she was given the self-acceptance scale from the California Psychological Inventory (Gough, 1957) to assess her level of chronic self-esteem. Clients were divided into high and low self-esteem subgroups for purposes of analysis by splitting the total distribution of scores at the median. Clients were assigned to experimental conditions on a random basis, without reference to their chronic self-esteem scores.

Self-esteem Enhancement Treatments

In order to establish rapport before the self-esteem enhancement treatment began, near the beginning of the first meeting each client was asked stand-ard questions about her daily activities, work, and family life, which elicited a moderate amount of self-disclosure. The counselor responded to the client's disclosures in a warm and sympathetic manner indicating his or her positive regard, and this attitude of acceptance was maintained throughout the first meeting regardless of the treatments that the client received. After asking the standard series of initial questions, the counselor consulted an assignment sheet which indicated the self-esteem enhancement treatment to be assigned to the client.

Task Self-esteem Enhancement

Clients who received this treatment were given an additional interview immediately after the moderate self-disclosure interview. It was designed to highlight their past successes, accomplishments, and strong points perti-nent to the achievement of success at dieting. Counselors followed a stand-ardized procedure such that they:

    1. elicited positive self-disclosure about past successes (e.g., the counse-lor asked questions about career accomplishments, even minor ones, and about personal resources the client had demonstrated in the past, such as perseverance);

2. spoke about personal strengths mentioned by the client and pointed out other resources revealed by the client's past activities that were not explicitly recognized by the client, asserting in each instance that such strengths or resources were directly applicable to dieting successfully;

3. concluded the supplementary interview with a few general questions about personal problems and then asked in a persuasive way if the client agreed that these were surmountable, not obstacles to successful dieting.

In the corresponding no-enhancement treatment, each counselor asked further questions about the client's daily routines and eating behavior, instead of asking about past successes or strong points pertinent to dieting. The counselor responded in the standard empathic and accepting manner.

General Self-esteem Enhancement
Clients who received this treatment were given a somewhat different type of additional interview, which was designed to highlight their past successes, accomplishments, and strengths pertinent to being generally successful despite any lack of immediate success at dieting. The standardized procedure followed by the counselors involved pointing out that each of the strong points or assets disclosed by the clients would continue to be a source of general success irrespective of the person's success at losing weight. (For example, a counselor told a client that she had her social leadership ability "going for her" regardless of how well she did at dieting.) The counselor avoided mentioning the applicability of the clients' strong points to successful dieting. Each counselor concluded the supplementary interview with the same standard questions about personal problems that were asked in the task self-esteem enhancement treatment, and asked in a persuasive way if the client agreed that these were surmountable, not obstacles to leading a generally successful and fulfilling life.

In the corresponding no-enhancement treatment, the counselor asked further questions about the clients' daily routines and eating behavior, just as in the no-enhancement condition for task self-esteem. Again, the counselor responded in the standard empathic and accepting manner.

A baseline control group consisted of subjects who received neither form of self-esteem enhancement treatment (as required by the factorial design), but these clients did receive the standard self-disclosure interview with consistently positive feedback from the counselor. The counselor's standard acceptance responses and other indications of positive regard after hearing the client's disclosures of daily routines and personal problems during the standard interview may have had the effect of enhancing self-esteem to some extent (see chap. 2).

Time Perspective Treatment
Just before this treatment, all clients were given standard recommendations about a 1200-calorie diet prepared by the Department of Dietetics at the Yale–New Haven Hospital. (In order to avoid unconscious variations in imparting the recommendations, the counselor played a tape recording in

his or her own voice that described the weight-reduction diet.) The counselor answered any questions that the clients had about the diet by repeating the appropriate parts of the standard instructions. Then the counselor spent 15 minutes presenting either a short-term or a long-term perspective with regard to sticking with the diet.

For the *short-term perspective,* clients were told that they should try to follow the diet and to think about it on a day-by-day basis. The counselor stated that worrying about all the hardships of the future could cause discouragement. The counselor explained that clients may have failed at dieting in the past because of a tendency to think too much about difficulties in the future. Clients were asked to structure the anticipated future into small steps and to approach the diet with the intention of living up to it for just one day at a time. At the end of the talk all clients given this treatment agreed that they would be able to follow the diet for just one day, and the counselor emphasized that each day that they successfully followed the diet could be seen as a separate accomplishment for which they could feel pride.

For the *long-term perspective,* clients were told that they should try to follow the diet and to think about facing up to the requirements of the diet for as long as was necessary in the future. The counselor made comments and asked questions according to a standardized procedure to convey the attitude that anticipating the difficulties that lie far ahead in the future could be beneficial to their success. The counselor told the clients to think about paying attention to food intake for as long as it would take to get their weight down and keep it down. The counselor explained that clients may have failed at dieting in the past because of a failure to accept the need to diet for as long as necessary. Clients were encouraged to think about the pride they could feel after they had maintained the diet for many months to achieve their target weight. The counselor tried to respond to the client in the same warm and reassuring manner as in the short-term treatment.

Standard Motivating Procedures

Two standard procedures were used during the initial session in all conditions to guarantee as fully as possible that all clients would be encouraged to build up their motivation to lose weight. First, at the beginning of the initial meeting all clients were given a modified decisional balance sheet to make salient all the personal and social incentives for losing weight, such as increased physical health and attractiveness (see chaps. 3 and 9). Second, all clients were told by the counselor that there was every reason to believe that they could be successful at dieting if they made enough effort. (See Weiner, Frieze, Kukla, Reed, Rost, & Rosenbaum, 1971, for a discussion of the importance of conveying attributions that personal effort will determine success.)

Dependent Measures

Dependent measures included (a) *objective weight loss,* assessed at the 4- and 8-week follow-up meetings with the counselor; (b) *attendance at follow-up meetings,* as a measure of compliance with one of the counselor's requests; (c) *weekly reports* of progress on the diet, which all clients were asked to mail back to the counselor summarizing their adherence to the diet, current weight, and thoughts during daily reflection periods; and (d) *attitudes* assessed by means of questionnaires given at each of the three meetings to measure changes in self-esteem and various other mediating psychological processes (e.g., feelings of mastery, helplessness, and self-confidence).

RESULTS

Effects of Time Perspective and Chronic Self-esteem

Table 14.1 shows that clients given instructions to diet on a day-by-day basis mailed back significantly more weekly reports about their progress on the

Table 14.1. Effects of time perspective and chronic self-esteem on adherence: mailing back weekly reports and objective weight loss

	Time perspective			
	Short term		Long term	
	High Self-esteem[a]	Low Self-esteem[b]	High Self-esteem[c],*	Low Self-esteem[a]
Weekly reports**	3.27	3.21	2.50	2.88
Pounds of weight loss at 4 weeks***	4.85	4.10	2.23	5.02
Pounds of weight loss at 8 weeks***	6.79	5.18	2.20	6.36

[a] $N = 26$.
[b] $N = 29$.
[c] $N = 24$.

* For the two measures assessed at the 8-week meeting: $N = 23$ in the high self-esteem–long-term condition.

** The only significant finding from an analysis of variance of scores for weekly reports is a main effect for time perspective: $F(1, 89) = 4.09$, $p < .05$.

*** For both measures of weight loss, there is the same significant finding—an interaction effect of time perspective with chronic level of self-esteem: Interaction F's = 5.14 and 6.02, $p < .03$ for each. In all instances the main effects are nonsignificant.

diet than did clients given instructions to face up to the diet for as long as it might take in the future ($p < .05$). This main effect bears out the predicted positive effect of a short-term perspective on a simple behavioral measure of clients' willingness to comply with the counselor's requests. No other main effects or interaction effects were found for this measure.

Weight loss, the primary behavioral indicator of successful dieting, was assessed by measuring the difference between the client's weight at the first meeting and her weight at each of the follow-up meetings.[2] Analysis of the weight loss data in Table 14.1 shows that there was no significant main effect for time perspective at either the 4- or 8-week follow-up sessions. However, there was a significant interaction effect between short-term versus long-term perspective and chronic self-esteem (for both measures, $p < .03$). Clients high in chronic self-esteem showed significantly more weight loss when given instructions to follow the diet on a day-by-day basis than when given instructions to face up to the diet for as long as it might take ($p < .03$). Clients low in chronic self-esteem, on the other hand, showed a trend in the opposite direction which is not statistically significant.

Table 14.1 indicates that chronic self-esteem itself was not predictive of weight loss. This finding might seem to be contrary to findings from two other studies carried out in the same diet clinic: Dowds, Janis, and Conolley (chap. 6) and Conolley, Janis, and Dowds (chap. 7) found that clients with low chronic self-esteem tended to lose more weight than did clients with high chronic self-esteem. But the present findings actually do agree with the earlier findings because as a standard procedure the counselors in both earlier studies brought the clients' attention to the long-term hazards and demands of dieting, such as the problems of gaining back weight and of being tempted by family members to eat fattening foods. When clients in the current study were given a long-term perspective, those low in chronic self-esteem showed significantly more weight loss than those high in chronic self-esteem (for both measures, $p < .02$). When clients were given instruc-

Table 14.2. Effects of time perspective and chronic self-esteem on attitudes at the end of the first meeting

	Time perspective			
	Short term		Long term	
Mean attitude ratings*	High self-esteem[a]	Low self-esteem[b]	High self-esteem[a]	Low self-esteem[c]
Respect for counselor**	48.3	48.5	44.8	47.2
Liking for counselor**	47.4	46.8	43.5	44.4
Hopefulness about diet**	46.5	47.5	45.2	44.8
Focusing on immediate dieting***	47.4	45.4	43.9	45.6

[a] $N = 23$.
[b] $N = 28$.
[c] $N = 25$.

*The higher the score on a 1 to 5 scale, the more positive the rating. All mean scores are multiplied by 10 in order to highlight differences.

**A main effect for time perspective is the only significant or near significant finding from an analysis of variance of scores on: (1) Respect for counselor: $F(1, 82) = 4.49$, $p < .05$; (2) Liking for counselor: $F(1, 83) = 3.59$, $p < .06$; (3) Hopefulness about diet: $F(1, 83) = 3.77$, $p < .06$.

***An interaction effect of time perspective with chronic level of self-esteem is the only near significant finding from an analysis of variance of scores on Focusing on immediate dieting: $F(1, 83) = 3.19$, $p < .10$.

tions to diet on a day-by-day basis, however, there was a slight, but nonsignificant difference in the opposite direction. One of the implications of the significant interaction effect is that situational factors, such as those affecting a person's time perspective, can influence the relationship between chronic self-esteem and adherence to a difficult decision.

Table 14.2 shows that the short-term approach had the predicted positive effect on attitudes expressed on the questionnaire given at the end of the initial session. Clients who were given instructions to diet on a day-by-day basis reported respecting the counselor ($p < .04$) and liking the counselor ($p < .06$) more than those who were given instructions to face up to the diet for as long as it would take. The clients given the short-term perspective also reported being more hopeful about dieting ($p < .06$).[3] There were no significant differences on any of the attitude measures for chronically high versus low self-esteem.

Up to this point the results partially support the expected positive effects of a short-term approach to dieting, but in some respects they are surprising. Clients with chronically high self-esteem benefited but those with chronically low self-esteem did not benefit from the short-term perspective as far as weight loss is concerned. Furthermore, when the significant main effects on respect and liking for the counselor and focusing on immediate dieting were examined, the relatively large differences proved to be for the clients with chronically high self-esteem (all p values $< .05$). The effects for the clients with chronically low self-esteem were not significant. In general, then, the findings in Table 14.2, like those in Table 14.1, indicate that clients with chronically high self-esteem were more responsive to the short-term time perspective treatment than clients with chronically low self-esteem.

Effects of Self-esteem Enhancement

Another hypothesis investigated in this study was that self-esteem enhancement by means of interviews that focus on the client's personal strengths would have positive effects on weight loss. As Table 14.3 shows, this hypothesis was not confirmed. Quite to the contrary, the differences in weight loss were in the opposite direction, although not statistically significant. (For general self-esteem enhancement treatment only, p values range from $< .10$ to $< .15$.) If the three groups that received self-esteem enhancement treatments are combined and contrasted with the single group of clients who were given no form of self-esteem enhancement, the results indicate that clients who received either or both forms of self-esteem enhancement did not lose as much weight as the controls ($p < .06$ for weight loss observed at the 8-week follow-up session).[4]

DISCUSSION

One of the main hypotheses tested in this study was that emphasizing a short-term perspective would increase the clients' sense of mastery and lead to greater adherence to dieting recommendations. This hypothesis was partially supported. Clients instructed to take a day-by-day approach to dieting were found to be more hopeful and to have more positive attitudes

Table 14.3. Effects of self-esteem enhancement on weekly reports and objective weight loss

	(1) General S. E. only ($N = 28$)	(2) Task S. E. only ($N = 26$)	(3) Both S. E. treatments ($N = 26$)*	(4) No S. E. enhancement ($N = 25$)
Weekly reports	3.04	3.19	2.77	2.92
Pounds of weight loss at 4 weeks	3.79	4.33	3.26	5.03
Pounds of total weight loss at 8 weeks**	4.26	5.34	4.41	6.97

* $N = 25$ for the 8-week measure.
** The only noteworthy finding from an analysis of variance is a near significant main effect for general self-esteem enhancement in the opposite direction from what was predicted: $F = 2.6$, $p < .10$.

about themselves and the counselor than did clients instructed to take a long-term approach that called attention to the trials and hardships to be expected in the future. Clients given the short-term perspective also mailed back more weekly progress reports, as expected.

Glass and Singer (1972, p. 156) suggest on the basis of evidence on effects of unpredictable loud noises and other cognitively disruptive stimuli that perceptions of uncontrollability are produced by perceiving an accumulation of unpredictable stresses, which creates a state of cognitive overload and feelings of helplessness. In line with this conception of perceived control, the present findings suggest that when people are confronted with stressful tasks such as dieting, their time orientation with regard to future stresses can influence feelings of helplessness. If people adopt a day-by-day approach to dealing with the problems of the same stressful tasks, they focus on small steps that can be mastered (such as living up to a diet for 24 hours, which they know anyone can do and which can lead to ultimate success if done repeatedly on each successive day). But if people take a long-term approach to a difficult course of action, focusing on the entire set of problems that may arise in the vast expanse of time that lies ahead of them in the future, the tasks may seem so endlessly demanding as to make them feel psychologically overwhelmed and hopeless. Thus, a person's time perspective when attempting to carry out a difficult course of action may be a crucial determinant of motivation to continue exerting the effort necessary for sustained adherence. (For comparisons with other approaches to enhancing a sense of personal control, see Fontaine, 1974; Langer, 1975; Rotter, 1966; Weiner et al., 1971; Wortman, 1975.)

For a stressful decision such as going on a diet, defensive avoidance is a frequent coping pattern which results in lack of psychological preparation for setbacks (see chap. 3). As Janis and Mann (1977) point out, a person's confidence or hopefulness about being able to find some way to cope with the distressingly unfavorable consequences of a decision is a major determinant of whether the person will resort to defensive avoidance. It seems likely that an intervention that gives clients a short-term time perspective helps to counteract this defective pattern of coping. Insofar as a short time perspective leads clients to focus on those parts of the long-term task that they can execute without undue suffering, about which they can feel hope for successful accomplishment, it could prevent defensive avoidance.

The present results on time perspective are similar to those obtained from a study of obese clients being treated by behavior modification techniques, reported by Bandura and Simon (1977) after the present study had been completed. Bandura and Simon found that clients who were instructed to adopt short-term subgoals on a daily basis ate less and lost more weight than clients who were instructed to adopt a longer term subgoal in terms of weekly accomplishments. In the current study, however, a major finding was that only the clients with chronically high self-esteem showed significantly more weight loss when given a short-term perspective than when given a long-term approach. For clients with chronically low self-esteem there was no significant effect. A plausible interpretation of this significant interaction effect is that the characteristic modes of coping and adaptation are different for people with relatively high as against low chronic self-esteem. Perhaps in the Bandura and Simon (1977) study most of the obese clients who volunteered or were selected for the behavior modification treatment tended to be like the clients who scored above the median on chronic level of self-esteem in the present study, which could account for their findings of a main effect of greater weight loss for those given the short-term time perspective.

Findings from a number of studies suggest that persons with chronically high self-esteem are more likely than those with chronically low self-esteem to take direct independent action as their preferred way of contending with impending threats or opportunities (see Marlowe & Gergen, 1969). In other words they are more predisposed to have a sense of self-efficacy and to exert personal control. When such persons are advised by a counselor, they may be sufficiently self-confident about their own capabilities to benefit from a day-by-day approach, which makes salient the decisive steps they can take on their own to exert personal mastery.

Clients with chronically low self-esteem may not benefit from a day-by-day approach because they are more externally oriented and require reassurance and support from others when confronted with threats or conflict. Perhaps externally oriented persons feel a chronic sense of helplessness about their ability to make decisions effectively on their own and attempt to rely primarily on social feedback from a counselor or others in their social networks (see Janis & Field, 1959; Marlowe & Crowne, 1961; Strickland &

Crowne, 1962).[5] Unlike persons with high self-esteem, who have relatively high self-confidence about succeeding on a difficult undertaking, such as a diet, those with low self-esteem may be so predominantly motivated by the desire to obtain social approval, reassurance, and guidance from the counselor that they are responsive only to the socially supportive features of the counseling situation. Because the counselor gave consistently positive feedback in all conditions, these contextual factors were extremely salient for everyone in the present study, which might explain the relatively large amount of weight loss for clients with chronically low self-esteem irrespective of the time perspective treatment they received.

If chronically low self-esteem persons are accustomed to coping with threats by relying on external social support, they might commonly feel threatened by situationally imposed demands that they exert personal mastery or internal control. In this study a significant interaction effect was obtained on an attitude item dealing with feelings of helplessness: Low self-esteem clients reported feeling somewhat more helplessness about dieting when given the short-term approach than when given the long-term approach, whereas high self-esteem clients showed a significant effect in the opposite direction. The defensiveness of low self-esteem persons in situations calling for skill and personal control is suggested in a study by Maracek and Mettee (1972). Students with extremely low chronic self-esteem performed significantly better on a simple laboratory task when successful performance could be attributed to chance (which allowed them to preserve an external orientation) than when successful performance was attributed to skill, which would make each student feel personally responsible.

A common thread running through the present findings and prior research on personality predispositions related to coping orientations may be the *learned helplessness* of persons with chronically low self-esteem. Their ostensible external orientation and reliance on social support from others may be traced to a chronic sense of personal inadequacy. This may explain why in the present study only the clients who have chronically high self-esteem showed greater adherence to the diet when they were given the short-term perspective, which increases feelings of personal control over eating behavior.

The self-esteem enhancement treatments produced the expected changes in attitude even though the treatments failed to produce the expected increase in adherence to the recommended diet. The findings from attitude questionnaires indicate that the self-esteem enhancement treatments were successful in increasing the clients' self-esteem, just as expected.[6] A moderate level of self-disclosure and positive feedback from the supportive counselor were held roughly constant in all conditions. Consequently it seems most probable that it was the *positive* self-disclosures (elicited by the self-esteem enhancement treatments) that influenced the changes in positive self-regard. Insofar as such changes in clients' self-ratings can be taken at face value, the present findings may have therapeutic applications when the object is primarily to enhance clients' self-esteem. Kroth (1973), for example, lists "greater self-acceptance" as one of the primary goals of counseling (p. 109).

Although both forms of the self-esteem enhancement treatment made clients feel better about themselves and improved related attitudes pertinent to dieting, these positive changes in verbal reports were not accompanied by greater adherence to the diet. Contrary to initial expectations, clients given the general self-esteem enhancement treatment showed greater failure to attend the 4-week follow-up meeting. Furthermore, clients given either or both forms of treatment designed to enhance self-esteem showed less success at dieting than clients given no form of self-esteem enhancement. It follows from these findings that making people feel better about themselves does not necessarily make them do better at tasks that require strong motivation. The findings underscore an obvious need for further inquiry on the conditions under which self-esteem enhancement has positive, as against negative, effects. One obvious possibility is that self-esteem enhancement will lower motivation to perform well when it induces a sense of complacency or self-satisfaction, which would lower the incentive to make sacrifices on a task such as sticking to a 1200-calorie diet. Janis's theoretical analysis of effective helping relationships (chap. 2) emphasizes the need for giving selective feedback in order to facilitate the counselor's essential norm-setting functions. In decision counseling intended to help people carry out difficult courses of action, giving unconditional positive regard is not likely to be an effective way to promote adherence.

Seligman's (1975) discussion of "learned laziness" assumes that noncontingent positive feedback, such as unearned praise, could have just such adverse effects as those found in the current study. Self-complacency would be particularly likely when clients believe that praise or positive evaluations from a counselor are attributable to their past accomplishments or to factors not related to current performance. In retrospect, the fact that in the present study the self-esteem enhancement treatments were presented *before* the clients started dieting and not in the context of their actually having successfully carried out praiseworthy actions may have prevented the treatments from having the intended positive effects. This implication is strengthened by evidence from a study by Eisenberger, Park, and Frank (1976) indicating that positive social feedback improves performance if it is experienced by the subjects as *contingent* on how they respond, which may enhance not only the incentive to comply but also their sense of control. In Smith's study (reported in chap. 16) showing positive effects of self-esteem enhancement, the enhancement treatment was given in the context of contingent acceptance.

The findings of this study reemphasize the importance of considering personality variables in planning counseling strategies for behavior change (see Bowers, 1973; Sarason & Spielberger, 1975). When taken alone, some potentially useful interventions, such as the short-term time perspective to enhance feelings of mastery, may show little effect on adherence to stressful decisions. But counseling interventions may emerge as therapeutically applicable treatments when examined in the context of differences in personality, as was found in the present study. By taking into account differences in chronic self-esteem and related self-feelings, it should be possible to select counseling interventions that are most likely to be effective for each client.

MAIN CONCLUSIONS

1. When the counselor gave overweight women in a weight-reduction clinic a day-by-day time perspective, the clients expressed more positive attitudes and appeared to have a greater sense of mastery than an equivalent group of clients who were given a long-term perspective focusing on the problems to be encountered in the future. The short-term orientation also had a significant positive effect on the clients' adherence to one of the recommendations made by the counselor: Clients given the day-by-day perspective mailed back a significantly larger number of weekly progress reports.

2. On the crucial measure of objectively assessed weight loss, the effect of time perspective was found to depend upon whether the client's chronic level of self-esteem was high or low. For clients with a relatively high chronic level of self-esteem, the day-by-day perspective resulted in a significantly greater amount of weight loss after 8 weeks than did the long-term perspective; but for clients with a relatively low chronic level of self-esteem, the opposite tendency was found (although this reverse trend by itself was not significant). This interaction effect might point to different characteristic modes of coping and adaptation for persons who differ in chronic level of self-esteem.

3. Contrary to initial expectations, the clients who were given self-esteem enhancement treatments showed less success at losing weight than the clients who were not given any such treatment. The self-esteem enhancement interventions proved to be partially successful, however, in improving the clients' self-appraisals, as manifested by their verbal self-reports, which may have clinical applications when the objective of counseling is primarily to enhance the clients' subjective feelings of self-esteem rather than to help clients carry out difficult courses of action.

NOTES

1. The resultant design had the following four cross-cutting factorial variables: chronic level of self-esteem (high vs. low), time perspectives (step by step vs. long term), task self-esteem enhancement (given vs. not given), and general self-esteem enhancement (given vs. not given).

2. In addition to the two measures of weight loss shown in Table 14.1, two other measures were also examined: percentage of weight loss (pounds lost/initial weight × 100) at 4 and 8 weeks. The results for percentage of weight loss were essentially the same as for pounds of

weight loss, again showing a significant interaction effect of time perspective with chronic level of self-esteem ($p < .03$, at 4 and 8 weeks). All four measures of weight loss were highly intercorrelated (correlations among the four measures ranged from .60 to .84). Because the criterion was of demonstrated weight loss, the few clients who did not show up for follow-up meetings despite repeated phone calls urging them to come in to be weighed were counted as having lost zero weight on each of the four measures.

3. When the sex of the counselor is included as a factor in the analysis of variance, which reduces error variance somewhat, the probability values for "liking for the counselor" and for "hopefulness" are significant beyond the .04 level.

4. Significant effects in the same direction were also found on failure to attend the 4-week follow-up meeting with the counselor. It was expected that general self-esteem enhancement would have a positive effect on attendance. But it turned out that 28% of the clients given the general self-esteem enhancement treatment did not come to the scheduled 4-week meeting compared with only 2% of the clients not given this form of self-esteem enhancement. This difference is statistically significant ($X^2 = 11.61$, $p < .02$, when adjusted by Yates's correction for discontinuity). There was, however, no significant effect of the general self-esteem en-hancement treatment on attendance at the 8-week follow-up session, or of the task self-esteem enhancement treatment on attendance at either the 4- or 8-week follow-up session. Neither of the self-esteem enhancement treatments had a significant effect on the number of weekly reports that clients mailed back to the counselor.

5. Findings by Baron and Ganz (1972), Phares and Lamiell (1974), and Watson and Baumal (1967) suggest a general equivalence between chronically high self-esteem and internal control, on the one hand, and between chronically low self-esteem and external control, on the other. A study by Riskind (1980) also supports the postulated equivalence of low self-esteem and external locus of control. In a sample of 20 medical patients in a hospital hemodialysis unit Riskind found that those patients who were low in self-esteem, as measured on Gough's self-acceptance scale, were significantly more "external" on Rotter's scale for locus of control ($p < .05$).

Baron and Ganz (1972) provide evidence that "externals" (who report generalized beliefs in the importance of chance and external control) perform best under conditions where external social feedback and approval can be expected for successful performance, while "internals" (who report generalized beliefs in the importance of skill and personal control) perform best where each person alone is responsible for decisions and judgments about performance. As with those who are chronically low in self-esteem, "external" persons lack self-confidence in the adequacy of their own actions and are highly reliant on external social support. Watson and Baumal (1967) studied the performance of "internals" and "externals" on skill and chance tasks. "Externals" performed best on a chance task where external factors were believed to determine successful performance, while "internals" performed best on a skill task (see also Houston, 1972).

If the assumption is correct that chronically high versus low self-esteem is equivalent to "internal" versus "external" locus of control, we can expect to find that both variables will interact with short-term versus long-term perspective in the same way. This line of reasoning suggests obvious directions for future research on responsiveness to different types of inter-ventions and recommendations made by counselors.

A number of studies indicate that persons with low self-esteem tend to be more responsive to social influences than those with high self-esteem, but other studies have reported the opposite outcome (see McGuire, 1969). One of the determinants of the relationship between self-esteem and influenceability may be the type of demand being made upon the person. Studies by Benson and Kennelly (1976) and Klein, Fencil-Mouse, and Seligman (1976) suggest that persons with low self-esteem are more debilitated than others by failures attributable to lack of personal competence. Apparently, they feel helpless and worthless when such failures occur. They may be more fearful than others of exposing their personal inadequacies when told that successful performance is not a matter of chance but requires skill and personal responsibility.

The above considerations are relevant to Averill's (1973) contention, after reviewing the literature on psychological stress, that increased personal control over impending threats does not always have positive effects. Chronic level of self-esteem may be a crucial moderating variable that determines the reactions of different people to opportunities to exercise greater control over what is going to happen to them.

6. Some of the evidence that self-esteem enhancement treatments were successful in enhancing clients' self-regard was obtained from the Quinlan and Janis self-esteem scale (Appendix). This scale measures a person's current state, as contrasted with his chronic trait, of self-esteem. Three components of a person's state of self-esteem are measured and an overall index is obtained of the average of the values for each of three components: self-pride, general self-confidence, and absence or self-derogation. These three components emerged from a factor analysis by the author based on the responses of 100 overweight women to the scale in previous research (Riskind and Janis, chap. 12).

General self-esteem enhancement was found to have positive effects, as expected, on clients' overall state of self-esteem ($p < .02$) and on their self-pride in past accomplishments ($p < .03$). Similar positive effects were found on other related attitudes when assessed by the questionnaire given at the end of the first meeting with the counselor. The predicted enhancement effects were significant for clients' hopefulness about success at dieting ($p < .04$), their willingness to diet ($p < .01$), their inclination to avoid attributing dietary setbacks to personal shortcomings ($p < .01$), and their belief that the counselor cared about their progress on the diet ($p < .02$). For task self-esteem enhancement most of the differences on these items were in the same direction, but none was statistically significant.

At the time of the 4-week follow-up meeting, task self-esteem enhancement turned out to have had a delayed positive effect on clients' overall state of self-esteem ($p < .01$), on their self-pride in past accomplishment ($p < .04$), and on their absence of self-derogation ($p < .05$). Task self-esteem enhancement also was associated with significantly lower feelings of being too weak and helpless to carry out a weight loss diet ($p < .001$). But at the time of the 8-week follow-up session there were no longer any significant effects of general self-esteem enhancement on state of self-esteem or on related attitudes.

SHORT-TERM COUNSELING IN A VARIETY OF SETTINGS

15 Effects of Self-disclosure and Interviewer Feedback: A Field Experiment during a Red Cross Blood Donation Campaign

WILLIAM L. MULLIGAN

This chapter describes experimental research in which the effects of amount of self-disclosure (moderate versus low) and interviewer feedback (positive versus neutral) were investigated in combination. The field setting was quite different from the one used in the preceding studies. It involved recruiting college men to contribute blood during a Red Cross blood donation campaign. This setting resembles a situation where a counselor advises the client to carry out a stressful course of action that the client had not previously contemplated, as when a physician recommends that a person should volunteer to donate his kidney for the altruistic purpose of saving a relative's life.

The research was designed to investigate further the following hypothesis derived from Janis's analysis (in chap. 2) of the crucial phases in a helping relationship: When attempting to help someone to carry out a difficult course of action, a counselor will be more effective in promoting compliance with a recommended course of action if he or she (1) induces a moderate amount of *self-disclosure* and (2) consistently responds to whatever the client reveals with *acceptance*. The combination of the two variables, according to the theoretical analysis, should result in more compliance than either consistent acceptance without much self-disclosure or self-disclosure without consistent acceptance.

The research presented earlier in this book supplies some supporting evidence for the beneficial effects of the two variables separately. The studies reported in chapters 9 and 10 show that when consistent acceptance by the counselor is held constant, inducing a moderate amount of self-disclosure tends to be more effective than inducing low disclosure. Three other studies, reported in chapters 6–8, show that with moderate disclosure held constant, giving consistent positive feedback (acceptance) tends to be

The research presented in this chapter is the author's doctoral dissertation, which was submitted to the Department of Psychology at Yale University. The author wishes to thank Dr. Janis, who was the main adviser, and the other members of the dissertation committee (Dr. Arnold Lazarus, Dr. David Mettee, and Dr. Fred Sheffield) for their guidance, support, and constructive criticisms throughout the course of this dissertation research.

more effective than giving neutral, ambiguous, or inconsistent positive feedback. By investigating the effects of self-disclosure and feedback in a different field setting, the present study provides a conceptual replication of the preceding investigations in a more complete test of the combined effects of the two variables.

The current study is concerned primarily with compliance with the interviewer's recommendation to volunteer as a blood donor for the Red Cross blood bank. Liking for the interviewer was also assessed as one component of attitude toward the interviewer. A number of prior studies on counseling have indicated that voluntary self-disclosure is correlated with liking (Fitzgerald, 1963; Jourard, 1959; Shapiro, McCarroll, & Fine, 1967; Worthy, Gary, & Kahn, 1969). But most of this correlational evidence can be interpreted as suggesting that liking precedes, rather than follows, voluntary self-disclosure. One of the subsidiary questions investigated in the present study involves the reverse causal sequence. Does eliciting a moderate amount of self-disclosure (under conditions of either positive or neutral feedback) lead to an increase in liking of the interviewer? If so, is the increased liking a plausible mediating factor that can account for the effects of self-disclosure on compliance with the interviewer's recommendations?

Yet another purpose of this study was to examine the effects of self-disclosure and interviewer feedback on subjective mood and emotional arousal. When a client is facing a stressful choice (such as whether to donate blood to the Red Cross), does self-disclosure increase or decrease anxiety? Social psychological research on affiliation (e.g., Schachter, 1959; Wrightsman, 1960) suggests that disclosure of realistic feelings of fear or uncertainty to another person reduces anxiety. But other investigations (e.g., Davis & Malmo, 1951; Dittes, 1957; Mowrer, 1964; Sarnoff & Zimbardo, 1961) suggest that disclosure of personal information about which the person feels embarrassed or ashamed can increase rather than decrease anxiety. Hence prior research does not provide a consistent answer. In order to investigate this question a stress induction was incorporated into the design of the current study by giving each subject a communication containing realistic information about the unpleasant experience that was in store for him if he complied with the request to donate blood to the Red Cross. The information was typical of that given by counselors who attempt to provide stress inoculation to their clients in order to prepare them psychologically for subsequent unfavorable consequences (see chap. 3).

The present study consists of two experiments which were carried out concurrently. Both investigated the effects of the same two independent variables—self-disclosure and interviewer feedback. The experiments differed only with respect to the content of the self-disclosures (past decisions only vs. past decisions plus current decisional conflict) elicited immediately before the dependent measures were taken. The major dependent variable involved an act of commitment: signing or not signing a Red Cross pledge card to donate blood. In each experiment there were 40 male undergraduates who were seen individually in 1-hour sessions that included a specific recommendation to donate blood to the American Red Cross.

THE FIRST EXPERIMENT: EFFECTS OF DISCLOSING DECISIONAL CONFLICTS OF THE RECENT PAST

Methods and Procedures

The subjects were students in an introductory psychology course at Yale University who had volunteered to participate in the study. They were randomly assigned to four conditions: (1) moderate disclosure with positive feedback, (2) moderate disclosure with neutral feedback, (3) low disclosure with positive feedback, and (4) low disclosure with neutral feedback.

Each subject in every condition was seen by two male psychologists in order to separate two different roles: the "proselytizing investigator" presented information, which was persuasive and stress inducing, on behalf of the Red Cross campaign, whereas the "interviewer" asked questions in the manner of a relatively nondirective counselor. The two psychologists alternated roles so that each was the proselytizing investigator for half the subjects and the interviewer for the other half in all four conditions.

At the beginning of the session each subject met the proselytizing investigator, who was dressed in a laboratory coat. Conspicuously displayed at one end of the table in the investigator's room was a variety of medical supplies (e.g., blood lancets, bandages, gauze, and alcohol) and there was a pronounced smell of alcohol. The subject was asked to read some materials regarding the American Red Cross Blood Donation Program. The communication was designed to induce a real-life decisional conflict by presenting very strong social, ethical, and personal reasons why the subject should donate blood. Each subject was also given stress inoculation materials consisting of a series of photographs (some of which were in color) with captions describing in a realistic way the temporary pain and discomfort involved in donating blood.

The proselytizing investigator truthfully informed each subject that (a) one of the main reasons for organizing the research project around the American Red Cross Blood Program was his personal feeling that the Red Cross's program served an important social function and needed all the volunteer support it could get, (b) the subject's decision would be regarded as a sincere commitment, and (c) if he signed a pledge card, that card would be forwarded to the Red Cross and a follow-up inquiry would be made to determine whether the pledge was honored. The subject was asked to postpone giving his decision until requested to do so later on, near the end of the interview.[1]

This series of procedures was designed to parallel those that occur in a medical clinic when the relative of a patient with kidney disease is asked to donate a kidney to save the patient's life. The relative is reminded of the strong social and moral arguments for making the donation but at the same time is given realistic information about the suffering and deprivations he will have to undergo and he or she is asked to think it over before committing himself (Fellner & Marhsall, 1970; Simmons, Klein, & Simmons, 1977).

Immediately after the initial session with the proselytizing investigator, the subject was taken to a separate room and introduced to the interviewer. The interviewer's opening comments were intended to put the subject at ease and to emphasize the differences between his and the investigator's roles in the study. The subject was told, for example, "Unlike Mr. _____ (the proselytizing investigator), I am *not* primarily interested in whether or not you decide to donate. . . . Although I personally think donating blood is a good thing to do, I am *primarily* interested in talking with you about a variety of experiences you have had and decisions you have made." In all conditions the interviewer gave this brief endorsement of the blood donation decision. Later, near the end of the session, he asked the subject whether he had decided to respond to the Red Cross appeal for blood donors. Each subject was reassured about the voluntary nature of the interview and the confidentiality of his statements.

In the *moderate self-disclosure* interview each subject was asked to talk about major, personal issues of the recent past. He was asked to list three of the most important personal life decisions he had made in the past few years or was in the process of making. The interviewer gave several examples (e.g., "One student decided to quit school for a while, another student decided to get married."). The interviewer selected for further questioning the two decisions that he thought were most consequential and focused his questions primarily on how the subject felt about each alternative. But the interviewer did not ask any probing questions to induce disclosure of intimate details that went beyond the subject's initial spontaneous comments even if he was vague or evasive. When talking about marital decisions, for example, the interviewer did not ask any questions about incompatibilities, quarrels, or sexual problems comparable to those used in the high self-disclosure interviews in the dieting clinic studies described in chapters 11–13.

The *low self-disclosure* interview was designed to minimize disclosure of significant information about the subject's personal life. The subject was asked to list a number of relatively unimportant deicisons he had made within a few weeks preceding the study. The interviewer gave each subject several examples of minor decisions (e.g., to see a movie, to play tennis, to do some light reading). From the list of decisions given by the subject, five of the least important were selected for further questioning. The interviewer's subsequent questions focused on objective facts and circumstantial details. Throughout the remainder of the low self-disclosure interview the subject was never asked to talk about any of his subjective feelings or areas of conflict.

Positive feedback included positive social reinforcement and reflective comments. When giving positive social reinforcement, the interviewer praised the subject for having given appropriate answers and for having done "good work" during the interview (e.g., "Very good, those are exactly the kinds of decisions I was looking for; I appreciate your trying as hard as you have to answer my questions."). Reflective comments attempted to concentrate on the essential content of the subject's answers in the manner described by Rogers (1961) (e.g., "So your parents wanted you to continue to attend church, but you felt religion was becoming less relevant each day.").

In the *neutral feedback* condition the interviewer tried to maintain a very businesslike exterior. He was silent a much greater percentage of the time than in the positive feedback condition, and his comments were limited to simple acknowledgment that the subject had spoken and had completed an answer to a question (e.g., "Uh-huh; O.K., the next question is. . . ."). It should be emphasized, however, that in this condition the interviewer's role was defined as requiring that he withhold explicit positive feedback rather than give negative feedback. Nonverbally the counselor displayed a friendly interest in everything the subject was saying. This type of feedback might have been perceived by the subject as mildly positive rather than neutral.

Immediately after the interview on major or minor decisions of the recent past, the interviewer asked the subject whether or not he decided to donate blood to the Red Cross. Those who said they would donate were asked if they would be willing to sign a pledge card and indicate several possible dates. After the interviewer obtained this measure of compliance with the recommendations that he had endorsed, an additional interview was conducted. For the subjects in the moderate disclosure condition the interviewer asked questions to elicit disclosure of feelings that were relevant to the decisional conflict about donating blood. For the subjects in the low disclosure condition the interviewer asked impersonal, non-ego involving questions such as What part of the country are you from? . . . What hobbies do you have? . . . What are your favorite academic subjects?.

At the end of each interview the proselytizing investigator once again took charge and gave the subject a final questionnaire that included items dealing with liking for and appraisals of the interviewer. Several measures of subjective mood and emotional arousal were also obtained after the interview (Mood Adjective Check List, Palmar Sweat Index, and Digit Symbol Test) along with Jourard's (1971) personality scale designed to differentiate between habitually high and low disclosure tendencies.

Results

Two items dealing with appraisals of the interviewer's "friendliness" and "warmth" were combined and used as a check on the adequacy of the positive versus neutral feedback treatments. As expected, the interviewer was rated more positively when he gave explicitly positive feedback ($p < .001$).[2]

In order to check on the adequacy of the interviews intended to elicit moderate versus low self-disclosure, tape recordings of all interview responses were examined by a psychologist who was blind with regard to experimental conditions. Again, as expected, the decisions that students in the high self-disclosure condition discussed were found to be consistently of a more intimate nature and were rated as being of much greater relevance to the students' personal goals and values than the decisions that the students in the low self-disclosure condition discussed.

Table 15.1. Compliance data from Experiment 1: percentage of subjects in each treatment condition who signed pledge cards committing themselves to donate blood

Self-disclosure treatment	Interviewer feedback		Combined
	Positive	Neutral	
Moderate self-disclosure	90%	50%	70%
Low self-disclosure	20%	50%	35%
Combined	55%	50%	52%

Note. $N = 10$ in each of the 4 groups.

As to the crucial results on compliance, the first finding is that there is a main effect for self-disclosure ($p < .05$). Students who had been given the moderate self-dislosure interview signed more pledge cards than those who had been given the low self-disclosure interview. But, as can be seen by examining the results in Table 15.1, this effect occurs only for those students who were given positive feedback by the interviewer. The interaction effect between self-disclosure treatment and interviewer feedback is statistically significant ($p < .05$).

The interaction effect indicates that, for moderate self-disclosure interviews, positive feedback led to greater compliance with the recommendation endorsed by the interviewer, but not for low self-disclosure interviews. Janis's theoretical analysis (chap. 2) is supported by the finding that the greatest compliance occurred, as predicted, in the group that received the moderate self-disclosure interview combined with positive feedback from the interviewer.

Objective follow-up evidence of behavioral adherence to the decision was also obtained which revealed that most students who signed pledge cards did, in fact, carry out their donation pledges. On the basis of an agreement to maintain the anonymity of the subjects, the American Red Cross checked the records of persons who actually came in to donate blood during the Yale Blood Drives and indicated how many in each group in this study did so. As expected, this follow-up adherence measure was highly correlated with the commitment measure: Those who signed the pledge cards were much more likely actually to donate blood than those who did not ($p < .001$). Analysis of the donation behavior of 29 students who had an opportunity to donate blood within 11 days of the end of the then-current Yale Blood Drive showed a significant interaction effect ($p < .05$), which is the same as the interaction effect found for signing of the pledge cards: Positive feedback from the interviewer led to more actual blood donations if the subjects were given the moderate self-disclosure interview but not if they were given the low self-disclosure interview.[3]

Liking for the interviewer was measured by a single questionnaire item: "How much did you like the interviewer?" The answers were scored on a scale ranging from –2 to +2. The meaning rating obtained from each group is shown in Table 15.2. The results indicate that subjects liked the interviewer

Table 15.2. Mean liking ratings of the interviewer (Experiment 1)

Self-disclosure treatment	Interviewer feedback		
	Positive	Neutral	Combined
Moderate self-disclosure	1.94	1.70	1.82
Low self-disclosure	1.82	1.63	1.72
Combined	1.88	1.66	1.77

Note. $N = 10$ in each of the 4 groups.

more if they were given positive feedback than if they were given neutral feedback ($p < .05$). Liking was not significantly affected by the self-disclosure treatment and there was no interaction effect paralleling that obtained for the compliance data shown in Table 15.1. These results suggest that liking for the interviewer did not mediate the relation between the treatments and compliance.[4]

THE SECOND EXPERIMENT: EFFECTS OF INDUCING ADDITIONAL DISCLOSURES OF THE CURRENT DECISIONAL CONFLICT

Methods and Procedures

The same two psychologists carried out the second experiment concurrently with the first one. The effects of the same two independent variables— amount of induced self-disclosure and type of feedback from the interviewer—were investigated in essentially the same way. The procedures were exactly the same, with only one important exception. In the second experiment the main measure of compliance was not obtained until after the subjects who were given the moderate disclosure interview had revealed a great deal more about themselves: The interviewer waited until each subject who had been given the moderate disclosure interview had also answered questions about his feelings concerning the here-and-now decisional issue as to whether to donate blood before asking whether he was willing to sign a pledge card. In Experiment 1, compliance measures were taken immediately after each subject in the moderate disclosure condition had discussed the past decisions that had nothing to do with the current decisional conflict about donating blood. In that experiment the interviewer asked the questions about the here-and-now decision after the compliance measure was taken. In Experiment 2, however, the compliance measure and the attitude measures were obtained at the end of the entire interview, after the subjects in the higher self-disclosure condition had answered all the questions about the here-and-now conflict as well as the questions about decisional conflicts of the recent past. Consequently the subjects were asked questions that involved substantially more disclosure of personal feelings than in the first experiment (including fear of physical pain or damage from donating blood and reluctance to respond to a humanitarian appeal to help other people, which could be construed as cowardice or callousness and therefore entail feelings of shame or guilt). But this interview did not attempt to induce as much self-disclosure as the "high" disclosure interviews used in the weight-reduction studies (chaps. 11–13), which included a wide variety of questions that probed for personal information that is usually not revealed to anyone or only to one's best friend. Therefore, the interview in the second experiment is designated as "moderately high self-disclosure."

Just as in the first experiment a content analysis of the tape recordings of the subjects' interview responses was made by a psychologist who was blind with regard to experimental conditions. This analysis showed that the moderately high self-disclosure interview in Experiment 2 did, in fact, elicit significantly more items of intimate personal information than the low disclosure interview in Experiment 2 and also significantly more than the moderate or low self-disclosure interviews in Experiment 1.

For subjects in the low disclosure condition the only difference between the two experiments was that in the second experiment the interviewer completed the entire interview, including some additional routine questions about the subject's background and interests (in order to equalize the length of the interviews) before obtaining the compliance measure. Thus, in the second experiment a slight augmentation of the low disclosure interview was compared with a substantial augmentation of the moderate disclosure interview.

This experiment was carried out before any of the studies indicating potentially unfavorable effects of inducing a high degree of self-disclosure had been completed. At the time, the changes introduced in Experiment 2 were expected to intensify the positive findings on the effects of self-disclosure combined with positive feedback, just as was found in the first experiment. Presumably there would be greater opportunity for self-esteem enhancement—and a corresponding increase in the interviewer's referent power—resulting from his giving positive feedback in response to the subjects' answers in the moderately high disclosure interview to questions about the immediate blood donation decision at hand. The results, however, did not bear out this expectation.

Results

The results for the primary compliance measure (*signing of pledge cards*) are shown in Table 15.3. Just as in the first experiment, there is a main effect

Table 15.3. Compliance data from Experiment 2: percentage of subjects in each treatment condition who signed pledge cards committing themselves to donate blood

Self-disclosure treatment	Interviewer feedback		
	Positive	Neutral	Combined
Moderately high self-disclosure	60%	90%	75%
Augmented low self-disclosure	60%	30%	45%
Combined	60%	60%	60%

Note. $N = 10$ in each of the 4 groups.

for self-disclosure, in this instance almost reaching the conventional level of significance ($p < .07$). This main effect is attributable to the interaction between self-disclosure treatment and interviewer feedback ($p < .07$). But the interaction effect is a reversal of the interaction obtained in the first experiment. It indicates that in the moderately high self-disclosure condition, neutral feedback produced greater compliance, whereas in the augmented low self-disclosure condition, positive feedback produced greater compliance.

Analysis of the follow-up behavioral data for those subjects who had an immediate opportunity to donate blood revealed a significantly greater tendency for subjects in the moderately high self-disclosure condition to make blood donations, according to Red Cross records. The proportion of subjects who actually donated was 54% in the moderately high self-disclosure condition as against only 15% in the augmented low self-disclosure condition. This main effect for level of self-disclosure is statistically significant ($p < .05$).[5]

Analysis of the results on *liking of the interviewer* (Table 15.4) revealed only one significant result, a main effect for interviewer feedback ($p < .01$).

This finding bears out the results obtained in the first experiment and in the weight-reduction studies (chaps. 6–8), again indicating that positive feedback leads to greater liking than neutral feedback.

Table 15.4. Mean liking ratings of the interviewer (Experiment 2)

Self-disclosure treatment	Interviewer feedback		Combined
	Positive	Neutral	
Moderately high self-disclosure	1.91	1.50	1.70
Augmented low self-disclosure	1.94	1.72	1.83
Combined	1.92	1.61	1.76

Note. $N = 10$ in each of the 4 groups.

Point biserial correlations were computed in order to determine if there was any relationship between liking for the interviewer and compliance. Liking was not significantly correlated with signing of pledge cards ($r = .18$) or with actual donation behavior ($r = -.06$). These results, like the comparable results in Experiment 1, imply that liking for the interviewer did not mediate the interaction effect of induced self-disclosure and interviewer feedback on compliance.

Significant interactions between self-disclosure treatment and interviewer feedback were obtained for the Mood Adjective Check List (MACL) scale on anxiety ($p < .01$), dysphoria ($p < .05$), elation ($p < .05$), and euphoria ($p < .05$). These results consistently indicate that for the moderately high self-disclosure interview, positive feedback had a more favorable effect on the subjects' mood, whereas for the augmented low self-disclosure interview, neutral feedback had a more favorable effect on their mood.

DISCUSSION

The results of the first experiment, which are consistent with the weight-reduction studies in chaps. 6–10, clearly support a major prediction from Janis's theoretical analysis of the helping relationship (chap. 2): The group that received the moderate self-disclosure interview and that was given positive feedback showed significantly greater compliance than any other group in terms of number of pledge cards signed. But unexpected results were obtained when the second, nearly identical experiment was run. The relatively higher level of induced disclosure was again more effective than the lower level of induced disclosure, but this time the neutral feedback in response to moderately high disclosure was more effective.[6]

The contrasting outcomes of the two experiments are depicted graphically in Figure 15.1. The markers indicating average amount of compliance for positive and neutral feedback combined show that in both experiments the relatively low level of self-disclosure, compared to moderate or moderately high self-disclosure, resulted in less compliance with the recommendation endorsed by the interviewer. The only discrepancy between the

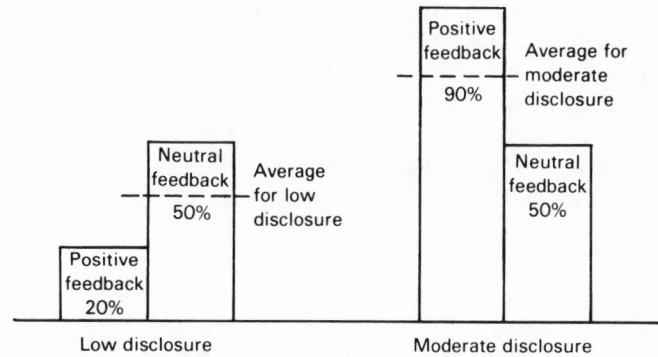

Experiment 1: In the moderate self-disclosure interview clients discussed recent personal decisions.

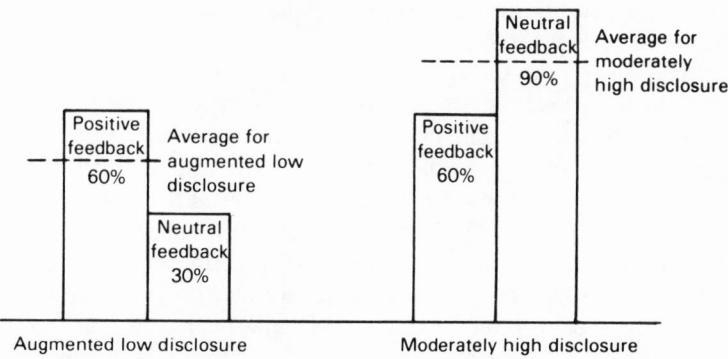

Experiment 2: In the moderately high self-disclosure interview clients discussed the current blood-donation decision in addition to other recent decisions.

Figure 15.1. Percentage of students who signed pledge cards to donate blood.

two experiments pertains to the effects of *neutral* compared with *positive* feedback. Neutral feedback, as was pointed out earlier, is in a sense misnamed because it is essentially a mild, nonexplicit form of positive feedback: The interviewer showed positive interest and a friendly attitude by his facial expressions and he avoided expressing any criticism or rejection.

What accounts for the unpredicted outcome of the second experiment? Why could it be that implicit acceptance (conveyed by the "neutral" feedback) leads to more compliance than explicit acceptance (conveyed by the "positive" verbal as well as nonverbal feedback) when the subjects are asked to talk about their current decisional conflict in a moderately high disclosure interview?

As is usually the case with results that were unpredicted before doing an experiment, one is impelled to look further into the data for an explanation. A replay of interview tapes revealed that in the second interview, dealing with the decision to give blood, the students in the moderately high disclosure condition were saying things such as "I don't really want to donate. I ought to, but I really wish I didn't have to. I do feel that I'd rather not." Students in the augmented low disclosure interview in Experiment 2 were not asked how they felt about donating blood and never expressed any such feelings.

A systematic content analysis of the moderately high self-disclosure interview tapes in the second experiment showed that subjects in both positive and neutral feedback conditions frequently expressed antidonation feelings (e.g., fear of needles, fear of giving blood, health concerns, negative experiences with doctors, resentment about being under pressure to give an immediate binding decision to donate blood). It seems likely, therefore, that explicit accepting feedback—given as the subjects were expressing such antidonation sentiments (e.g., "I can understand your feelings....") —would serve to reinforce an antidonation stance. Many of the students who received this positive feedback during the moderately high disclosure interview may have learned essentially that they would continue to receive noncontingent positive feedback regardless of what they felt or said about donating blood. Whenever a student said he felt reluctant to donate, the interviewer's positive feedback could have increased the likelihood that he would decide not to sign a pledge card. Neutral feedback given after the students had expressed counterdonation responses would be much less likely to be construed as noncontingent acceptance and would therefore be much less likely to encourage them to act on whatever antidonation feelings they expressed. This interpretation would also account for another finding: Subjects given positive feedback during the moderately high disclosure interview reported feeling *less anxiety* afterward than those given neutral feedback, perhaps because they felt reassured by the explicitly accepting interviewer that it was perfectly all right as far as he was concerned to decide not to donate.

Studies of verbal conditioning (e.g., Greenspoon, 1955; Krasner, 1958; Marlowe, 1962; Salzinger, 1959) have consistently shown the importance of contingent rather than random or indiscriminately positive reinforcement. Heller, Davis, and Myers (1966) conclude that although positive feedback consistently produces greater liking, "indiscriminate approval by an interviewer may be an inefficient method of inducing behavior change, because it retards the learning of new responses by rewarding erroneous as well as appropriate behavior" (p. 506). If subjects in the present study were motivated by a need for approval, the interviewer's approval would have to be made contingent upon their prodonation responses in order to maximize the likelihood of compliance.

The preliminary theoretical framework presented by Janis (chap. 2) takes account of the value of making acceptance contingent upon the client's expression of willingness to try to carry out the interviewer's recommendations. According to Janis's formulation the subject could be given unconditional positive acceptance during the first phase of treatment in order to establish a trusting relationship in which the subject comes to rely on the counselor for enhancement of self-esteem. Then during the second phase acceptance is made contingent upon the expression of responses that are compatible with the goal. Given the results obtained in the present studies, it seems likely that for decisions about which the subjects feel negativistic or extremely ambivalent at the outset, noncontingent reinforcement given during the first phase may sometimes work against the counseling goals.

Accordingly, two addenda to Janis's formulation are suggested whenever counselors are attempting to induce clients to comply with their recommendations, such as those given by physicians in medical clinics. One suggestion involves controlling the content of the material disclosed. Initially the interviewer could ask the subject to make disclosures that are *not directly relevant* to the decision about which he or she is in conflict (donating blood in the present study). As the client makes nonrelevant disclosures, the interviewer can maintain a stance of noncontingent acceptance. Once it appears that sufficient rapport is established, the interviewer could ask the subject to make disclosures that are *directly relevant* to the current decisional conflict. During this second phase the interviewer could make his or her acceptance contingent upon the subject's favorable comments about trying to carry out the recommended course of action. Thus, in the first phase the counselor can maintain a position of unconditional acceptance of the person, whereas in the second phase the counselor can function as a norm-sender and differentially reinforce responses that are in favor of, or at least not antagonistic to, the recommended means for attaining the goal that the client agrees he or she wants to attain.

A second suggestion is that it might be maximally effective for a counselor to give approval on a contingent basis from the beginning of the counseling relationship. This approach assumes that starting off with unconditional acceptance, as described by Rogers (1961), may in many cases not be necessary for a successful outcome when the objective is to help clients commit themselves and adhere to a difficult course of action. Such an approach would make no attempt to operate in two discrete phases, one for establishing rapport and the other for eliciting compliance. An advantage of making social reinforcement contingent from the beginning of the helping relationship is that it may avoid the severe crisis which is likely to occur if the counselor begins with noncontingent acceptance and subsequently changes to contingent acceptance. But, of course, this alternative solution runs the risk of failing to build up a sufficiently positive relationship. The counselor's approval may not become enough of an incentive for the client to adopt and carry out a difficult or stressful set of recommendations. The central point underlying both suggestions is that the counselor should at no time give positive feedback that would reinforce the subject immediately after he or she has disclosed feelings or attitudes that are antagonistic to the recommended course of action.[7]

The results of the Colten and Janis study (chap. 9) do not seem to support some of the assumptions just made. In that experiment the moderate self-disclosure interview elicited comments from the clients about their current decisional conflict about going on a diet to lose weight and all clients were given consistently positive feedback by the interviewer. Contrary to what might be expected from the foregoing discussion of the undesirability of giving noncontingent acceptance, the results showed that the moderate self-disclosure treatment tended to produce more behavioral compliance with the counselor's recommendations than the low self-disclosure treatment. In that study, however, all subjects came voluntarily to the clinic in order to obtain help in carrying out their decision to lose weight. During the moderate self-disclosure interviews, few clients expressed any reluctance to go on a diet and when they did the interviewer was careful to avoid making positive comments that might have the unintended effect of reinforcing the wrong choice. But if a sizable proportion of clients at a weight-reduction clinic were to express opposition or reluctance to comply with the recommendations, as in the present study, it might be difficult for a counselor who is attempting to give noncontingent positive feedback to avoid making some accepting comments that could be construed by the client as acceptance of the client's decision to reject the recommended course of action.

Turning now to the findings on attitude toward the interviewer, we note first that both of the present experiments show that positive feedback led to greater liking for the interviewer, as measured by one qustionnaire item. These findings are consistent with those from weight-reduction experiments (chaps. 6 and 7) and from earlier social psychological research on liking for strangers (Backman & Secord, 1959; Deutsch & Solomon, 1959; Dickoff, 1961; Jones, Gergen, & Davis, 1962; Newcomb, 1956, 1961). But the data obtained in both of the current experiments indicate that liking for the interviewer was not affected by self-disclosure and was not positively correlated with compliance. These findings appear to be inconsistent with the conformity literature, which indicates that conformity and liking are frequently correlated (see Hare, 1976). One explanation for this discrepancy is that the compliant behavior investigated in prior studies of conformity was much less stressful than that investigated in the present study. Positive feedback alone may increase the likelihood that subjects will be influenced to modify their ratings in conformity with mild social pressure from an experimenter when they are asked to judge a painting or to give their opinions about a remote political or social issue. Other factors, however, may enter in when subjects are asked to do something as stressful as committing themselves to donate blood.

In any case the results on the questionnaire item dealing with liking for the interviewer imply that liking did not mediate the relation among self-disclosure, interviewer feedback, and compliance. In other words the results seem to indicate that subjects did not comply with the interviewer's recommendations simply because they like him. But, of course, the check mark that subjects make in response to a questionnaire item about liking the interviewer may pertain to a rather superficial or conventional view of the other person as tolerable, as someone who does not deserve to be disliked. It may not mean that he is someone who is regarded with affection and high esteem and whose approval they want to have. If so, the crude measure of liking may not be a valid one for investigating the mediating attitude toward the interviewer that is specified in Janis's theoretical analysis.

The main results reported in this chapter appear to be compatible with a formulation that emphasizes approval seeking as a mediating variable, but additional research is obviously needed to test the hypothesis that acceptance of an interviewee's self-disclosures by an interviewer heightens the interviewee's need for approval (or fear of disapproval) from the interviewer. If this hypothesis is correct, approval seeking may turn out to be the critical variable underlying compliance with an interviewer's recommendations after the interviewer has induced a moderate amount of self-disclosure and has given either implicit or explicit positive feedback.

MAIN CONCLUSIONS

1. The positive effects of eliciting a moderate degree of self-disclosure, compared with eliciting a low degree of self-disclosure, was confirmed in a field setting quite different from the dieting clinic in which earlier confirmations were obtained. This study was conducted during a Red Cross campaign at a time when recruiters were asking college men to volunteer to donate blood, which is a minor stressful dilemma that may be comparable in some essential ways to the major stressful dilemma arising when a physician or health-care counselor recommends that a person should volunteer to donate his or her kidney or some other organ for the altruistic purpose of saving a relative's life. The results show that eliciting moderate or moderately high self-disclosure tended to produce more compliance with the recommendations endorsed by the interviewer than eliciting low disclosure, most pronouncedly under conditions where the interviewer did not ask any questions about the current decisional conflict about donating blood and gave consistently positive feedback.

2. When the disclosures induced by the counselor were relevant to the

current decisional conflict and contained admissions of the subjects' reluctance to adopt the recommended course of action, more compliance was produced when the counselors gave neutral feedback than when they gave explicit positive feedback. The positive feedback may have indirectly reinforced the wrong decision from the recommender's standpoint despite the precautions taken to avoid doing so.

3. Positive feedback from the interviewer during a low, moderate, or moderately high self-disclosure interview led to an increase in ratings of liking for the interviewer, as measured by an item on an attitude questionnaire. But this increased liking, which does not necessarily imply increased affection for the interviewer or greater incentive to seek his approval, apparently did not mediate compliance with the interviewer's recommendations.

NOTES

1. Each subject was also exposed to a supplementary procedure that confronted him with the more immediate but very minor threat of having a blood sample taken by means of an ear prick at the end of the session. The investigator told each subject that the ear prick was routinely given to everyone, regardless of his donation decision, in order to provide a "first hand, concrete experience of part of the procedure of donating blood." (It was true that at Red Cross Bloodmobiles an ear prick was always taken in order to obtain an initial blood sample from every prospective donor.) A photograph of a donor receiving an ear prick was included in the stress inoculation materials. The investigator added that discussion of any questions the subject might have regarding the ear prick should be temporarily postponed until after the interview (at which time each subject learned that he had a free choice as to whether to undergo the ear prick procedure). The dependent measures, including subjective reports of arousal, failed to provide clear-cut evidence that this ear prick procedure had the intended effect of inducing at least a mild degree of anticipatory fear or anxiety and therefore this supplementary procedure did not provide any relevant data.

2. An analysis of variance of combined scores on ratings of the interviewer showed that a significant main effect for type of interviewer feedback held for both Experiments 1 and 2 ($F(1, 64) = 36.52$, $p < .001$). An analysis of variance that included the two interviewers as an additional variable showed that this main effect also held for both psychologists who served as interviewers. Essentially the same results were found for both interviewers for other dependent variables investigated in the two experiments: signing pledge cards, actual donations of blood, liking for the interviewer, and liking for the study as a whole.

3. The data for proportions obtained for signing of pledge cards that committed the person to the donation decision (and also for the follow-up on actual donation behavior) were analyzed by means of a formula for analysis of variance suggested by Sheffield (1957). This analysis of variance, which was specifically designed for the multidimensional analysis of discontinuous data, yielded a significant interaction effect for the signing of pledge cards: $F = 4.90$, $p < .05$).

The follow-up data from Experiments 1 and 2 combined revealed that, of the 45 subjects who signed a pledge card, 30 (67%) actually carried out their pledges; whereas, of the 35 subjects who did not pledge to donate, 8 (23%) subsequently donated blood during a Red Cross blood drive ($\chi^2 = 15.14$, $df = 1$, $p < .001$).

Unfortunately, a minority of the subjects in Experiment 1 could not be scheduled for their interviews until just after the Red Cross's Fall Blood Drive at Yale University had ended and therefore had to wait about 3 months for an opportunity to donate blood during the Spring Blood Drive. More specifically, of the 40 subjects in the first experiment, 11 were seen too late for the Fall Blood Drive. The follow-up behavioral data for those 11 subjects do not show any trend but the number of cases is too small to warrant statistical analysis. The essential point is that the significant interaction effect for the follow-up behavioral data pertains only to those subjects who had the opportunity to donate blood within less than 2 weeks; the percentages of those subjects who actually donated blood, according to the Red Cross records, were as follows:

(1) moderate self-disclosure with positive feedback   4 out of 8 = 50%
(2) low self-disclosure with positive feedback   1 out of 7 = 14%
(3) moderate self-disclosure with neutral feedback   2 out of 8 = 25%
(4) low self-disclosure with neutral feedback   3 out of 6 = 50%

For the very small number of cases in each of the four conditions, the first group exceeded two of the other groups but not the fourth group. These findings for the follow-up behavioral measure partially replicate the findings for signing of pledge cards. The interaction effect is again significant, ($p < .05$), but the group given the moderate self-disclosure interview with positive feedback did not exceed the group given the low self-disclosure interview with neutral feedback.

4. In order to examine further the relationship between liking of the interviewer and the blood donation decisions, point biserial correlations were computed. These calculations revealed that liking of the interviewer was uncorrelated with signing the pledge card to donate blood ($r = -.06$) and negatively correlated with the follow-up behavioral measure of adherence ($r = -.34$, $p = .02$). The latter correlation indicates that subjects who liked the interviewer the most were least likely to donate blood. The explanation for this unexpected reversal of the predicted relationship might lie in the fact that at the very end of the initial session all subjects given the moderate disclosure interview were permitted to express their qualms or reluctance about donating blood without being given any selective or contingent feedback by the interviewer. After going through such an interview the subjects who liked the interviewer the most may have been more likely than the others to feel that the interviewer was so accepting that it would make no difference to him whether someone actually donated blood.

Additional minor findings from Experiment 1 were as follows:

(1) Results on a questionnaire item that asked about "liking for the study as a whole" yielded the same interaction effect as was found for behavioral compliance ($F(1, 32) = 4.91$, $p < .05$).

(2) Two measures of subjective mood (Mood Adjective Check List [MACL] scales for Anxiety and Elation) indicated that the subjects were significantly aroused by the stress inoculation communication given in all treatment conditions, but other measures (Palmar Sweat Index, Digit Symbol Test, and other MACL scales) failed to show significant changes.

(3) No significant effects of self-disclosure or interviewer feedback were found for any scales from the Mood Adjective Check List, or for the Palmar Sweat Index or the Digit Symbol Test.

(4) Habitual self-disclosure type (as measured by Jourard's [1971] questionnaire) failed to show any significant relationships to any of the dependent measures and did not enter into any significant interaction effects.

5. The same type of analysis of variance was used as for the comparable data in Experiment 1 (see n. 3). Just as for the signing of pledge cards, the highest percentage of actual blood donations was found in the group that had received the moderately high self-disclosure interview with neutral feedback (72%), which was more than double the percentage for the group that had received the same moderately high self-disclosure interview with positive feedback (33%). In the two groups that had received the augmented low self-disclosure interview, only a small percentage actually donated blood (14% for those who had been given positive feedback and 17% for those who had been given neutral feedback).

6. As a further check on the differential findings from the two experiments, a three-way analysis of variance was carried out for the compliance measure by combining the data from both experiments. This analysis, as expected, revealed a significant third-order interaction effect for (a) interviewer feedback and (b) induced level of self-disclosure, with (c) content of material disclosed (Experiment 1 vs. 2): $F = 9.15$, $p < .01$.

7. Research on conflict resolution (e.g., Bixenstine & Wilson, 1963; Deutsch, Epstein, Canavan, & Gumpert, 1967; Harford & Solomon, 1967) has consistently shown that a position of unconditional cooperation followed by conditional cooperation is a less effective strategy

than conditional cooperation followed by unconditional cooperation. More simply, these studies indicate that beginning with a high degree of benevolence and decreasing it subsequently is an ineffective strategy for eliciting desired responses.

Note by the Editor. In the studies carried out in the Yale Weight-Reduction Clinic (chaps. 5–14) and in other clinical settings (chaps. 4 and 16–19) the counselors were trained to avoid reinforcing undesirable actions. They were especially cautious about this whenever a client asserted reluctance or doubt about doing what the counselor was recommending. For example, if a client were to say that he or she lacks the will power to carry out the recommended 1200-calorie diet, the counselor typically would say something like this: "It's good to be honest about having that feeling because it is necessary to realize that it's part of your problem."

Mulligan's second suggestion (that counselors might elicit more compliance with their recommendations if they give approval on a contingent basis from the beginning of the initial interview) was subsequently investigated by Quinlan and Janis in the field experiment in the Yale Weight-Reduction Clinic, reported in chap. 11. That study showed that clients who were given noncontingent positive feedback throughout the entire initial interview lost about the same amount of weight after 1 month and mailed back about the same number of weekly reports as clients who were given contingent positive feedback from the beginning of the interview. It is quite possible, of course, that in certain settings (such as weight-reduction clinics, in which clients very seldom express counternorm intentions) it makes no difference whether the counselor gives noncontingent or contingent feedback throughout the entire interview, whereas in other settings contingent feedback may prove to be more effective, as suggested by Mulligan.

16 Effects of Self-esteem Enhancement on Teachers' Acceptance of Innovation in a Classroom Setting

ARTHUR D. SMITH

The present investigation is primarily based upon the theoretical analysis of self-esteem dynamics put forward by Janis (chap. 2). According to Janis's formulation, an individual becomes reliant upon a helper for self-esteem enhancement if he or she has disclosed personal information that is normally withheld, provided that the disclosures are received with positive acceptance. As a result the individual becomes increasingly motivated to comply with the helper's recommendations. Janis hypothesizes that in a self-disclosing situation, attraction to the helper and changes in self-esteem mediate the relationship among degree of self-disclosure, quality of feedback, and adherence to the helper's recommendations.

The present study was designed primarily to investigate the relationship between enhancement of self-esteem and adherence to a counselor's recommendations. Specifically, the major purpose is to test the hypothesis that trainees in a workshop for improving the effectiveness of public school teachers will be more responsive to a counselor's recommendations if they are given positive feedback (rather than neutral feedback) in regard to their professional capabilities under conditions where they engage in a moderate degree of self-disclosure. This investigation attempts to determine whether teachers who are given positive feedback focusing on their professional skills will show the expected increase in self-esteem and greater adherence to recommendations that require changes in the teaching methods they use in their classrooms.

This study is based on a dissertation presented to the faculty of the graduate school of Yale University in candidacy for the Ph.D. degree. In the process of completing this dissertation I have been aided by the suggestions and criticisms of many friends and scholars. Among those I should like to mention especially are obligations to my advisor, Professor I. L. Janis, for his assistance, advice, and encouragement throughout the preparation of the study. I am also indebted to committee members Professors R. P. Abelson, W. Kessen, P. M. Powell, and D. M. Quinlan for guidance and editorial comments.

My thanks are also due to Dr. Richard Mastain, who was Executive Director of the New Haven Education Improvement Center at the time this study was carried out, for his valuable assistance in conducting the workshops and in providing some of the experimental materials. Dr. Mastain, who had developed the workshop program, was the instructor in the present study.

Although there is reason to believe that Janis's formulation will apply across all levels of chronic self-esteem, some prior studies suggest that individuals with high, medium, and low self-esteem differ in their responses to self-disclosure and positive feedback (e.g., Holstein, Goldstein, & Bem, 1971; Maracek & Mettee, 1972).[1] The chronic level of self-esteem, therefore, may be an important determinant in the process Janis has described. A subsidiary purpose of the current investigation was to observe the relationship between a measure of chronic self-esteem and the effects of self-esteem enhancement.

In order to test a related personality determinant that might be predictive of responsiveness to positive feedback, all subjects were also administered a locus-of-control measure. The locus-of-control construct, which derives from Rotter's social learning theory, might prove to be related to the degree to which people attribute reinforcements to their own actions (Rotter, 1966). Persons who feel that they control their own destiny are located on the internal end of the continuum; persons who feel controlled by outside forces (whether fate, luck, chance, or powerful others) are at the external end of the continuum (Rotter, 1966). External locus-of-control has been found to be related to poor achievement behavior (Coleman, Campbell, Hobson, & McPartland, 1966), greater conformity (MacDonald, 1972; Odel, 1959), and positive reaction to influence attempts (Biondo & MacDonald, 1971; Ritchie & Phares, 1969).

METHOD

Overview of Procedure

The setting for the present study was a workshop for inner-city elementary school teachers who generally lack opportunities for positive feedback in their daily environment.[2] All subjects engaged in self-disclosure of their learning skills and their feelings, specifically about their professional roles and competence. But unlike the earlier experiments involving self-disclosure (chaps. 6–15), where positive feedback was given immediately after each of the subject's answers during self-disclosure interviews, positive feedback (self-esteem enhancement) in the present study was applied to the teachers' performances and spontaneous comments in the workshop.

The main independent variable was self-esteem enhancement. All subjects were given pre- and immediate post-self-esteem measures. Various behavioral indicators were used to assess subsequent adherence to the counselor's recommendations, which pertained to innovative teaching methods requiring the use of diagnostic techniques in the classroom.

The study was carried out with 40 elementary school teachers in a training workshop designed to improve their classroom competencies. The workshop, which met twice during one month, was based on a previously developed training program in diagnostic arithmetic techniques. The purpose of the workshop was to increase the teachers' ability to make differential diagnoses of students' specific difficulties in arithmetic and to prescribe learning experiences based on an accurate diagnosis of the individual student's needs. The author was assisted by the male workshop instructor, who had developed this program. During the workshop the author acted as a tutor and counselor. The instructor was kept blind to the treatment conditions and he was the one who made detailed recommendations regarding the use of diagnostic tests and various other materials introduced during the workshop. The recommendations were endorsed in a standard way by the counselor. This division of labor was adopted in order to prevent differential treatment in the way the recommendations were given to the experimental and control subjects.

At the beginning of the first workshop session, all subjects completed: (a) the Self-Acceptance Subtest of the California Personality Inventory (CPI), consisting of 34 true–false items; (b) the Rotter IE Scale, consisting of 22 forced choice items (with 6 filler items) designed to measure the degree to which an individual believes that reinforcements are contingent upon his or her own behavior; and (c) a self-disclosure questionnaire, consisting of 2 essay questions concerning the subjects' feelings about themselves as teachers and about teaching as a profession. Subjects were asked to take the essay questions home and return them at a later session. All subjects did, in fact, do so.

One month after the last workshop session all subjects were again asked to complete the Self-Acceptance Subtest (CPI) in order to assess changes in the subjects' self-esteem scores. They were assured that the results of all measures would be confidential and that the author would contact them individually with information about their test results (which was subsequently done).

Procedures for Observation of Behavioral Changes

Performance Criteria (in the context of the teachers' classrooms)
Two weeks after the workshops were completed, as an occasion to talk about the results of the personality measures, the author visited each teacher's classroom, including all those who were in the experimental and control groups. (The school system would not give permission for anyone other than the counselor or the instructor to visit the classrooms, and the instructor, a high-level administrator, was unavailable.) While visiting each classroom, the author took advantage of the opportunity to note and to unobtrusively collect objective evidence of the use of diagnostic arithmetic techniques by the teacher that could be attributed to the workshop experience. School teachers and administrators at each school were given no warning of the visit and had no way of knowing that these unobtrusive measures were being made.

Indicators

Five performance variables (behavioral measures) were examined:

1. The teacher's use of diagnostic tests, either those provided in the workshop or very similar ones developed by the teacher.
2. The teacher's use of mimeographed or written exercises designed to remedy an individual's diagnosed arithmetic learning problems, which were obtainable only from the workshop instructor.
3. The teacher's use of games and puzzles recommended by the instructor during the workshop.
4. The teacher's use of mimeographed worksheets, forms, and drawings for diagnosing arithmetic deficiencies, which were available only from the workshop instructor.
5. The teacher's chalk drawings on her blackboard to illustrate concepts of likeness or difference in geometric shapes, which exactly duplicated the ones demonstrated and explained by the workshop instructor.

While in each classroom, the author examined the surface of every desk and the blackboards for evidences of the use of diagnostic tools. Each teacher was rated on a scale of 0–5 for evidence of the five indicators listed above. One point was assigned for clear, visible evidence of each of the five indicators; a score of 0 was recorded where the indicator was not directly observable in the classroom. Thus, ratings of presence–absence of the five indicators involved no inferences and could be made with almost perfect reliability. The author was also able to collect samples of arithmetic tests in 21 classrooms without regard to whether they were experimental or control. These samples were turned over to the workshop instructor, who was blind to the experimental conditions. He evaluated them for evidence of specific diagnostic procedures recommended during the workshop.

Subjects

The subjects were 40 female elementary school teachers of grades 1–4, who volunteered in response to a letter inviting all interested teachers to participate in a 2-week workshop sponsored by the local school system. Prior to the first workshop session eligible teachers were sent a stamped, self-addressed postcard, on which they were asked to indicate the times when they could come for the meetings. Volunteers were assigned to conditions on the basis of their answers about meeting times, which were found to be uncorrelated with potentially relevant personality or background variables. All subjects who expressed a preference for the first part of the week ($N = 19$) were assigned to the workshop that met on Tuesdays (control condition). Subjects who preferred the latter part of the week ($N = 21$) were assigned to the workshop that met on Thursdays (experimental condition). There were only slight, nonsignificant differences on personality test variables, age, years of experience, and ethnicity between the control and the experimental groups.

Experimental Conditions

In both experimental and control conditions the instructor provided the training expertise and made all recommendations and suggestions about possible applications of workshop materials in a classroom setting. The author, acting as a tutor and counselor, circulated in the workshop classroom and provided assistance on an individual basis. In the control condition he functioned exclusively as a tutor, making comments appropriate to the work task at hand ("Are you ready for the next step?" "If you need help raise your hand." "If there is something you don't understand, please ask about it." "Help each other as much as you can."). In the experimental group the author functioned in the same way as a tutor but he also took on the role of counselor. He made the same types of comments about the work tasks as in the control group, but in addition he discussed briefly the problems each teacher was having. His comments consisted of positive reinforcement statements on each teacher's skills, designed to function as self-esteem enhancement feedback (e.g., "You're making excellent progress." "No one understands this the first time." "You're doing exceptionally well." "You have a real talent for this." "I really like what you're doing.").

In all other respects the workshop procedures were identical. Each workshop lasted 2 hours. Workshops were held every other week for a month, a combined total of 8 hours (4 hours for the control group and 4 hours for the experimental group). In order to avoid unintentional variations that could give rise to differential demands, the tutor-counselor abstained from repeating the recommendations being made by the instructor. But because the tutor-counselor was working in collaboration with the instructor, his role and his manner conveyed that he agreed with the instructor's recommendations and would be pleased to see them carried out. Throughout the workshop the instructor remained blind to the experimental conditions; he did not hear anything the tutor-counselor was saying to any of the teachers.

RESULTS

Enhancement of Self-esteem

The procedure designed to enhance self-esteem was evaluated by examining changes on the Self-Acceptance Subtest (CPI). Table 16.1 presents the mean pre- and posttest scores for both the experimental and control groups. The results of an analysis of variance indicate that the increase in self-esteem was significantly greater in the experimental group than in the control group ($p < .01$).[3] Because the groups did not differ in initial self-esteem, we can conclude that the experimental procedure had the intended effect of enhancing self-esteem beyond the effect of participation in the workshop per se.

Table 16.1. Comparison of pre- and posttreatment means on self-esteem (self-acceptance subtest of the California Personality Inventory)

	Pretreatment	Posttreatment	Increase
Group			
Experimental	13.2	19.4	6.1
Control	13.7	15.6	1.9

Note. N = 21 in the experimental group; N = 19 in the control group.

Adherence to Recommendations

An individual's total adherence score was computed on a scale of 0–100 based on the five behavioral variables already described (20 points for one index, 40 for two, and so on). An analysis of variance of the total scores showed that adherence was significantly higher in the experimental group than in the control group ($p < .01$). Additional results indicate that the experimental group was significantly higher than the control group on each of the five variables.[4] Table 16.2 shows the percentage of subjects receiving a positive score on each of the performance variables for both the experimental and control group. In every instance the experimental group has a significantly higher percentage for a given performance variable than does the control group.

Table 16.2. Percentage of teachers in the experimental and control groups who were unobtrusively observed to adhere to workshop recommendations on each of five performance variables

Performance variable	Experimental	Control
1. Use of diagnostic tests	90	41
2. Use of individual printed diagnostic worksheets	77	21
3. Use of games, puzzles	90	41
4. Use of worksheets for entire classroom	62	32
5. Use of chalk drawings on blackboard	86	53

Note. N = 21 in the experimental group; N = 19 in the control group.

The results thus support the major hypothesis that positive self-esteem-enhancing feedback from a counselor produces an increase in adherence to recommendations endorsed by the counselor.

Personality Measures

A secondary purpose of this investigation was to observe personality differences in relation to the effects of self-esteem enhancement. Accordingly, an attempt was made to determine whether the scores on self-esteem and locus of control measures can be used to predict performance outcomes. An analysis of variance on the sum of adherence scores in relation to each of these two personality measures revealed that neither had a significant main effect. Locus of control was not in any way predictive of indicators of adherence to the recommendations made in the workshop. But self-esteem (as measured by the pretreatment scores on the CPI subtest) enters into a significant interaction effect ($p < .002$), indicating that initial self-esteem is predictive of responsiveness to the self-esteem enhancement treatment given by the counselor to the experimental group.

The nature of the interaction is apparent in Table 16.3, which gives the percentages of low self-esteem and high self-esteem subjects in both the control and experimental groups who adhered to one or more of the five specific recommendations listed in Table 16.2. An analysis of variance of these data reveals that adherence is jointly determined by a significant

Table 16.3. Comparison of teachers in the experimental and control groups who obtained low and high self-esteem scores on the pretreatment questionnaire: percentage of each subgroup who subsequently adhered to at least one recommendation

Group	Low self-esteem	High self-esteem	Total
Experimental	86%	76%	81%
Control	20%	50%	35%

Note. $N = 10 \pm 1$ in each of the 4 groups.

interaction ($p < .002$) between initial level of self-esteem and the self-esteem enhancement treatment. A Tukey multiple comparison test indicates that there is a nonsignificant difference in adherence scores between the high self-esteem control group and the high self-esteem experimental group. There is, however, a significant difference between the two low self-esteem groups ($p < .01$). The findings show that it was the low self-esteem individuals who were responsive to self-esteem enhancement treatments when responsiveness is measured by the indicators of adherence.

DISCUSSION

The results on the effects of self-esteem enhancement conform very closely to the predicted outcome. Both the experimental group and the control group showed an increase in self-esteem from before to after the workshop (as measured on the CPI subtest). Changes in self-esteem were, however, significantly greater in the experimental group that received the self-esteem enhancement treatment. That group also showed significantly greater adherence to recommendations made in the workshop than did the control group. The increases in self-esteem change and in adherence to workshop norms are attributable to the positive feedback treatment given by the counselor.

The workshop was in actuality being given to increase diagnostic skills for teaching arithmetic. The teacher's responses may have been less defensive and more genuine than they would have been had they been aware of what observations were being made. This is especially true in regard to adherence, since the subjects did not know that their subsequent use of the new methods of teaching would be assessed, and they did not realize that the counselor was going to make such an assessment when he visited each classroom to inform the teacher about her personality test scores.

Although the present study was not specifically designed to explore mechanisms mediating differential effects on persons with high self-esteem and low self-esteem, some observations bear on them. One salient finding is that the counseling treatment designed to enhance self-esteem was relatively more effective in inducing adherence to the workshop recommendations among teachers with initially low self-esteem scores (before the workshop began) than for teachers with initially high self-esteem scores (see Table 16.3). This finding suggests that chronically low self-esteem subjects may be more susceptible than others to counseling procedures that enhance self-esteem.[5]

Yet there is an alternate explanation if we assume that the self-report questionnaire measures a situational (state of self-esteem) rather than a chronic personality variable. Observations in the inner-city schools suggest that most teachers initially feel good about themselves and their profession, but a combination of disillusionments, frustrations, and unsatisfactory work conditions tends to create a situationally induced lowering of self-esteem. Thus, the subjects (inner-city school teachers) were engaged in an occupational role which for various reasons tends to produce states of low self-esteem. Among them are constant pressures from the principal and other superiors in the school system to whom a teacher is accountable, the scathing criticism of teachers and public schools in the mass media, overcrowded classrooms, and intractable children who disrupt the classroom. Perhaps the most important factor is the ambiguity inherent in much of what a teacher tries to accomplish in his or her classroom with little in the way of constructive help from superiors or from fellow teachers who are equally harassed. All these factors may combine to produce a lower state of self-esteem (as opposed to a chronic personality trait). Thus teachers such as those in the present study, whose pretreatment scores on the self-esteem measure (CPI subtest) are low, may be exhibiting a situationally induced state resulting from the nature of their occupation and hence they may be quite responsive to positive feedback from sources they consider credible and relevant.

It seems likely that many of our low self-esteem subjects were in a situationally induced state of low self-esteem, which made them especially responsive to the self-esteem enhancing treatment they received from the counselor, who was perceived as an experienced and well-qualified helper. He was also viewed as an "insider." The teachers knew that both the instructor and the counselor had high status in the local school system and had previous pertinent experience (20 and 12 years, respectively) as teachers and administrators in public school systems. The results of the present study may apply only to teachers in comparable circumstances where their state of self-esteem (rather than chronic level) is initially low.

The only ambiguity in the results pertains to the foregoing alternative interpretations of the finding of differential enhancement effects for high and low initial self-esteem subjects. The main effect of the self-esteem enhancement treatment is consistent with Janis's theoretical model (chap. 2) of changes in self-esteem in relation to adherence to a counselor's recommendations.

MAIN CONCLUSIONS

1. Positive effects of a counselor's self-esteem enhancement treatment were found in an investigation involving 40 inner-city elementary school teachers attending a mathematics teaching workshop. Compared with those in an equivalent control group, the teachers in the experimental group given positive feedback focusing on their professional capabilities under conditions where they spontaneously disclosed personal shortcomings, showed: (a) a significant increase in self-esteem and (b) a significant increase in openness to innovation as measured by objective performance indicators of adherence to the recommendations about new teaching methods made by the workshop instructor and endorsed by the counselor. The findings are consistent with the theoretical analysis of the effects of positive feedback (chap. 2).

2. The positive effect of the self-esteem enhancement treatment by the counselor occurred primarily among teachers who obtained low pretreatment scores on a measure of self-esteem. The low scores may reflect a state of low self-esteem resulting from the frustrations and harassments that beset teachers in inner-city schools rather than a chronic personality trait.

NOTES

1. Holstein, Goldstein, and Bem (1971) found that chronic self-esteem was correlated with need for approval, which in turn was predictive of reactions to social feedback. Subjects high in need for approval expressed more liking for a positive evaluator. Similar findings are reported by Milburn, Bell, and Koeski (1970), who found that subjects with chronically high need for

approval were more responsive to evaluative feedback, both positive and negative. Jacobs, Berscheid, and Walster (1971) also found that persons with chronically low self-esteem responded most strongly to positive feedback, provided that the feedback was explicit and clearly positive. If the feedback was positive but not explicit, persons with high self-esteem reacted more favorably, indicating that those with low self-esteem find it difficult to accept ambiguous positive feedback. Maracek and Mettee (1972) present evidence suggesting that a person's acceptance of signs of success is a direct function of chronic level of self-esteem. They found in a laboratory study of manual skills that persons with chronically low self-esteem either rejected success or attributed it to chance. Maracek and Mettee conclude from the results of their study that explicit positive feedback tends to be rejected by those for whom it is inconsistent with an existing self-image. This study implies that persons with chronically low self-esteem will be less likely to respond positively to positive feedback that is intended to enhance self-esteem and will be correspondingly less likely to comply with the recommendations of an accepting counselor. The main conclusion that follows from the prior research is that individuals with varying levels of chronic self-esteem will respond differently to those positive social reinforcements that are capable of enhancing self-esteem.

2. Results from a pilot study comparing student teachers ($N = 22$) with more experienced teachers ($N = 22$) suggest that the teaching situation may tend to lower self-esteem—for example, as a result of ambiguous demands, unclear role definitions, negative feedback from their superiors and colleagues and from the children in their classrooms. Overall, teachers who had been working in inner-city schools for 1 to 5 years were found to have a significantly lower mean for self-esteem (on the California Personality Inventory) than student teachers who were just starting in the inner-city schools.

3. A repeated measures analysis showed that both groups had higher posttest scores on self-esteem ($F = 148.54$, $df = 1/34$, $p < .01$). The interaction effect of self-esteem enhancement with time of testing was highly significant ($F = 77.3$, $df = 1/34$, $p < .01$). A separate analysis of variance was computed on the pretreatment scores on self-acceptance (CPI) for the experimental and control groups as a check on randomization. The means for the two groups did not differ significantly ($F = 1.03$, $df = 1/36$). Thus there was no initial difference in self-esteem scores between the two groups.

4. A multivariate analysis of variance was computed using each of the five performance variables in the total adherence score as a separate dependent variable. The large multivariate main effect for the experimental group is sufficiently reliable ($F = 14.005$, $p < .001$) to permit univariate testing within each variable. The F values and p values obtained from the univariate analysis of variance for enhancement effects are as follows: use of diagnostic tests, 13.3, $p < .01$; worksheets for individual, 15.8, $p < .01$; diagnostic games and puzzles, 13.5, $p < .01$; group worksheets for class, 3.8, $p < .10$; blackboard sketches and diagrams, 6.0, $p < .10$; change in self-esteem, 54.4, $p < .01$.

Two of the performance variables required the teacher to use the workshop's diagnostic approach with her entire class, while the other three required applying the diagnostic approach to individual students, which was a primary emphasis of the workshop. The most highly significant results ($p < .001$) were obtained for diagnostic work with individual students by the experimental group.

A multivariate analysis of covariance with initial self-esteem as covariate was also computed. The covarying of initial self-esteem increased the F values only slightly and p values were essentially the same.

A principal component factor analysis was computed on the five performance variables and change in self-esteem. The factor structure was such that one general factor emerged. In addition, two specific factors also met Kaiser's criterion of eigen values greater than 1.0. Neither the principal components nor the vari-max orthogonal factors indicated that the group and individual tests could be separated. This evidence of a single large factor indicates that the experimental treatment leads to fairly uniform adherence on the measures.

5. The results bearing on the predictive value of self-esteem scores are consistent with the relatively extensive set of findings indicating that people who negatively evaluate themselves

are more conforming to situational demands (Marlowe & Crowne, 1961; Strickland & Crowne, 1962); more responsive to social reinforcement under verbal conditioning procedures (Crowne & Strickland, 1961; Marlowe, 1962; Marlowe, Beecher, Cook, & Doob, 1964); less likely to express aggression (Fishman, 1965); and sometimes more responsive to persuasion and social influence (Berkowitz & Lundy, 1957; Janis & Field, 1959; Lesser & Abelson, 1959; Leventhal & Perloe, 1962).

In addition to studies showing low self-esteem subjects as more responsive to social influence, research by Dittes (1959) and others indicates that low self-esteem persons are more affected by the evaluative nature of social feedback. In Dittes's (1959) study low self-esteem persons who were made to feel accepted by a group were more attracted to the group than those not accepted. This relationship was significantly stronger for low self-esteem subjects than for high. The notion here is that individuals with low self-esteem can ill afford to be rejected and tend to be exceedingly responsive to acceptance. Conversely, for subjects with high self-esteem being accepted should not be especially notable since it happens frequently (see Jacobs, Berscheid, & Walster, 1971; Jones & Panitch, 1967; Maracek & Mettee, 1972).

17 Increasing Adherence to a Stressful Decision via the Balance-Sheet Procedure: A Field Experiment on Attendance at an Exercise Class

MICHAEL F. HOYT AND IRVING L. JANIS

Various gain–loss models of the decision-making process, derived from Lewin's (1951) topological analysis of conflict resolution, have been proposed (e.g., Blau, 1964; Homans, 1961; Janis, 1959; Thibaut & Kelley, 1959). As Janis (1959) has suggested, the anticipated gains (or benefits) and the anticipated losses (or costs) can be exhaustively categorized in four major types of consequence: (a) utilitarian gains or losses to self; (b) utilitarian gains or losses for significant others; (c) approval or disapproval from significant others; (d) self-approval or -disapproval (see chap. 3). The first type refers to the expected effects of the decision with respect to the satisfaction of tangible personal objectives, while the second pertains to the tangible goals of important individuals and groups with whom the decision maker is associated or identified. The anticipated social approval or disapproval of reference groups and reference persons constitutes the third type of consequence. The final type pertains to self-appraisals based on internalized standards and ego ideals.

Attention to negative as well as positive consequences of all four types is necessary not only for making optimal choices but also for minimizing postdecisional regret when unanticipated consequences materialize. A number of studies, reviewed in chapter 3, point to the value of stress inoculation and informational preparation for equipping persons to deal with unfavorable consequences of their decisions. Janis (1972) has documented the deleterious effects that incomplete consideration of possible consequences has had in the realm of American foreign policy decision making.

A tool that is useful in helping persons to consider more thoroughly the consequences of an impending decision is the "decisional balance-sheet

This chapter is a slightly revised version of an article published in the *Journal of Personality and Social Psychology*, 1975, *31*, 833–839. We wish to thank Fred D. Sheffield for helpful suggestions concerning the statistical analysis and criticisms of the first draft of the manuscript. Grateful appreciation is also expressed to Donald Tonry and Joni Barnett of the Yale Department of Athletics, Physical Education, and Recreation, for their kind cooperation. Additional thanks are extended to Helen R. Siporin for her service as an experimenter.

procedure" developed in a series of pilot studies by Janis (see chap. 3). College seniors who were given this procedure for career choices added pros and cons for each alternative that they had not mentioned earlier when interviewed about the anticipated consequences. In a pilot study more than half the 18 subjects given the balance-sheet procedure reported changing their evaluations of the alternative they had most preferred, whereas only 1 of the 18 control subjects did so. This observation suggests that aside from whatever long-term effect the balance-sheet procedure might have, it can produce an immediate self-persuasion effect. This immediate effect might be similar to that which occurs in certain types of role playing when a person writes an essay in favor of a counterattitudinal position and becomes more aware of the supporting arguments (see Collins & Hoyt, 1972; Janis & Gilmore, 1965).

The pilot work was followed up by Mann (1972) in a similar study using high school seniors who were trying to decide which college to attend. The balance-sheet procedure again proved effective. On posttest measures taken approximately 6 weeks after the students had notified the colleges of their decisions, subjects given the balance-sheet procedure showed less postdecisional regret and were able to be more objective about the consequences than were control subjects.

In the initial study on self-disclosure by Colten and Janis (chap. 9), women who had come to a diet clinic underwent (a) either a moderate or low self-disclosure interview (with the interviewer providing consistently positive feedback) and then (b) either a balance-sheet procedure (pertaining to the pros and cons of going on the recommended diet vs. other alternatives) or a control interview that gave the clients essentially the same information but without suggesting that they consider the pros or cons of alternative courses of action. Those subjects who underwent both the moderate self-disclosure interview and the decisional balance-sheet procedure showed significantly more adherence to the recommendations than the others. They sent in more weekly reports concerning their dieting and were significantly more successful in losing weight.

The present study was designed to obtain additional information regarding the effects of (a) the decisional balance-sheet procedure versus a control procedure and (b) slight versus no self-disclosure elicited under the restricted conditions of a brief telephone interview.

METHOD

Design Overview

The setting for our research was a women's early-morning exercise class conducted at the Yale gymnasium. We used records of class attendance to obtain an unobtrusive behavioral measure as the dependent variable. Attendance at such classes is voluntary. As the initial excitement of the class wanes and other morning activities beckon, a decisional conflict arises for many participants regarding whether to continue attending the class on a regular basis.

Early in the semester, women who had started attending an exercise class were interviewed via telephone. During the telephone conversation we presented four different conditions to represent our two independent variables: relevant vs. irrelevant balance-sheet procedure and low vs. no disclosure.

After receiving an introductory explanation and a request to have a pencil and paper at hand, each woman was first assigned on a random basis to an exercise-relevant or -irrelevant balance-sheet procedure. Those in the relevant balance-sheet condition were asked to consider carefully and to write out all the advantages and disadvantages that would result, for themselves and significant others, from their regular participation in the exercise class. Women randomly assigned to the irrelevant balance-sheet condition, on the other hand, were asked to consider carefully and to write out all the pros and cons involved in a different health-oriented decision, reducing or abstaining from cigarette smoking. (Nonsmokers completed balance sheets concerning their ongoing decision not to smoke.) Thus, in contrast to the balance-sheet studies cited above, wherein comparisons were made between balance-sheet experimental and no-balance-sheet control groups, the present study compared the two types of balance-sheet treatment (relevant vs. irrelevant). This may be a somewhat superior procedure in that there is a greater equivalence across treatment conditions with respect to holding constant the nature of the subject–interviewer interaction and the amount of cognitive work required of the subject.

Immediately after completing the relevant or irrelevant balance-sheet procedure, each subject was randomly assigned to either the low or no self-disclosure treatment. Women in the low self-disclosure condition were asked to read their balance-sheet entries aloud to the telephone interviewer (with the interviewer responding in a positive, accepting manner). Those in the no self-disclosure condition were instructed to scan their entries silently. Although our telephone intervention was brief and superficial in contrast to the more intimate, face-to-face interviews used in other self-disclosure studies, it seemed worthwhile to add this minimal self-disclosure treatment in order to test the limits of self-disclosure effects under conditions similar to those of brief counseling by telephone. Relative to other studies of self-disclosure (chaps. 9–13 and 15), this treatment would fall near the very low end of the self-disclosure continuum.

All interviews were conducted in the same way, including the same standard introduction and the same concluding remarks. At the end of every interview a brief tape-recorded message in the interviewer's own voice was played recommending regular and frequent attendance at the exercise class.

Behavioral records were obtained unobtrusively of every subject's attendance for a 7-week period after the telephone interview. This was done in the following way. The exercise class met three times weekly and class participants were asked by the gymnasium instructors to sign an attendance sheet each time they came. Similar sheets were posted outside most of the gymnasium facilities. Care was taken to avoid any perceptible connection between the attendance sheets and the telephone intervention. Subjects gave no indication to the class instructors of having surmised any such connection.

We collected the data to test our expectation that subjects in the relevant balance-sheet condition, having given careful attention to the advantages to be gained and the disadvantages to be overcome, would adhere more to the decision by attending the exercise class more regularly than would irrelevant balance-sheet subjects, who had focused their attention on the pros and cons involved in a different health decision. We were also interested in determining whether the very small amount of self-disclosure elicited in the telephone interview was sufficient to have a discernible effect.

Ten additional members of the same exercise class were randomly as-signed to a no-treatment control group. The purpose of collecting attend-ance data for this supplementary group was to obtain a baseline rate of attendance for comparison with the experimental treatment groups in the 2 × 2 after-only experimental design.

Subjects

Fifty women served as subjects. The majority were wives of Yale faculty members; there were also a few women graduate students and wives of male graduate students. Each subject had signed a class enrollment sheet during the second week of class, on which she had indicated her phone number. From this list 10 subjects were randomly assigned to each of the four experi-mental treatment conditions (relevant vs. irrelevant balance sheet × low vs. no self-disclosure); the remaining 10 were in the untreated control group.

Procedure

All 40 of the subjects in the four experimental groups were telephoned during the third week of the semester. Two interviewers, one male and one female, each contacted half the subjects. After introducing himself or her-self as "a graduate student doing a study in cooperation with the Yale Physical Education Department ... concerning people's decisions to engage in health-improvement programs," the interviewer went on to assure the subject of the confidential nature of the study and asked if the subject would give 10–15 minutes to answer some questions. All agreed to do so. (A few subjects had to be called back at a more convenient time.)

After asking a few background questions (age, physical education activi-ties, whether subject smoked cigarettes, and so forth) and then giving the subject the time to get some writing materials, the interviewer continued:

[Balance-sheet instructions] "Past research has shown that a very useful way for people to consider some decision they've made or are making—like deciding to take an exercise class or not smoking cigarettes—is to write down the advantages and disadvantages that will result from their decision. Oftentimes, in going through the process of actually writing down the considerations involved in a decision, people think of benefits and difficulties they did not originally realize were involved—and it's useful for them to be aware of these. What I would like you to do is spend the next couple of minutes writing down the benefits you hope to gain from taking the exercise class [not smoking] and the difficulties and problems you expect to encounter.

The way I'd like you to do that is this: At the top left of your page, write down GAINS TO SELF and list all the gains and benefits that will result from your regularly attending exercise class [cutting down or not smoking]. Don't tell me what you're writing, just try to include as many considerations as you think are relevant. Be sure to be frank and candid, including all personal considerations that may affect your regularly attending the class ['not smoking']. Take about a minute to do that; I'll signal you when a minute's up."

After 1 minute, the interviewer went on:

"Now, on the top right side of your page, write LOSSES TO SELF, and again list all you can think of, being frank and honest. Here you'll want to include any difficulties, inconveniences, or expenses you may encounter."

In similar fashion, the subject was instructed to make the headings GAINS TO IMPORTANT OTHERS, LOSSES TO IMPORTANT OTHERS, APPROVAL FROM OTHERS, DISAPPROVAL FROM OTHERS, SELF-APPROVAL, and SELF-DISAPPROVAL. The interviewer gave a brief explanation of what kinds of entries might go under each heading and paused 1 minute for each while the subject thought and listed her entries. Finally, the interviewer instructed the subject to make a last category, EXTRAS, and to enter there any considerations she had not already placed in one of the other categories.

For the subjects randomly assigned to the low self-disclosure interview, the interviewer asked to have all the entries read aloud. Those assigned to the no self-disclosure condition were asked to spend the same amount of time reading the entries silently to themselves. Subjects in both conditions were asked to think about the implications of what they were reading, reviewing the benefits they could gain from the decision (the exercise program or not smoking) and the difficulties to be overcome.

Throughout the low disclosure interview the interviewer responded to everything said by the subjects in an affirmative, accepting manner, invariably offering positive feedback. Balance-sheet entries that were favorable to following the desired course of action were met with responses such as "Good," "Uh-huh," and "That's an advantage," whereas negative entries were responded to with phrases such as "Yes, that can be a problem" and "It's good that you're aware of that."

As the final step in the interview for subjects in all experimental conditions, the interviewer played a standard 2-minute tape recording (in his or her own voice) that strongly recommended regular and frequent attendance at the exercise class. After the tape recording the interviewer answered any questions that the subject had (by repeating the appropriate statements made earlier) and concluded by requesting that the subject not discuss the phone call with any members of her class because "it's important for each person to generate her own list of balance-sheet entries, without priming or forethought."

RESULTS

How did our various treatments affect attendance? An analysis of variance indicated that one variable, the balance-sheet treatment, had a significant main effect ($p < .001$). The self-disclosure and experimenter variations had no significant main effects and there were no significant interaction effects.

Table 17.1. Mean number of times subjects attended class

| | Balance sheet | |
Condition	Relevant	Irrelevant
Self-disclosure		
Low	11.6	5.4
None	12.1	6.2

Note. $N = 10$ for each cell. The mean for untreated control subjects = 5.6. The main effect for relevant vs. irrelevant balance sheet is significant: $F = 13.79$, $p < .001$.

As seen in Table 17.1 the balance-sheet procedure had a markedly positive effect: The mean weekly attendance of subjects in the relevant balance-sheet condition was about double that of the irrelevant balance-sheet subjects. For the untreated control group, attendance was about the same as for the irrelevant balance-sheet group ($p < .50$) and was significantly less than for the relevant balance-sheet group ($t(28) = 2.87$, $p < .01$).

Figure 17.1 shows that the week-by-week attendance for the relevant balance-sheet group was consistently higher than for the irrelevant balance-sheet group throughout the entire period of 7 weeks.[1] The data for the untreated control group (shown by the broken line in the figure) deviate only slightly over the 7-week period from the data for the irrelevant balance-sheet group.

DISCUSSION

The results offer straightforward evidence for the effectiveness of the balance-sheet procedure. Merely hearing the 2-minute recorded pep talk advocating regular and frequent attendance was not enough, nor was considering an irrelevant health-related decision sufficient to increase class attendance. There was essentially no difference between the attendance of

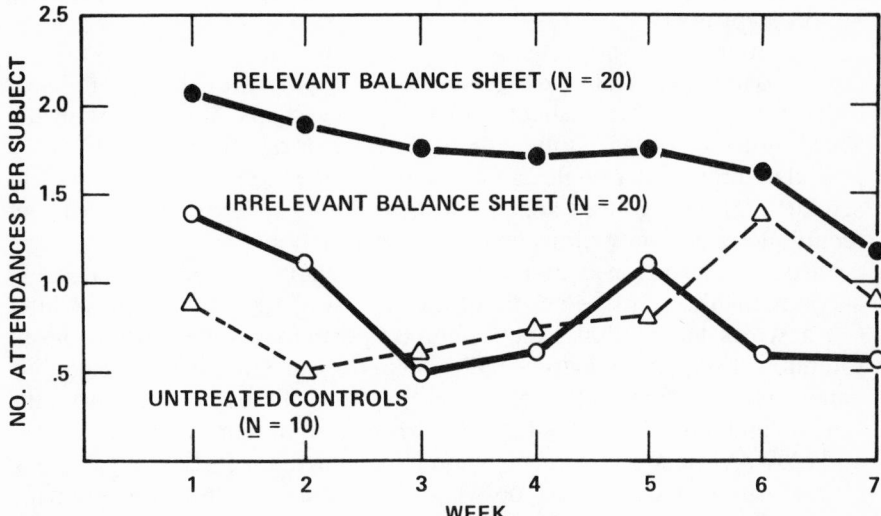

Figure 17.1. Week-by-week attendance for the relevant balance-sheet group, the irrelevant balance-sheet group, and the untreated control group.

irrelevant balance-sheet and no-treatment (baseline) control subjects. Comparison of the untreated control subjects with those in the relevant balance-sheet condition, however, shows that, as predicted, the relevant balance sheet had a substantial effect on subsequent behavior. The subjects who completed balance sheets relevant to attending the exercise class attended class about twice as often as did other subjects.

It is not surprising that the self-disclosure variable had no discernible effect. Previous studies on the effects of moderate versus low self-disclosure (reported in chaps. 9, 10, and 15) involved substantially more intense, interpersonally more meaningful encounters with the interviewer than the brief telephone interaction in the present experiment. We noticed that the balance-sheet entries of the slight self-disclosure subjects were so abbreviated (e.g., "better health," "inconvenience of driving to gym," and "friends will admire") that it was probably unlikely that the subjects felt any significant sense of self-disclosure at all or that the interviewer's responses would be perceived as being particularly empathic and accepting. Furthermore, Janis's preliminary model of the helping relationship (chap. 2) postulates that after having received acceptance in response to their initial self-disclosures, subjects are more motivated to follow recommendations made by a counselor as a way of continuing to receive the counselor's approval. In the present experiment, however, no expectation was created that there would be any future interaction with the interviewer or that the interviewer would be monitoring the subject's attendance; therefore, it does not seem reasonable to expect that subjects would become motivated to attend the exercise class as a way of winning the (unknown and unknowing) interviewer's approval.

Prior studies have shown that when people are making personal decisions they tend to benefit from the careful consideration of pros and cons induced by a systematic balance-sheet procedure (see chaps. 3 and 9). With the success of the present study—dramatic behavioral effects over a 7-week period as a result of a single 15-minute telephone interview—we expect to see further investigations and applications of the decisional balance-sheet technique in a variety of decision-making situations.

Earlier we mentioned two alternative mediating processes that could account for the positive effects of the relevant balance-sheet procedure: (1) a stress inoculation effect, whereby participants are better able to tolerate subsequent negative feedback (in the current study, for example, embarrassment from failing to perform certain of the exercises correctly, fatigue, and muscular aches resulting from attending the exercise classes) and (2) a self-persuasion effect, whereby the participants become aware of more positive incentives that outweigh the negative incentives for carrying out the given course of action (in this case, attending the exercise class). If stress inoculation were the predominant effect we would expect to find that the superiority in attendance resulting from the relevant compared with the irrelevant balance-sheet procedure would appear gradually, week by week, as the participants encountered more and more instances of minor negative consequences and perhaps one or two major setbacks that might tempt them to quit. But if the positive effects are attributable primarily to self-persuasion we would expect to find an immediate effect, as typically occurs when role playing or authoritative persuasive communications are used to promote a recommended course of action. The week-by-week attendance data in Figure 17.1 show that there was, in fact, an immediate effect that appeared in the very first week after the telephone interview and that continued without being augmented during the subsequent 6 weeks. These findings favor an interpretation of the observed effect of the relevant balance-sheet procedure in terms of self-persuasion rather than stress inoculation.

We know from the content of the balance sheets read to the interviewer by the subjects in the slight self-disclosure condition that generally they listed many favorable consequences of the decision and relatively few unfavorable ones. This mobilization of predominantly positive incentives may be similar to what happens in role-playing experiments when a person is induced to write an essay in support of an assigned position on an issue with which he is familiar under conditions of favorable sponsorship (see Collins & Hoyt, 1972; Elms & Janis, 1965; Janis & Gilmore, 1965). In the present experiment the subjects were asked to fill out the balance sheet for only one alternative and it was one to which they had already committed themselves. Furthermore, the interviewer was associated with a prestigeful educational institution and was unambiguously in favor of the decision. Under less favorable conditions a relevant balance-sheet procedure would probably be less effective and might even have the reverse effect. These and other plausible limiting conditions for the observed positive effect of the relevant balance-sheet procedure obviously require further investigation.

MAIN CONCLUSIONS

1. After a short telephone interview with women who were enrolled in a gymnasium exercise class, those who completed balance sheets that prompted careful consideration of the consequences of their decision showed greater subsequent adherence than those who did not. The women who filled out the balance sheet showed significantly more attendance over a 7-week period than women given an equivalent interview during which they filled out an irrelevant balance sheet (on smoking); the latter group's rate of attendance did not differ from that of control subjects, who received no treatment at all.

2. Degrees of self-disclosure (having the subjects read their balance-sheet entries aloud to the interviewer vs. having them read the entries silently) did not affect attendance, most probably because the brief and superficial treatment was not strong enough to engender a meaningful sense of self-disclosure.

NOTES

1. An additional analysis of variance ($2 \times 2 \times 2 \times 7$) was carried out for the data from these two groups using subjects' weekly attendance during the 7 consecutive weeks as a repeated measures factor. The results for the two experimental variables and the experimenter variation were the same as reported above, the only significant finding being a main effect for the balance-sheet variable. A significant main effect for variations in weekly attendance was also obtained, $F(6, 192) = 4.51$, $p < .001$. The latter F pertains to the observation that for both the relevant and the irrelevant balance-sheet conditions there was a gradual decrement in attendance from the first to the seventh week. There was no significant interaction effect ($F < 1$), indicating no difference between balance-sheet conditions with respect to the rate of decrement.

18 Effects of Outcome Psychodrama as a Supplementary Technique in Marital and Career Counseling

IRVING L. JANIS AND DONNA-MARIA LA FLAMME

Outcome psychodrama is a new type of intervention for improving the quality of personal decision making (see chap. 3). This chapter describes the pilot studies that led us to regard outcome psychodrama as a promising technique to supplement the balance-sheet procedure for use in decision counseling. It also summarizes a field experiment intended specifically to test the effect of outcome psychodrama in counteracting defective information-processing patterns. The experiment, which was conducted in a career-counseling clinic, also included an assessment of the balance-sheet procedure. The unexpected negative findings of the experiment illustrate the need for systematic evaluation of new counseling interventions in order to determine which clients, if any, will benefit.

PILOT STUDIES ON OUTCOME PSYCHODRAMA

Outcome psychodrama, which focuses on nonsalient consequences, was developed as an intervention designed to neutralize resistance and defensive avoidance tendencies that interfere with careful examination of decisional issues, particularly when the client is inclined to bolster his or her choice just before becoming fully committed to a new course of action (see Janis & Mann, 1977, pp. 379–388). The outcome psychodrama procedure requires clients to project themselves into the future and to act out a scenario that elaborates on the consequences of choosing each major alternative. The improvisations required of the client by the procedure are intended to bring to the surface some of the less obvious consequences of the leading alternatives that otherwise might be ignored. The cognitive balance-sheet procedure, which also induces clients to look ahead to the potentially favorable and unfavorable consequences of implementing the main alternatives, can be combined with the relatively more emotional outcome psychodrama procedure in order to stimulate a more complete exploration of the pros and cons.

Outcome psychodrama as an intervention for use in decision counseling was developed by Janis in a series of pilot studies. He first used it in interviews with clients having serious marital problems who came to a marital counseling clinic for aid in making a decision about whether or not to seek a divorce. One woman, for example, who in three earlier interviews had consistently described her marriage as nothing but misery and seemed fully convinced that the only solution was to divorce her unfaithful husband, was asked to imagine that one year had gone by since she made her decision. Mrs. Stern, as we shall call her, was told that she would be asked to go through this procedure twice, once as if she had decided to obtain a divorce and a second time as if she had made a genuine effort to keep her marriage going. She was asked to imagine that she had come back to see the counselor for a follow-up interview, and to tell him what had happened during the interim year. Mrs. Stern chose to enact the divorce alternative first. After a brief warm-up period (in which she had to be encouraged to describe her feelings in the present tense instead of using conditional phrases such as "I suppose I would feel..."), Mrs. Stern began giving an imaginative account of what her life would be like after the divorce. During the first ten minutes, her statements merely repeated what she had already said in earlier interviews about relief from constant quarreling and other improvements in her daily life that she expected as a result of being rid of her husband. But when asked whether she now felt fairly contented living independently, she blurted out, "No, I feel lonely and miserable, I miss my husband terribly, my life is completely empty now," and she burst into tears. This was the first time in any of the interviews that she displayed any intense emotion and the first time that she alluded to any affectionate feelings toward her husband.

During the second part of the procedure, devoted to enacting a follow-up interview a year after her decision to continue the marriage, Mrs. Stern continued to explore the positive aspects of her relationship with her husband, including (again for the first time) her exclusive sexual attachment to him and her fear of being frigid with any other man. In the final part of the interview, while reviewing what she had said during the psychodramatic enactments, she expressed her surprise at the strong feelings that had momentarily overwhelmed her and said, "I have so much reason to hate him I guess I hadn't been willing to admit to myself that I still love him and will miss him." Thus the psychodramatic enactments enabled Mrs. Stern to gain access to deep-seated emotional attitudes toward her husband that she had defensively avoided acknowledging to herself.

Once these formerly preconscious components became part of her conscious balance sheet, she could make a more thorough assessment of the alternatives and work out more realistic plans for implementation. As it turned out, Mrs. Stern felt convinced that despite her newly acknowledged attachment to her husband, his constant mistreatment of her was so intolerable that she should obtain a divorce. In a final session, one month after the psychodramatic enactments, Mrs. Stern spoke about a definite plan to avoid the loneliness of the separation by moving into an apartment with a girlfriend. It seems probable that this plan was at least partly shaped by the increased awareness she had gained from the psychodramatic enactments of the losses she would sustain from going through with a divorce. (Janis & Mann, 1977, pp. 380–381)

In marital counseling interviews with 6 other women and two men, Janis used the same outcome psychodrama procedures. All 8 clients showed signs of having become more vigilant, especially by thinking out loud about important new considerations regarding the choice alternatives that they had not mentioned in earlier interviews. The technique was sufficiently effective in helping the clients to uncover preconscious worries, hopes, and other previously unverbalized feelings pertaining to the decision that it appeared to be worthwhile to develop the procedure further in another pilot study.

A similar psychodramatic procedure was next tried out by Janis in career counseling with 15 male Yale College seniors, after each had received a preliminary interview concerning the pros and cons of his career alternatives. Each senior was also asked to fill out a balance sheet beforehand. The seniors were then instructed to enact a 1-year follow-up interview for each of the two leading alternatives. However, such instructions did not seem fruitful in this setting until a revised psychodrama scenario was constructed which required the seniors to conceive of themselves as telling a *friend* about a *crisis* situation in which "everything that could go wrong had gone wrong." Additional pilot work in this setting on the positive scenarios appeared to be relatively unproductive. Consequently, the procedure that was finally adopted asked the seniors to focus exclusively on the crisis scenario, which required them to elaborate on the unfavorable consequences of each alternative. When this scenario was used, the seniors became aware of important entries for their balance sheets, which they had not mentioned earlier, as a result of the psychodramatic enactments. For 12 of the 15 seniors, new considerations emerged during the psychodramas that affected the final evaluation of their career alternatives. Four students were so impressed by the undesirable consequences that surfaced during their improvised performance of the psychodrama that they reversed their preferences. Other students became more convinced of the correctness of their original first choice. Practically all the seniors seemed to acquire a more realistic view of their main alternatives.

From this pilot work, outcome psychodrama appears potentially useful as a supplement to the balance-sheet procedure, especially if the technique is introduced to clients who are on the verge of making up their minds about what they were going to do without having thoroughly considered the pros and cons of the leading alternatives. But there are potential drawbacks because the procedure highlights the disastrous consequences that might ensue, which could have a demoralizing effect and reduce the quality of decision making if the client were to lose hope of finding a satisfactory solution. Consequently it is essential to determine whether the procedure has the intended effect of improving decision making and whether it has unintended negative side effects.

A FIELD EXPERIMENT IN A CAREER COUNSELING CLINIC

Following up on the prior clinical observations and pilot work, LaFlamme and Janis (1977) carried out a systematic assessment of the effects of using outcome psychodrama in career counseling. The participants in this field experiment were 80 volunteers who came to our career counseling clinic in response to announcements in local newspapers.[1] After answering the counselor's initial series of structured questions about the nature of the decision and the possible alternatives, each client was randomly assigned to one of four conditions: (1) outcome psychodrama only; (2) outcome psychodrama combined with the balance-sheet procedure (following the procedure described by Janis & Mann, 1977, pp. 405–409); (3) the balance-sheet procedure only; and (4) control (given the Strong–Campbell Vocational Interest Inventory and an additional interview about past decisions to occupy the same amount of time as the outcome psychodrama or the balance-sheet procedure).

The standard instructions for the outcome psychodrama asked the client to imagine that a year had gone by after the decision was made and that it was now clear how successful or unsuccessful it proved to be. The first scenario involved telling a friend that the decision has worked out very badly and explaining exactly what has gone wrong. A second scenario involved telling a friend that the decision has worked out well and explaining in what ways. Each client was asked to enact both scenarios for the two leading alternatives, so that he or she engaged in four separate psychodramatic enactments. For each of the four, the counselor played the role of the friend. In this role the counselor sympathetically asked questions such as "How did that happen?," "What happened then?," and "How do you account for that?" After the outcome psychodrama was completed, each client was asked to write down any new considerations (pros and cons for either alternative) that had emerged during the enactment of the four scenarios.

After receiving either the experimental or control treatment, all clients were told about two services that the clinic had arranged for their use (devised partly for the purpose of obtaining behavioral measures of the effects of the treatments). The first involved the availability of a set of books on a variety of vocational choices, which we arranged to be held on reserve at the New Haven Public Library and at one of the Yale libraries. Clients were informed that the books could be used for free and that the information contained in them would be helpful to them in trying to make a decision. The second was the Yale Information Service (which we set up for the purpose of the study). Clients were told that they could write to this free service asking for specific information about all sorts of jobs, such as the special types of training required.

All clients were also given a set of daily report forms and were asked to keep a record each day of activities related to their career decision. The clients were instructed to mail back the forms at the end of each week.

Contrary to expectation, our results showed that the clients given the outcome psychodrama procedure engaged in less information seeking activity than those who were not given the procedure (see Table 18.1). On one of the measures (number of letters requesting information mailed to the Information Service) the difference was statistically significant ($p < .05$);

on the other (number of relevant library books used) the difference was in the same direction but was nonsignificant. Thus, instead of improving the information seeking behavior of the clients as was expected, outcome

Table 18.1. Effects of the outcome psychodrama versus no outcome psychodrama on three behavioral measures

	No outcome psychodrama	Outcome psychodrama
Mean number of requests for information from Yale Information Service	.31	.08
Mean number of library books on career choices used	1.80	1.32
Mean number of diary sheets mailed to the clinic	2.85	2.44

Note. $N = 40$ in each group. The only statistically significant difference is for the first item (requests for information): $p < .05$.

psychodrama tended to have the opposite effect. On the third behavioral measure (adherence to the counselor's request to mail back weekly reports) the outcome psychodrama had no observable effect. The balance-sheet procedure was found to have no significant effect on any of the three behavioral measures.

Table 18.2. Effects of four experimental conditions on state-of-self-esteem measured four weeks later: mean self-esteem scores

	No outcome psychodrama	Outcome psychodrama
Balance sheet	43.97	45.66
No balance sheet	47.70	43.36

Note. $N = 20$ in each cell. Neither main effect is statistically significant. The interaction effect is marginally significant ($F = 3.10$, $p < .10$). For those who had not been given the balance-sheet procedure the effect of outcome psychodrama is a significant decrease ($p < .05$).

The outcome psychodrama was not found to have the expected favorable effect on the clients' state of self-esteem, as measured by the Quinlan and Janis scale (see Appendix). In fact, Table 18.2 shows that when only the outcome psychodrama was used, the clients' level of self-esteem was reduced ($p < .05$). When preceded by the balance-sheet procedure, however, the outcome psychodrama did not have this unfavorable effect; it resulted in slightly (but not significantly) higher self-esteem scores. Just as for all the behavioral measures in Table 18.1, the main effect of the balance-sheet procedure on self-esteem scores was not statistically significant.

The results in the first two rows of Table 18.1 imply that the outcome psychodrama had a detrimental effect on information seeking. Of course it is conceivable that the clients engaged in less information seeking after the psychodramatic procedure because it had the positive effect of making them realize that their current career was more advantageous than an alternative they had thought to be much more attractive. After becoming aware of the unfavorable consequences of the seemingly attractive alternative, which they had not thought about until engaging in the psychodrama, they might realistically decide to give up the idea of changing from their present career and therefore lose interest in obtaining information about other careers. But it seems improbable, from what the clients said, that the outcome psychodrama tended to eliminate the clients' decisional conflicts. Further, the data in Table 18.2 indicate that when clients were not given the balance-sheet procedure, the outcome psychodrama had the adverse effect of lowering their self-esteem.

The negative results obtained in the present study contrast sharply with the positive results reported by Janis from his pilot work on the effects of outcome psychodrama with senior college students described earlier in this chapter and with the three controlled field experiments utilizing the balance-sheet procedure, all of which showed that the procedures had beneficial effects (see chaps. 3, 9, and 17). In all the previous work in which either the balance-sheet or the outcome psychodrama procedures were used, the subjects were predominantly in the later stages of decision making. They had already performed a substantial amount of information seeking behavior prior to the interview. In the current study, however, the majority of the clients were not in the later stages of decision making. Most of the clients had just begun to become familiar with the decisional problem. Some had spent hardly any time at all obtaining information about alternatives or even thinking about the alternatives; they were dissatisfied with the kind of work they were doing but felt extremely insecure about the possibility of doing anything else. For such ill-prepared clients the dire negative consequences of the leading alternatives made salient by the outcome psychodrama procedure might reduce self-confidence and make them lose hope of finding an adequate solution. The results in Table 18.2 show that if clients were first given the balance-sheet procedure, which enhances awareness of the consequences of each alternative, the outcome psychodrama did not have an unfavorable effect on self-esteem. But when clients were given only the outcome psychodrama, it had the effect of reducing self-esteem. When clients have not previously thought about negative consequences, exposing them to the strong images of unfavorable outcomes generated by the psychodramatic enactments may be so demoralizing that they are unintentionally induced to adopt the defective coping pattern of defensive avoidance (see chap. 3). Perhaps when a client is in an early stage of decision making, the use of outcome psychodrama promotes a defensive reaction, whereas if the client has progressed to a later stage of decision making, the identical procedures might promote vigilance. What we are suggesting is that the ultimate success or failure of the procedure may depend on the client's current stage of decision making.

Before the LaFlamme and Janis experiment was carried out, we thought that the risk of demoralizing the client through the use of the outcome psychodrama would be very slight, especially since the images of unfavorable consequences are generated entirely by the client rather than supplied by the counselor. The unexpected negative findings remind us once again of the need for systematic evaluation before a new intervention procedure is applied on a large scale to clients who seek help from counselors. All too often, counselors rely exclusively on their clinical experience when it comes to using new procedures, which ultimately could prove to be detrimental rather than beneficial. Even very conscientious counselors who want to provide the best possible services to their clients will sometimes try out a new procedure with a series of cases to see if it looks promising (usually without bothering to do a systematic evaluation of changes). If an innovative clinician sees a series of cases in which a new procedure appears to be helpful, with no apparent detrimental effects, he or she is likely to apply it across the board to all types of clients and to recommend that it be widely used by other professional counselors. But, as the LaFlamme and Janis study shows, even after promising results have been obtained from a pilot study, a new procedure applied in a different context with a different type of client could prove to be ineffective or even harmful to the objectives of the counseling. The evidence of detrimental effects (with clients who sought help about their ill-defined career dilemmas) despite the positive results obtained in the initial pilot work (with college seniors who were dealing with clear-cut choices for which they were well informed) provides empirical grounds for being skeptical about applying new interventions before they have been carefully tested with samples of the population for which they are intended.

Where does this leave us on the practical issue of when, if ever, outcome psychodrama should be used? Obviously, in view of the negative results from the LaFlamme and Janis study we cannot recommend outcome psychodrama for routine use in decision counseling. Nevertheless, the promising results from the pilot studies suggest that the technique might prove to be useful with carefully selected clients if limited to those in the later stages of decision making who appear to be quite robust with regard to self-confidence about finding good solutions to their dilemmas. Counselors who think it is worthwhile to try out the procedure should, of course, use it with caution, being alert to possible signs of demoralizing effects, which may require additional steps to help the client regain a hopeful outlook. In any case we must await further systematic research to assess the effects of the procedure before formulating any definitive generalizations about when and with whom outcome psychodrama could be used effectively to increase vigilance with minimal risks of producing demoralization.

MAIN CONCLUSIONS

1. Pilot studies in a marriage counseling clinic for men and women contemplating divorce and in a career counseling program with college seniors suggest that outcome psychodrama can be helpful to clients who are on the verge of committing themselves to a new course of action. The procedure appears to make them sharply aware of worries, hopes, and previously unverbalized feelings pertaining to the decision, which enables them to take a more comprehensive view of the consequences of their choice.

2. A field experiment conducted in a career decision clinic with 80 males and females who wanted to change their jobs or their careers failed to support the positive view concerning the value of outcome psychodrama derived from the pilot studies. Contrary to expectations, outcome psychodrama had the effect of decreasing the clients' information seeking behavior and, if they had not been given the balance-sheet procedure, tended to lower their level of self-esteem. Most of the clients in this study were in the early stages of decision making and felt insecure about making any major change in their vocational choice. A plausible explanation of the adverse effects is that such clients lose confidence about finding an adequate solution to their problem as a result of the vivid images of disastrous failure generated by participating in the psychodrama scenarios that focus on unfavorable outcomes. The apparently beneficial effect of outcome psychodrama observed in the pilot studies may be restricted to clients in the later stages of decision making, for whom the decision is well structured and is approached in a fairly confident manner as a result of their having already spent considerable time working on it.

NOTES

1. The men and women who received the services of the clinic represented a wide range of ages and ethnic and educational backgrounds. Upon initially telephoning the clinic, each client was told that the purpose of the clinic was to aid each person in helping himself or herself make a better quality decision about career alternatives. Many callers declined to participate when they learned that the clinic could not provide job placement, vocational testing, or psychotherapy. We excluded a few others because they were unable to say anything more than that they were discontent with what they were doing and could not mention any alternative. The first 80 individuals who agreed to participate were selected for the study and scheduled for initial appointments.

Upon arriving at the clinic, each client was interviewed by 1 of the 4 counselors (2 men and 2 women) who participated in this study. Each counselor worked with 5 clients in each of four experimental conditions.

19 Reduction of Psychological Stress in Surgical Patients

ELLEN J. LANGER, IRVING L. JANIS, AND JOHN A. WOLFER

INTRODUCTION

Prior research provides evidence that stress tolerance can be increased by increasing perceived control over the aversive stimuli (e.g., Pervin, 1963), the availability of a distractor (e.g., Kanfer & Goldfoot, 1966), and information about the threatening event (e.g., Lazarus & Alfert, 1964). The study reported in this chapter indicates the applicability of some of these findings obtained from the laboratory to a natural setting. The main purpose was to compare and evaluate two strategies for reducing stress, one emphasizing cognitive control over aversive events and the other providing realistic information and reassurance. The two strategies are based on principles derived from an analysis of coping patterns (chap. 3) as well as laboratory research. They were tested on hospital patients about to undergo major surgery.

Coping Device

The first of the two strategies involves the cognitive reappraisal of anxiety-provoking events. The subjects are told that attention to and cognitions about an aversive event influence the amount of stress one experiences with regard to that event (see Ellis, 1962; Meichenbaum, 1977; Meichenbaum, Turk, & Burstein, 1975). They are encouraged to exercise cognitive control through selective attention so as to focus on the positive instead of the negative aspects of the stressful events they encounter. This strategy is in keeping with experimental evidence on the effectiveness of both distraction and perceived control in reducing stress. It makes the expected gains salient and provides an active means of coping with stress under the patient's own control. The patient knows that he or she can initiate it at any time and in any situation.

This research was conducted while the senior author was an NIMH predoctoral fellow (1F01 MH 5454-01) and was partially supported by Grant no. GS-30514X to Irving L. Janis, principal investigator, from the National Science Foundation. The present chapter is a slightly modified version of an article previously published in the *Journal of Experimental Social Psychology*, 1975, *11*, 155–165.

The relationship between perceived control and pain tolerance has been explored in numerous laboratory studies. For example, Pervin (1963) showed that subjects are less anxious when they control the administration of shock than when the experimenter controls it, even though the amount of external stimulation is the same. Other investigators have also found that when subjects believe that they have some control over impending aversive stimuli, the stimuli are rated as less aversive (e.g., Bowers, 1968; Corah & Boffa, 1970; Geer, Davison, & Gatchel, 1970; Glass & Singer, 1972; Kanfer & Seider, 1973).

In terms of coping patterns for dealing with stress (chap. 3), the coping device can be expected to promote vigilance rather than defensive avoidance by encouraging an optimistic reappraisal of anxiety-provoking events, which builds up the surgical patient's hopes for a satisfactory outcome. Without encouraging denial of realistic threats, it encourages the patient to feel confident about being able to deal effectively with whatever losses or setbacks are subsequently encountered.

Preparatory Information

The second stress-reducing strategy consists of supplying patients with information regarding the impending surgical experience to prepare them psychologically. On the basis of field and laboratory studies, Janis (1958, 1971) has suggested that successful stress inoculation can be produced in persons facing severe stress by giving them preparatory communications containing accurate warnings about what to expect, together with pertinent reassurances. According to this conception, preparatory communications are effective when they arouse a moderate level of anticipatory fear, which leads to the constructive "work of worrying," i.e., mentally rehearsing the impending threats and developing realistic, self-delivered reassurances that prevent subsequent emotional shock, severe disappointment in protective authorities, and feelings of helplessness when the threats materialize.

Evidence from a number of laboratory experiments indicates that preparatory communications can reduce the emotional impact of confrontations with stressful stimuli. Lazarus and Alfert (1964), for example, found much less fear manifested on physiological-arousal measures and on self-rating measures when young men, before they witnessed distressing scenes in a film depicting a primitive circumcision rite, were given preliminary information and reassurance that the procedure was harmless. When prior information about aversive stimulation is accompanied by reassurances, pain tolerance tends to increase (Staub & Kellett, 1972), whereas when such information is given without reassurances, pain tolerance tends to decrease (Kanfer & Goldfoot, 1966).

Many field investigations with hospitalized patients also suggest the potential value of preparatory communications that correctly predict stressful events and make recommendations about how to cope with them (see Janis & Mann, 1977, pp. 155–158). In most of the studies, however, it is not clear whether the effects are attributable to the information intended as stress inoculation or to other variables, such as contact with a counselor who provides social support.

The present study sought to evaluate the effectiveness of a coping device, a somewhat new but familiar strategy, and to compare it with a preparatory information procedure that did not include explicit coping suggestions. We predicted that the coping device would effectively reduce pre- and postoperative stress. But because the preparatory information directed attention to the threatening event, an initial mild increase in stress was predicted, and hence its effectiveness would be seen only postoperatively. In order to be able to test these predictions and to assess the value of a treatment that combined both strategies, a control group and a coping-plus information group were also included in the experimental design.

METHOD

Subjects

The experiment was carried out at the Yale–New Haven Hospital with 60 adult surgical patients. All the patients were about to undergo elective operations for which the prognoses were generally favorable. The operations included hysterectomies, hernia repairs, and cholecystectomies, as well as less serious major surgical procedures such as transuretheral resections and tubal ligations. Subjects were assigned to conditions on a stratified random basis, so that the experimental groups were equated on five relevant background factors: type of operation, seriousness of operation, sex, age, and religious affiliation.

Procedures

The effectiveness of two different methods for relieving operative stress was investigated in a 2 × 2 factorial design. One variable consisted of presenting versus not presenting the cognitive coping device; the other consisted of presenting versus not presenting the preparatory information that briefly described the discomforts of the pre- and postoperative experience.

A short time after being admitted to the hospital, each patient was approached by a female psychologist dressed in a laboratory coat, who introduced herself and stated that she was a psychologist studying preoperative stress. In order to allay fears that the patient might have been singled out because of special psychological problems, the psychologist added that she was visiting all preoperative patients on that floor. After obtaining the patient's consent, the investigator conducted one of four standardized interviews.

(1) Coping Device Only
This condition involved presenting a prepared communication that included explanations and examples of the coping strategy.[1] The communica-

tion began with a standard introduction asserting that most people are somewhat anxious before an operation but that people can often control their own emotions if they know how to. The counselor explained that it is rarely events themselves that cause stress but rather the views people take of them and the attention they give to those views. To facilitate under-standing, the coping device was introduced by way of an analogy. Each male patient was told to imagine playing an exciting football game and was asked if he thought he would have noticed receiving a minor cut. After he answered in the negative, he was told that if, on the other hand, he had been at home reading a boring newspaper and received a paper cut, he probably would have nursed it attentively. Female patients were asked to imagine rushing to finish preparations for a dinner for 15 people and receiving a minor cut in the process. The point of these sex-typed examples was that the patient actually controlled the amount of stress experienced.

The patients were told that nothing that happens is either all positive or all negative and that it is the wise person who finds alternative views of threatening situations to avoid becoming overly stressed. Illustrative ex-amples from everyday life of alternative ways of viewing seemingly negative events (e.g., losing one's job) were provided. Patients were then asked to generate examples from their own lives and to present positive alternative views of the events. The communication then went on to relate the coping device to the hospital experience. If there are indeed at least two ways of interpreting every experience, there must be a positive non-stress-provoking view of being in the hospital. Attention was called to the positive or com-pensatory aspects of undergoing surgery in a good hospital, focusing on the improvement in health, the extra care and attention the patient would receive, the probable weight loss (if appropriate), and the rare opportunity to relax, to take stock of oneself, to have a vacation from outside pressures, and the like. The counselor suggested that the patient rehearse these realistic positive aspects whenever he or she starts to feel upset about the unpleasant aspects of the surgical experience. The patients were assured that this approach was not equivalent to lying to oneself. The coping device did not encourage denial but rather encouraged maintaining an overall optimistic view by taking account of the favorable consequences and rein-terpreting the unfavorable ones.

As a final check on comprehension of the recommendation, the patient was given the following event to interpret: "Suppose that some emergencies have come up so that your operation has to be delayed for a few days. How would you view this positively?" If the patient did not give the expected type of response, he or she was given additional details and examples.

(2) Preparatory Information Only
This communication began with the same introduction, stating that most people are somewhat anxious when they have an operation, but added that it is often because they do not have enough information about what to expect. The same basic information was then given to all subjects in this

condition. After asking the patients what was likely to happen in preparation for the operation, the counselor told about the nature of and reasons for such practices as skin preparation, preoperative medication, and anesthesia. The second half of the information was addressed to the postoperative experience. Again the patients were questioned about their expectations. The patients were then informed that the surgery might be followed by gas pains, slight nausea, constipation, and difficulty in urinating. They were also alerted to the possibility that, after the anesthetic had worn off, some pain might be experienced around the incision area as a result of the surgical procedure itself. All the information consisted of simple facts available in standard nursing manuals concerning operative care and usual sources of discomfort. The probable pains and discomforts were made analogous to commonplace experiences rarely accompanied by stress. Additional statements of a reassuring nature called attention to the high quality of the hospital staff.

(3) Combination of Preparatory Information and Coping Device

After an introduction that combined the key statements used in each of the two preceding conditions, the patients were given the preparatory communication concerning discomforts and operative care. Then they were given the explanation of the coping device. In an attempt to hold constant the amount of interaction with the psychologist, the combined condition was limited to approximately the same amount of time as the sessions in either condition alone. This was accomplished by using fewer examples (but still enough to ensure understanding) and a condensed discussion of each.

(4) Control

The purpose of this interview was to control for the possible effects on a surgical patient of the mere encounter with an interested psychologist. The interview was introduced in the same way as the three experimental conditions, asserting that most people are somewhat anxious before an operation and that a patient's view of hospital routines may influence the stress he or she is undergoing. It was conducted in the same manner and lasted about the same amount of time as the other sessions. In order to avoid a discussion about fears concerning the present operation, the patients were asked relatively neutral questions relevant to the surgical experience, such as: Have you ever been in the hospital before? When did you first go to the doctor for this ailment? How long did you know you were going to have the operation before you came to the hospital? When did you last see your doctor? Could you tell me about the admitting procedure? All conversation was directed toward hospital routines; no questions were asked about the unpleasant aspects of the impending operation.

The sessions for each of the four treatments lasted approximately 20 minutes. All physicians, nurses, and others on the hospital staff were kept blind as to each patient's psychological treatment.

Dependent Measures

Behavioral ratings and direct behavioral measures were used in order to evaluate the stress-reducing properties of the various treatments. Immediate effects on the patients' emotional state were assessed by obtaining behavioral ratings from nurses on the surgical ward. Before the interview the nurse who had admitted the patient to the hospital was asked to complete a short questionnaire evaluating the patient's level of stress in comparison with most other major elective preoperative patients. The first question asked about the patient's level of anxiety and provided anchors on a 7-point scale at (1) extremely anxious, (4) moderately anxious, and (7) not at all anxious. The second question asked: How well is the patient dealing with stress and discomforts? Again there was a 7-point scale with anchors at (1) not at all well, (4) moderately well, and (7) extremely well. The nurse was told to answer the preinterview questionnaire on the basis of the impressions she had formed during the admitting procedure. Approximately 15 minutes after the psychologist's visit was completed, the same nurse was asked to revisit the patient and to complete the same questionnaire once again. The instructions stated that the nurse should ignore her previous ratings because the patient may have changed in either direction. All nurses were kept blind with respect to psychological treatments given to the patients.

In addition to the nurses' blind ratings, data on overt behavioral indicators of postoperative stress were also recorded. The total number of pain relievers and sedatives the patients requested and their length of stay in the hospital were taken from the patient's record. Physiological measures were also obtained: blood pressure and pulse readings were recorded by the nurses before and 15 minutes after the interview and then again immediately before and about 1 hour after the operation.

RESULTS

Nurses' Preoperative Evaluations

Changes from immediately before to immediately after the psychologist's interview were assessed for each patient on the basis of the nurses' blind evaluations of the patients' level of anxiety and ability to cope with stress. Table 19.1 presents the mean change scores for each experimental condition. A positive score reflects an improvement in successful coping. As expected, the cognitive-reappraisal procedure was effective in increasing preoperative stress tolerance, as indicated by significant changes in the nurses' ratings of anxiety and of the patients' ability to cope.[2]

Postoperative Behavioral Measures

The four groups were compared on the basis of the mean number of pain relievers requested by patients during postoperative convalescence. The mean numbers of requests per patient were 5.13 for cognitive reappraisal and preparatory information, 3.36 for cognitive reappraisal only, 5.13 for preparatory information only, and 9.27 for the controls. As expected, the

Table 19.1. Mean changes in nurses' preoperative ratings of stress and percentage of patients who requested drugs during postoperative convalescence

	(a)	(b)	(c)	(d)	(e)
	Rated anxiety[a]	Rated ability to cope[a]	Percentage req. pain relievers	Percentage req. sedatives	Percentage req. pain relievers and sedatives
Cognitive reappraisal and preparatory information	.53	.53	73%	87%	67%
Cognitive reappraisal only	.40	.67	64%	72%	50%
Preparatory information only	−.20	−.13	80%	87%	73%
Controls: no cognitive reappraisal and no preparatory information	.13	0	93%	100%	93%

Note. $N = 15$ in each group for preoperative measures; $N = 14$ or 15 for postoperative measures.
[a]A positive change score indicates improvement, i.e., lower anxiety or higher ability to cope.

control group, which was given neither the preparatory information nor the coping device, requested significantly more pain-relieving drugs than any of the other three groups.[3] Table 19.1 (cols. c and d) shows the percentage of patients in each group who made at least one request for pain relievers and the percentage who made at least one request for sedatives. On both these postoperative measures and on the combined measures (col. e), the results for preparatory information, compared with the controls, are in the expected direction but are not large enough to be statistically significant. The cognitive-reappraisal procedure, however, clearly had a significant effect on both measures of stress tolerance.[4] In order to highlight the pronounced effect of the cognitive-reappraisal procedure on postoperative stress tolerance, Figure 19.1 depicts graphically the differences between the group that received the procedure and the control group.

DISCUSSION

It is exceedingly difficult to carry out an experimental treatment that consists largely of obtaining a certain category of responses from an interviewee in a field setting, such as a surgical ward, with the exacting control possible in a laboratory analogue. However, insofar as the present results corroborate previous experimental findings they may be viewed as a meaningful extension of laboratory findings to a real world problem, reducing the

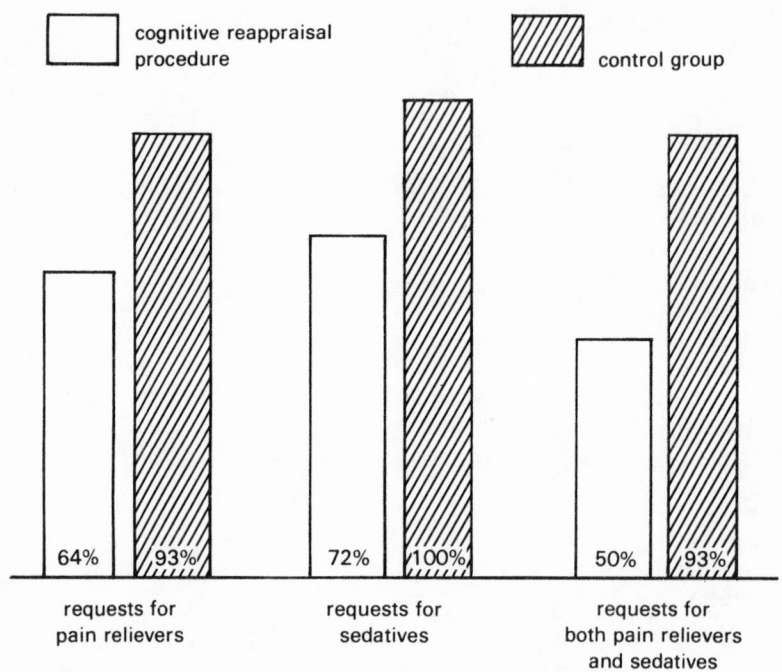

Figure 19.1. Comparison of patients given a cognitive-reappraisal procedure during preoperative counseling ($N = 14$) with control patients ($N = 15$).

stresses of surgery. A coping device derived largely from laboratory studies on distraction and perceived control, which encourages cognitive reappraisal of anxiety-provoking events, calming self-talk, and intentional cognitive mastery through selective attention, appears to be an effective means of increasing both pre- and postoperative stress tolerance. Unlike the control and information-only groups, subjects taught this approach showed an immediate positive change as evidenced by the nurses' blind ratings of the patients' level of anxiety and ability to cope with discomfort. This relatively rapid decrease in anxiety and increase in apparent coping ability in the groups given the cognitive-reappraisal procedure may be partly attributed to the reassuring effect of the procedure. Although the immediate fears of these patients were recognized and discussed, fears about the pre- and postoperative procedures and about the pains and discomforts they might experience were not stimulated. The patients' generally negative view of their physical condition, hospitalization, and the impending operation were reinterpreted by directing their attention to the favorable aspects of their present situation.

In addition to being urged to focus their attention on positive features of the operation, the patients given the cognitive-reappraisal procedure, unlike those in the information-only and control groups, were explicitly told that they could exert more influence over what they will experience than they might have realized. Cognitive reappraisal was portrayed as a mechanism for controlling one's emotions. This heightened perception of personal mastery may also have contributed to greater stress tolerance by reducing the additional stress generated by feelings of helplessness that so often occur among hospitalized patients.

The patients who received the cognitive-reappraisal procedure proved to be superior to those who did not on two postoperative measures of stress tolerance, pain relievers and sedatives requested. There was a similar but nonsignificant trend for length of stay in the hospital.[5] The data are consistent with the expectation that the cognitive-reappraisal procedure helps surgical patients deal with potentially anxiety-provoking situations as they arise.

In the information-only group, on the other hand, very specific details of the pre- and postoperative procedures were discussed. This had the initial effect of making the impending operation more anxiety arousing. Although the negative effects of the communication apparently dissipated by the time the postoperative measures were taken, no clear evidence of a positive postoperative effect was found. It must be emphasized that the preparatory information was given in a very brief preoperative session (only about 10 minutes was spent on it). From a brief presentation the patients could acquire more realistic conceptions of the postoperative discomforts to be expected, which could stimulate them to develop spontaneously some effective coping mechanisms. But they may still be tuned in, so to speak, to the pains and discomforts. Focusing on expected suffering appears to be a less effective means, as far as tolerating temporary postoperative pains is concerned, than focusing on the positive gains to be expected from undergoing the discomforts of surgery.

The results of this field experiment suggest that it would be beneficial to incorporate a procedure like that employed in the cognitive-appraisal procedure into nurses' intake interviews with patients. It may also be valuable to use laboratory as well as other field settings that permit precise experiments to be conducted in order to determine mediating processes. A major question that remains to be answered is whether the positive effects of the cognitive-reappraisal procedure are attributable primarily to an increase in perception of personal mastery over the stressful event, distraction, calming self-talk, or some other mediating changes. If dependable answers are obtained, more effective counseling devices might be developed to help many different types of medical and surgical patients who decide to undergo treatments that entail anxiety-provoking consequences.

MAIN CONCLUSIONS

1. Positive effects were obtained with a coping device that involves cognitive reappraisal of anxiety-provoking events, which encourages calming self-talk and cognitive control through selective attention. Patients about to undergo major surgery who were exposed to the cognitive-reappraisal procedure displayed increased stress tolerance before the operation, as indicated by nurses' blind ratings of the patients' preoperative anxiety and ability to cope. The procedure also had a marked effect on postoperative measures of stress tolerance: number of pain relievers requested and proportion of patients requesting sedatives.

2. Giving patients about to undergo major surgery a brief (10 minute) exposure to preparatory information about what to expect did not produce any significant effects on postoperative measures of stress tolerance.

NOTES

1. A more complete description of the coping strategy can be found in Langer and Dweck, 1973.

2. A separate analysis of variance was computed for each of the two measures. Both measures showed a significant main effect for the cognitive-reappraisal treatment ("anxiety": $F(1, 56) = 5.60$, $p < .05$; "ability to cope": $F(1, 56) = 12.59$, $p < .01$). Whereas the cognitive-reappraisal procedure was expected to reduce stress, an initial mild increase in stress was anticipated for patients receiving only the preparatory information. A contrast analysis describing this outcome (which set the two cognitive-reappraisal groups equal to each other and superior to the control group, which, in turn, was superior to the information-only group) yielded reliable results for both ratings ("anxiety": $F(1, 56) = 4.63$, $p < .05$; "ability to cope": $F(1, 56) = 7.06$, $p < .05$).

3. Comparison between the control group and the three experimental groups yielded $F(1, 55) = 4.44$, $p < .05$. The main effects and interaction did not reach conventional levels of significance.

The data on pain relievers, sedatives, and length of stay are based on 59 cases because the husband of one patient in the coping condition refused to sign the release for his wife to have a hysterectomy.

4. When the proportions are transformed into arc sines, the analysis yields a significant main effect only for the cognitive-reappraisal procedures ($Z = 1.75$, $p < .04$). (See Langer & Abelson [1972] for a discussion of the use of the arc sine transformation in this context.)

The main effect for the cognitive-reappraisal procedure and the interaction effect are significant at $p < .025$ ($Z = 2.02$, in both instances). The last column in Table 19.1 gives the proportion of patients in each group who requested both pain relievers and sedatives. Once again, the analysis yielded a significant main effect for the coping strategy ($Z = 2.24$, $p < .02$) and a significant interaction ($Z = 1.74$, $p < .05$).

A multivariate analysis of the physiological measures (systolic blood pressure, diastolic blood pressure, and pulse rate obtained before and after the psychologist's visit, and before and after the operation) failed to reveal any systematic variation. The measures did not differ among the groups, in contrast to the behavioral ratings and drug request measures that indicated differential stress among patients in the four conditions. Furthermore, the physiological measures did not differ within groups over time, although one might expect patients to be more stressed immediately prior to the operation than at earlier times. It is noteworthy that the changes in blood pressure and pulse do not correlate significantly with the behavioral measures of stress or with each other. The correlations of changes in pulse with changes in blood pressure ranged from -.02 to .10. Since the two physiological measures did not correlate with each other or with the behavioral measures of stress, they do not appear to be promising dependent variables for assessing the effects of preparatory procedures on stress tolerance in surgical patients. Perhaps some other physiological measures, such as variability in heart rate (Porges, 1972), rather than changes in heart rate per se, will prove to be more valid for investigating changes under stress.

5. Although the groups do not differ reliably on mean length of stay in the hospital, the direction of the differences is the same as for pain relievers and sedatives: cognitive reappraisal and preparatory information, 6.2 days; cognitive reappraisal only, 5.6 days; preparatory information only, 7.2 days; controls, 7.6 days.

PART
5
SYNTHESIS

20 Personality Differences in Responsiveness to Counseling Procedures

IRVING L. JANIS

Do clients with different personality traits or other predispositional characteristics react differently to short-term counseling procedures? One important purpose of posing this question in reexamining the evidence from the field experiments reported in this volume is to try to identify the types of clients for whom each procedure is ineffective or perhaps even detrimental. It is a truism among professionals and research workers in medical psychology, behavior modification, and psychotherapy that no psychological procedure works well for everyone, that any successful procedure is helpful only for some people but not for others (see Lazarus, 1975).

In this chapter I shall use two different bases for singling out predispositional variables that seem worth pursuing in subsequent research. One basis is the most promising *empirical results* from the research described in chapters 4–19 on adherence to stressful courses of action. The other basis is *theory*, which comes from inferences about sources of individual differences with respect to the critical phases in supportive helping relationships (chap. 2) and the five coping patterns discussed by Janis and Mann (chap. 3). The latter inferences derived from the conflict theory analysis of decision making, as we shall see, suggest several predispositional variables that have been neglected in personality research but that may account for some of the variance in behavior change.

Obviously, it is always difficult to draw definitive conclusions from studies of relationships between predispositional attributes and behavior changes because such studies are correlational and therefore alternative interpretations in terms of hidden third factors cannot be precluded. Nevertheless, if observed correlations or interactions between predispositional measures and treatments prove to be well replicated in a series of studies, they can provide dependable information about who is likely to respond in what way.

LEVEL OF SELF-ESTEEM

The theoretical analysis of critical phases in helping relationships presented in chapter 2 alerts us to the potential importance of the clients' initial level of self-esteem as a determinant of responsiveness to supportive counseling.

The theory postulates that when people have the intention of changing to a difficult course of action, such as dieting, the incentive value of gaining the approval of a counselor or an adviser can help to get them started and to continue. A supportive norm-sending adviser can build up and use potential motivating power, acording to the theory, if he or she meets the main conditions specified for the three critical phases (see Table 2.1). When those conditions are met, the client builds up an image of the counselor as a quasi-dependable source of self-esteem enhancement: The person who seeks help comes to realize that he or she will mostly receive spontaneous acceptance, including when revealing weaknesses and shortcomings, *except* when he or she fails to make a sincere effort to live up to a *limited* set of norms. This modified expectation of partly contingent acceptance from the helper allows the client to look forward to receiving genuine acceptance and approval from the helper much of the time—and perhaps even practically all the time—provided that he or she makes a sincere effort to follow just a few rules recommended by the helper pertaining to only a specific sphere of personal behavior.

This theoretical analysis leads us to expect that it is worthwhile to investigate individual differences in initial level of self-esteem because such differences might be related to the outcome of supportive counseling. But the theory does not state exactly what the relationship will be. One plausible hypothesis is that clients initially low in self-esteem are most demoralized and therefore most in need of self-esteem bolstering to counteract their lack of confidence about succeeding on a difficult new course of action. According to this hypothesis the initially low self-esteem clients will show relatively little adherence to the counselor's recommendations if the counselor gives neutral feedback or shows signs of being critical or detached, but will show a marked increase in adherence if the counselor consistently meets the optimal conditions for functioning as a quasi-dependable source of self-esteem enhancement. The clients with initially high self-esteem, on the other hand, will be relatively self-confident about succeeding to start with and therefore will show a relatively high degree of adherence irrespective of variations in the counselor's acceptance behavior.

An alternative hypothesis, which also seems quite plausible in light of clinical observations, is that clients with low self-esteem are not initially more demoralized or less self-confident than others but are more dissatisfied with themselves as they now are, which inclines them to be more strongly motivated to obtain whatever self-esteem enhancement they can from living up to the counselor's norms and from achieving success on a difficult task, such as dieting. Clients with an initially high level of self-esteem, on the other hand, being less discontented with themselves, are less motivated to work hard to make use of the opportunity for self-esteem enhancement offered by the relationship with the counselor or by succeeding at the difficult task at hand. The predictions that follow from the second hypothesis are different from those that follow from the first one. The second hypothesis leads us to expect that clients initially low in self-esteem will show more adherence to the counselor's recommendations than clients with initially high self-esteem for all forms of counseling (including when the counselor gives primarily neutral feedback, although they may do even better when the counselor is explicitly accepting).

Turning now to the available evidence from the eight field experiments that included personality measures, we find more support for the second hypothesis than for the first. In the initial field experiment in a weight-reduction clinic (chap. 6 by Dowds, Janis, and Conolley), the clients' scores on the Janis and Field self-esteem scale were found to be related to successful adherence to the counselor's recommendations, regardless of whether the counselor gave positive or neutral feedback in response to self-disclosures. During the 2-month follow-up period, clients with relatively low self-esteem scores (below the median) mailed back significantly more weekly reports and reported following the diet to a significantly greater extent than clients with relatively high self-esteem scores. There was a difference in the same direction for weight loss over the 2-month period, but the difference was not large enough to be statistically significant.

The differences between low and high self-esteem clients were replicated and emerged even more strongly in the pair of field experiments that followed (chap. 7 by Conolley, Janis, and Dowds). The low self-esteem clients (assessed in the same way) lost more weight than the high self-esteem clients; this time the difference was significant. And again the clients with low self-esteem scores returned a significantly larger number of weekly reports, on the average, over the 2-month follow-up period and reported following the diet for a significantly greater number of days.

Thus, the results from both studies indicate that the clients who benefit most from the type of short-term counseling provided in the dieting clinic are those who initially have a relatively low level of self-esteem, as manifested by their answers to questions about feelings of personal inadequacy, self-blame, and lack of confidence in dealing with people. These differences were observed irrespective of the type of feedback given by the counselor.

In a completely different setting, involving brief counseling sessions for elementary school teachers who were attending a workshop on new methods of arithmetic instructions, Smith (chap. 16) found that low initial self-esteem was related to adherence to recommendations when the teachers were given individualized counseling treatment designed to enhance their self-esteem. In Smith's study the counseling treatment consisted of making encouraging comments about the teachers' progress and their potentialities for mastering the new instructional methods despite whatever problems they were having. The teachers who were most responsive to the self-esteem enhancement counseling, as manifested by unobtrusive behavioral measures of subsequent adherence to the workshop recommendations in their own classrooms, were those who initially obtained low self-esteem scores on the California Personality Inventory. (For the control group, which was given a tutoring treatment that did not involve giving positive feedback that might enhance self-esteem, no relationship was found between initial level of self-esteem and subsequent adherence to the recommendations.) Smith points out that the initial low self-esteem scores of those who responded best to the counseling treatment do not necessarily imply a chronically low level of self-esteem. All of them were working at inner-city schools under adverse conditions that make for disillusionment and lowering of self-esteem. Their low self-esteem scores could reflect, therefore, a situationally induced state caused by the stresses of their work, which might make them especially responsive to a brief counseling treatment that involves self-esteem enhancement.[1]

Smith's experiment showed that adherence to recommendations was determined by the interaction of a personality measure (initial level of self-esteem) and a counseling treatment variable (self-esteem enhancement). Another example of an interaction effect of the same kind was found in a counseling study in the Yale Weight-Reduction Clinic by Riskind (chap. 14). Using the self-acceptance scale from the California Personality Inventory (Gough, 1957) to assess level of self-esteem, Riskind found that when the clients were given a long-term perspective that emphasized difficulties to be expected in the future, those clients with initially low self-esteem scores showed more adherence, including more weight loss. This is essentially the same finding obtained in the two prior studies in the weight-reduction clinic that showed low self-esteem to be related to high adherence (chaps. 6 and 7); the counselors in both those earlier studies had called the clients' attention to the long-term demands and difficulties of dieting. But Riskind discovered that the relationship between self-esteem and adherence was reversed when clients were encouraged to adopt a short-term (day by day) approach to dieting, which fostered a sense of personal mastery. Under these conditions of greater personal mastery, clients who obtained high self-esteem scores showed more adherence. Riskind suggests that persons who differ in chronic level of self-esteem may have different characteristic modes of coping that influence their responses to situational conditions requiring personal responsibility and mastery rather than dependency on support from others.

I suspect that many other situational variables will also be found to affect the relationship between level of self-esteem and responsiveness to a counselor's recommendations. Perhaps if subsequent research focuses on counseling variables that give rise to interaction effects, it will become possible to formulate some dependable generalizations.

Another type of interaction effect that needs to be looked into involves the different components that go into the self-esteem scales that are currently in use. For example, one scale may primarily tap the subjects' chronic level of self-esteem while another may tap the subjects' temporary state during recent days or weeks, induced by the current life situation, and a third may tap the subjects' mood of the moment. These diverse components of a heterogeneous personality scale that purports to measure self-esteem might not be related to adherence in the same way. The analysis of coping patterns in chapter 3 provides theoretical grounds for expecting that chronically low self-esteem makes for a coping pattern of defensive avoidance, which leads to low adherence, whereas a temporary state of current dissatisfaction with oneself could function as a positive incentive that leads to vigilance and high adherence.

The need for a similar type of differentiation is indicated by seemingly contradictory findings from two other studies carried out in our weight-reduction clinic. In chapter 10 Quinlan, Janis, and Bales noted that overweight women who reported on a questionnaire that they felt guilty about their lack of control over their eating behavior showed more successful adherence to the diet after 2 months than those who reported less guilt. This result appears to be in line with the previous findings on the relationship between low self-esteem and adherence. But the study by Janis and Quinlan reported in chapter 13, which used a comparable interview procedure with a small sample of overweight women, indicates that those who initially expressed low self-confidence about succeeding at the task of dieting were *less* likely to lose weight. Lack of self-confidence is, of course, generally regarded as a component of low self-esteem. If we were to regard it that way, we would be obliged to say that these findings on level of self-confidence contradict the other findings on level of self-esteem because they show exactly the reverse relationship. But there may not be any contradiction here because the two measures may not be measuring the same thing. In subsequent work with predispositional measures, it would appear to be worthwhile to separate the two components into independent scales, one dealing with demoralization as manifested by lack of self-confidence about future success at solving the overweight problem and the other dealing with shame or guilt about failure to exercise sufficient self-control to solve the problem. As was mentioned earlier, the shame or guilt component of self-esteem might increase a person's motivation to adopt a new course of action, whereas the demoralization component implies a lack of hope, which according to the conflict theory of coping with decisional stress (chap. 3) makes for defensive avoidance in the form of procrastinating, shifting responsibility to others, or bolstering the current course of inaction.

FIELD DEPENDENCE

Field dependence assessed by the Embedded Figures Test was described by Witkin and his associates (1962) as indicating high dependence on environmental cues and lack of psychological differentiation. This variable has been found in some studies to be correlated with a number of interrelated personality characteristics, including passivity, submissiveness, indistinct body image, and low self-esteem, but the results have been somewhat inconsistent (see Horn, 1976, pp. 448–450). In a study in the Yale dieting clinic by Green (chap. 8), field dependence was found to be predictive of clients' acquiescent behavior during the initial interview but not of subsequent adherence to the recommended diet. As expected, the clients who obtained the highest scores on field dependence (based on the Embedded Figures Test) displayed fewer signs of withdrawal during the interview, expressed more positive feelings toward the counselor, and also expressed greater willingness to accept the recommended diet than those who obtained lower scores. These reactions can be regarded as manifestations of a strong need for approval from the counselor. But what happens afterward, when these dependent clients have to carry out their good intentions without being in contact with the counselor? During the 5 weeks following the initial interview the clients who scored high on field dependence showed *less* adherence than the others: they mailed back fewer weekly reports and were less successful in losing weight.

In terms of the theoretical analysis of phases in the development of an effective supportive relationship with a counselor (chap. 2), the high scoring clients on field dependence might be more responsive than others to cues suggesting interest and acceptance on the part of the counselor in Phase 1 and perhaps also in Phase 2, when the counselor gives specific recommendations, but less tolerant of separation from the counselor in Phase 3. Thus, despite getting off to a very good start in the initial session at the clinic, the field dependent clients appear to do relatively poorly at home when it comes to adhering to a difficult course of action without having contact with a supportive counselor.

INDIVIDUAL DIFFERENCES IN COPING STYLE

Having examined the meager findings bearing on relationships between predispositional measures and adherence observed in our short-term counseling studies, we turn next to predispositional variables that are suggested by the theoretical analysis of coping patterns as being potentially predictive of adherence to a stressful course of action. It will be recalled that three conditions are essential for vigilant search and appraisal, according to the conflict-theory analysis of coping patterns in response to threats or opportunities that induce changes in behavior (see chap. 3): (1) belief that there are serious risks for whichever available course of action is chosen, (2) belief that it is realistic to be optimistically hopeful about finding a better alternative solution than the objectionable ones that are being contemplated, and (3) belief that there is adequate time in which to search and deliberate before a decision is required. A person who is generally unresponsive to authentic information that promotes one or another of these beliefs would be expected to show a consistently defective coping pattern that generally would lead either to no change at all or to a poorly worked out decision without adequate contingency planning, which would soon be followed by reversal of the decision in response to setbacks or acute post-decisional regret.

There are various bits and pieces of evidence from prior research on personality differences that appear to be in line with these assumptions. For example, a number of studies employing Byrne's (1964) repression-sensitization scale and Goldstein's (1959) closely related coper versus avoider test suggest that persons diagnosed as chronic repressors or avoiders tend to minimize, deny, or ignore any warning that presents disturbing information about impending threats. Such persons appear to be predisposed to display the characteristic features of defensive avoidance and, unlike those who are predisposed to be vigilant, do not respond adaptively to preparatory information that provides realistic forecasts about stressful experiences to be expected along with reassurances. Some confirmatory findings are to be found in the reports on two field experiments conducted on surgery wards by Andrew (1970) and DeLong (1971). In both studies, patients awaiting surgery were given Goldstein's test in order to assess their preferred mode of coping with stress and then were given preparatory information. The reactions of the following three groups were compared: (1) copers, who tended to display vigilance or sensitizing defenses; (2) avoiders, who displayed avoidant or denial defenses; and (3) nonspecific defenders, who showed no clear preference. In Andrew's (1970) study preparatory information describing what the experience of the operation and the postoperative convalescence will be like had an unfavorable effect on the rate of physical recovery of avoiders but a positive effect on nonspecific defenders. Copers recovered well regardless of whether they were given the preoperative information. In DeLong's (1971) study avoiders were found to have the poorest recovery regardless of whether they were given the preparatory information; copers showed the greatest benefit from the preparatory information.

Although not completely consistent with each other, the findings from the two studies appear to agree in indicating that persons who display defensive avoidance tendencies do not respond well to preoperative counseling that offers preparatory information. This conclusion seems to be in line with evidence on stress tolerance obtained in some (although not all) of the laboratory stress experiments in which differences between repressors (or avoiders) and sensitizers have been studied. For example, Davidson and Bobey (1970) found that repressors showed a decrease in tolerance for experimentally induced pain after an initial exposure to the painful stimulus whereas sensitizers showed a trend in the opposite direction. In a laboratory experiment by Olson and Zanna (1978), which required subjects to make a minor decision, repressors displayed selective exposure by avoiding exposure to dissonance-producing perceptions whereas sensitizers did not.[2]

Complicated findings on another predispositional attribute were obtained

by Auerbach, Kendall, Cuttler, and Levitt (1976) in a study of stress inoculation for dental surgery. Using Rotter's (1966) personality measure of locus
of control, these investigators found that "internals" (patients who perceive themselves as having control over the outcome of events) responded
positively to specific preparatory information about the surgical experiences to be expected, showing high stress tolerance during the recovery
period. In contrast, "externals" (patients who perceive themselves as primarily under the control of external circumstances) obtained lower adjustment ratings when provided with the specific preparatory information. But
subsidiary findings show the reverse outcome when the patients were given
general preparatory information that was not directly relevant to their
surgical experiences.

As is so often the case with the correlational data obtained in personality
research, the findings can be interpreted in a number of different ways and
it is difficult to determine which interpretation is best. For example, because
prior research shows that "externals" tend to be more defensive than "internals," the main finding could be viewed as consistent with the hypothesis
that persons who are predisposed to adopt a defensive avoidance coping
pattern fail to evince increased stress tolerance when given preparatory
information about the specific stress experiences that are to be expected.
An alternative interpretation would be in terms of the importance of perceived control: Maybe only those patients who are capable of perceiving
themselves as influencing what happens develop adequate coping responses
when given preparatory information about anticipated stress. In any case
the complex findings suggest that in order to increase the percentage who
benefit from stress inoculation it will be necessary to hand-tailor the preparatory information in a way that takes account of the coping style of
different individuals.

When oportunities for stress inoculation are made available, personality
factors may play a role in determining who will choose to take advantage of
those opportunities and who will not. A study by Lapidus (1969) of pregnant
women indicates that when preparatory information about the stresses of
childbirth is offered free of charge, passive-submissive women who are
most in need of stress inoculation are unlikely to obtain it if it is left up to
them to take the initiative. On various indicators of field dependence-
independence, cognitive control, and flexibility, the pregnant women who
chose to participate in a program that offered psychological preparation for
childbirth differed significantly from those who chose not to participate.
The participants were more field independent and displayed stronger tendencies toward active mastery of stress than the nonparticipants, many of
whom showed signs of strong dependency and denial tendencies.

In order to take account of individual differences in coping style and
other personality predispositions it may be necessary for health counselors
in clinics and hospitals to set up a number of different preparation programs rather than just one standard program. Clients would probably have

to be screened in advance for their knowledge about the consequences of the treatment they have agreed to undergo as well as for their capacity to assimilate unpleasant information. At present, until more analytic research is carried out on responsiveness to each of the major components of stress inoculation, health-care professionals will have to use their best judgment in selecting what they think will be the most effective preparatory information and coping recommendations for each particular individual facing a particular type of stress.

HYPOTHESES DERIVED FROM CONFLICT THEORY

The evidence from the various studies I have just cited is suggestive but bears only indirectly on the major implications of Janis and Mann's conflict-theory analysis of coping patterns (chap. 3). The following hypotheses specify how, according to the theory, personality predispositions are expected to be conducive to faulty decision making in response to challenging communications or events that call attention to serious risks from continuing the same old defective course of action or inaction:

1. Some persons have a consistently low capacity for assimilating information about risks, for example, as a result of low intellectual ability, which prevents comprehension of warnings about impending threats, or lack of vivid imagery, which dampens the emotional impact and the subsequent salience of the warnings. Such persons will generally show *unconflicted adherence* to their old course of action in response to challenging events or communications that motivate most other people to change their behavior. They will, however, show *unconflicted change* to a new course of action, without adequate preparation for avoiding acute post-decisional regret, on those relatively rare occasions when the following two conditions are present: (a) the challenge is so powerful that it is above the person's high threshold for assimilating information about the risks of continuing the old course of action and (b) the information about the risks entailed by the new course of action is not sufficiently impressive to be above the person's high threshold.
2. Some persons have a consistently low capacity for assimilating information that for most people promotes optimism about available opportunities and resources for finding an acceptable solution to the challenging event or communication, for example, because of pessimistic expectations resulting from a chronic mood of depressive self-disparagement. Such persons will generally display a *defensive avoidance* pattern (in the form of chronic procrastination, shifting of responsibility to someone else, or bolstering of the least objectionable alternative with rationalizations), which involves denying or minimizing the risks and interferes with developing plans that lead to stable changes in behavior.
3. Some persons have a consistently low capacity for assimilating information that leads most people to expect to have sufficient time for search

and appraisal before being required to make a choice among alternative courses of action. They may, for example, have a chronic sense of time urgency, as has been found among "type A personalities," who are at high risk with regard to coronary heart disease (Glass, 1977). For such persons, *hypervigilance* will frequently be displayed in response to challenging events or communications, which leads to impulsive and ill-considered decisions that are unstable.

The examples of predispositional variables given in the above propositions refer to personality traits that are so broad in scope that they would affect any type of decision, whether it pertains to health, career, marriage, social affiliations, or even policy making in an executive role. But most psychologists have learned to be skeptical about being able to make significant predictions on the basis of such broad predispositional attributes because so much prior research reveals that personality traits, as measured by the most widely used tests and rating scales, often fail to show high consistency across different situations and do not account for very much of the variance in observable behavior change (see Mischel, 1968). More recent studies, however, indicate that general personality traits are not quite in such bad shape as they seemed in 1968 (see Sechrest, 1976). In any case the above propositions do not necessarily have to be so imperialistic in scope; they can be reformulated in terms of less sweepingly broad predispositions that pertain to a more limited domain of decision making. In a less imperialistic version the propositions could be confined to the home territory of just one type or subtype of decision, such as those pertaining to health risks.

In my opinion there is no reason to be pessimistic about the prospects of finding consistent individual differences in the three types of capacities specified in the above propositions. I expect that in some persons such capacities (or thresholds) may be consistently high and in others consistently low because of a variety of causes, including both chronic personality characteristics and current social circumstances, such as recent exposure to demoralizing or sensitizing events that could affect a person's responsiveness to information bearing on just one type of decision.

The theoretical analysis based on the Janis and Mann model provides suggestive leads for reinterpreting some seemingly paradoxical findings. Consider, for example, studies of patients who have recently had a heart attack and who are temporarily depressed, worried about the possibility of having another attack, and preoccupied with the poor prospects for recovering fully. Some evidence suggests that these patients are more likely to fail to adopt the recommended course of action necessary for rehabilitation than the equally ill patients who show less depression and less anxiety (Gentry, Foster, & Haney, 1972; Hackett, Cassem, & Wishnie, 1968; McGill, 1975). This observation has been interpreted as suggesting that those heart patients who deny their illness do better in the rehabilitation programs than those who do not engage in denial. This formulation creates a paradox because of the other observations I have already cited indicating that denial of illness generally has adverse effects on patients' decision making and can be pathogenic. But I suspect that "denial" vs. "nondenial" may not be the appropriate terms to describe the patients' reactions. Instead, the crucial difference may be between developing and maintaining some degree of *hope* about solving the health problem despite current suffering vs. remaining *hopeless* about the value of doing anything. That is to say, the second hypothesis stated above might provide an explanation: Those coronary heart disease patients who become pessimistic about finding a satisfactory solution to their current health problem—whether their pessimism is attributable to lifelong personality predispositions, recent untoward events, pessimistic communications from a physician, or lack of social support—tend to be relatively unresponsive to information that encourages most others to have a hopeful outlook about finding a satisfactory solution to the health problems posed by suffering from heart disease. As a result they may shift responsibility and pin all their hopes on the physicians' protective powers, displaying a pattern of defensive avoidance. This denial of personal responsibility is antithetical to adopting and adhering to the recommended courses of action required for rehabilitation. Alternatively, defensive avoidance may take the form of bolstering a business-as-usual stance, which consists of doing nothing about the hazards.

Some of the evidence on level of self-esteem that was reviewed earlier in this chapter is also pertinent to the second hypothesis (concerning pessimism as a determinant of defensive avoidance). Among overweight persons who come to our weight-reduction clinic, the majority of cases who obtain low self-esteem scores on personality scales may not be asserting a lack of confidence about succeeding on the diet but, rather, expressing feelings of guilt or shame about their past failures to control overeating, which is a different component of low self-esteem. Nevertheless, in a minority of clients who obtain low self-esteem scores we have observed what appears to be a syndrome of pessimism combined with manifestations of defensive avoidance, usually in the form of procrastination or shifting responsibility to others. In these cases pessimism about finding a successful solution to their overweight problem seems to stem from a variety of different causes. For example, some men and women are so chronically depressed that they expect to fail at dieting and at any other undertaking that requires self-control; others who usually have fairly high confidence about being able to exercise self-control may believe from bitter past experience that their spouses will sabotage their efforts at dieting as soon as they succeed in losing 4 or 5 pounds. Whatever the cause, however, the relatively pessimistic cases, who express very low confidence about attaining their goal of bringing their weight down to a normal level and keeping it down, have been found to be more likely to fail to adhere to the recommended diet than those who are more hopeful (see chaps. 11 and 13). This observed phenomenon might again be explained by the second hypothesis, which is compatible with the recent reemphasis on *self-efficacy* as a key determinant of successful behavior change by Bandura (1977) and other behavior theorists.

   In future research, investigations of individual differences in self-confidence and in feelings of hope should provide the type of data needed for more rigorous testing of the second hypothesis. The use of appropriate questions in pretreatment interviews and questionnaires should make it possible to determine whether such individual differences are related to manifestations of the defensive avoidance pattern and whether those manifestations, in turn, are predictive of failure to adhere to a counselor's recommendations.

   Appropriate questions could also be devised for use in pretreatment interviews and questionnaires in order to assess individual differences in the predispositional variables specified by the first and third hypotheses. Obviously it should be worthwhile to start off using pertinent measures that are already in the literature, such as the measure of time urgency developed by Glass (1977), which was suggested in the formulation of the third hypothesis on hypervigilance. If such measures fail to discriminate very well, the next step should be to develop new measures designed to tap more directly the predispositional factors specified in the set of three hypotheses. Those theoretically based measures might prove to be more predictive of behavior change than the predispositional measures currently being used in research on attitude change, therapy, and counseling.

NOTES

   1. Among those overweight clients who came to the dieting clinic, low self-esteem might also have been situationally induced as a result of distressing circumstances quite different from those besetting the teachers. Nevertheless, we should be open-minded about the possibility that in the dieting clinic, as well as in the teachers' workshop, the relatively low self-esteem scores of those who proved to be most responsive to the counseling procedures may indicate a *chronic* personality characteristic. Replications in other counseling settings might reveal that those clients who initially manifest low self-esteem are generally the ones who respond best, regardless of whether there are specific situational circumstances that could account for their low self-esteem. This generalization does not appear to be very plausible, however, in light of evidence from a large number of attitude change studies that have investigated the relationship between level of self-esteem and responsiveness to persuasive communications. Although some of the attitude change studies yield the predicted relationship between low self-esteem and high responsiveness to social influence, just as was observed in the field experiments on counseling, other attitude change studies show no relationship at all and still others show the opposite relationship (see McGuire, 1969). Inconsistent findings may arise partly because situational factors interact with level of self-esteem as determinants of responsiveness to social influence.

   2. Evidence from a correlational study of surgical patients appears to contradict the implications of all the predispositional studies just discussed bearing on vigilance versus defensive avoidance. Cohen and Lazarus (1973) report that patients who were rated as "vigilant" before the operation showed more negative postoperative reactions than those rated as "avoidant." This finding seems not only to contradict the earlier surgery findings but also to go against the expectation from the conflict theory model that people who are vigilant will cope with unfavorable consequences of their decisions much better than those whose dominant coping pattern is defensive avoidance or hypervigilance. But there are two important considerations

that need to be taken into account. One is that Sime (1976) attempted to replicate Cohen and Lazarus's (1973) finding using the same categories but was unable to do so. When there are disagreements like this, one suspects that either there are unrecognized differences in the ways in which the variables were assessed or the relationship between the two variables is determined by an interacting (but uninvestigated) third variable, such as severity of the patient's illness.

A second consideration has to do with the way Cohen and Lazarus define *vigilance*. A careful examination of their procedures reveals that they did not differentiate between hypervigilance and vigilance. The investigators state that they classified as vigilant any patient who sought out information about the operation (which hypervigilant people do even more than vigilant ones) or who were sensitized in terms of remembering the information and displaying readiness to discuss their thoughts about the operation. (Again, hypervigilant people tend to be much more preoccupied with information about threatening consequences than those who are vigilant.) The one example Cohen and Lazarus give of a so-called vigilant reaction would be classified as "hypervigilant" according to the criteria given in Janis and Mann (1977, pp. 74, 205–206): "I have all the facts, my will is all prepared [in the event of death] . . . you're put out, you could be put out too deep, your heart could quit, you can have shock. . . . I go not in lightly." Consequently, the correlation observed by these investigators might be attributable to the relationship between preoperative *hypervigilance* and low tolerance for postoperative stress, which has been observed by other investigators (Auerbach, 1973; Janis, 1958; Leventhal & Sharpe, 1965). Auerbach (1973), for example, found that surgical patients who showed a high state of preoperative anxiety relative to their normal or average level (as assessed by the State-Trait Anxiety Inventory developed by Spielberger, Gorsuch, & Lushene, 1970) obtained poorer scores on a measure of postoperative adjustment than those who showed a relatively moderate level of preoperative anxiety.

In Auerbach's study the postoperative adjustment of the patients who showed moderate preoperative anxiety was found to be superior to the patients who showed either relatively low anxiety or relatively high anxiety before the operation. In disagreement with contradictory findings reported by Cohen and Lazarus (1973) and by several other investigators, Auerbach's data tend to confirm Janis's (1958) earlier finding of a curvilinear relationship between the level of preoperative anxiety and postoperative adjustment. Such data are consistent with the "work of worrying" concept, which assumes that vigilance in surgical patients (manifested by a moderate level of preoperative fear or anxiety) is beneficial for postoperative adjustment (Janis, 1958; Janis & Mann, 1977). But it is essential to take note of the disagreements in the correlational results obtained from many nonintervention studies in the research literature on the relationship between level of preoperative fear or anxiety and postoperative adjustment, which can be affected by a number of extraneous variables that are difficult to control even when they can be recognized (see Cohen & Lazarus, 1979). It would not be worthwhile, it seems to me, for investigators to carry out more such correlational studies because even a dozen or two of them cannot be expected to settle the issue. I think it is realistic, however, to hope for dependable conclusions about the postoperative effects of arousal of vigilance before surgery—and also about the interacting effects of such arousal with personality charcteristics —if a few more well-controlled *intervention* studies are carried out in which preparatory information designed to induce vigilance is used as an independent variable and is not confounded with social support or with any other potentially potent variable.

21 Implications of the Field Experiments for Theory and Practice

IRVING L. JANIS

In this chapter I shall reexamine the entire set of findings from the 23 field experiments reported in this book for the purpose of trying to answer fundamental theoretical and practical questions about short-term counseling. The most important questions are when, how, and why short-term counseling can be effective. Whenever possible, the answers will be given in the form of empirical generalizations that appear to be warranted by the evidence now at hand.

Some of the issues to be discussed pertain to practical implications for improving the effectiveness of short-term counseling. Much of the discussion, however, will focus on fundamental questions that require reevaluating the main theoretical assumptions about helping relationships that I and my colleagues had started with (presented in chap. 2). Those assumptions, which originally were based solely on clinical observations, have been put to the test in many of our field experiments, so that it is now possible to modify and reformulate them on a firmer empirical basis.

Readers who have examined the conclusions from each of the preceding studies may at this point be somewhat unclear about exactly how well the model has stood up to the test. Although findings from most of the studies support the model, there are some that do not. Can the anomalous findings be integrated with the supportive findings? I believe they can. In this chapter I shall sketch out an integrative perspective, which attempts to take account of all the evidence on psychological factors that influence counselor effectiveness.

IS SHORT-TERM COUNSELING EFFECTIVE?

The first question that has to be answered before we consider any explanatory hypotheses is a simple empirical one: Does short-term counseling of the type we investigated actually work? Although our studies were designed to be analytic experiments rather than descriptive evaluation research, many of the findings nevertheless can be used to answer this initial empirical question.

By and large, the field experiments show that short-term counseling is effective at least for a sizable minority of the clients and sometimes, when special procedures are used, for the majority. A fairly high percentage of the clients in our studies obtained short-term benefits from the two or three counseling sessions that each client typically was given. For a smaller, but nevertheless substantial percentage, some of the short-term counseling procedures we investigated proved to have highly significant long-term effects as well, extending over a period of many months and, in one instance, many years. It must be recognized that most of the evidence is from studies in antismoking and weight-reduction clinics whose clients voluntarily come for help because they are motivated to change their behavior.

The very first field experiment reported in this volume (chap. 4 by Janis and Hoffman) provides clear-cut evidence of the effectiveness of short-term counseling in helping people to get started on cutting down on cigarette smoking. After five weekly meetings with the counselor all the various treatments groups (irrespective of whether or not the counselor arranged for the clients to form partnerships) had a marked decrease in number of cigarettes smoked. The majority of the clients showed a marked reduction in smoking over the 5-week period. Control data from other studies in the same antismoking clinic, using clients who had been kept on a waiting list for 5 or more weeks, indicate that in the absence of the short-term contact with the counselor no change at all is to be expected over that time interval. The evidence in chapter 4 consistently indicates that clients can be helped to start cutting down on cigarette smoking if they meet for a few sessions with a counselor in an antismoking clinic.

When we look at the long-term effects in the same study we see that the outcome depends on whether the counselor had used the supplementary procedure of assigning his clients to partnerships, with instructions to phone each other every day for 5 weeks. The clients who had been given this supplementary procedure during the period when they came for weekly sessions with the counselor showed a highly significant sustained effect after 1 year and also after 10 years. The control clients, who were not given the supplementary partnership treatment, showed no substantial decrease in smoking after 1 year or after 10 years. Later on I shall discuss the factors that are most likely to account for the success of the partnerships. For the present, it suffices to conclude from this field experiment that counselors in antismoking clinics who use educational films and other communications about the unhealthy consequences of smoking, together with interviews and discussions that encourage the clients to commit themselves to stop smoking, can help them succeed in getting started on a difficult new regimen of reducing cigarette consumption. But counselors apparently need to introduce special procedures during the few counseling sessions they conduct, such as setting up client partnerships, in order to increase their clients' long-term success.

In a comprehensive review of the relevant research on the effectiveness of antismoking clinics Hunt and Bespalec (1974) reported that counseling is generally effective in helping people cut down on cigarette consumption for several weeks but the majority relapse within a few months. Nevertheless, according to these authors a substantial minority show long-term success in abstaining, particularly among those smokers who receive counseling treatments that provide educational information and social support. The findings from the Janis and Hoffman study are consistent with those conclusions.

Essentially the same conclusions can be applied to successful dieting, as was shown by the first of the two experiments conducted in a weight-reduction clinic by Nowell and Janis (chap. 5). Again, the short-term counseling sessions were effective in helping clients in all treatment conditions to get started on a rigorous low-calorie diet (when assessed 3 weeks after the first session). By using the special device of setting up partnerships, the counselors were able to help their clients attain longer term success in losing weight (when assessed after a period of 2¼ months). A second experiment reported by Nowell and Janis, however, indicates that under certain conditions—which seem to involve promising the clients too much—the effectiveness of short-term counseling is not increased by setting up partnerships (see the last section of chap. 5).

Subsequent studies in the Yale Weight-Reduction Clinic reveal that even when counselors limit their contacts to only two or three sessions with each client and do not set up any client partnerships, they are generally effective in accomplishing the stated purpose of the counseling clinic, which is to get the clients started on a low-calorie diet. In one study after another we find significant decreases in weight, on the average, for each short-term counseling treatment when assessed after about 1 or 2 months. And again the evidence from the clinic's waiting lists shows over and over again that when the clients receive no counseling treatment the average amount of weight loss over either a 1- or 2-month period is zero. Some counseling treatments, of course, were found to be much more effective than others, but even the least effective treatments generally resulted in a significant average amount of weight loss over a period of about 2 months.

Similar results on the effectiveness of short-term counseling come from our research project's studies in other settings. In these studies the counselor's recommendations deal with different types of clients making a variety of different kinds of decisions: students deciding to donate blood during a Red Cross campaign (Mulligan, chap. 15), public school teachers deciding to adopt a new method of teaching arithmetic (Smith, chap. 16), young and middle-aged women deciding to attend an early morning exercise class (Hoyt & Janis, chap. 17), and hospitalized men and women being prepared to undergo elective surgery (Langer, Janis, & Wolfer, chap. 19). In each of these settings one or two sessions with a supportive counselor was found to make a significant difference in the degree of adherence to the decision when assessed from 1 to 7 weeks later.

It must be emphasized that the favorable effects of counseling that we have observed in the 23 field experiments pertain primarily to *short-term adherence* to the counselors' recommendations. When long-term adherence is assessed at 9 months or 1 year after the counseling contact has ended, we find mixed results. Some counseling treatments have detectable long-term effects and some do not. Other investigators who have studied the effectiveness of both short-term and long-term contact with physicians or health counselors have reported essentially the same mixed results, usually with the majority of clients showing backsliding about 1 or 2 months after having started to adhere to the physicians' or counselors' recommendations. (See the reviews of the literature by Hunt & Matarazzo [1973], Marston [1970], and Stone [1979].)

This brings us to a central practical issue of present-day counseling research: How can the long-term effectiveness of counselors be increased? A good psychological theory of helping relationships should be able to supply promising answers to this question by pointing to key factors that determine the extent to which counselors will have a positive influence on their clients long after all contact has terminated. We shall return to this problem shortly when we discuss the effects of self-disclosure, positive feedback, and other factors specified by the theoretical model presented in chapter 2. Before reviewing the evidence bearing on those factors, let us first examine briefly a well-known factor that has repeatedly been suggested in the literature on counseling as a means for increasing the effectiveness of short-term counseling.

DOES INCREASING THE AMOUNT OF CONTACT WITH THE CLIENT INCREASE THE COUNSELOR'S EFFECTIVENESS?

Some clients in our weight-reduction clinic say that they want more contact with the counselor than our short-term counseling arrangement provides. A few openly ask for added sessions, a few others telephone the clinic from time to time to ask questions of their counselors. Occasionally, clients complain in the follow-up interview about the limited number of times they could talk with the counselor (see chap. 13 by Janis & Quinlan). The efforts of those clients to have more contact might be regarded as justifiable by quite a few practicing counselors; large numbers of practitioners deliberately arrange to have many more than just two or three sessions with each of their clients. Some psychologists claim that the number of times the counselor is in contact with the client is more important in producing persistent change than what the counselor says or does. This claim is made by an American Psychological Association Task Force on Health Research in a survey article in *American Psychologist* (1976), but the only evidence cited is from an unpublished study on promoting toothbrushing. Other investigations, left out of that survey, do not support any such generalization. Romanczyk (1974), for example, found that overweight clients who had been given "full" behavior-change treatments in a series of six weekly meetings with the counselor were not more successful in losing weight than overweight clients who were given only one session before and one session after a 4-week interval. During the interval the latter clients were asked to carry out recommendations to change their eating habits without any contact at all with the counselor. Those clients lost significantly more weight than control subjects who were not given the recommendations, and after 3 months they were just as successful as the ones given three times as many sessions.

A more recent experiment by Carter, Rice, and DeJulio (1977) randomly assigned overweight clients to a group treatment program that had either 10 weekly sessions or only 4 sessions over the 10-week period. Their data show that the clients given fewer sessions lost significantly more weight by the end of the treatment program and 6 months later. In direct contrast to the claim made by the APA Task Force, these investigators conclude their report by posing an embarrassing question for counselors and therapists: Are they perhaps doing a disservice to their clients by seeing them too often?

Is there any evidence from the studies of one-to-one counseling bearing on the claim that additional sessions are worthwhile? In order to answer this question we must look into studies that compare the effectiveness of different amounts of contact between counselor and client while holding constant all other relevant factors, such as the type of client being treated, the type of counseling procedure being used, and the type of problem being dealt with. Our studies provide some direct and some indirect evidence bearing on the issue. As far as our evidence goes, it does not indicate that the effectiveness of the type of counseling provided in a setting such as our weight-reduction clinic would be increased by increasing the amount of counselor–client contact.

Of all the investigations carried out in the Yale dieting clinic (a total of 16 field experiments), the one in which the clients had the largest number of sessions with the counselor was the study by Nowell and Janis (chap. 5). All clients in that study (whether or not they were assigned to the condition involving daily phone calls with their partners) had a series of *three* weekly meetings with the counselor, which included interviews and discussions similar to those conducted in other investigations. And yet the clients given this relatively greater amount of contact with the counselor did not lose significantly more weight than those given only one session and a follow-up interview in other studies carried out in the same weight-reduction clinic. For example, the clients given three weekly counseling sessions in the Nowell and Janis pair of experiments did not show a significantly greater amount of weight loss than the clients who received only one counseling session in the Riskind experiment (chap. 14) when measures were obtained at a comparable interval (after about 2 months). From these observations we infer that the short-term counseling we provide in our clinics is not too short; there is no reason to expect that three times more of the same would produce better results.

Confirmatory findings indicating no consistent benefit from additional contact between counselor and client comes from the study by Quinlan, Janis, and Bales (chap. 10). In this field experiment systematic comparisons were made between clients randomly assigned to a condition in which they were given a series of four weekly telephone calls by the counselor during the month following the initial face-to-face interview and those clients randomly assigned to a control condition in which they had no additional contact after the initial face-to-face interview. Eight weeks later the clients who had been given the additional contact via phone calls from the counselor were not doing any better at losing weight than the controls. Additional findings from this study reveal that the effects of the extra contact varied, depending upon the type of initial interview the clients had been given. The clients who had been asked to disclose a moderate amount of favorable personal information about their current assets and past achievements showed considerably *more* weight loss if they were given the added telephone contact. In contrast the clients who had been asked to disclose a moderate amount of both favorable and unfavorable personal information showed *less* weight loss if they were given the added contact.

A replication of the latter finding, showing a negative effect from additional telephone contact, was obtained in a recently completed (unpublished) study conducted in the Yale Weight-Reduction Clinic by Blechman, Janis, and Bales. In this study clients were given a standard moderate disclosure interview, eliciting both favorable and unfavorable information about the self. On a random basis half the clients were asked to commit themselves to a contract and the other half not. Those given the high commitment treatment received a series of four phone calls from the counselor during the 2 weeks after the initial interview, whereas those given the control treatment received no phone calls. The results were that the clients in the high commitment treatment involving added telephone contact with the counselor were *less* successful in losing weight than the controls.

Follow-up interviews in the two studies of telephone contact suggest that one of the reasons why the telephone calls from the counselor had unfavorable effects was that some clients thought the purpose was to keep them under surveillance and they disliked being required to report to the counselor on their eating delinquencies. Whether or not this is a correct or complete explanation, the evidence indicates that more contact is not necessarily better and sometimes can be worse. Our evidence certainly does not support the conclusion that what a counselor does is less important than repeated contact with the client, as claimed by the American Psychological Association Task Force on Health Research (1976). On the contrary the results from the weight-reduction studies just reviewed consistently indicate that what the counselor does during the periods of contact is a much more important determinant of the clients' adherence to a low-calorie diet than the amount of contact.

Obviously, further studies are needed in a variety of different counseling settings in order to determine the conditions under which additional contact has beneficial effects and the conditions under which it has detrimental effects (such as mobilizing resistances and fostering buck-passing dependency rather than vigilance). For the present, the only general conclusion we can draw with any certainty from our studies of adherence to dieting recommendations is essentially the same as the negative one that follows from Romanczyk's (1974) study of changing eating habits. We are led to conclude that by and large the treatments we used in our studies of short-term counseling in the Yale Weight-Reduction Clinic, which proved to be fairly effective with a sizable percentage of clients, would not yield better results if we were to offer the same kinds of treatment somewhat more intensively by giving the clients three or four times as many counseling sessions, either face-to-face or via telephone.

DOES POSITIVE FEEDBACK RESULT IN MORE ADHERENCE TO THE COUNSELOR'S RECOMMENDATIONS?

Our studies of self-disclosure and positive feedback, designed to test basic theoretical assumptions, also help to answer a fundamental practical question that confronts all counselors: What is the most effective way to conduct the initial session? This is an extremely important issue especially in short-term counseling, when the initial session comprises most, if not all, of the counseling that is provided.

The theoretical model with which we started (chap. 2) assumes that a counselor's motivating power can be built up if he or she does certain things in order to take on the role of a quasi-dependable source of self-esteem enhancement for each client. According to this model, at the beginning of a supportive relationship there are two principal variables that determine the motivating power of the counselor, both of which involve specific kinds of verbal behavior on the part of the counselor in his or her interactions with the clients: first, encouraging or eliciting some degree of *self-disclosure* and second, responding to self-disclosures with *positive feedback* in the form of acceptance statements. We shall review first the evidence on the effects of positive feedback, which is much less complicated than the evidence on the effects of eliciting different amounts of self-disclosure.

The field experiment by Dowds, Janis, and Conolley (chap. 6) and the replication of it by Conolley, Janis, and Dowds (chap. 7) show the same outcome. Both these experiments conducted in the Yale Weight-Reduction Clinic clearly indicate that consistently positive feedback from the counselor has favorable effects when given during an interview that induces a moderate amount of self-disclosure. In both experiments consistently positive feedback was compared with consistently neutral feedback and with predominantly positive feedback marred by a single instance of very mild negative feedback. Of the three forms of feedback treatment it was the consistently positive that was found to result in the most favorable attitudes toward the counselor and also in the greatest adherence to the counselor's recommendations, as manifested by weight loss 2 months later. (Unexpected findings from these experiments indicating that under certain conditions neutral feedback can also be highly effective will be discussed later in this chapter.)

The findings on the favorable effects of consistently positive feedback have also been replicated in an unpublished doctoral dissertation by Chang (1977), designed under the supervision of Edward Conolley. In a weight-reduction clinic at the University of Southern California, modeled after the one at Yale, Chang compared consistently positive feedback with an ambiguous type of neutral feedback (no response at all from the counselor except for impassive or skeptical facial expressions). He found significantly more weight loss after a period of about 3 weeks among the clients who had been given positive feedback during their initial interview, irrespective of whether the interview questions induced only positive or only negative disclosures about the self.

Further evidence that consistently positive feedback fosters adherence to the counselor's recommendations comes from another study in the Yale Weight-Reduction Clinic by Greene (chap. 8), which introduced a variation in physical proximity that had not been investigated in the earlier studies. Greene found that when the seating arrangement for the interview placed the client at a normal distance of about 2 feet from the counselor, positive verbal feedback had the expected favorable effect, as shown by significantly greater weight loss 5 weeks after the interview. But when the seating arrangement placed clients at a relatively far distance from the counselor (5 feet away), which they apparently interpreted as a nonverbal sign of withdrawal or detachment, the favorable effect of positive verbal feedback was lost. These results point to the same conclusion suggested by subsidiary findings from the earlier experiments in the Yale clinic: In order for positive feedback to be effective, the counselor must use it *consistently* throughout the interview, abstaining from saying or doing anything that could be construed by the clients as withdrawing from them or criticizing them.

Additional confirmatory results, which also involve limiting conditions, were obtained in a pair of field experiments by Mulligan (chap. 15), conducted during a Red Cross campaign to elicit blood donations from college students. Mulligan found that consistently positive feedback from the interviewer, compared with neutral feedback, increased the amount of adherence to the interviewer's recommendation to donate blood to the Red Cross. This was the outcome when the interview elicited self-disclosures that were not directly relevant to the current decisional conflict. But the opposite outcome was obtained when the interview included the additional issue of whether or not to donate blood, which gave the clients the opportunity to express their reluctance to do so. These findings imply that although positive feedback may generally be more effective than neutral feedback in response to a person's self-disclosures, it can be less effective if it reinforces the "wrong" decision from the recommender's standpoint. Even though counselors deliberately attempt to avoid reinforcing "bad intentions," they may inadvertently do so by expressing understanding and empathy during interviews in which clients talk about not wanting to carry out a recommended healthful or socially desirable course of action.

In all the studies just cited, positive feedback took the form of making acceptance statements in response to whatever the clients disclosed about themselves. For example, if a woman who comes for help in the weight-reduction clinic comments favorably about herself as being a prudent and conscientious person, the counselor would respond with a reinforcing comment such as "It's clear that you do have a lot going for you." If the client says something unfavorable about herself by reporting an incident to illustrate her lack of self-control, the counselor would respond with an empathic comment that conveys understanding and continued acceptance, such as "It's quite understandable that you would feel self-critical at such times and would want to change." Additional ways of presenting positive feedback can be used when clients are being monitored after they have started carrying out a difficult task like dieting. The counselor can make favorable comments about the progress that the clients are making and express his or her belief that they have whatever it takes to succeed at the task. This form of self-esteem enhancement was used in a field experiment by Smith (chap. 16) in the setting of a weekend workshop for primary school teachers in which they were being instructed in a difficult new method for teaching arithmetic. On a random basis half the teachers in the workshop were privately given this form of positive feedback by a counselor, focusing on their professional capabilities, during the period when they were attempting to learn and to practice the new procedures. Unobtrusive observations made 2 weeks later revealed that those teachers were using the recommended new procedures in their own classrooms to a much greater extent than were the teachers in the control group, who had received the same instruction and the same amount of practice but without the self-esteem enhancement feedback from the counselor.

Riskind (chap. 14) investigated a different type of self-esteem enhancement in the weight-reduction clinic but found that it did *not* have the intended effect of increasing adherence to the counselor's recommendations. He used a "positive disclosure" interview about the clients' assets, capabilities, aspirations, and past achievements, some of which involved activities having nothing to do with dieting. In response to the positive self-disclosures the counselor made explicitly positive comments. One form of self-esteem enhancement treatment consisted of pointing out personal strengths and resources that were applicable to dieting successfully. Another consisted of emphasizing the clients' assets that would help them to be generally successful in life despite any lack of immediate success in dieting. On a random basis one group of clients was given the first form of treatment, a second group was given the second form, a third group was given both, and a fourth group was given neither.

Riskind's results indicate that both forms of self-esteem enhancement made clients feel much better about themselves (as indicated by their responses on a posttreatment questionnaire), but both failed to have the intended effect on adherence to the low-calorie diet. Contrary to expectations, clients given the self-esteem enhancement treatments showed less weight loss after 8 weeks than those not given either treatment.

Riskind's self-esteem enhancement treatments may have failed to help the clients adhere to the diet for two reasons. In some clients the unearned praise from the counselor may create doubts about the counselor's sincerity; in other clients it may foster complacency, which would reduce their motivation to diet rigorously.

A modified version of the same type of self-esteem enhancement procedure was used with some degree of success in a field experiment by Quinlan, Janis, and Bales (chap. 10). This time the positive disclosure interview was confined to questions relevant to the overweight problem, and the counselor's comments encouraged the clients' expectations of success at dieting without using "hard sell" statements about the clients' hitherto unrecognized assets. And this time the positive disclosure interview proved to be effective both in increasing self-confidence about carrying out the tasks of dieting (as indicated by immediate posttreatment questionnaire responses) and in increasing adherence to the diet (as indicated by subsequent weight loss 2 months later), provided that the interview was followed during the first month by weekly telephone calls from the counselor. In the absence of such telephone calls, however, the positive disclosure interview was relatively ineffective. These findings lead us to surmise that among many of the clients given the self-confidence enhancement interview there were still some residual doubts about the counselor's sincerity, which did not clear up until the counselor demonstrated genuine interest by making the phone calls.

Whether or not this explanation accounts for the negative findings on adherence in Riskind's study, the crucial point is that in six of the seven pertinent studies consistently positive feedback from the counselor (compared with inconsistently positive and/or neutral feedback) had the effect of significantly increasing adherence to the counselor's recommendations. The tentative conclusion that seems warranted from the series of studies is an affirmative answer to the key question of this section, but with some provisos added: When short-term counseling sessions induce a moderate degree of self-disclosure, the degree to which the clients subsequently adhere to the counselor's recommendations will be increased if the counselor responds to the self-disclosures during the sessions by giving positive feedback, provided that it is given consistently and within the obvious limits of plausibility and credibility.

WHEN CLIENTS ARE GIVEN CONSISTENTLY POSITIVE FEEDBACK, DOES INDUCING SELF-DISCLOSURE INCREASE THE COUNSELOR'S EFFECTIVENESS?

Sociolinguists point out that no matter how trivial the topic of conversation may be, every verbal interchange entails at least a slight degree of self-disclosure (see Labov & Fanshel, 1977). But, of course, the amount of self-disclosure by clients that occurs during an initial counseling interview can vary tremendously, depending largely on the questions asked by the interviewer. (The correlation between types of question being asked and amount of self-disclosure elicited is expected to be high when the interviewer is a respected professional counselor, but it would be lower when the interviewer is seen as someone interested only in collecting information in a public opinion poll or, worse yet, a nosy stranger prying into the interviewees' personal life for illegitimate or exploitative purposes.)

In a number of our studies we have investigated the effects of different levels of self-disclosure by varying the content of the counselor's questions, while holding constant the personality of the counselor, the length of the interview, the recommendations being made, and everything else we could think of that might affect the outcome. In these studies, systematic content analysis of the clients' answers to the counselor's questions consistently indicates very large and significant differences in the amount of self-disclosure and degree of intimacy of the disclosures actually induced by interviews designed to elicit a moderate versus a low level of disclosure and also between those designed to elicit a high versus a moderate level. According to the interviewer's notes, the self-disclosures elicited from the clients generally were given in a spontaneous manner with tone of voice and facial expressions conveying feelings congruent with the intimate information being revealed.

From my own observations of a wide range of different levels of self-disclosure elicited in interviews by professional counselors in many different clinical settings, I rate the routine intake interviews conducted in our weight-reduction clinic as eliciting a relatively "low" level of self-disclosure. These routine interviews are limited to questions about food preferences, eating habits, and related events of daily life. At the opposite extreme are "high" disclosure interviews, which contain intimate questions about current or past joys and sorrows, body image, sex life, guilt feelings about misbehavior, secret longings, and other such personal information that is sometimes elicited by probing clinicians but is likely to be withheld from most, if not all, members of one's family and close friends. Intermediate between "high" and "low" is the "moderate" type of self-disclosure interview, which includes questions about personal strengths and weaknesses, sources of worry, aspirations, and the like, all of which are likely to be discussed openly with good friends and sympathetic relatives but seldom with strangers, unless they are being consulted as professional counselors.

The theoretical analysis of helping relationships in terms of self-esteem enhancement (chap. 2) asserts that there are two main conditions which, in combination, build up the motivational power of the counselor. One condition involves eliciting self-disclosure and the other giving positive feedback. Although the theoretical analysis is vague about the upper limit of self-disclosure that might be optimal, it implies the following general hypothesis: Counselors will be more effective in inducing adherence to their recommendations if they first elicit a moderate degree—rather than a very low degree—of self-disclosure in the initial session with each of their clients, provided that they give positive feedback in the form of acceptance responses and display no signs of indifference, rejection, or hostility.

Several experiments in our research project were designed to investigate this self-disclosure hypothesis. The first such experiment, which was conducted in the Yale Weight-Reduction Clinic by Colten and Janis (chap. 9), can be interpreted as tending to confirm the hypothesis. Under conditions where the counselor consistently gave positive feedback in response to whatever the clients said, those who were given only a low disclosure interview showed less adherence to the counselor's recommendations (including less weight loss) than those who were given a moderate disclosure interview combined with a balance-sheet procedure. The latter procedure elicited additional self-disclosures concerning the favorable and unfavorable consequences they would expect to personally experience if they adopted one or another of the alternative courses of action they were considering for dealing with their overweight problem.

Two more experiments conducted in the Yale Weight-Reduction Clinic by Quinlan, Janis, and Bales (chap. 10) yield partially confirmatory evidence in support of the self-disclosure hypothesis, together with some indications of limiting conditions. One of their experiments showed that there was a significantly favorable effect on subsequent adherence when the counselors elicited a moderate degree as against a low degree of self-disclosure from the clients. This outcome (more weight loss after 8 weeks resulting from the moderate disclosure interview) was found, however, only under certain conditions that were also present in the Colten and Janis (chap. 9) study: namely, when (1) a standard type of intake interview was given containing questions about both positive and negative aspects of the self and (2) no contact occurred between the counselor and the clients during the interval between the initial session and the first follow-up interview. When those conditions were changed (by giving interviews that elicited only positive self-disclosures or by having weekly telephone conversations during the 4 weeks following the initial session), the outcome was not the same. In short, the effects of moderate versus low self-disclosure interact in a complex way with type of disclosure and with amount of contact. The most successful of all the conditions investigated in the two experiments (with regard to weight loss after 8 weeks) was one in which *moderate* (rather than low) disclosure was elicited in an interview that was confined to *positive disclo-*

sures only (similar to what is typically done in vocational-counseling interviews) and was followed by weekly telephone conversations for 4 weeks after the first moderate disclosure interview.

The complicated interaction effects seem to detract somewhat from the findings that are confirmatory. (We can only guess about why the standard low disclosure interview was more effective than the standard moderate disclosure interview when the counselor had weekly telephone interviews with the clients during the 4 weeks after the initial session.) Some suggestive evidence from self-reports, however, appears to be consistent with the theoretical assumptions from which the self-disclosure hypothesis was derived. In this pair of experiments there are indications that (a) eliciting self-disclosures about personal shortcomings had a favorable effect with regard to subsequent weight loss when it mobilized a self-confrontation in the clients that generated shame and guilt about continuing to be overweight and (b) eliciting self-disclosures about personal assets had a favorable effect insofar as it built up the clients' self-confidence about achieving future success in changing their undesirable behavior. This combination is consistent with the theoretically derived expectation (from the assumptions presented in chap. 2) that as a result of being perceived as an enhancer of the client's self-esteem, a counselor's referent power will increase if he or she consistently gives acceptance and encouragement while conducting a moderate (rather than low) self-disclosure interview.

A more direct test of the crucial combination of variables is provided by Mulligan's research (chap. 15), which was conducted with male college students in the setting of a Red Cross blood donation campaign. Mulligan confirmed the positive effects on compliance of eliciting a moderate degree of self-disclosure compared with eliciting a low degree of disclosure. He assessed compliance with the interviewer's recommendation by a behavioral measure: the students' signing of pledge cards to donate blood, which was found to be highly correlated with actually making the donation of blood. As I mentioned earlier, Mulligan also found that positive feedback resulted in more compliance than neutral feedback did, provided that the clients were not given the opportunity to discuss their disinclinations to donate blood by being asked to talk about their current decisional conflict. The most effective set of conditions, then, was just what was expected on the basis of the theoretical analysis of supportive helping relationships (chap. 2): when the interviewer (1) gave a *moderate self-disclosure* (rather than low disclosure) interview and (2) gave consistently *positive feedback* (rather than neutral feedback) in response to the disclosures but (3) *avoided expressing acceptance of the client's reluctance to comply* (by not asking any questions about willingness to comply).

The confirmatory results from Mulligan's research help to preclude the possibility that the theoretical analysis of the first critical phase in the development of motivating power on the part of a counselor or interviewer, with its emphasis on moderate self-disclosure and positive feedback, holds only for people who are especially defective in self-control. All the other supporting evidence, except for Smith's study of the effects of positive feedback on women teachers who were seeking help in improving their teaching skills (chap. 16), comes from studies of women who could be regarded as chronically lacking in self-control because they could not control their overeating without external help. Mulligan's findings indicate that inducing a moderate level of self-disclosure and giving positive feedback have essentially the same positive effects on healthy young males (who are not seeking help of any kind) as those we have repeatedly observed among female clients in the weight-reduction clinics.

The available evidence from our studies does not support the notion that the more disclosure the better. Two weight-reduction studies—one by Quinlan and Janis (chap. 11) and the other by Riskind and Janis (chap. 12)—show that eliciting a relatively high level of self-disclosure, as defined at the outset of this section, results in less behavioral adherence to the counselor's recommendations than eliciting a moderate level of disclosure. The high self-disclosure interviews used in these studies elicited a great deal of confidential material about the client's weaknesses and shortcomings that seldom, if ever, is disclosed even to intimate friends. They are similar to the probing intake interviews used by some depth psychologists who treat people seeking help to control their eating, smoking, or drinking habits. The findings suggest that, in the absence of additional sessions devoted to psychotherapeutic treatments, such intake interviews are likely to be far less effective in helping the clients change their behavior than those that elicit only a moderate amount of personal information.

Since one set of experiments shows that moderate disclosure is more effective than low disclosure and another set shows that high disclosure is less effective than moderate disclosure, the obvious inference is that the relationship between amount of induced disclosure and adherence to the counselor's recommendations is nonlinear. The curve for adherence as a function of self-disclosure would be expected to take the form of an inverted U-shaped function, just as has been found for other types of independent variables that have both facilitating and inhibiting effects (see Janis, 1967; McGuire, 1969). This implication of the findings will have to be tested systematically in parametric studies that vary the amount of self-disclosure within each experiment from very low through intermediate levels to very high. As a first approximation to such an experiment, Mulligan's research provides pertinent data on four different levels of self-disclosure, ranging from very low to relatively high (see Figure 15.1). For those subjects who were given positive feedback by the interviewer, the predicted inverted U-shaped curve emerges if we plot the compliance measure (signing a Red Cross pledge card to donate blood) against amount of self-disclosure induced by the interviewer.[1] In agreement with the prior experiments on the effects of self-disclosure, Mulligan's data show that the moderate disclosure interview was more effective than either the low disclosure or the relatively high disclosure interviews.

What accounts for the relatively detrimental effects of high disclosure? Fairly consistent answers to this question are implied by the process data obtained from the various experiments on self-disclosure (chapters 9–12 and 15) and also from the more sensitive indicators obtained from the small sample study by Janis and Quinlan (chap. 13). In the latter study each client in the weight-reduction clinic was given an intensive process interview immediately after the initial high disclosure or moderate disclosure interview. Two main types of detrimental effects were observed. First, numerous signs indicate that participating in a high self-disclosure interview makes the clients somewhat demoralized, despite all the positive comments and acceptance statements made by the counselor. After having revealed all sorts of personal weakness, some clients feel dissatisfied with themselves, as well as with the counseling session, and their self-confidence is shaken. When this occurs, the clients feel less certain than ever that they can succeed in carrying out difficult tasks, such as adhering to a low-calorie diet. An initial counseling session that elicits high disclosure from the clients apparently runs the risk of lowering rather than enhancing self-esteem, even when the counselor gives consistently positive feedback.

The second type of detrimental effect, suggested by more indirect and subtle indicators, is a relative increase in conflict about entering into a dependent relationship with the counselor. Many of the clients given a high disclosure interview express vague uneasiness and dissatisfaction about the counseling session. When an effort is made to pin down what is bothering them, some clients admit being concerned about having lost the respect of the counselor or about the threat of somehow being hurt as a result of becoming too trusting, too affectionate, or too dependent upon the counselor. A few explicitly express a sense of vulnerability from having revealed so much. Other clients seem to manifest overinvolvement in the emerging dependent relationship by saying that they really want the counselor to give them more time and more directive advice, not just about the problem at hand (such as being overweight) but also about other problems that were discussed in the high disclosure interview (such as marital difficulties).

The clients given a moderate or low self-disclosure interview seem less likely to regard the counselor as someone who could become an affectionate parental figure or a savior who will solve their problems by telling them exactly what to do. At the end of the initial session they appear to accept with more emotional equanimity a businesslike relationship with the counselor and do not feel deprived because of the limited amount of help offered them. They regard the counselor as friendly, genuinely helpful, and doing a good job; they seem less likely to be hoping to bask in the warmth of intimacy with an affectionate, indulgent parent figure.

HOW CAN THE POTENTIALLY UNFAVORABLE EFFECTS OF HIGH DISCLOSURE INTERVIEWS BE MITIGATED?

Although there is clear-cut evidence from a number of our studies showing that high self-disclosure interviews run the risk of being less effective in inducing clients to adhere to the counselor's recommendations than moderate disclosure interviews, many counselors can be expected to continue to ask personal questions that elicit high disclosure in their intake interviews. Even if they become familiar with the evidence and believe it to be correct, there are two major reasons why they are likely to do so. First, a counselor may be convinced that he or she cannot properly evaluate a client's problem and work out an appropriate counseling strategy without learning about how the problem is related to other important aspects of the person's life, which requires obtaining a great deal of personal information during the intake interview. Counselors who are aware of the potential drawbacks of eliciting intimate disclosures may feel that it is still worthwhile to obtain the intimate material they regard as essential for adequate diagnosis, relying on their clinical skills to counteract whatever drawbacks may become apparent. Second, many clients who come to a counselor for help are in a perturbed state, thoroughly prepared to talk about what is bothering them. They want to reveal their most pressing difficulties. If the counselor were to try to discourage men and women who are primed to tell their personal story, especially the ones who believe that they should "let it all hang out," those clients would be disappointed and perhaps become less responsive than if they were permitted to unburden themselves despite the drawbacks. (In our studies we regularly encounter a small minority of clients who spontaneously start revealing all sorts of intimate information that is not asked for during low or moderate self-disclosure interviews.)

For these two reasons, despite whatever evidence accumulates on the detrimental effects, I expect that at least for a minority of clients, if not for the majority, intake interviews that elicit high self-disclosure are here to stay. Accordingly, it is worthwhile to continue research on the subsidiary problem of determining the conditions under which people can tolerate a relatively high degree of self-disclosure. Such research could increase our understanding of the psychology of intimacy and point to practical ways of preventing or counteracting potentially unfavorable consequences.

A few leads have emerged from the research carried out in the Yale Weight-Reduction Clinic and in other settings. One hypothesis suggested by intensive process interviews (discussed in chap. 13) is that the decrease in self-confidence and other unfavorable effects resulting from an initial high self-disclosure interview might be counteracted if a retrospective interview were conducted immediately afterward. A *retrospective* interview is one in which the counselor asks the clients to discuss their reactions to the earlier high disclosure interview, allowing them to ventilate whatever misgivings and self-derogatory feelings might have been generated. This type of supplementary interview would, of course, require positive feedback from the counselor to reassure each client that he or she is not despised or thought to be a hopeless case. A crucial component for counteracting the demoralizing effects of high disclosure would be clear-cut signs that the counselor continues to regard the client as worthy of respect and to have high hopes of success on the task at hand, despite all the personal weaknesses and past failures revealed by the client in the intake session.

No systematic study has been done as yet on the effects of a supplementary retrospective interview following high disclosure. But we do have some evidence that a role-playing procedure conveying signs of positive regard on the part of the counselor after a high disclosure interview can have the expected counteracting effect. Riskind and Janis (chap. 12) tried out in the weight-reduction clinic a new procedure designed to build up expectations of social approval by inducing clients to participate in a psychodrama. The scenario focused on the approval they could expect to receive from the counselor if they succeeded in adhering to the recommended diet. In the absence of any such approval training, the clients given a high disclosure interview were relatively unsuccessful in losing weight compared with those given a moderate disclosure interview. But when the social approval training was given right after the interview, the high disclosure interview proved to be relatively more effective than the moderate disclosure interview. The findings indicate that the relatively adverse effects of inducing high disclosure can be modified by the approval training, as manifested by amount of weight loss 5 weeks later.

Those findings can be plausibly interpreted in the following way: Clients who were not given the social approval training felt that they had created an unfavorable impression on the counselor as a result of all the derogatory information they had revealed about themselves during the high self-disclosure interview. They had little hope, therefore, of changing the counselor's basically negative attitude toward them even if they were to do all the things recommended. In contrast, when clients were given the approval training after the interview, their hopes in this regard were at least partially restored, so that they left the session in a "steamed up" state similar to those who had received the moderate self-disclosure interview without approval training. Consequently, during the weeks following the interview the expected approval of the counselor may have functioned as an incentive for adhering to the diet only among those high self-disclosure clients who had received the approval training. The important point is that the evidence from the Riskind and Janis study (chap. 12) supports the assumption that the potentially adverse effects of eliciting a high degree of self-disclosure can be attenuated and perhaps overcome by using special procedures to restore the motivating power of the counselor.

WHAT ELSE CAN COUNSELORS DO
TO INCREASE THEIR EFFECTIVENESS?

Aside from the research on self-disclosure and positive feedback, many studies reported in this book present evidence bearing on new procedures that practitioners who engage in short-term counseling might add to their standard procedures in order to increase their effectiveness. The following eight supplementary procedures look promising in light of the evidence now available.

Setting up Partnerships

The most impressive evidence pertains to the effectiveness of treating clients in pairs, with instructions to function as partners during the intervals between counseling sessions. First of all, there is the Janis and Hoffman study (chap. 4), which found that clients in an antismoking clinic who were assigned to high-contact partnerships were more successful in cutting down on cigarette smoking than those who were assigned to low-contact partnerships or to the control group. The high-contact partnerships were created by the counselor by meeting with the partners once a week and instructing them to phone each other every day for 5 weeks. Long-term follow-up interviews conducted 1 year and 10 years after the clinic treatment was terminated revealed that the clients who had been assigned to the high-contact partnerships were continuing over a very long period of time to be significantly more successful than the others in abstaining from cigarette smoking. These findings suggest that any counselor dealing with clients who want to change unhealthy habits like smoking may find it highly efficient to meet with 2 clients at a time, and perhaps even to meet with small groups of perhaps 4 to 8 clients, by assigning pairs to the same type of partnership set up in the Janis and Hoffman study. Obviously, however, the question of whether a counselor typically can save time and still be just as effective if he or she conducts sessions with two to four sets of partners simultaneously would have to be answered empirically by subsequent conceptual replication studies.

Additional evidence from the Janis and Hoffman study suggests that the prime conditions specified in chapter 2 for the development of effective helping relationships were met by the high-contact partnerships. The partners disclosed a fair amount of personal information to each other, as well as to the counselor, bearing mostly on temptations that made it difficult to cut down on smoking, withdrawal symptoms, and related problems. The partners' disclosures to each other generally were accompanied by mutual acceptance. Hence the conditions for the first phase of acquiring motivational power were met. At each of the weekly meetings, the counselor explicitly conveyed the expected norm by encouraging the partners to make genuine efforts to stop smoking. An analysis of tape recordings of the partners' conversations showed that they repeated this antismoking norm to each other. In their spontaneous conversations that were recorded during the clinic sessions, the clients in successful partnerships were much more likely than the other clients to praise each other for success in cutting down, to criticize each other for backsliding, and to be skeptical about excuses for not making any improvement. Hence the conditions were met for the second phase, which involved using the motivating power acquired during the first phase. The importance of the norm-sending requirement in the second phase was underlined by evidence from a supplementary study: When the same counselor in the same antismoking clinic set up high-contact partnerships without meeting with the clients to endorse the antismoking norm, the partnerships were not at all effective in helping to reduce the amount of cigarette smoking.

With regard to the third phase, the partners who had been meeting with the counselor could look forward to maintaining contact with each other when the time came to terminate the meetings of the three-person groups. This could reduce the disruptive effects of separation from the counselor. Evidence from follow-up interviews indicates that the partners did, in fact, remain in contact with each other for a month or so, on the average, after the final meeting with the counselor.

Because contact between the partners dropped off during the subsequent months the extraordinarily high degree of success of the partnerships in reducing their cigarette smoking, found 1 year and 10 years after the termination of the counseling sessions, cannot be attributed to the partners continuing to give each other direct social support. It appears most likely that the success of the high-contact partnerships is attributable to the increase in motivational power of the three-person clinic group headed by the counselor as group leader, which augmented the degree to which the clients internalized the norms set by the leader.

Confirmatory results from the study by Nowell and Janis (chap. 5) on the effectiveness of high-contact partnerships in a dieting clinic can be interpreted in essentially the same way.

Phase 1: The partners made personal disclosures to each other as well as to the counselor and they received positive feedback in the form of acceptance responses.

Phase 2: At each meeting of the three-person group in the clinic the counselor repeatedly conveyed the norm (to stay on the prescribed low-calorie diet in order to lose weight).

Phase 3: The partners responded to the loss of contact with the counselor by deciding to remain in contact with each other after the last session at the clinic; in follow-up interviews they reported having continued to maintain contact for an average of 3 weeks. Although many of the partners were no longer in contact with each other 6 weeks later, they were still markedly more successful in not overeating, as manifested by their weight loss, than the clients in the two groups that had not been asked by the counselor to form high-contact partnerships.

The success of the partnerships apparently depends upon how the counselor handles the partnership arrangements. We have seen, for example, that no advantages are to be expected when the counselor fails to function as a norm sender. If the other essential conditions for the three critical phases are not met, according to my theoretical analysis (chap. 2), the partnerships cannot be expected to be successful.

Another condition for a successful outcome, indicated by a serendipitous finding in the Nowell and Janis study (chap. 5), is that the counselor does *not* tell the partners that they are very similar and well-matched on attitudes and background. Contrary to what might be expected from prior research on perceived similarity (e.g., Byrne & Griffitt, 1969), giving clients such information apparently generates overoptimistic expectations that lead to disappointment. This adverse effect is avoided if the partners are told that an attempt was made to match them but that there are some divergences.

Undoubtedly, additional conditions essential for effective partnerships will be discovered in subsequent research. From the evidence now at hand, however, it does not seem premature to conclude that setting up high-contact partnerships can be an effective adjunct to counseling in anti-smoking and weight-reduction clinics—and perhaps in a variety of other clinical settings as well—provided that the counselor takes account of the essential requirements specified in the analysis of the three critical phases in effective helping relationships.

Aside from setting up partnerships, what other things could a counselor do to increase his or her effectiveness in helping people carry out difficult decisions? In answer to this question, I shall summarize several additional procedures (described in chaps. 3, 9, and 17–19), which appear to be promising types of intervention for counteracting defensive avoidance and promoting vigilant decision making in some clients, although probably not in all who come for decision counseling.

The "Awareness-of-Rationalizations" Technique

This procedure requires the client to examine typical "excuses" used by heavy smokers and to state which ones he or she uses. It has been found to be effective in increasing smokers' acceptance of warning messages (endorsed by the counselor), such as American Cancer Society films about the harmful effects of cigarette smoking (see pp. 62–64). Comparable procedures might prove to be useful for other types of personal decisions.

Emotional Role-playing

Even more effective with heavy smokers is a psychodramatic procedure in which the client plays the role of a lung cancer victim at the time of receiving the bad news from a physician. After the psychodrama the client is likely to show a marked increase in feelings of personal vulnerability to the threat of lung disease and also a sharp decrease in cigarette consumption, an effect that has been found to persist more than a year after the role-playing session (see Janis & Mann, 1977, pp. 350–354).

Stress Inoculation for Postdecisional Setbacks

This procedure consists of giving clients (a) detailed information about the unfavorable consequences of the new course of action they have decided to carry out, and (b) positive information that fosters self-reassurances and effective coping mechanisms. Evidence of the value of stress inoculation for fostering adherence to stressful courses of action comes from controlled field experiments of surgical patients, medical patients undergoing painful medical treatments, employees who have decided to take a new job, and elderly persons being relocated to a nursing home or hospital (see pp. 70–71). But preparatory information about unfavorable consequences of a chosen coures of action such as undergoing surgery may sometimes fail to increase stress tolerance (see chap. 19). The task for the next stage of research will be to test explanatory hypotheses concerning the effective components of stress inoculation for different types of persons and circumstances, which will help to identify the conditions under which stress inoculation is effective.

The Balance-sheet Procedure

This type of intervention was originally developed to aid college students and high school students to focus on neglected consequences of the career or training alternatives available to them (see pp. 65–69). The procedure requires clients to write down all the favorable and unfavorable consequences they can think of for each of the alternatives they are considering; they are also asked to look over a detailed list of potentially relevant considerations as an aid in making their own list of pros and cons. The balance-sheet procedure was used in three studies reported in this volume. In the study by Colten and Janis (chap. 9) it was found to contribute to success in dieting among clients who came to the weight-reduction clinic, as manifested by their weight loss. The field experiment by Hoyt and Janis (chap. 17) showed that the balance-sheet procedure was effective in helping healthy women who had decided to attend an early morning exercise class to stick with their decision, as testified by their attendance records. This study, which was originally published in 1975, was replicated by Wankel and Thompson (1977) in an experiment with 100 women who were members of a physical fitness club but had become inactive. Taking account of comparisons with a control group, they found that attendance rates were significantly increased for a group given the decisional balance-sheet procedure used by Hoyt and Janis and also for a group given an attenuated form of the procedure restricted to positive outcomes only. Their findings bear out the Hoyt and Janis hypothesis that the positive effects are mediated by a self-persuasian effect similar to that observed in certain experiments on role playing when people are required to improvise arguments in support of an assigned conclusion.

In a third study (reported in chap. 18) by LaFlamme and Janis, the balance-sheet procedure had no observable effect on the information-seeking activity of clients who came to a career counseling clinic, most of whom were in the early stages of deciding on a shift in career. It seems likely that this procedure is of value only in the later stages of decision making, after clients have already learned a great deal about the available alternatives, as in the case of Yale seniors for whom such procedures were found to be effective as aids for making career choices. When the balance-sheet procedure is successful in increasing the clients' subsequent adherence to a difficult course of action, the effective mediating variables may prove to be increased vigilance, self-disclosure, stress inoculation, and/or self-persuasion (see chaps. 3, 9, and 17).

Encouraging a Short-term Perspective for the Recommended Action

In order to increase the clients' sense of mastery, control, and self-confidence about succeeding on a difficult course of action, a decision counselor can structure the task as a series of short-term accomplishments and focus on features of the long-term task that can easily be mastered (see chap. 14 by Riskind). For example, clients in a weight-reduction clinic are encouraged to think about living up to the diet for the next 24 hours, which practically everyone can do. They are told that approaching the task step by step, just one day at a time, can be the key to ultimate success if they do so repeatedly. In a controlled field experiment Riskind found that overweight clients who were encouraged to adopt this short-term perspective expressed a greater sense of personal control and displayed more compliance with the counselor's recommendation to send in weekly reports than those who were encouraged to adopt a longer time perspective. But the results were somewhat complicated with regard to adherence to the diet itself, as measured by weight loss 2 months later. The day-by-day perspective was found to be more effective than the long-term perspective in increasing weight loss only for those clients who initially expressed a relatively high level of self-esteem. In order to be used effectively to promote adherence, therefore, this time-perspective intervention may require the counselor to assess each client's level of self-esteem in the initial session so as to withhold it from those with relatively low self-esteem.

Outcome Psychodrama

The purpose of this procedure is to induce clients to explore more fully the consequences of the leading alternatives (see chap. 18 by Janis and LaFlamme). Clients are asked to act out a scenario that involves projecting themselves into the future in order to explore a potential outcome as though it has actually occurred, such as "The decision has worked out badly." They are required to use their imaginations in order to improvise what specifically could happen, which may enable them to become more aware of expectations and attitudes not previously verbalized even to themselves.

In Janis's pilot studies, outcome psychodrama was used in marital counseling and career counseling. Clients on the verge of committing themselves to a new course of action appeared to benefit from it. For such clients, all of whom were in the later stages of decision making, the procedure seemed to be a promising means for helping them gain access to preconscious worries and other previously unverbalized feelings about alternative courses of action. But negative results were obtained from a field experiment by Janis and LaFlamme in a career decision clinic for men and women who wanted to change their jobs or careers, almost all of whom were in the early stages of decision making (see chap. 18). These clients did not seem to benefit from the procedure. Worse yet, it appeared to have an adverse effect on some of them, lowering their self-confidence about finding a good solution and decreasing vigilant information seeking. Consequently, the procedure cannot be recommended for routine use in decision counseling. It might prove to be of value, however, for selected clients in the later stages of decision making, provided that their self-confidence is not shaky and the counselor is prepared to be responsive to any signs of demoralizing effects when the scenarios involve exploring undesirable outcomes.

A Cognitive-Reappraisal Procedure for Coping with Postdecisional Stress

This procedure, which was investigated in a field experiment by Langer, Janis, and Wolfer (chap. 19), was designed to counteract the detrimental effects of defensive avoidance and to promote vigilance after a person has already become committed to a difficult course of action. The experiment assessed the effectiveness of the procedure when introduced by a professional counselor during brief counseling sessions with patients who had recently decided to undergo a major operation. In the hospital setting stress is very high and defensive avoidance is a frequent coping pattern. The cognitive-reappraisal procedure consists of building up hope for successful long-term outcomes by encouraging an optimistic but realistic reappraisal of stressful postdecisional events that might otherwise make the person regret his or her decision. Without encouraging denial of impending threats, the procedure encourages the patients to feel confident about being able to deal effectively with whatever losses or setbacks are subsequently encountered. The patients are advised to think about all the compensatory positive aspects whenever they start to feel upset about the unpleasant aspects of the surgical experience.

The procedure proved to be effective in reducing both pre- and post-operative stress. The data for testing the predictions were obtained from an analysis of the nurses' blind ratings of preoperative stress and by unobtrusive objective measures of postoperative behavior (the number of times the patient requested pain-relieving drugs and sedatives). The findings consistently show that the procedure had a markedly favorable effect on stress tolerance. The same kind of cognitive-reappraisal intervention involving positive self-talk has been applied and evaluated in clinics for helping people manage anxiety, anger, and pain (see Meichenbaum & Turk, 1976). Similar interventions probably can be developed to prevent defensive avoidance tendencies and to foster an effective vigilant coping pattern among clients facing any kind of postdecisional stress, including setbacks entailed by marital and career decisions, as well as health decisions.

HOW WELL DOES THE THEORETICAL MODEL OF THE COUNSELOR'S MOTIVATING POWER (PRESENTED IN CHAPTER 2) STAND UP WHEN EVALUATED IN LIGHT OF THE AVAILABLE EVIDENCE?

By and large, the model based on observations of effective vs. ineffective long-term counseling and psychotherapy appears to stand up fairly well for short-term counseling. That is to say, the findings from the field experiments on short-term counseling reported in this volume provide a great deal of confirmatory evidence that the variables specified by the theoretical analysis do have significant effects in the predicted direction on the clients' adherence to counselors' recommendations. Nevertheless, some changes are needed in the theoretical formulations in order to take account of additional unpredicted findings.

The First Phase

Most of the studies deal with the variables in the first critical phase of the counselor–client relationship, which relate to the conditions under which counselors build up their motivating or referent power (see Table 2.1). Three conditions are stipulated:

(1) Encouraging clients to engage in a moderate level of self-disclosure vs. not doing so.
(2) Giving positive feedback (acceptance and understanding) vs. giving neutral or negative feedback in response to self-disclosures.
(3) Using self-disclosures to give insight and cognitive restructuring vs. giving little insight or cognitive restructuring.

Unlike the first two, the third one is not an essential condition but nevertheless is expected to augment somewhat the motivating power of a counselor. The positive findings for the cognitive restructuring procedure described in chapter 19 can be interpreted as supporting this expectation.

The first two conditions, which are assumed to be essential for building up the counselors' motivating power, are embodied in the basic proposition that was investigated in various ways in the series of studies reported in chapters 6–16. The basic proposition is that counselors will be most successful in inducing their clients to live up to specific recommendations, such as adhering to a low-calorie diet, if they start off by encouraging a moderate level of *self-disclosure* and respond to the client's disclosures by giving *positive feedback* in the form of explicit acceptance responses. Earlier in this chapter we have seen that most of the findings pertinent to the effects of self-disclosure and of positive feedback are consistent with this proposition. Additional findings, however, were unexpected and indicate that the basic proposition needs to be modified by inserting some essential provisos.

One proviso (which is suggested by Mulligan's study in chap. 15, summarized on p. 348) is that the counselor must *avoid ambiguity* when expressing understanding and empathy in response to clients' disclosures about not wanting to carry out the course of action recommended by the counselor. Ambiguity can inadvertently reinforce the "wrong" decision. The counselor can avoid this error by making favorable comments about the client's honesty (for admitting reluctance to do what is recommended) and then explicitly labeling the client's resistance to the recommended course of action as a problem to be overcome in order for the client to achieve his or her goals.

A second major proviso is that the positive feedback from the counselor must be given *consistently,* with no deviating comments and no nonverbal cues that could be construed by clients as indicating criticism, insincerity, rejection, or exploitative intent. In the summary of the research dealing with the effects of positive versus neutral feedback presented earlier in this chapter, I pointed out that in six out of a series of seven pertinent field experiments, the investigators found that consistently positive feedback from the counselor resulted in a significant increase in subsequent adherence to the counselor's recommendations, just as predicted by the theoretical model. But from three of the confirmatory studies carried out in the weight-reduction clinic we obtained the following surprising, additional results, which were not predicted:

(1) The study reported in chapter 6 showed that positive feedback from the counselor throughout a moderate disclosure interview resulted in more subsequent adherence to dietary recommendations (as manifested by weight loss) only if the counselor also gave a positive evaluation to each client's performance when he imposed a minor task (a motivation test). If the counselor told the client that she did not perform so well as expected on the minor task, neutral feedback from the counselor throughout the interview resulted in more subsequent adherence than did positive feedback.

(2) The study reported in chapter 7 showed that positive feedback throughout a moderate disclosure interview resulted in more subsequent adherence to dietary recommendations (as manifested by weight loss) only if the minor task (a motivation test) imposed by the counselor was relatively easy. If the minor task was very difficult (making the clients feel that they failed), neutral feedback throughout the interview resulted in more subsequent adherence than did positive feedback.

(3) The study reported in chapter 8 showed that positive feedback throughout a moderate disclosure interview in a face-to-face session re-

sulted in more subsequent adherence to the dietary recommendations (as manifested by weight loss) only if the counselor seated himself at a normal distance from the client (about 2 feet away). If the counselor seated himself at a relatively remote distance (about 5 feet away), neutral feedback throughout the interview resulted in more subsequent adherence than did positive feedback.

To these unpredicted findings we must add that the study in chapter 14 not only failed to obtain the expected increase in adherence but obtained a decrease in adherence (as manifested by amount of weight loss) when the counselor gave a supplementary interview in which he responded with consistently positive feedback to whatever answers the clients gave to a series of questions that were designed to elicit self-disclosures only about the clients' personal assets and past successes. The counselor's acceptance of these positive self-disclosures may have induced in some clients a sense of complacency or self-satisfaction which could lower the overweight clients' motivation to make the effort to adhere to the recommended dietary restrictions. Also, because the counselor gave unearned praise, sometimes accompanied by favorable comments about personal strengths that the clients had not mentioned, some clients may have been skeptical about the counselor's sincerity.

All these unexpected findings, from four different investigations of weight loss, indicate that under certain conditions we can expect that counselors will *not* increase their effectiveness if they respond with positive feedback during an interview that elicits a moderate level of self-disclosure. Counselors can be expected to fail if they give a great deal of unearned praise or if they are somewhat inconsistent about giving positive feedback in response to the self-disclosures elicited from their clients. The inconsistency may take the form of making just one slight criticism of a client's behavior (chap. 6), demanding the client to carry out a difficult task that is not directly pertinent to the problem for which the client is seeking help (chap. 7), or presenting nonverbal cues that can be construed as signs of detachment or withdrawal, as when the counselor sits at a relatively remote distance from the client (chap. 8). It must be emphasized that in all three studies each one of these disturbing events was presented in such a mild form that the investigators had not expected it to have any adverse effect at all. Nevertheless, each proved to have a profoundly disturbing and long-lasting effect which was revealed by significantly less weight loss at the time of the follow-up interview 5 to 8 weeks later. The findings suggest that if counselors for any reason find it necessary to expose clients to a disturbing event, such as giving clients an unfavorable rating on a test, they will be better off (from the standpoint of motivating the clients to adhere to their recommendations) if they give neutral feedback, rather than positive accepting feedback, throughout the entire intake interview.

Most surprising is the evidence that the disturbing events, as I have been calling them, actually had a favorable effect on clients who were given neutral feedback. The study in chapter 6 showed that the amount of adherence of the clients who received neutral feedback, when assessed by weight loss 8 weeks later, proved to be significantly higher if they had been given an unfavorable rather than favorable rating on the extraneous motivation test. The studies in chapter 7 (in which the disturbing event consisted of a high demand made during the motivation test) and in chapter 8 (in which the disturbing event consisted of a remote seating arrangement) showed the same trend, again implying that among clients who are given neutral feedback, subsequent adherence might be increased by inserting one or another of these disturbing events into the intake interview.

The paradoxical findings just reviewed suggest that building up an image of the counselor as a firm, demanding authority figure by withholding positive feedback throughout the entire initial session, and by occasionally expressing mild disapproval or withdrawal, can sometimes have considerable motivating power. Nevertheless, in each of the three experiments, when counselors gave neutral feedback along with one or another disturbing event (unfavorable rating, high demand, or remote seating), they were not so successful in inducing subsequent adherence as when they gave consistently positive feedback (with no disturbing event). The difference is statistically significant, however, in only one of the studies (chap. 7). If this trend continues and proves to be statistically significant in subsequent conceptual replications of these field experiments with clients who meet with a counselor individually or in groups, it will carry the implication that when counselors are seen by their clients as nurturant supportive helpers they tend to be more successful in inducing adherence than when they are seen as businesslike authority figures who are critical, withdrawn, or excessively demanding.

By a nurturant supportive helper I mean a person who is seen by the clients as someone who can be counted on to enhance their self-esteem, provided only that they make a conscientious effort to do what he or she recommends. The evidence I have reviewed indicates that counselors can build up this kind of image and thereby elicit increased adherence if, as specified in Phase 1 of the theoretical model for acquiring referent power, they induce a moderate degree of self-disclosure and give positive feedback, with due regard to the provisos inferred from the unpredicted findings. But the evidence bearing on the provisos suggests that in the first stage, when counselors are starting to build up their motivating power in this way, that power is rather fragile. Clients evidently are extremely sensitive to cues that might show that the counselor has a low opinion of them or will be too hard to please. Any little comment or gesture by the counselor could unintentionally be misconstrued as a sign of rejection and greatly reduce the counselor's motivating power. Clinical observations from longer term counseling, however, suggest that if the counselor continues to express positive regard most of the time during subsequent sessions, clients can tolerate quite well an occasional criticism of their behavior and an occasional stringent demand that might have had an adverse effect if presented during the first session. That is to say, the motivating power of the counselor might be expected to increase and to become much more robust if the counselor continues to meet the conditions for Phase 1 during the second, third, and fourth sessions. The fragility we noted in our studies might, therefore, prove to be characteristic only of *short-term counseling that is limited to just one initial session* before the client is expected to adhere to a diet or to carry out some other recommended course of action, as in ten of the eleven studies reported in this book that investigated the variables in Phase 1.

What I am saying here may at first seem like a contradiction of what I said earlier in this chapter about the effects of increasing the number of sessions. The main conclusion from the available evidence on frequency of contact was that the number of sessions per se is less important as a determinant of adherence than what the counselor does during each session. That conclusion does not preclude the plausible suggestion that, if the counselor continues to do the appropriate things specified for Phase 1 to build up his or her motivating power, each additional session will strengthen the positive effect, contribute to building up a more robust relationship, and lead to more adherence.

The Second Phase

For Phase 2 of the theoretical model (Table 2.1), the various studies in this volume provide only fragmentary evidence, which bears on three of the following five variables:

(4) Making directive statements or endorsing specific recommendations regarding actions the client should carry out vs. abstaining from any directive statements or endorsements.

(5) Eliciting commitment to the recommended course of action vs. not eliciting commitment.

(6) Attributing the norms being endorsed to a respected secondary group vs. not doing so.

(7) Giving selective positive feedback after making recommendations vs. giving noncontingent acceptance or predominantly neutral or negative feedback.

(8) Giving communications and training procedures that build up self-control attributions and a sense of personal responsibility vs. giving no such communications or training.

For variable 4, which involves making directive statements or endorsements, indirect evidence comes from the first study in which adherence to recommendations (assessed by reported number of cigarettes smoked per day) was found to increase when clients in an antismoking clinic were assigned to partnerships (chap. 4). The partners not only phoned each other every day to disclose mutual problems but also met once a week with a *norm-sending* counselor for 5 weeks. A supplementary study of 20 smokers (reported on pp. 89–90) showed that in the absence of any contact with a directive counselor at the clinic (except for an initial phone call in which partners were assigned), the partnerships had a brief effect of decreasing cigarette consumption during the first month, but after that backsliding occurred in all cases. In contrast, when the same type of partners attended five weekly meetings with a directive counselor who explicitly endorsed the antismoking recommendations, they showed a marked and sustained reduction in cigarette consumption that was still observable 10 years later.

Similar findings concerning the need for contact with a directive leader were cited from an earlier study by Miller and Janis (1973). This study showed that student partnerships without any exposure to norm-sending communications had the opposite effect from what was intended. Instead of providing mutual support that would improve the students' morale and adjustment to college life, the partnerships had an adverse effect.

After obtaining this indirect evidence from two studies, I surmised that clients who come to a clinic for help with their smoking, overeating, or any other such problem of self-control would not be likely to benefit from whatever treatments they were given if the counselors were to abstain from making any recommendations. Consequently, it seemed to me to be unethical to assign any such clients to the control treatment condition required to carry out an experiment designed to test variable 4 in Phase 2 of the theoretical analysis.

No systematic research has been carried out as yet on two of the other variables listed under Phase 2 in Table 2.1: attributing the norms being endorsed to a respected secondary group, and giving selective positive feedback after the recommendations are presented. These variables are represented in the experiments conducted in clinical settings, such as the weight-reduction clinic, in that we arrange for the counselors to endorse recommendations that are truthfully attributed to appropriate medical authorities and to give contingent positive feedback after presenting the recommendations, so as to avoid reinforcing the clients' reluctance to comply. The only study in which a systematic variation was introduced was the one in chapter 11, in which the effects of noncontingent vs. contingent feedback throughout the initial interview were systematically compared. The findings on weight loss and other behavioral measures of adherence showed that it was equally effective to give either contingent or noncontingent positive feedback throughout the initial interview. But this outcome might hold only in certain types of clinical settings, such as weight-reduction clinics, in which clients seldom express any intentions that go counter to the counselor's recommendations. In other settings, contingent reinforcement throughout the initial interview might prove to be more effective, as is suggested by the study in chapter 15, discussed earlier in this chapter, in which the counselors' noncontingent positive feedback appears to have inadvertently reinforced the subjects' reluctance to comply with the recommendation to donate blood to the Red Cross.

The other two subsidiary variables listed in Phase 2 (eliciting commitment and building up attributions of self-control and personal responsibility) could be investigated to some extent without posing ethical issues concerning responsibility to offer genuine help to clients in clinical settings. Such research does not necessarily require assigning clients to control conditions that are expected to have unfavorable effects that might undermine the effectiveness of whatever else the counselor might do in an effort to help the clients. Prior research on one of the variables (commitment) suggests that it can have positive effects on adherence to difficult decisions, but the limiting conditions remain to be determined. (See the review of the research literature in Janis & Mann, 1977, chap. 11, and in Kiesler, 1971). In several pilot studies in our weight-reduction clinic, my colleagues and I have compared the standard commitment procedure used in all such studies (chaps. 6–14) with an additional procedure intended to make commitment even more salient. The standard procedure involves asking clients at the end of the session if they are willing to try conscientiously to stick to the recommended low-calorie diet; the additional procedure involves asking clients to sign contracts asserting that they will avoid eating their favorite fattening foods and will conscientiously stay on the diet for as long as it takes to reach their target weight.

In these pilot studies we have found no evidence of any effect of the additional commitment on adherence (as measured by weight loss). These unpromising findings may be attributable to the use of the standard commitment procedure as the control condition, which may be so potent that it is already at the ceiling as far as commitment effects are concerned. We have been reluctant to take the next step in pursuing commitment effects in our weight-reduction clinic, which would be to compare the standard commitment procedure with a control condition in which no commitment at all is elicited. Again, the reason is that ethical standards require that we do not use a control condition which prior research indicates could run the risk of undermining the effectiveness of the counseling sessions, which would deprive the clients of genuine help. In future research some way might be found to investigate commitment effects in field experiments without violating ethical standards, perhaps by carrying out the research in a setting like that used in chapter 15 (in which clients were encouraged to contribute blood to the Red Cross drive), where the interviewers do not recruit subjects by offering a genuine clinical service but can nevertheless make legitimate recommendations.

The remaining variable specified for Phase 2—building up attributions of self-control and personal responsibility—was systematically investigated in the study reported in chapter 12, which included a special procedure intended to promote long-term adherence by training clients to give themselves self-approval for successful adherence to dieting rules. Each client was asked to engage in two psychodramatic enactments in order to "look into the future." One of the role-playing scenarios stipulated failure to follow the diet and the other stipulated success. While acting out each scenario in turn, the client was required to say out loud what she would think of herself, particularly her thoughts and feelings concerning self-pride. Unexpectedly, the results came out in the opposite direction from what was predicted for clients who were given a standard type of intake interview that induced a moderate degree of self-disclosure. Those clients also expressed less confidence about their ability to diet successfully and more self-derogation than clients who were not given the self-approval training. Evidently the attempt to get the clients to focus on their own personal responsibility and to anticipate self-approval for successful dieting had a boomerang effect.

Perhaps enacting the failure scenario (which was always done first) had such a demoralizing effect that it could not be counteracted by enacting the success scenario. In any case the unfavorable outcome from the psycho-dramatic self-approval procedure has made us very wary about trying out any similar procedure because of the danger that it may do the clients more harm than good. Nevertheless, my colleagues and I are now trying out other approaches that we think may prove to be more effective for building up self-control attributions and a sense of personal responsibility in a way that will facilitate long-term adherence.

What little evidence is available bearing on the facilitating conditions listed for Phase 2 seems to be consistent with the theoretical model (except perhaps for the last variable since the one attempt to represent it in a field experiment yielded an outcome opposite from what was predicted). But the variables for Phase 2 remain largely uninvestigated, partly because of ethical considerations.

The Third Phase

Ethical constraints again loom large when it comes to investigating the first of the following four variables specified for handling termination (Phase 3 in table 2.1), but not for the last two:

(9) Giving reassurances that the counselor will continue to maintain an attitude of positive regard vs. giving no such reassurances.

(10) Making arrangements for phone calls, exchange of letters, or other forms of communication that foster hope for future contact, real or symbolic, at the time of terminating face-to-face meetings vs. making no such arrangements.

(11) Giving reminders that continue to foster self-control attributions and a sense of personal responsibility vs. giving no such reminders.

(12) Building up the client's self-confidence about succeeding without the aid of the counselor vs. not doing so.

In all the studies carried out in clinical service settings, before saying good-bye the counselors always convey reassurance that they will continue to maintain a positive attitude toward each client, often by explicitly express-ing their confidence that the client has what it takes to achieve and retain self-control over the problem behavior if he or she makes a genuine effort. Taking account of extensive clinical observations of clients' spontaneous fear of being rejected in resonse to the termination crisis, we have not tested the hypothesis that withholding this type of reassurance will have a demoralizing effect on many clients.

There is no reason to expect, however, that if such reassurances are given, demoralization or any other such adverse effect will result from withholding the other conditions specified for promoting a satisfactory outcome to the termination crisis. Accordingly, there appears to be no basis for ethical objections to investigating those three ameliorative variables.

Arrangements for future contact were systematically varied in the experimental research reported in chapter 10, in which half the clients had weekly telephone calls from the counselor after the initial session, while the other half had no contact at all until the brief follow-up session 1 month later. The latter (low contact) condition corresponds to the standard amount of contact arranged in all other studies in the Yale Weight-Reduction Clinic. The arrangement to have the additional telephone contact had complicated effects on adherence, including both favorable and unfavorable outcomes, depending upon whether the clients had been induced to disclose positive or negative personal information and whether the level of self-disclosure was low or moderate. Nevertheless, it is noteworthy that under certain conditions (moderate level of disclosure in an interview that elicited only positive personal information), arranging for the additional telephone contact was found to result in much more weight loss than any other condition in this experiment or in any other experiment reported in this volume (a mean weight loss of 10 pounds after 8 weeks). Consequently it appears worthwhile to continue investigating this enigmatic variable to find out how and why it results in such a marked increase in success under certain limited conditions and why it reduces success under other conditions.

Variable 11 in Phase 3, which involves reminders that encourage self-reliance, is very similar to variable 8 in Phase 2. Both variables were investigated in combination in the study reported in chapter 12 on weight reduction, which yielded results indicating that the attempts at building up reliance on self-approval rather than on approval from others failed to increase adherence (as measured by subsequent weight loss) and appeared to have reduced the clients' self-confidence at the end of the initial interview.

We cannot be at all optimistic about the kind of self-approval training used in that field experiment, without making major changes. Nevertheless, we need not be pessimistic about finding some way to foster self-reliance that will increase rather than decrease self-confidence. One possibility, for example, would be to drastically modify the procedure described in chapter 12 by focusing only on expected successful outcomes in the future and leaving out possible failures.

A new approach to transforming other-directed to self-directed approval motivation is suggested by clinical observations in the Yale Weight-Reduction Clinic, particularly from process interviews such as the ones used in the study reported in chapter 13. These observations fit in with a hypothesis suggested in chapter 12 which asserts that transitory dependency on the counselor helps the client get started on a stressful course of action but continued adherence requires that the client develop self-attributions of personal responsibility, with a corresponding decline in dependency upon the counselor. Our clinical observations seem to be in agreement with those of Davison and Valins (1969), who conclude from their research in a completely different setting that behavior change is more likely to be maintained when clients attribute the cause of the change to themselves instead of to an outside agent. A direct implication of this conclusion is that people who seek help in self-regulation will be more likely to adhere in the long run to a new course of action, such as dieting, if the counselor stresses the client's own role in whatever behavior change occurs (see Brehm, 1976, p. 168).

I have noticed that some of our most successful clients go through a progression of steps in which other-directed approval motivation seems to be transformed into self-directed approval motivation, much as was proposed in chapter 12 by Riskind and Janis. First, they start off feeling that with the counselor's help they will be able to stick to the diet. The second step comes during the first week or so of dieting, when they begin to feel like "I can do it on my own most of the time, as long as you are still available to give me some support and encouragement." The third step comes after they start losing some weight when they see that, in fact, they have basically been doing it on their own for a while. They feel, "At first I needed your help, but now I can do it on my own with a little support from someone else besides you." Finally, the last step comes when they realize that they are able to control their eating. Then they feel, "I can do it entirely on my own and I have already shown that I can do it." I have the impression that the final attitude of self-reliance is predominant among those clients who are most successful at resisting temptations to backslide.

I suspect that this sequence of steps, moving from dependency to self-reliance, could be facilitated in many clients if counselors give their clients step-by-step guidance in self-talk about personal responsibility. In the initial session the counselors might make a frank statement about the problem of dependency and set up the ultimate goal of self-reliance after describing the successive steps. Then, at the appropriate times, they could encourage the clients to try to move on to the next step. For example, in a telephone conversation with a client who reports having lost weight for 2 successive weeks, a counselor might remind the client of the third step in the sequence and raise the question as to which one of the clients' friends or relatives might be most suited to function as an additional helper. Later on, after the client has demonstrated weight loss in a follow-up interview, the counselor could encourage self-talk that embodies the final attitude of self-reliance as specified by variable 12 in Phase 3. This type of procedure is currently being tried out in a pilot study to see if it looks sufficiently promising to warrant systematic testing in a field experiment.

HOW FAR HAVE WE GONE IN ATTAINING OUR PRIMARY GOAL — TO HELP TRANSFORM THE ART OF COUNSELING INTO A SCIENCE?

A little way, in my judgment, but not very far. In the opening chapter I pointed out that in our research on short-term counseling my colleagues and I were attempting to move ahead on the two-fold task of formulating testable theoretical ideas and of obtaining systematic evidence bearing on them. The theoretical model based on observations of successful versus unsuccessful long-term counseling has proved to be useful in guiding the choice of variables for most of the studies of short-term counseling reported in this volume. The key variables pertaining to the first phase of forming an effective counselor–client relationship, as we have just seen, have stood up quite well in replicated field experiments as determinants of adherence to counselors' recommendations. The variables specified for Phases 2 and 3, however, must be regarded as an unfinished agenda on which research work is still in progress. For some of those variables, fragmentary findings have been obtained, and they appear to be sufficiently promising to warrant further systematic investigation. From unexpected findings in the research completed so far, we have obtained a few fresh leads, particularly bearing on the crucial mediating role of building up the clients' self-confidence about improving their self-control, which also appear well worth pursuing. But all these small advances carry us only a short distance and we cannot console ourselves with the overoptimistic view that they have brought us to the verge of a big breakthrough.

Those of us carrying out research on helping relationships, like psychologists working on many other problems of human behavior, evidently must resign ourselves to snail-like progress. As we systematically test the most promising hypotheses, using the best available research methods, we would like to achieve some quantum jumps in the science of counseling. But can we realistically expect much more than a slow accumulation of piecemeal evidence that may tell us a little something that is dependable about when, how, and why counselors can succeed in helping clients achieve their goals? If not, we need to function like a good counselor to ourselves, to build up our own hope and self-confidence about being successful in the long run.

NOTES

1. In order to perceive the inverted U-shaped function shown by Mulligan's data in Fig. 15.1, it is necessary to order the different levels of self-disclosure in the two concurrent experiments from highest to lowest. The results for those given positive feedback by the interviewer are as follows:

Level of self-disclosure	Percentage complying by signing pledge cards to donate blood to the Red Cross
1. *Relatively high*: The moderate disclosure interview combined with questions about the current decisional conflict about donating blood (from Experiment 2)	60
2. *Moderate*: All questions restricted to past decisional conflicts on important personal issues, such as career choice (from Experiment 1)	90
3. *Fairly low*: The very low disclosure interview with additional low disclosure questions to make the interview the same length as the relatively high disclosure interview (from Experiment 2)	60
4. *Very low*: All questions restricted to minor decisions such as which movie to go to (from Experiment 1)	20

The results for the subjects who were given neutral feedback, however, do not yield an inverted U-shaped curve; the percentages corresponding to the ones just given for positive feedback are as follows: (1) 90%, (2) 50%, (3) 30%, (4) 50%. With neutral feedback the relatively high disclosure interview is more effective than any other level of disclosure. The divergences between the neutral feedback and the positive feedback data are somewhat surprising because in this face-to-face interview situation neutral feedback was essentially a form of mild positive feedback. Although the interviewer said little except "Um hum," he smiled, nodded, and looked interested in what the subject was saying, thus giving paralinguistic responses that undoubtedly conveyed interest in and acceptance of whatever the subject was saying. One explanation for the divergence suggested by Mulligan (chap. 15) is that inadvertently the interviewer's positive verbal feedback tended to reinforce the wrong responses when the relatively high disclosure interview was given because some subjects expressed anxiety and reluctance about complying with the request to donate blood. An alternative explanation, suggested by process interviews and questionnaire data from later studies in other settings, is that relatively high disclosure made the subjects so aware of their personal weaknesses and shortcomings that they could no longer accept the counselor's positive feedback as credible, which would incline them to believe that the interviewer was insincere and perhaps would try to manipulate their behavior after giving them many compliments. Whether one or the other or both detrimental processes are operating in this type of interview situation will remain an open question until replications are carried out in which pertinent process data are obtained.

The possibility that inducing a relatively high degree of self-disclosure might result in negative attitudes toward the interviewer was investigated in Mulligan's study and in the other experiments on the effects of self-disclosure. In all these studies, questionnaire data were obtained immediately after the disclosure interview on attitudes toward the interviewer. The findings consistently indicate that when positive feedback is given throughout the interview, inducing relatively high disclosure does *not* result in less favorable attitudes toward the interviewer than inducing moderate or low levels of disclosure. But these attitudes, as assessed by postinterview questionnaires, are not predictive of compliance with the interviewer's recommendations. The absence of the expected relationship could be due to the low validity of the attitude measures. Clients tend to give conventionally polite answers when printed questionnaires are given right after an interview. There is some evidence that the clients' answers on the printed questionnaires do not correspond to the attitudes they express during an intensive supplementary interview in which they are encouraged to speak freely and at length about how they felt during the self-disclosure interview (see chap. 13).

Appendix: Assessing State of Self-esteem

DONALD M. QUINLAN AND IRVING L. JANIS

Self-esteem, or the level of regard one holds for oneself, has been a concept in diverse areas of psychology. Two different lines of approach have been used in the study of self-esteem. The individual trait method treats self-esteem as a consistent, stable trait of the individual. Experimental studies using this approach divide subjects into high and low self-esteem groups and examine differences in how they respond to various experimental conditions that are known to affect performances. A second approach has been to investigate the effects of specific treatments, such as giving praise or criticism, that temporarily influence a person's level of self-esteem. In this line of work, self-esteem is an intervening variable affected by the experimental conditions that produce a change in performance on a dependent variable such as mood, level of effort, or expectations about being successful in the future.

The literature on anxiety has a parallel dual approach, described most explicitly by Spielberger, Gorsuch, and Lushene (1970) in their work on *state* and *trait* anxiety. Their trait scale refers to stable individual characteristics, while their state scale pertains to the fluctuations that a person shows in different circumstances.

A STATE OF SELF-ESTEEM (SSE) QUESTIONNAIRE

In order to measure changes in a person's level of self-esteem, such as those induced by certain of our experimental treatment conditions, we have devised an 18-item questionnaire. Each subject is asked to make explicit comparisons between his or her current state and how he or she usually feels. The cover-sheet instructions state:

> Please answer the following questions by describing how you feel *right now*—not how you felt yesterday or even an hour ago, but how you feel at the present moment.
>
> Every person has different moods from one day to the next, and sometimes even from one hour to the next. At times, a person may be in a good mood and feel more satisfied with himself than usual. At other times the same person may be in a bad mood and feel less satisfied with himself than usual. We want you to answer these questions by comparing the

feelings you have *right now* with the feelings that you *usually* have. Check one answer to each question.

The checklist of answers for each question is a 5-point scale, with each point having a full-length verbal description. Each question begins with "As compared with how you usually feel: Right now how _____ do you feel...." with modifications suited to each content item. For example, the first item is:

1. As compared with how you usually feel: Right now, how <u>confident</u> do you feel about dealing with whatever important problems may arise in your life?
   ___ Much more confident than usual
   ___ Somewhat more confident than usual
   ___ About the same as usual
   ___ Somewhat less confident than usual
   ___ Much less confident than usual

The content of each of the items is as follows:

Item	Label
Each item begins with the introductory phrase: **As compared with how you usually feel, right now:**	
1. How <u>confident</u> do you feel about dealing with whatever important problems may arise in your life?	Confident
2. How <u>optimistic</u> do you feel about your chances for having a full and satisfying life?	Optimistic
3. When you think over your personal weaknesses and shortcomings, how <u>shameful</u> do you feel they are?	Shameful
4. How much does your <u>conscience</u> bother you?	Bothered by conscience
5. How much do you feel that <u>you deserve to be admired and respected</u> by the people who know you well?	Admired
6. When you think about the worst thoughts or desires you have, how bad (<u>immoral</u>) do you feel those thoughts and desires are?	Immoral
7. When you think over what you have accomplished in your life, how <u>satisfied</u> do you feel with yourself?	Satisfied
8. How <u>guilty</u> do you feel about bad things that you have done in the past?	Guilty
9. How <u>insecure</u> do you feel about what may happen to you in the future?	Insecure
10. How much do you <u>respect yourself</u> as a worthwhile person?	Having self-respect

11. When you think over your personal strengths and   Having pride
    assets, how much pride do you feel?
12. How much do you feel that you deserve to be   Deserving
    criticized and rejected by the people who know   criticism
    you well?
13. When you think about the best thoughts and in-   Having good
    tentions you have, how good (moral) do you feel   intentions
    those thoughts and intentions are?
14. How discouraged do you feel about the things you   Discouraged
    are trying to accomplish?
15. How much do you like yourself as a person?   Liking self
16. How ashamed do you feel about your shortcom-   Ashamed
    ings and failures?
17. How dissatisfied do you feel about yourself as a   Dissatisfied
    person?
18. How much self-confidence do you feel about   Self-confident
    achieving your main goals in life?

ITEM SELECTION

The items were selected to measure multiple aspects of self-esteem. One set
of items assesses positive feelings about the self, about the future in general,
and about being admired by others. Another set assesses the more negative
aspects, such as feeling insecure, deserving criticism, and feeling one's
intentions are bad. A balance of positive and negative self-descriptions was
intentionally included, not only to balance "yea-saying" and "nay-saying"
response sets but also to allow individuals to express a full range of feelings
both about themselves and about reactions they expect from others.

When we started using the SSE questionnaire in large-scale field experiments we conducted some in-depth process interviews after the experimental sessions were over. The subjects' comments about this scale were
generally satisfactory but raised questions about certain of the items that
had not created any apparent difficulty in our earlier pilot studies. Several
clients singled out one or more of the questions as being "too personal" or
otherwise raising uncomfortable feelings. Taking account of their comments we have deleted four questions for our current and future use of the
questionnaire: 3, shameful weaknesses; 4, conscience bother you; 6, bad
(immoral) thoughts or desires; and 12, deserve to be criticized and rejected.

FACTOR ANALYSIS

In order to find the number of factors represented in the responses to the
State of Self-Esteem questionnaire and to reduce the number of variables, a
principal components factor analysis was performed on the responses
obtained immediately after the interviews of 74 women in the Riskind and

Janis study (chap. 12). Two factors had an eigenvalue substantially greater than 1.0 (i.e., the factor accounts for more than any single item). The third factor, however, was marginal, with an eigenvalue of 1.25.

The three factors were labeled: (1) self-pride (Items 5, 7, 10, 11, 13, 15), (2) self-confidence (Items 1, 2, 9, 14, 18) and (3) absence of self-derogation (Items 3, 4, 6, 8, 12, 16, and 17).

A further analysis of the SSE questionnaire was conducted using the replies of more than 100 clients in the Quinlan, Janis, and Bales study (chap. 10). Using the previous factor solutions from the Riskind and Janis study, we

Table A1. Factor analysis of the state of self-esteem questionnaire: factor loadings from the Quinlan, Janis, and Bales study

Questionnaire item	Week 1[a]		Week 4[b]		Week 8[c]	
	Self-confidence	Self-blame	Self-confidence	Self-blame	Self-confidence	Self-blame
1. Confident	.666	.204	.809	.398	.853	.416
2. Optimistic	.669	.213	.797	.426	.866	.398
3. Shameful	.260	.681	.352	.814	.447	.756
4. Bothered by conscience	.246	.707	.364	.759	.389	.826
5. Admired	.664	.237	.838	.351	.868	.396
6. Immoral	.168	.612	.450	.790	.493	.771
7. Satisfied	.718	.058	.860	.212	.901	.295
8. Guilty	.101	.737	.383	.725	.481	.760
9. Insecure	.069	.377	.281	.775	.317	.867
10. Having self-respect	.792	.012	.885	.306	.907	.341
11. Having pride	.735	−.010	.847	.280	.891	.356
12. Deserving criticism	.199	.391	.254	.817	.387	.837
13. Having good intentions	.667	.224	.768	.452	.810	.455
14. Discouraged	−.217	.355	.221	.768	.239	.857
15. Liking self	.779	−.029	.900	.231	.903	.311
16. Ashamed	−.021	.825	.374	.792	.330	.876
17. Dissatisfied	.014	.615	.151	.864	.276	.856
18. Self-confident	.800	.140	.831	.302	.853	.366

Note. Factor 1 = Confident, optimistic, admired, satisfied, having self-respect, having pride, having good intentions, liking yourself, self-confident: 1, 2, 5, 7, 10, 11, 13, 15, 18. Factor 2 = Shameful, bothered by conscience, immoral, guilty, insecure, deserving criticism, ashamed, dissatisfied: 3, 4, 6, 8, 16, 17, 9, 12 (underlined items deleted in new form).
[a] *N* = 130.
[b] *N* = 108.
[c] *N* = 105.

found that the self-pride scale had poor reliability after the first session. A principal-axis factor solution was performed on each of the three administrations of the questionnaire: at the time of the first interview, at the 4-week follow-up, and at the 8-week follow-up. Whereas the initial questionnaire suggested that a three-factor solution met the usual criteria, both the 4- and 8-week data strongly pointed to a two-factor solution. One factor has to do with *self-confidence,* the second with *self-blame.*[1] The factor loadings of the varimax rotation are shown in Table A1.

The results pointing to two factors show that each item loads highly on only one scale. The content of the items comprising the two factors suggests that they are internally consistent unipolar scales.

Cronbach's alpha, which provides an indication of test reliability, was computed for the scales specified at the bottom of Table A1, with the four objectionable items omitted. The self-confidence scale item sums yielded high reliabilities (alpha = .91, .97, and .99 for the initial visit, the 4-week follow-up, and the 8-week follow-up, respectively). The self-blame scale, although it consists of only four items, yielded satisfactory reliabilities (the corresponding alphas were .74, .91, and .95). Thus in two ways, the scales show reliability: The factorial structure remains highly similar for three administrations over an 8-week period, and the internal consistencies of each of the scales are fairly high.

TEST-RETEST RELIABILITY

For a trait scale, the stability of the scores obtained at different times with regard to indicating the same level of a chronic or temporally stable personality characteristic is a desirable feature. For a *state* scale, however, this form of reliability is not necessarily desirable. If the initial scores correlate with a second trial too closely, especially if an appreciable amount of time has elapsed, then the scale is suspect of measuring stable trait qualities rather than changing states. On the other hand, if there were no correlation at all, one would wonder whether the state scale was too unstable to be useful.

The test–retest correlations for the self-confidence and self-blame scales (Table A2) are, as expected, in the moderate range ($r = .20–.40$). The coef-

Table A2. Test–re-test reliability of the two main factors: self-confidence and self-blame at weeks 1, 4, and 8

	Self-confidence		Self-blame	
	Week 4	Week 8	Week 4	Week 8
Week 1	.41*	.22**	.36*	.27*
Week 4	—	.43*	—	.20

*$p = < .01$.
**$p = < .05$.

ficients are high enough to suggest some stability over time but not so high as to preclude the relative independence of the "state" variable.

DISCRIMINANT VALIDITY

For a *state* of self-esteem scale to provide useful and valid information, it is important that whatever the scale measures be distinguishable from scales of the *trait* of self-esteem. In the Quinlan, Janis, and Bales study (chap. 10), two measures related to the trait of self-esteem were employed: the Self-Acceptance Scale from the California Psychological Inventory (Gough, 1957) and the Depressive Experiences Questionnaire (Blatt, D'Afflitti, & Quinlan, 1976). The latter questionnaire yields three scales, each of which has been found to be related to relevant measures in a normal population: dependency, self-criticism and efficacy. The correlations of these three scales with the self-confidence and self-blame scales from our SSE questionnaire are presented in Table A3. All the correlations are quite low. None is larger than .29 and only 6 of the 24 correlations are significant. The correlations in Table A3 do not form a consistent pattern, and they are not so high as to suggest that our scales are simply reflecting the "trait" properties of the standard measures of chronic level of self-esteem.

Table A3. Correlations of state of self-esteem scales with trait measures

	CPI Self-acceptance	Depressive Experience Questionnaire		
		Dependency	Self-criticism	Efficacy
Week 1[a]				
Self-confidence	.04	.07	−.08	.29*
Self-blame	−.06	.23**	.08	−.09
Week 4[b]				
Self-confidence	.05	.00	−.01	.09
Self-blame	−.12	.24**	.13	−.02
Week 8[c]				
Self-confidence	.16	−.07	−.22**	.27*
Self-blame	−.12	.12	.23**	−.17

  *$p < .01$.
  **$p < .05$.
  [a] $N = 125$.
  [b] $N = 110$.
  [c] $N = 105$.

REACTIVITY

One of the dangers of asking questions like those in the State of Self-esteem questionnaire is that it will call the subjects' attention to certain aspects of the experimental treatments so as to sensitize them or convey anticipations of the expected outcome. This problem of reactivity seems unlikely, however, given the Quinlan, Janis, and Bales results. None of the significant effects of the treatments on weight loss was paralleled by significant differences on either of the self-esteem scales.

CONSTRUCT VALIDITY

Do the State of Self-esteem scales measure changes in feelings about the self? Some data bearing on validity are provided by the correlations of weight loss with changes on self-esteem scale scores, presented in Table A4.

Table A4. Correlations between changes in self-esteem and weight loss, from the data in the Quinlan, Janis, and Bales study

Self-esteem changes	Weight loss	
	Week 4	Week 8
Self-confidence: weeks 1–4	.41*	.42*
Self-confidence: weeks 1–8	.33**	.33**
Self-blame: weeks 1–4	−.28**	−.23***
Self-blame: weeks 1–8	−.26**	−.19

* $p < .001$.
** $p < .01$.
*** $p < .05$.

There is a highly significant correlation between weight loss and changes in self-confidence. The correlation between weight loss and changes in self-blame are lower in magnitude but significant and in the approprirate direction. *Initial* self-confidence and self-blame do not predict weight loss (r [142] $< .18$). Rather, weight loss is reflected by changes on the SSE scales: an increase in self-confidence and a decrease in self-blame.

SUMMARY

Initial analysis of the State of Self-esteem questionnaire yielded three factors. Subsequent analysis yielded two scales that remained factorially consistent over time: self-confidence and self-blame. Within-scale estimates of reliability were high. The scales did not correlate more than marginally with standard measures of trait of self-esteem. The scales do not appear to be highly reactive to experimental conditions. Consistent with construct validity, there were significant correlations with objectively measured weight loss. Further work on the validity of the State of Self-esteem scales is needed to determine whether the two factors are differentially responsive to specific treatments that are expected to induce changes in self-confidence and self-blame.

NOTES

1. Throughout the chapters in this book, the self-blame scale is referred to as "guilt." For future use, we recommend the term "self-blame."

References

Abelson, R. P. Script processing in attitude formation and decision making. In J. S. Carroll and J. W. Payne (Eds.), *Cognition and social behavior*. Hillsdale, N.J.: Lawrence Erlbaum Associates, 1976.

Albert, S., & Dabbs, J. Physical distance and persuasion. *Journal of Personality and Social Psychology,* 1970. *15,* 265–270.

Alcoholics Anonymous. New York: A. A. World Service, 1939.

Altman, I., & Taylor, D. *Social penetration: The development of interpersonal relationships.* New York: Holt, Rinehart & Winston, 1973.

American Psychological Association Task Force on Health. Contributions of psychology to health research: Pattern, problems and potentials. *American Psychologist,* 1976, *31,* 263–274.

Andrew, J. M. Recovery from surgery, with and without preparatory instructions, for three coping styles. *Journal of Personality and Social Psychology,* 1970, *15,* 223–226.

Argyle, M., & Dean, J. Eye-contact, distance, and affiliation. *Sociometry,* 1965, *28,* 289–304.

Aronson, E. Some antecedents of interpersonal attraction. In W. Arnold & D. Levine (Eds.), *Nebraska Symposium on Motivation* (Vol. 17). Lincoln: University of Nebraska Press, 1969.

Aronson, E. *The social animal* (2nd ed.). San Francisco: W. H. Freeman, 1976.

Atthowe, J. Behavior innovation and persistence. *American Psychologist,* 1973, *28,* 34–41.

Auerbach, S. M. Trait-state anxiety and adjustment to surgery. *Journal of Consulting and Clinical Psychology,* 1973, *40,* 264–271.

Auerbach, S. M., Kendall, P. C., Cuttler, H. F., & Levitt, R. Anxiety, locus of control, type of preparatory information and adjustment to dental surgery. *Journal of Consulting and Clinical Psychology,* 1976, *44,* 809–818.

Averill, J. R. Personal control over aversive stimuli and its relationship to stress. *Psychological Bulletin,* 1973, *80,* 286–303.

Backman, C. W., & Secord, P. F. The effect of perceived liking on interpersonal attraction. *Human Relations,* 1959, *12,* 379–384.

Bandura, A. *Principles of behavior modification.* New York: Holt, Rinehart, & Winston, 1969.

Bandura, A. Self-efficacy: Toward a unifying theory of behavioral change. *Psychological Review,* 1977, *84,* 191–215.

Bandura, A., & Simon, K. The role of proximal intentions in self-regulation of refractory behavior. *Cognitive Therapy and Research,* 1977, *1,* 177–193.

Baron, R. M., & Ganz, R. L. Effects of locus of control and type of feedback on the task performance of lower-class black children. *Journal of Personality and Social Psychology,* 1972, *21,* 124–130.

Barrett-Leonard, G. T. Dimensions of therapist response as causal factors in therapeutic change. *Psychological Monographs,* 1962, *76* (43, Whole No. 562).

Baudry, R., & Wiener, A. The pregnant patient in conflict about abortion: A challenge for the obstetrician. *American Journal of Obstetrics and Gynecology,* 1974, *119,* 705-711.

Becker, E. *The structure of evil.* New York: Braziller, 1968.

Bennis, W. G., Berlew, D. E., Schein, E. H., & Steele, F. I. Some interpersonal aspects of self confirmation. In W. G. Bennis et al. (Eds.), *Interpersonal dynamics* (3rd ed.). Homewood, Ill.: Dorsey, 1973.

Benson, J. S., & Kennelly, K. J. Learned helplessness: The results of uncontrollable reinforcements or uncontrollable aversive stimuli? *Journal of Personality and Social Psychology,* 1976, *34,* 138-147.

Bergman, A. B., & Werner, R. J. Failure of children to receive penicillin by mouth. *New England Journal of Medicine,* 1963, *268,* 1334-1338.

Berkowitz, L., & Lundy, R. M. Personality characteristics related to susceptibility to influence by peers or authority figures. *Journal of Personality,* 1957, *25,* 306-316.

Berscheid, E., Boye, D., & Darley, J. M. Effects of forced association upon voluntary choice to associate. *Journal of Personality and Social Psychology,* 1968, *8,* 13-19.

Berscheid, E., & Walster, E. *Interpersonal attraction* (2nd ed.). Reading, Mass.: Addison and Wesley, 1978.

Best, J. H., Bass, F., & Owen, L. E. Mode of service delivery in a smoking cessation program for public health. *Canadian Journal of Public Health,* 1977, *68,* 469-473.

Biondo, J., & MacDonald, A. P. Internal-external measures of control and response to influence attempts. *Journal of Personality,* 1971, *39,* 407-419.

Bixenstine, V., & Wilson, K. Effects of level of cooperative choice by the other player on choices in a Prisoners Dilemma Game (Part 2). *Journal of Abnormal and Social Psychology,* 1963, *67,* 139-147.

Blatt, S. J., D'Afflitti, J. P., and Quinlan, D. M. Experiences of depression in normal young adults. *Journal of Abnormal Psychology,* 1976, *85,* 383-389.

Blau, P. M. *Exchange and power in social life.* New York: Wiley, 1964.

Blechman, E. A. The role of problem solutions and problem solving in behavioral interaction. Unpublished manuscript, Yale University, 1977.

Bordin, E. *Research strategies in psychotherapy.* New York: Wiley, 1974.

Bowers, K. S. Pain, anxiety, and perceived control. *Journal of Consulting and Clinical Psychology,* 1968, *32,* 596-602.

Bowers, K. S. Situationism in psychology: An analysis and a critique. *Psychological Review,* 1973, *80,* 307-336.

Brammer, L. M., & Shostrom, E. L. *Therapeutic psychology: Fundamentals of actualization counseling and psychotherapy.* Englewood Cliffs, N.J.: Prentice Hall, 1968.

Breen, D. *The birth of a first child: Toward an understanding of femininity.* London: Tavistock, 1975.

Brehm, S. *The application of social psychology to clinical practice.* New York: Halsted Press (Wiley), 1976.

Brewer, R. E., & Brewer, M. .B. Attraction and accuracy of perception in dyads. *Journal of Personality and Social Psychology,* 1968, *8,* 188-193.

Broadhurst, A. Applications of the psychology of decisions. In M. P. Feldman and A. Broadhurst (Eds.), *Theoretical and experimental bases of the behavior therapies.* London: Wiley, 1976.

Brownell, K. D., Heckerman, C. L., & Westlake, R. J. Therapist and group contact as variables in the behavioral treatment of obesity. Paper presented at the annual meeting of the Association for the Advancement of Behavior Therapy, New York, December, 1976.

Bugental, D. E., Kaswan, J. W., & Love, L. R. Perception of contradictory meanings conveyed by verbal and nonverbal channels. *Journal of Personality and Social Psychology,* 1970, *16,* 647–655.

Byrne, D. Interpersonal attraction and attitude similarity. *Journal of Abnormal and Social Psychology,* 1961, *62,* 713–715.

Byrne, D. Repression-sensitization as a dimension of personality. In B. Maher (Ed.), *Progress in experimental personality research.* New York: Academic Press, 1964.

Byrne, D. *The attraction paradigm.* New York: Academic Press, 1971.

Byrne, D., & Buehler, J. A. A note on the influence of propinquity upon acquaintanceships. *Journal of Abnormal and Social Psychology,* 1955, *51,* 147–148.

Byrne, D., & Griffitt, W. A developmental investigation of the law of attraction. *Journal of Personality and Social Psychology,* 1966, *4,* 699–702.

Byrne, D., & Griffitt, W. Similarity and awareness of similarity of personality characteristics as determinants of attraction. *Journal of Experimental Research in Personality,* 1969, *3,* 179–186.

Caplow, T., & Forman, R. Neighborhood interaction in a homogeneous community. *American Sociological Review,* 1950, *15,* 357–366.

Carkhuff, R. R. *The art of helping.* Amherst, Mass.: Human Resources Development Press, 1972.

Carkhuff, R. R., & Pierce, R. M. *Trainer's guide: The art of helping.* Amherst, Mass.: Human Resources Development Press, 1975.

Carroll, J. S., & Payne, J. W. (Eds.). *Cognition and social behavior.* Hillsdale, N.J.: Lawrence Erlbaum Associates, 1976.

Carter, E. N., Rice, H. P., & DeJulio, S. Role of the therapist in the self-control of obesity. *Journal of Consulting and Clinical Psychology,* 1977, *45,* 503.

Cartwright, D., & Zander, A. (Eds.). *Group dynamics: Research and theory* (3rd ed.). New York: Harper & Row, 1968.

Chang, P. *The effects of quality of self-disclosure on reactions to interviewer feedback.* Unpublished doctoral dissertation. University of Southern California, 1977.

Charney, E., Bynum, R., Eldredge, D., MacWhinney, J. B., McNabb, W., Scheiner, A., Sumpter, E. A., & Iker, H. How well do patients take oral penicillin? A collaborative study in private practice. *Pediatrics,* 1967, *40,* 188–195.

Clore, G. L., & McMillan, K. L. Role playing, attitude change, and attraction toward a disabled other. Unpublished paper, University of Illinois, 1970. Cited in J. S. Wiggins and others, *The psychology of personality.* Reading, Mass.: Addison-Wesley, 1971.

Cochran, D. J., Hoffman, S. D., Strand, K. H., & Warren, P. Effects of client/computer interaction on career decision-making processes. *Journal of Counseling Psychology,* 1977, *24,* 308–312.

Cohen, F., & Lazarus, R. S. Active coping processes, coping dispositions, and recovery from surgery. *Psychosomatic Medicine,* 1973, *35,* 375–384.

Cohen, F., & Lazarus, R. S. Coping with the stresses of illness. In G. S. Stone, F. Cohen, & N. E. Adler (Eds.), *Health psychology.* San Francisco: Jossey-Bass, 1979.

Coleman, J. S., Campbell, E. Q., Hobson, C. J., & McPartland, J. *Equality of educational opportunity* (Superintendent of Documents Catalog No. FS5.238:38001). Washington, D.C.: Government Printing Office, 1966.

Collins, B. E., & Hoyt, M. F. Personal responsibility-for-consequences: An integration and extension of the "forced compliance" literature. *Journal of Experimental Social Psychology,* 1972, *8,* 558–593.

Collins, B. E., & Raven, B. H. Group structure: Attraction, coalitions, communication and power. In G. Lindzey & E. Aronson (Eds.), *The handbook of social psychology* (Vol. 4). Reading, Mass.: Addison-Wesley, 1969.

Corah, N. L., & Boffa, J. Perceived control, self-observation, and response to aversive stimulation. *Journal of Personality and Social Psychology,* 1970, *16,* 1–4.

Cormier, W. H., & Cormier, L. S. *Interviewing strategies for helpers: A guide to assessment, treatment and evaluation.* Monterey, Calif.: Brooks/Cole, 1979.

Corsini, R. J. Counseling and psychotherapy. In E. F. Borgatta & W. W. Lambert (Eds.), *Handbook of personality theory and research.* Chicago: Rand McNally, 1968.

Cozby, P. C. Self-disclosure: A literature review. *Psychological Bulletin,* 1973, *79,* 73–91.

Cronbach, L. J. Beyond the two disciplines of scientific psychology. *American Psychologist,* 1975, *30,* 116–127.

Crowne, D. P., & Marlowe, D. *The approval motive.* New York: Wiley, 1964.

Crowne, D. P., & Strickland, B. R. The conditioning of verbal behavior as a function of the need for social approval. *Journal of Abnormal and Social Psychology,* 1961, *63,* 395–401.

Darley, J. M., & Aronson, E. Self-evaluation vs. direct anxiety reduction as determinants of the fear–affiliation relationship. In B. Latane (Ed.), *Studies in social comparison.* New York: Academic Press, 1966.

Darley, J. M., & Berscheid, E. Increased liking as a result of the anticipation of personal contact. *Human Relations,* 1967, *20,* 29–40.

Davidson, P. O., & Bobey, M. J. Repressor–sensitizer differences on repeated exposure to pain. *Perceptual and Motor Skills,* 1970, *31,* 711–714.

Davis, F. H., & Malmo, R. B. Electromyographic recording during interview. *American Journal of Psychiatry,* 1951, *107,* 908–916.

Davis, M. S. Variations in patients' compliance with doctor's orders: Analysis of congruence between survey responses and results of empirical investigations. *Journal of Medical Education,* 1966, *41,* 1037.

Davis, M. S. Variation in patients' compliance with doctors' orders: Medical practice and doctor–patient interaction. *Psychiatry in Medicine,* 1971, *2,* 31–54.

Davison, G. C., & Valins, S. Maintenance of self-attributed and drug attributed behavior change. *Journal of Personality and Social Psychology,* 1969, *11,* 25–33.

DeCharms, R. *Personal causation: The internal affective determinants of behavior.* New York: Academic Press, 1968.

Deignan, G. M. Perceptual, interpersonal and situational factors in cooperation and competition. *Dissertation Abstracts International,* 1970, *31,* 1371. (Abstract)

DeLong, D. R. *Individual differences in patterns of anxiety arousal, stress-relevant information and recovery from surgery.* Unpublished doctoral dissertation, University of California, Los Angeles, 1971.

Deutsch, M., Epstein, Y., Canavan, D., & Gumpert, P. Strategies of inducing cooperation: An experimental study. *Journal of Conflict Resolution,* 1967, *11,* 345–360.

Deutsch, M., & Solomon, L. Reactions to evaluations by others as influenced by self-evaluation. *Sociometry,* 1959, *22,* 93–112.

Dickoff, H. *Reactions to evaluations by another person as a function of self-evaluation and the interaction context.* Unpublished doctoral dissertation, Duke University, 1961.

Dittes, J. E. Extinction during psychotherapy of GSR accompanying "embarrassing" statements. *Journal of Abnormal and Social Psychology,* 1957, *54,* 187–191.

Dittes, J. E. Attractiveness of the group as function of self esteem and acceptance by the group. *Journal of Abnormal and Social Psychology,* 1959, *59,* 77–82.

Dosey, M., & Meisels, M. Personal space and self-protection. *Journal of Personality and Social Psychology,* 1969, *11,* 93–97.

Egbert, L., Battit, G., Welch, C., & Bartlett, M. Reduction of post-operative pain by encouragement and instruction. *New England Journal of Medicine,* 1964, *270,* 825–827.

Egan, G. *The skilled helper: A model for systematic helping and interpersonal relating.* Monterey, Calif.: Brooks/Cole, 1975.

Eisenberger, R., Park, D. C., & Frank, M. Learned industriousness and social reinforcement. *Journal of Personality and Social Psychology,* 1976, *33,* 227–232.

Ellis, D. *Reason and emotion in psychotherapy.* New York: Lyle Stuart, 1962.

Ellsworth, P. C., & Carlsmith, J. M. Effects of eye contact and verbal content on affective response to a dyadic interaction. *Journal of Personality and Social Psychology,* 1968, *10,* 15–20.

Ellsworth, P. C., & Ross, L. Intimacy in response to direct gaze. *Journal of Experimental Social Psychology,* 1975, *11,* 592–613.

Elms, A., & Janis, I. L. Counter-norm attitudes induced by role-playing. *Journal of Experimental Research in Personality,* 1965, *1,* 50–60.

Etzioni, A. *The active society.* New York: Free Press, 1968.

Exline, R., & Winters, L. C. Affective reactions and mutual glances in dyads. In S. Tomkins & C. E. Izard (Eds.), *Affect, cognition, and personality.* New York: Springer, 1965.

Fellner, C. H., & Marshall, J. Kidney donors: The myth of informed consent. *American Journal of Psychiatry,* 1970, *126,* 1245–1251.

Festinger, L. Architecture and group membership. *Journal of Social Issues,* 1951, *7,* 152–163.

Festinger, L. A theory of social comparison processes. *Human Relations,* 1954, *7,* 117–140.

Festinger, L. *Conflict, decision and dissonance.* Stanford: Stanford University Press, 1964.

Field, P. Effects of tape-recorded hypnotic preparation for surgery. *International Journal of Clinical and Experimental Hypnosis,* 1974, *22,* 54–61.

Fishman, C. Need for approval and the expression of aggression under varying conditions of frustration. *Journal of Personality and Social Psychology,* 1965, *2,* 809–811.

Fiske, P. W., Hunt, H. F., Luborsky, L., Orne, M. T., Parloff, M. B., Reiser, M. F., & Tuma, A. H. The planning of research on effectiveness of psychotherapy (Report of workshop sponsored and supported by Clinical Projects Res. Rev. Comm., NIMH). *Archives of General Psychiatry,* 1970, *22,* 22–32.

Fitzgerald, M. P. Self-disclosure and expressed self-esteem, social distance and areas of the self revealed. *Journal of Psychology,* 1963, *56,* 405–412.

Fontaine, G. Social comparison and some determinants of expected personal control and expected performance in a novel task situation. *Journal of Personality and Social Psychology,* 1974, *29,* 487–496.

Frank, J. The bewildering world of psychotherapy. *Journal of Social Issues,* 1972, *28,* 27–44.

Freedman, N., O'Hanlon, J., Oltman, P., & Witkin, H. A. The impact of psychological differentiation on kinetic behavior in varying communicative contexts. *Journal of Abnormal Psychology,* 1972, *79,* 239–258.

French, J. R., & Raven, B. The bases of social power. In D. Cartwright (Ed.), *Studies in social power.* Ann Arbor: University of Michigan, 1959.

Garfield, S. L. Research on client variables in psychotherapy. In A. E. Bergin and S. L. Garfield (Eds.), *Handbook of psychotherapy and behavior change.* New York: Wiley, 1971.

Garfield, S. L., & Bergin, A. E. (Eds.). *Handbook of psychotherapy and behavior change: An empirical analysis* (2nd ed.). New York: Wiley, 1978.

Geer, A. H., Davison, G. C., & Gatchel, R. I. Reduction of stress in humans through nonveridical perceived control of aversive stimulation. *Journal of Personality and Social Psychology,* 1970, *16,* 731–738.

Gentry, D., Foster, S., & Haney, T. Denial as a determinant of anxiety and perceived health in the coronary care unit. *Psychosomatic Medicine,* 1972, *34,* 39.

George, A. L. The Chinese Communist intervention in the Korean War. In A. George and R. Smoke (Eds.), *Deterrence in American foreign policy: Theory and practice.* New York: Columbia University Press, 1974.

George, A. L. *Presidential decisionmaking in foreign policy: The effective use of information and advice.* Boulder, Colo.: Westview, 1980.

Gergen, K. J. *The psychology of behavior exchange.* Reading, Mass.: Addison-Wesley, 1969.

Glass, D. C. *Behavioral antecedents of coronary heart disease.* New York: Erlbaum, 1977.

Glass, D. C., & Singer, J. E. *Urban stress: Experiments on noise and social stressors.* New York: Academic Press, 1972.

Goldstein, A. P. Relationship-enhancement methods. In F. H. Kanfer and A. P. Goldstein (Eds.), *Helping people change.* New York: Pergamon Press, 1975.

Goldstein, M. J. The relationship between coping and avoiding behavior and response to fear-arousing propaganda. *Journal of Abnormal and Social Psychology,* 1959, *58,* 247–252.

Gomersall, E. R., & Myers, M. S. Breakthrough in on-the-job training. *Harvard Business Review,* 1966, *44,* 62–72.

Gottschalk, L., & Gleser, G. C. *The measurement of psychological states through content analysis.* Berkeley: University of California Press, 1969.

Gough, H. G. *Manual for the California Psychological Inventory.* Palo Alto, Calif.: Consulting Psychologists Press, 1957.

Greene, L. R. Effects of field dependence on affective reactions and compliance in dyadic interactions. *Journal of Personality and Social Psychology,* 1976, *34,* 569–577.

Greene, L. R. Effects of verbal evaluative feedback and interpersonal distance on behavioral compliance. *Journal of Counseling Psychology,* 1977, *24,* 10–14.

Greenspoon, J. The reinforcing effect of two spoken sounds on the frequency of two responses. *American Journal of Psychology,* 1955, *68,* 409–416.

Greenwald, H. *Decision therapy.* New York: Wyden, 1973.

Gullahorn, J. Distance and friendship as factors in the gross interaction matrix. *Sociometry,* 1952, *15,* 123–134.

Hackett, T. P., Cassem, N. H., & Wishnie, H. A. The coronary care unit: An appraisal of its psychological hazards. *New England Journal of Medicine,* 1968, *279,* 1365.

Hackman, R., & Morris, C. G. Group tasks, group interaction process, and group performance effectiveness: A review and proposed integration. In L. Berkowitz (Ed.), *Advances in experimental social psychology* (Vol. 8). New York: Academic Press, 1975.

Hall, E. T. *The hidden dimension.* New York: Doubleday, 1966.

Hamilton, E. *Three Greek plays—translated with introductions by Edith Hamilton.* New York: Norton, 1958.

Hare, A. P. *Handbook of small group research* (2nd ed.). New York: Free Press, 1976.

Harford, T., & Solomon, L. The effects of a "reformed sinner" vs. a "lapsed saint" strategy upon cooperative behavior in the Prisoner's Dilemma Game. *Journal of Conflict Resolution,* 1967, *11,* 104–110.

Harris, J. E. The computer: Guidance tool of the future. *Journal of Counseling Psychology,* 1974, *21,* 331–339.

Haymes, M. Technique for measuring self-disclosure from tape recorded interviews. In S. Jourard (Ed.), *Self-disclosure: An experimental analysis of the transparent self.* New York: Wiley, 1971.

Heller, K., Davis, J. D., & Myers, R. A. The effects of interviewer style in a standardized interview. *Journal of Consulting Psychology,* 1966, *30,* 501–508.

Helmreich, R. L., & Collins, B. E. Situational determinants of affiliative preference under stress. *Journal of Personality and Social Psychology,* 1967, *6,* 79–85.

Henderson, J. B., Hall, S. M., & Lipton, H. L. Changing self-destructive behaviors. In J. C. Stone, F. Cohen, & N. E. Adler (Eds.), *Health psychology.* San Francisco: Jossey-Bass, 1979.

Hillis, R. E. Some effects of socioeconomic-educational similarity on the interpersonal communication process. *Dissertation Abstracts,* 1969, *29* (8-A), 2801. (Abstract)

Hoffman, D. Effect of ad-lib and fixed daily contact between partners who agree to cut down on smoking. Unpublished research report, Yale University, 1968.

Holstein, C. M., Goldstein, J. W., & Bem, D. J. The importance of expressive behavior, sex, and need approval in inducing liking. *Journal of Experimental and Social Psychology,* 1971, *7,* 534–544.

Homans, G. C. *Social behavior: Its elementary forms.* New York: Harcourt, Brace, & World, 1961.

Hood, T. C., & Back, K. W. Self-disclosure and the volunteer: A source of bias in laboratory experiments. *Journal of Personality and Social Psychology,* 1971, *17,* 130–136.

Hoopes, M. H., & Scoresby, A. L. Commitment to change: Structuring the goals and ground rules for counseling. In J. K. Krumboltz & C. E. Thoresen (Eds.), *Behavioral counseling: Cases and techniques.* New York: Holt, Rinehart & Winston, 1969.

Horn, J. L. Human abilities: A review of research and theory in the early 1970s. In M. Rosenzweig and L. W. Porter (Eds.), *Annual review of psychology* (Vol. 27). Palo Alto: Annual Reviews, 1976.

Houston, B. K. Control over stress, locus of control, and response to stress. *Journal of Personality and Social Psychology,* 1972, *21,* 249–255.

Hunt, W. A., & Bespalec, D. A. An evaluation of current methods of modifying smoking behavior. *Journal of Clinical Psychology,* 1974, *30,* 431–438.

Hunt, W. A., & Matarazzo, J. D. Three years later: Recent developments in the experimental modification of smoking behavior. *Journal of Abnormal Psychology,* 1973, *81,* 107–114.

Jacobs, T. J. Posture, gesture and movement in the analyst: Cues to interpretation and countertransference. *Journal of the American Psychoanalytic Association,* 1973, *21,* 77–92.

Jacobs, L., Berscheid, E., & Walster, E. Self-esteem and attraction. *Journal of Personality and Social Psychology,* 1971, *17,* 84–91.

Jackson, D. *Personality research form manual.* Goshen, New York: Research Psychologists Press, 1967.

Janis, I. L. Problems related to the control of fear in combat. In S. A. Stouffer, Lumsdaine, A. A., Lumsdaine, M. H., Williams Jr., R. M., Smith, M. B., Janis, I. L., Star, S. A., and Cottrell Jr., L. S., *The American soldier: Volume 2. Combat and its aftermath.* Princeton University Press, 1949.

Janis, I. L. *Psychological stress.* New York: Wiley, 1958.

Janis, I. L. Motivational factors in the resolution of decisional conflicts. In M. R. Jones (Ed.), *Nebraska Symposium on Motivation* (Vol. 7). Lincoln: University of Nebraska Press, 1959.

Janis, I. L. *Progress Report.* United States Public Health Service Grant MH-08564 for research on factors influencing tolerance for deprivation, Yale University, 1965. (Mimeo).

Janis, I. L. Effects of fear-arousal on attitude change. In L. Berkowitz (Ed.), *Advances in experimental social psychology* (Vol. 3). New York: Academic Press, 1967.

Janis, I. L. Group identification under conditions of external danger. In D. Cartwright & A. Zander (Eds.), *Group dynamics: Research and theory* (3rd ed.). New York: Harper & Row, 1968.

Janis, I. L. *Stress and frustration.* New York: Harcourt, Brace, Jovanovich, 1971.

Janis, I. L. *Victims of groupthink: A psychological study of foreign-policy decisions and fiascos.* Boston: Houghton Mifflin, 1972.

Janis, I. L. Effectiveness of social support for stressful decisions. In M. Deutsch & H. Hornstein (Eds.), *Applications of social psychology.* Hillsdale, N.J.: Erlbaum, 1975.

Janis, I. L. Personality differences in decision making under stress. In K. R. Blankstein, P. Pliner, & J. Polivy (Eds.), *Assessment and modification of emotional behavior.* New York: Plenum Publishing Corp., 1980.

Janis, I. L. Stress inoculation in health care: Theory and research. In D. Meichenbaum & M. Jaremko (Eds.), *Stress prevention and management: A cognitive-behavioral approach.* New York: Plenum, in press.

Janis, I. L., & Field, P. B. Sex differences and personality factors related to persuasibility. In C. I. Hovland & I. L. Janis (Eds.), *Personality and persuasibility.* New Haven: Yale University Press, 1959.

Janis, I., & Gilmore, L. B. The influence of incentive conditions on the success of role playing in modifying attitudes. *Journal of Personality and Social Psychology,* 1965, *1,* 17–27.

Janis, I. L., & Mann, L. Effectiveness of emotional role playing in modifying smoking habits and attitudes. *Journal of Experimental Research in Personality,* 1965, *1,* 84–90.

Janis, I. L., & Mann, L. *Decision making: A psychological analysis of conflict, choice, and commitment.* New York: Free Press, 1977.

Janoff-Bulman, R. Self-blame in rape victims: A control-maintenance strategy. Paper presented at American Psychological Association Meetings, Toronto, 1978.

Johnson, J. E., & Leventhal, H. Effects of accurate expectations and behavioral instructions on reactions during a noxious medical examination. *Journal of Personality and Social Psychology,* 1974, *29,* 710–718.

Jonas, G. Profiles: Visceral learning I. Dr. Neal E. Miller. *New Yorker Magazine,* 1972, *48,* 34–57.

Jones, E. E. *Ingratiation: A social psychological analysis.* New York: Appleton-Century-Crofts, 1964.

Jones, E. E., Gergen, J. J., & Davis, K. E. Some determinants of reactions to being approved or disapproved as a person. *Psychology Monographs,* 1962, *76,* No. 521.

Jones, E. E., Jones, R. G., & Gergen, K. J. Some conditions affecting the evaluation of a conformist. *Journal of Personality,* 1963, *31,* 270–288.

Jones, E. E., & Nisbett, R. E. The actor and the observer: Divergent perceptions of the causes of behavior. In E. E. Jones, D. E. Kanouse, H. H. Kelley, R. E. Nisbett, S. Valins, & B. Weiner (Eds.), *Attribution: Perceiving the causes of behavior.* Morristown, N.J.: General Learning Press, 1971.

Jones, S. C., & Panitch, D. The self-fulfilling prophecy and interpersonal attraction. *Journal of Experimental Social Psychology,* 1967, *7,* 356–366.

Jourard, S. M. Self-disclosure and other-cathexis. *Journal of Abnormal and Social Psychology,* 1959, *59,* 428–431.

Jourard, S. M. *Disclosing man to himself.* Princeton: Van Nostrand, 1968.

Jourard, S. *The transparent self* (Rev. ed.). New York: Van Nostrand Reinhold, 1971.

Justice, M. *Field dependency, intimacy of topic and interpersonal distance.* Unpublished doctoral dissertation, University of Florida, 1970.

Kanfer, F. H., & Goldfoot, D. A. Self-control and tolerance of noxious stimulation. *Psychological Reports,* 1966, *18,* 79–85.

Kanfer, F., & Seider, M. L. Self-control: Factors enhancing tolerance of noxious stimulation. *Journal of Personality and Social Psychology,* 1973, *25,* 381–389.

Kaplan, K. J., Firestone, I. J., Degnore, R., & Moore, M. Gradients of attraction as a function of disclosure, probe intimacy and setting formality: On distinguishing attitude oscillation from attitude change—study one. *Journal of Personality and Social Psychology,* 1974, *30,* 638–646.

Kasl, S. V. Issues in patient adherence to health care regimens. *Journal of Human Stress,* 1975, *1,* 5–18.

Kasl, S. V., & Mahl, G. M. The relationship of disturbances and hesitations in spontaneous speech to anxiety. *Journal of Personality and Social Psychology,* 1965, *1,* 425–433.

Katz, A. M., & Hill, R. Residential propinquity and marital selection: A review of theory, method, and fact. *Marriage and Family Living,* 1958, *20,* 27–35.

Katz, D., Sarnoff, I., & McClintock, C. G. Ego-defense and attitude change. *Human Relations,* 1956, *9,* 27–46.

Kaufmann, H. Similarity and cooperation received as determinants of cooperation rendered. *Psychonomic Science,* 1967, *2,* 73–74.

Kelly, F. D. Communicational significance of therapist proxemic cues. *Journal of Consulting and Clinical Psychology,* 1972, *39,* 173–181.

Kennedy, R. Premarital residential propinquity. *American Journal of Sociology,* 1943, *48,* 580–584.

Kiesler, C. A. (Ed.). *The psychology of commitment.* New York: Academic Press, 1971.

Kiesler, C. A., & Sakumura, J. A test of a model for commitment. *Journal of Personality and Social Psychology,* 1966, *3,* 349–353.

Kirscht, J. P., & Rosenstock, I. M. Patients' problems in following recommendations of health experts. In G. C. Stone, F. Cohen, & N. E. Adler (Eds.), *Health psychology.* San Francisco: Jossey-Bass, 1979.

Klein, D. C., Fencil-Mouse, E., & Seligman, M. E. P. Learned helplessness, depression, and the attribution of failure. *Journal of Personality and Social Psychology,* 1976, *33,* 508–516.

Koch, S. Language communities, search cells, and the psychological studies. In J. K. Cole (Ed.), *Nebraska Symposium on Motivation, 1975* (Vol. 23). Lincoln: University of Nebraska Press, 1976.

Kohut, H. *The restoration of the self.* New York: International Universities Press, 1977.

Konstadt, N., & Forman, E. Field dependence and external directedness. *Journal of Personality and Social Psychology,* 1965, *1,* 490–493.

Krasner, L. Studies of the conditioning of verbal behavior. *Psychological Bulletin,* 1958, *55,* 148–170.

Kroth, J. A. *Counseling psychology and guidance.* Springfield, Ill.: C. F. Thomas, 1973.

Krumboltz, J. D. (Ed.). *Revolution in counseling.* Boston: Houghton Mifflin, 1966.

Labov, W., & Fanshel, D. *Therapeutic discourse.* New York: Academic Press, 1977.

LaFlamme, D., & Janis, I. L. Effects of the balance-sheet and the outcome psychodrama procedures on career decision-making processes. Unpublished study, Yale University, 1977.

Lampel, A. K., & Anderson, N. H. Combining visual and verbal information in an impression-formation task. *Journal of Personality and Social Psychology,* 1968, *9,* 1–6.

Langer, E. J. The illusion of control. *Journal of Personality and Social Psychology,* 1975, *32,* 311–328.

Langer, E. J., & Abelson, R. P. The semantics of asking a favor: How to succeed in getting help without really trying. *Journal of Personality and Social Psychology,* 1972, *24,* 26–32.

Langer, E. J., & Dweck, C. S. *Personal politics.* Englewood Cliffs, N.J.: Prentice-Hall, 1973.

Langer, E. J., Janis, I., & Wolfer, J. Reduction of psychological stress in surgical patients. *Journal of Experimental Social Psychology,* 1975, *1,* 155–166.

Langer, E. J., & Rodin, J. The effects of choice and enhanced personal responsibility for the aged: A field experiment in an institutional setting. *Journal of Personality and Social Psychology,* 1976, *34,* 191–198.

Lapidus, L. B. Cognitive control and reactions to stress: Conditions for mastery in the anticipatory phase. *Proceedings of the 77th Annual Convention of the American Psychological Association,* 1969, *4,* 569–570.

Lazarus, R. S. *Psychological stress and the coping process.* New York: McGraw-Hill, 1966.

Lazarus, R. S. Psychological stress and coping in adaptation and illness. In S. M. Weiss (Ed.), *Proceedings of the National Heart and Lung Institute Working Conference on Health Behavior.* Washington, D.C.: DHEW (Publication No. [NIH] 76-868), 1975.

Lazarus, R. S., & Alfert, E. The short circuiting of threat by experimentally altering cognitive appraisal. *Journal of Abnormal and Social Psychology,* 1964, *69,* 195–205.

Lefcourt, H. M. Recent developments in the study of locus of control. In B. A. Maher (Ed.), *Progress in experimental personality research* (Vol. 6). New York: Academic Press, 1972.

Lefcourt, H. M. The function of the illusions of control and freedom. *American Psychologist,* 1973, *28,* 417–425.

Lefcourt, H. M., & Siegel, J. M. Reaction time performance as a function of field dependence and autonomy in test administration. *Journal of Abnormal Psychology*, 1970, *76*, 475–481.

Lesser, G. S., & Abelson, R. P. Personality correlates of persuasibility in children. In C. I. Hovland & I. L. Janis (Eds.), *Personality and persuasibility*. New Haven: Yale University Press, 1959.

Lester, D., & Brockopp, G. W. (Eds.), *Crisis intervention and counseling by telephone*. Springfield, Ill.: Thomas, 1973.

Leventhal, H., & Niles, P. A field experiment on fear arousal with data on the validity of qustionnaire measures. *Journal of Personality*, 1964, *32*, 459–479.

Leventhal, H., & Perloe, S. I. A relationship between self-esteem and persuasibility. *Journal of Abnormal and Social Psychology*, 1962, *64*, 385–388.

Leventhal, H., & Sharpe, E. Facial expressions as indicators of stress. In C. Izard and S. Tompkins (Eds.), *Studies of emotion*. New York: Springer, 1965.

Levinger, G., & Breedlove, J. Interpersonal attraction and agreement: A study of marriage partners. *Journal of Personality and Social Psychology*, 1966, *3*, 367–372.

Levinger, G., & Rausch, H. L. (Eds.). *Close relationships: Perspectives on the meaning of intimacy*. Amherst: University of Massachusetts Press, 1977.

Levinger, G., & Snoek, J. D. *Attraction in relationships: A new look at interpersonal attraction*. New York: General Learning Corporation, 1972.

Levy, J. M., & McGee, R. K. Childbirth as crisis: A test of Janis' theory of communication and stress resolution. *Journal of Personality and Social Psychology*, 1975, *3*, 171–179.

Lewin, K. *Field theory in social science*. New York: Harper, 1951.

Ley, P., & Spelman, M. S. Communications in an out-patient setting. *British Journal of Social and Clinical Psychology*, 1965, *4*, 114–116.

Lichtenstein, E., & Danaher, B. G. Modification of smoking behavior: A critical analysis of theory, research, and practice. In M. Hersen, R. M. Eisler, & P. M. Miller (Eds.), *Progress in behavior modification* (Vol. 3). New York: Academic Press, 1976.

Linton, H. B. Dependence on external influence: Correlates in perception, attitudes and judgment. *Journal of Abnormal and Social Psychology*, 1955, *51*, 502–507.

Little, K. B. Personal space. *Journal of Experimental Social Psychology*, 1965, *1*, 237–247.

Luborsky, L. Helping alliances in psychotherapy: The groundwork for a study of their relationship to its outcome. In J. L. Claghorn (Ed.), *Successful psychotherapy*. New York: Brunner/Mazel, 1976.

Luborsky, L., Todd, T. C., & Katcher, A. H. A self-administered social assets scale for predicting physical and psychological illness and health. *Journal of Psychosomatic Research*, 1973, *17*, 109–120.

Ludwig, L. M., & Ellsworth, P. C. Some effects of observation set on the interpretation of nonverbal cues. Unpublished manuscript, Yale University, 1976.

MacDonald, A. P., Jr. Internal–external locus of control change-techniques. *Rehabilitation Literature*, 1972, *33*, 44–47.

Maisonneuve, J., Palmade, G., & Fourment, C. Selective choices and propinquity. *Sociometry*, 1952, *15*, 135–140.

Mann, L. Use of a "balance sheet" procedure to improve the quality of personal decision making: A field experiment with college applicants. *Journal of Vocational Behavior*, 1972, *2*, 291–300.

Mann, L., & Janis, I. L. A follow-up study on the long-term effects of emotional role playing. *Journal of Personality and Social Psychology*, 1968, *8*, 339–342.

Maracek, J., & Mettee, D. R. Avoidance of continued success as a function of self-esteem certainty and responsibility for success. *Journal of Personality and Social Psychology*, 1972, *22*, 98–107.

Marlowe, D. Need for social approval and the operant conditioning of meaningful verbal behavior. *Journal of Consulting Psychology*, 1962, *26*, 79–83.

Marlowe, D., Beecher, R. S., Cook, J. B., & Doob, A. N. The approval motive, vicarious reinforcement and verbal conditioning. *Perceptual Motor Skills*, 1964, *19*, 523–530.

Marlowe, D., & Crowne, D. P. Social desirability and response to perceived situational demands. *Journal of Consulting Psychology*, 1961, *25*, 109–115.

Marlowe, D., & Gergen, K. J. Personality and social interaction. In G. Lindzey & E. Aronson (Eds.), *The handbook of social psychology* (Vol. 3, 2nd ed.). Reading, Mass.: Addison-Wesley, 1969.

Marston, M. V. Compliance with medical regimens: A review of the literature. *Nursing Research*, 1970, *19*, 312–323.

Marwell, G., & Schmitt, D. R. Dimensions of compliance-gaining behavior: An empirical analysis. *Sociometry*, 1967, *30*, 350–364.

May, R. *Love and will.* New York: W. W. Norton, 1969.

McClean, P. D. Depression as a specific response to stress. In I. G. Sarason and C. D. Spielberger (Eds.), *Stress and anxiety* (Vol. 3). New York: Wiley, 1976.

McGill, A. M. Review of literature on cardiovascular rehabilitations. In S. M. Weiss (Ed.), *Proceedings of the National Heart and Lung Institute Working Conference on Health Behavior.* Washington, D.C.: DHEW (Publication No. NIH 76-868), 1975.

McGuire, W. J. Selective exposure: A summing up. In R. P. Abelson, E. Aronson, W. J. McGuire, T. N. Newcomb, M. J. Rosenberg, & P. H. Tannenbaum (Eds.), *Theories of cognitive consistency: A sourcebook.* Chicago: Rand McNally, 1968.

McGuire, W. J. The nature of attitudes and attitude change. In G. Lindzey and E. Aronson (Eds.), *The handbook of social psychology* (Vol. 3, 2nd ed.). Reading, Mass.: Addison-Wesley, 1969.

McGuire, W. J. The yin and yang of progress in social psychology: Seven koan. *Journal of Personality and Social Psychology*, 1973, *28*, 446–456.

McWhirter, R. M., & Jecker, J. D. Attitude similarity and inferred attraction. *Psychonomic Science*, 1967, *7*, 225–226.

Mehrabian, A., & Ferris, S. J. Inference of attitudes from nonverbal communications in two channels. *Journal of Consulting Psychology*, 1961, *31*, 248–252.

Mehrabian, A., & Weiner, M. Decoding of inconsistent communications. *Journal of Personality and Social Psychology*, 1967, *6*, 109–114.

Meichenbaum, D. H. *Cognitive-behavior modification: An integrative approach.* New York: Plenum, 1977.

Meichenbaum, D. H., & Turk, D. C. The cognitive-behavioral management of anxiety, anger, and pain. In P. O. Davidson (Ed.), *The behavioral management of anxiety, depression and pain.* New York: Brunner/Mazel, 1976.

Meichenbaum, D. H., Turk, D., & Burstein, S. The nature of coping with stress. In I. Sarason & C. Spielberger (Ed.), *Stress and anxiety* (Vol. 2). New York: Wiley, 1975.

Melamed, B. C., & Siegel, L. J. Reduction of anxiety in children facing hospitalization and surgery by use of filmed modeling. *Journal of Consulting and Clinical Psychology*, 1975, *43*, 511–521.

Mettee, D. R. Changes in liking as a function of the magnitude and effect of sequential evaluations. *Journal of Experimental Social Psychology*, 1971, *7*, 157–172.

Mettee, D. R., Taylor, S. E., & Fisher, S. The effect of being shunned upon the desire to affiliate. *Psychonomic Science*, 1971, *23*, 429–431.

Milburn, T. W., Bell, N., & Koeski, G. F. Effect of censure or praise and evaluative dependence on performance in a free-learning task. *Journal of Personality and Social Psychology,* 1970, *15,* 43-47.

Miller, G. A. The magical number seven, plus or minus two. *Psychological Review,* 1956, *63,* 81-97.

Miller, J. C. Boundary scale. Unpublished test, 1968.

Miller, J. C., & Janis, I. L. Dyadic interaction and adaptation to the stresses of college life. *Journal of Consulting Psychology,* 1973, *3,* 258-264.

Miller, N., & Dworkin, B. R. Critical issues in therapeutic applications of biofeedback. In G. E. Schwartz & J. Beatty (Eds.), *Biofeedback: Theory and research.* New York: Academic Press, 1977.

Mischels, W. *Personality and assessment.* New York: Wiley, 1968.

Moran, P. A. *An experimental study of pediatric admission.* Unpublished master's thesis, Yale University School of Nursing, 1963.

Morganstern, K. P. Behavioral interviewing: The initial stages of assessment. In M. Hersen & A. S. Bellack (Eds.), *Behavioral assessment: A practical handbook.* New York: Pergamon Press, 1976.

Mowrer, O. H. *The new group therapy.* Princeton: Van Nostrand, 1964.

Nay, W. R. *Behavioral intervention.* New York: Gardner, 1976.

Nevill, D. Experimental manipulation of dependency motivation and its effects on eye contact and measures of field dependence. *Journal of Personality and Social Psychology,* 1974, *29,* 12-79.

Newcomb, T. M. The prediction of interpersonal attraction. *American Psychologist,* 1956, *11,* 575-586.

Newcomb, T. M. *The acquaintance process.* New York: Holt, Rinehart & Winston, 1961.

Niles, P. *The relationship of susceptibility and anxiety to acceptance of fear-arousing communications.* Unpublished Ph.D. dissertation, Yale University, 1964.

Nisbett, R., & Ross, L. *Human inference: Strategies and shortcomings of social judgment.* Englewood Cliffs, N.J.: Prentice-Hall, 1980.

Odell, M. Personality correlates of independence and conformity. Unpublished manuscript, Ohio State University, 1959.

Okun, B. F. *Effective helping: Interviewing and counseling techniques.* North Scituate, Mass.: Duxbury Press, 1976.

Olson, N., & Zanna, M. P. A new look at selective exposure. *Journal of Experimental Social Psychology,* 1979, *15,* 1-15.

Pervin, L. A. The need to predict and control under conditions of threat. *Journal of Personality,* 1963, *31,* 570-587.

Phares, E. J., & Lamiell, J. T. Internal–external control and defensive preferences. *Journal of Consulting and Clinical Psychology,* 1974, *42,* 872-878.

Phillips, L. *Human adaptation and its failures.* New York: Academic Press, 1968.

Pollack, I. W., & Kiev, A. Spatial orientation and psychotherapy: An experimental study of perception. *Journal of Nervous and Mental Disease,* 1963, *137,* 93-97.

Porges, S. Heart rate variability and deceleration as indexes of reaction time. *Journal of Experimental Psychology,* 1972, *92,* 103-110.

Quinlan, D. M., & Blatt, S. J. Field articulation and performance under stress: Differential predictions in surgical and psychiatric nursing training. *Journal of Consulting and Clinical Psychology,* 1972, *39,* 517.

Radloff, B. What is the next thing I want to do with my life? *Carnegie Quarterly,* 1977, *25,* 3-5.

Radloff, R., & Helmreich, R. *Groups under stress: Psychological research in Sealab II.* New York: Appleton-Century-Crofts, 1968.

Rae-Grant, Q. The art of being a failure as a consultant. In J. Zusman and D. L. Davidson (Eds.), *Practical aspects of mental health consultation.* Springfield, Ill.: Charles C. Thomas, 1972.

Reece, M. M., & Whitman, R. N. Expressive movements, warmth, and verbal reinforcement. *Journal of Abnormal and Social Psychology,* 1962, *64,* 234–236.

Reed, H. B., & Janis, I. L. Effects of a new type of psychological treatment on smokers' resistance to warnings about health hazards. *Journal of Consulting and Clinical Psychology,* 1974, *42,* 748.

Riskind, J. H. Relationship between locus of control and self-esteem in hemodialysis patients. Unpublished manuscript. Texas A & M University, 1980.

Ritchie, E., & Phares, E. J. Attitude change as a function of internal–external control and communication status. *Journal of Personality,* 1969, *37,* 429–443.

Rodin, J. Cognitive-behavioral strategies for the control of obesity. Paper presented at Conference on cognitive-behavior therapy: Applications and issues. Los Angeles, September, 1978.

Rodin, J., & Janis, I. L. The social power of health-care practitioners as agents of change. *Journal of Social Issues,* 1979, *35,* 60–81.

Rodin, J., & Langer, E. Long-term effects of a control-relevant intervention with the institutionalized aged. *Journal of Personality and Social Psychology,* 1977, *35,* 897–902.

Rogers, C. R. *Client-centered therapy.* Boston: Houghton Mifflin, 1951.

Rogers, C. R. The necessary and sufficient conditions of therapeutic personality change. *Journal of Consulting Psychology,* 1957, *21,* 95–103.

Rogers, C. R. *On becoming a person.* Boston: Houghton Mifflin, 1961.

Rogers, C. R., & Dymond, R. F. (Eds.). *Psychotherapy and personality change.* Chicago: University of Chicago Press, 1954.

Rokeach, M. Long-range experimental modification of values, attitudes, and behavior. *American Psychologist,* 1971, *26,* 453–459.

Romanczyk, R. G. Self-monitoring in the treatment of obesity: Parameters of reactivity. *Behavior Therapy,* 1974, *5,* 531–540.

Rosenfeld, H. M., & Jackson, J. Temporal mediation of the similarity-attraction hypothesis. *Journal of Personality,* 1965, *33,* 649–656.

Rotter, J. B. Generalized expectancies for internal vs. external control of reinforcement. *Psychological Monographs,* 1966, *80* (1, Whole No. 609).

Rubin, Z. *Liking and Loving.* New York: Holt, Rinehart & Winston, 1973.

Sackett, D. L. The magnitude of compliance and noncompliance. In D. L. Sackett & R. B. Haynes (Eds.), *Compliance with therapeutic regimens.* Baltimore: Johns Hopkins University Press, 1977.

Sackett, D. L., & Haynes, R. B. (Eds.). *Compliance with therapeutic regimens.* Baltimore: Johns Hopkins University Press, 1977.

Salzinger, K. Experimental manipulation of verbal behavior: A review. *Journal of General Psychology,* 1959, *61,* 65–94.

Sarason, I. G., & Spielberger, C. D. (Eds.), *Stress and anxiety* (Vol. 2). New York: Wiley, 1975.

Sarnoff, I. R., & Zimbardo, P. G. Anxiety, fear, and social affiliation. *Journal of Abnormal and Social Psychology,* 1961, *62,* 356–363.

Schachter, S. *The psychology of affiliation*. Stanford, Calif.: Stanford University Press, 1959.

Scheflen, A. *Body language and social order: Communication as behavioral control.* Englewood Cliffs, N.J.: Prentice-Hall, 1972.

Schein, E. H. *Process consultation*. Reading, Mass.: Addison-Wesley, 1969.

Schimek, J. G. Cognitive style and defenses: A longitudinal study of intellectualization and field independence. *Journal of Abnormal Psychology*, 1968, *73*, 575–580.

Schmidt, R. L. *An exploratory study of nursing and patient readiness for surgery.* Unpublished master's thesis, School of Nursing, Yale University, 1966.

Schmitt, F. E., & Wooldridge, P. J. Psychological preparation of surgical patients. *Nursing Research*, 1973, *22*, 108–116.

Schulz, R. Effects of control and predictability on the physical and psychological well being of the institutionalized aged. *Journal of Personality and Social Psychology*, 1976, *33*, 563–573.

Scriven, M. Maximizing the power of causal investigations: The modus operandi method. In C. V. Glass (Ed.). *Evaluation studies: Review annual* (Vol. 1). Beverly Hills: Sage, 1976.

Sechrest, L. Personality. In M. R. Rosensweig & L. W. Porter (Eds.), *Annual review of psychology* (Vol. 27). Palo Alto, Calif.: Annual Reviews, Inc., 1976.

Seligman, M. E. P. *Helplessness: On depression, development, and death.* San Francisco: Freeman, 1975.

Shapiro, D. *Neurotic styles.* Austen Riggs Center Monograph (Series No. 5). New York: Basic Books, 1965.

Shapiro, J. G. Agreement between channels of communication in interviews. *Journal of Consulting Psychology*, 1966, *30*, 535–538.

Shapiro, J. G., McCarroll, J. E., & Fine, H. Perceived therapeutic conditions and disclosure to significant others. Arkansas Rehabilitation Research and Training Center, *Discussion Papers*, Vol. 1, 1967.

Shaw, M. E. *Group dynamics.* New York: McGraw-Hill, 1971.

Sheffield, F. D. Comment on a distribution-free factorial-design analysis. *Psychological Bulletin*, 1957, *54*, 425–428.

Shepard, R. N. On subjectively optimum selections among multi-attribute alternatives. In M. W. Shelley & G. L. Bryan (Eds.), *Human judgments and optimality.* New York: Wiley, 1964.

Shewchuk, L. A. Special report: Smoking cessation programs of the American Health Foundation. *Preventive Medicine*, 1976, *5*, 454–474.

Sigall, A., & Aronson, E. Opinion change and the gain–loss model of interpersonal attraction. *Journal of Experimental Social Psychology*, 1967, *3*, 178–188.

Sime, A. M. Relationship of preoperative fear, type of coping, and information received about surgery to recovery from surgery. *Journal of Personality and Social Psychology*, 1976, *34*, 716–724.

Simmons, R. G., Klein, S. D., & Simmons, R. L. *Gift of life: The social and psychological impact of organ transplant.* New York: Wiley-Interscience, 1977.

Smith, M. B. Criticism of a social science (Review of *The Context of Social Psychology*, J. Israel & H. Tajfel [Eds.]). *Science*, 1973, *180*, 610–612.

Spielberger, C. D., Gorsuch, R. L., & Lushene, R. E. *Manual for the state-trait anxiety inventory.* Palo Alto, Calif.: Consulting Psychologist Press, 1970.

Spinoza, B. *Ethics.* A. Boyle (Ed.). New York: Dutton, 1910.

Staub, E., & Kellett, D. Increasing pain tolerance by information about aversive stimuli. *Journal of Personality and Social Psychology,* 1972, *21,* 198-208.

Stone, G. C. Patient compliance and the role of the expert. *Journal of Social Issues,* 1979, *35,* 34-59.

Storms, M. D., & Thomas, G. C. Reactions to physical closeness. *Journal of Personality and Social Psychology,* 1977, *35,* 412-418.

Strickland, B. R., & Crowne, D. P. Conformity under conditions of simulated group pressure as a function of the need for social approval. *Journal of Social Psychology,* 1962, *58,* 171-181.

Strong, S. R. Counseling: An interpersonal influence process. *Journal of Counseling Psychology,* 1968, *15,* 215-224.

Strong, S. R., & Matross, R. Change processes in counseling and psychotherapy, *Journal of Counseling Psychology,* 1973, *20,* 25-37.

Strong, S. R., & Schmidt, L. D. Expertness and influence in counseling. *Journal of Counseling Psychology,* 1970, *17,* 81-87.

Strupp, H. H. *Psychotherapy and the modification of abnormal behavior.* New York: McGraw-Hill, 1971.

Taylor, D. A., Altman, I., & Sorrentino, R. Interpersonal exchange as a function of rewards and costs and situational factors: Expectancy confirmation-disconfirmation. *Journal of Experimental Social Psychology,* 1969, *4,* 324-338.

Tedeschi, J. T. Attributions, liking, and power. In T. Huston (Ed.), *Foundations of interpersonal attraction.* New York: Academic Press, 1974.

Tedeschi, J. T., & Lindskold, S. *Social psychology: Interdependence, interaction, and influence.* New York: Wiley, 1976.

Thibaut, J. W., & Kelley, H. H. *The social psychology of groups.* New York: Wiley, 1959.

Toomey, M. Conflict theory approach to decision making applied to alcoholics. *Journal of Personality and Social Psychology,* 1972, *24,* 199-206.

Truax, C. B. Effective ingredients in psychotherapy: An approach to unravelling the patient-therapist interaction. *Journal of Counseling Psychology,* 1963, *10,* 256-263.

Truax, C. B., & Carkhuff, R. R. *Toward effective counseling and psychotherapy.* Chicago: Aldine, 1967.

Truax, C. B., & Mitchell, K. M. Research on certain therapist interpersonal skills in relation to process and outcome. In A. Bergin & S. Garfield (Eds.), *Handbook of psychotherapy and behavior change.* New York: Wiley, 1971.

Turk, D. C., & Genest, M. Regulation of pain: The application of cognitive and behavioral techniques for prevention and remediation. In P. Kendall & S. Hollon (Eds.), *Cognitive-behavioral interventions: Theory, research and practices.* New York: Academic Press, 1979.

Tversky, A., & Kahneman, D. Judgment under uncertainty: Heuristics and biases. *Science,* 1974, *185,* 1124-1131.

Vernon, D. T. A., & Bigelow, D. A. Effect of information about a potentially stressful situation on responses to stress impact. *Journal of Personality and Social Psychology,* 1974, *29,* 50-59.

Walster, E., Berscheid, E., & Walster, G. W. New directions in equity research. In L. Berkowitz and E. Walster (Eds.), *Advances in experimental social psychology* (Vol. 9). New York: Academic Press, 1976.

Walster, E., Walster, G. W., & Berscheid, E. *Equity: Theory and research.* Boston: Allyn and Bacon, 1978.

Wankel, L. M., & Thompson, C. Motivating people to be physically active: Self-persuasion vs. balanced decision making. *Journal of Applied Social Psychology,* 1977, *7,* 332–340.

Wanous, J. P. Effects of a realistic job preview on job acceptance, job attitudes and job survival. *Journal of Applied Psychology,* 1973, *58,* 321–332.

Watson, D., & Baumal, E. Effects of locus of control and expectation of future control upon present performance. *Journal of Personality and Social Psychology,* 1967, *6,* 212–215.

Weiner, B., Frieze, I., Kukla, A., Reed, L., Rost, S., & Rosenbaum, R. M. Perceiving the causes of success and failure. In E. E. Jones, D. E. Kanouse, H. H. Kelley, R. E. Nisbett, S. Valins, & B. Weiner (Eds.), *Attribution: Perceiving the causes of behavior.* Morristown, N.J.: General Learning Press, 1971.

Winer, B. J. *Statistical principles in experimental design.* New York: McGraw-Hill, 1962.

Witkin, H. A., Oltman, P. K., Raskin, E., & Karp, S. A. *Manual for the embedded figures test.* Palo Alto, Calif.: Consulting Psychologist Press, 1971.

Wolfer, J. A., & Visintainer, M. A. Pediatric surgical patients' and parents' stress responses and adjustment as a function of psychologic preparation and stress-point nursing care. *Nursing Research,* 1975, *24,* 244–255.

Worthy, M., Gary, A. L., & Kahn, G. M. Self-disclosure as an exchange process. *Journal of Personality and Social Psychology,* 1969, *13,* 59–63.

Wortman, C. B. Some determinants of perceived control. *Journal of Personality and Social Psychology,* 1975, *31,* 282–294.

Wrightsman, L. S., Jr. Effects of waiting with others on changes in level of felt anxiety. *Journal of Abnormal and Social Psychology,* 1960, *61,* 216–222.

Wylie, R. C. *The self concept.* Lincoln: University of Nebraska Press, 1961.

Yablonsky, L. *Synanon: The road back.* New York: McMillan, 1967.

Zimbardo, P. G., & Formica, R. Emotional comparison and self-esteem as determinants of affiliation. *Journal of Personality,* 1963, *31,* 141–162.

Index